MOSES OF OXFORD

Elie Wiesel lectures to 1,500 Oxford students
on the Joys of Purim

Rabbi Shmuel Boteach

MOSES OF OXFORD

A JEWISH VISION OF A UNIVERSITY AND ITS LIFE

2

Introduction to Volume 2 by
Danah Zohar

André Deutsch

First published in Great Britain in 1994 by
André Deutsch Ltd
106 Great Russell Street
London WC1B 3LJ

ISBN 0 233 98878 5

Cataloguing-in-Publication data available for this title
from the British Library

Printed in Finland
by WSOY

Contents

VOLUME TWO

Introduction

by Danah Zohar

The night before I was to meet Rabbi Shmuley Boteach for the first time I had a terrifying dream. I knew nothing about him, nothing about his age or background or affiliation with any particular Jewish sect, but in my dream he appeared as a stern and demanding Chasid. He was dressed in a long, black caftan, had side curls and a long, grey beard and he scowled at me with eyes that blazed with religious intensity and yet were cold from lack of any human warmth. Because of the dream, I nearly cancelled my appointment to see him.

I felt that I was on shaky ground in going to see any rabbi. Though I had converted to Judaism as a young student at Harvard University twenty years before, I had a thoroughly Christian background, my appearance was distinctly non-Jewish, and since my marriage to an Englishman with Christian loyalties I had been attending local Church of England services regularly on Sunday mornings. I felt that my Jewish credentials were just about nil.

The reason for going to see a rabbi was a ceaseless campaign on the part of our children, who were four and six years old at the time. Each had acquired a best friend at school who was Jewish, and they jointly announced to us one day that *they* wished to be Jewish. They knew I had become Jewish sometime in the past, so, they argued, why shouldn't they? At first my husband and I laughed and reminded them that our family was Christian. We told them they could join what religion they liked when they were sixteen, but in the meantime our roots as a family were in the local Christian community. The children didn't accept this and didn't give up. Now forced to go to church on Sunday mornings, they would sit in the pew with their eyes rolled towards the ceiling and say, 'This is ridiculous. Jews don't go to *church*!'

In the end, rather than damaging the children by completely refusing to acknowledge their feelings, I promised I would go to see a rabbi, explain the situation, and ask how we might learn to do a few Jewish ceremonies at home. That was how I came to contact Shmuley Boteach.

On the morning of my appointment my worst fears seemed confirmed. On the outside of his house on Oxford's Cowley Road there was a gigantic sign that said 'Chabad House of Oxford' and the door was opened by a woman whose natural hair was covered by the traditional scarf worn by ultra-Orthodox Jews. I had some vague knowledge of these Chabad, or Lubavitch, Jews, their '*mitzvah* tanks' that swooped down on the unsuspecting non-observant with exhortations to prepare for the imminent coming of the Messiah and their Orthodox interpretation of the Torah. Their zeal frightened me.

'You're Chasidim, aren't you?' I asked as the rabbi's wife gestured me towards the sitting room and she confirmed that, yes, they were. During the hour that I waited for her husband to appear (it wasn't long before I joined the many who reckon on 'real time', 'Jewish time' and 'Shmuley time'), I rehearsed several speeches that might enable me to survive unscathed the confrontation I dreaded. The room was lined with imposing Hebrew texts, a picture of the grey-bearded Lubavitcher rebbe, and banners proclaiming the coming of the Messiah. The only familiar feature was a ten-month-old baby playing with her building bricks at my feet, little Chaya Mushka, the eldest of what was to become Shmuley's brood of children.

Just at the moment when a mixture of panic and impatience was about to make me flee, a breathless young American dressed in casual trousers and a short, brown leather bomber jacket bounded into the room carrying a large packet of nappies under each arm. I assumed he was a university student who had done some shopping for the rabbi's wife.

'Hi, I'm Shmuley,' he said as he apologized for being late. He didn't shake my hand, nor has he ever since, despite a long and warm friendship, because Chasidim never touch women who aren't their wives.

'You mean *you're* the rabbi?' I gasped in undisguised relief. My relief was mixed with some disquiet on first glance, just because of his youth. In a way I had felt some comfort in the idea of taking my family's confused religious situation to a wise, older man, but Shmuley didn't disappoint me. It is one of the extraordinary things about his service in Oxford that, though the same age as many of his L'Chaim Society members, Shmuley has combined youth and its informality with an unquestionable authority and uncanny wisdom that command instant and abiding respect from both students and older members of the community. I've never once felt the twenty-five years that divide our ages when talking to him. The great Talmudic scholar and mystic Adin Steinsaltz says this is a natural gift of the Chabad *Shliach* (youth group leader) wherever you find him – that despite his youth he is able to draw on the wisdom and authority of the three thousand-year-old tradition he represents.

Shmuley drew on all that authority in his first meeting with me. He asked to see my conversion certificate and said that as far as he was concerned both the children and I were Jews and we were welcome in his community. But more than that, he said my husband was welcome.

'Come as a family whenever you like,' he repeated. I told him that could raise problems.

I had lived in Israel for four years as a Jew, but I felt like a fraud the whole time because no one knew my true background and I was constantly pretending to be something more than I was. In the Christian community I attended with my husband I also felt like a fraud because I wasn't really Christian any more and didn't believe what those around me believed. I could no longer bear pretending. My husband, too, had a similar problem. Though he had been brought up as a Christian, his own father was a Jew and my husband looks very Jewish. He is very interested in Jewish thinking. Whenever he is in a Jewish crowd, people put their arms around him and say, 'Don't worry. You're really one of us.' But he is and he isn't and he feels uncomfortable pretending to be more than he is. Shmuley understood and accepted all this at once.

'You'll come here as you are and you don't have to pretend anything,' he said, and he was as good as his word. The L'Chaim Society has provided a deeply religious and nourishing community for our family where, for the first time, we are free just to be ourselves and let our confused feelings and ideas about religion sort themselves out. In consequence, without pressure or pretence, Judaism has come to play a stronger role in all our lives and is at least one highly valued focus for our religious feelings. Our children enrolled themselves in Hebrew school at the synagogue and we always observe Shabbat at home.

In fact, nearly two-thirds of the L'Chaim Society's twelve hundred members are non-Jews. At the Sabbath table on Friday nights there is always a rich assortment of people – black students from America, Chinese and Southeast Asian Buddhists, the occasional Muslim and lots of young Jews for whom the society is the first real exposure to any sort of Jewish learning or ritual. Our good friends, a young Christian priest and his family, have always felt at home there. Seeing Shmuley dressed up in his outrageous clown costume for Purim, the priest's son described him as 'a pretty funny reverend'. There is no other religious community like it in Oxford. It must be rare to find it anywhere.

Yet I think it is very important to stress that there is no 'ecumenicism' at the L'Chaim Society. Nothing is watered down to accommodate the lowest common denominator – the student who knows nothing or the visitor of another faith. The traditions and the ethos of the society are unashamedly Jewish. No one can doubt Shmuley's own deep adherence to tradition or ever forget his Orthodox ideas and credentials. It's the true miracle of the society that it can be led by such a firmly observant Jew and yet be so open to and accepting of others and their ways. Indeed, something even more remarkable lies in this particular association – I think it is *just because* Shmuley has his strong Chabad principles and deep adherence to his own tradition that he can be the inspiration he is to all of us who come with more shaky beliefs or with other beliefs entirely. We all draw on his faith and observance in important ways that make us more secure, even more bold, in our own ways, even if they are different. Some of us may disagree vehemently with his ideas (for instance, about evolution!), but it is impossible not to respect the way he holds them.

I want to close with a few words about the incredible atmosphere at the L'Chaim Centre. Judaism stresses the holiness of the everyday, and it is the everyday that is glorified at L'Chaim. The simple matter of taking a meal together becomes a weekly celebration during the Sabbath meal on Friday night. There is singing and dancing (often on the tables), and every week Shmuley's amazing wife Debbie performs what a Christian would call the miracle of the loaves and the fishes. Having set the table for the thirty or forty expected guests, she never bats an eye when fifty or sixty more hungry students turn up with their friends to be fed. Tables appear out of nowhere, settings are placed, and vast quantities of extra food are carried from the kitchen. No one ever leaves L'Chaim hungry.

During the week, there is constant activity at the centre. Classes, seminars, debates, conversations, music, eating, the constant possibility of impromptu Chasidic dancing. People drop in off the street and Shmuley puts down the three telephones into which he is talking simultaneously to share a bagel and a joke. Shmuley's children seem to be everywhere. His marriage with Debbie seems particularly blessed and is a focus of joy and stability for everyone around them. The secretaries and the au pairs never seem to be Jewish and the obvious pleasure they take in all the activity and craziness that surrounds them adds something too. L'Chaim is more than a student society. It's a whole vision of life. For those of us who were young in the 60s, it's 'a happening'.

SECTION FIVE

SCIENCE AND THE JEWISH CONTRIBUTION TO KNOWLEDGE

Chapter Forty-five

JEWISH RATIONALISM: THE ONLY WAY FORWARD

On 9 December 1993, the Oxford University L'Chaim Society hosted Mikhail Gorbachev, the former President of the Soviet Union, and one of the most significant figures after the Second World War. It was with great pleasure and pride that we welcomed everyone to the first annual Elie Safra Lecture Series. Two years ago Mr Edmond Safra, to whom this book is dedicated, emerged as principal supporter and benefactor of our L'Chaim Society, and thus, when his eldest brother passed away in February 1993, it was with deep humility and respect that we inaugurated this annual lecture series in memory of Mr Elie Safra.

Throughout the world the Safra family name is synonymous with acts of loving kindness and generosity, and the name of Mr Edmond Safra in particular carries with it the nobility of ambassador of the Jewish nation and a loyal servant of his people, safeguarding their welfare everywhere. The first lecture in this series by Ambassador Morris Abram concerned Israel's place in the UN, and so it was also a great honour for us to welcome Mr and Mrs Javier Perez de Cuellar as our guests at the Gorbachev lecture as well.

Mr Gorbachev's visit marked a historic occasion for Oxford, as he is a man who has shaped world events and heralded an age of change. Not since the Second World War has there been such a whirlwind of influence through the offices of one man.

A Five-year Dream

This event was also of particular importance for me since it marked the culmination of a five-year dream that began the very day I was to embark from New York as an emissary of the Lubavitcher rebbe to assume my position as rabbi to the Jewish students of Oxford University. Although I was very busy with minute details about my departure, I was pulled as if by a magnet to Manhattan on the occasion of one of the largest public receptions that New York had ever seen. A gentleman from the Soviet Union was to lecture at the United Nations, and the whole city was in uproar. Thousands of people and police lined the streets to catch a glimpse of this one man whose charismatic political leadership was stealing international headlines and taking the world by storm. His name was Mikhail Gorbachev.

On hearing what he had said at the UN, a call for vastly reducing America's and the Soviet Union's nuclear arsenals and ground forces in Europe, I was greatly impressed by his political and humanitarian vision for peace and the betterment of the world. I saw his appearance at the United Nations as an outstanding event because it revealed a man motivated by the high ideal of making the world a better and freer place; and he was prepared and willing to use the secular power and influence vested in him as the President of the Soviet Union to achieve it. This channelling of resources I thought remarkable because he did not claim to be motivated by any religious belief, and yet he was prepared to act for the good of man against the background of a world where political power is so often wielded for cynical or expedient ends. It was a privilege to witness this, and it reconfirmed my vehement belief that causing good and creating a better world is the highest calling of humanity. I also believe that this should never, and can never, be achieved through exclusively religious actions. Perhaps the greatest tribute I can accord Mr Gorbachev is that when he relinquished the reins of power he left the world in a far better state than when he commenced office. In this he provides each and every one of us with a challenge: we too must leave an indelible mark, our stamp on the world, for the benefit of humanity. The prints we leave on anything we touch should have enhanced the lives and happiness of our brothers and sisters everywhere.

On a personal note Mr Gorbachev's UN début speech marked our first meeting, though I am not sure that Mr Gorbachev would immediately remember me. As he passed me in his big black Zil limousine leaving the United Nations, he smiled and waved in a friendly way in my direction, a gesture which touched me. It was only when I turned around that I realized there were about four hundred other people standing behind me.

Whatever the truth behind our first meeting, I became determined that one day he would speak for the L'Chaim Society, and I spent five years working towards making this dream a reality, calling the Gorbachev Foundation in Moscow and Mr Gorbachev's interpreter's home phone number on many occasions. Even though I had the faith that one day Mr Gorbachev would pay us the great honour of speaking for us, it was in some ways difficult to believe he was finally here.

Gorbachev and the Chanuka Tradition

December 9 1993 was a particularly auspicious and appropriate day for Mr Gorbachev to be speaking for us. Mr Gorbachev's lecture coincided with the first day of the Jewish festival of Chanuka, which is the most universal of the Jewish festivals, one that celebrates the light of God, goodness in the world, and the freedom of peoples from religious and political oppression.

The festival originates in the victory of the Maccabean Jews over their Greek oppressors in the land of Israel over two thousand years ago. Then King Antiochus, the profane and deranged king of Assyrian Greeks, attempted to destroy Judaism, and to impose his idolatrous and pagan practices on the Jews. The Jews were forbidden on pain of terrible death to practise their faith, and Antiochus committed obscene sacrilege in the Temple in Jerusalem. Eventually the Maccabees rebelled and miraculously defeated the might of the Greeks. They restored the Temple, rekindled the lights of the Menorah, and kept it burning by a miracle. Ever since then, the light of the Chanuka Menorah has become a universal symbol of religious and political freedom to all people. It also reminds us that nowhere does light shine so brightly than in darkness, and nowhere does the light of humanity show more clearly than in a morally impoverished world that cries out for goodness.

Fortunately, the event was very successful. Fifteen hundred students sat enraptured as Mr Gorbachev outlined his vision for a new world era of peace. I invited Mr Edmond Safra to light a beautiful menorah on stage while two Oxford students sang 'Moaz Tur'. Mr Gorbachev spoke for over an hour on the urgency of international co-operation in fostering a new way forward for positive change. At the end, Mr Edmond Safra presented Mr Gorbachev with a silver antique Russian menorah, over 100 years old, which Mr Gorbachev is going to place in the Gorbachev Foundation Museum as a permanent symbol of religious freedom.

Anger from Jewish Organizations

However, although the event went well on the whole, it was not without its own difficulties. In every press interview on the subject of Mr Gorbachev's visit, I was asked why a Jewish organization was hosting Mr Gorbachev. I was astonished at the question. *Why were we hosting Mr Gorbachev*?

I answered these critics by telling them that Mr Gorbachev had acted in the same tradition of Chanuka: restoring religious liberties, allowing for greater freedom and tolerance and enabling many Jews to emigrate unhindered to their homeland in Israel. Thus he serves as one of the greatest sources of inspiration to the world in general, and an example to our students in particular, and it was an honour of the highest order to host him.

But even this did not satisfy our detractors. The visit was co-ordinated with the First Artist Corporation in London, to whom we owe special thanks for the exceptional support of Jon Smith and Victoria Charlton.

They phoned one day to tell me, much to my surprise, that a Jewish group had made threats against our safety. The British Special Branch had called the head of the First Artist Corporation to warn him that we were being threatened by a group who claimed that Gorbachev was a menace, a torturer of Jews, and an operative of the KGB, and that it was absurd that a Jewish group should host him. An article even appeared in *New Moon* magazine criticizing the fact that we were hosting this event.

In this chapter, I would like to consider Mr Gorbachev's contribution to the world, and why it was that the L'Chaim Society decided to honour him.

Maimonides Fathers Jewish Rationalism

Eight hundred and fifty years ago, Moses Maimonides was confronted with a generation which, having been deeply influenced by Greek philosophy and western ideology and thought, was assimilating and losing its Jewish faith. The Jews of that generation were not prepared to act and be religious when they felt that Judaism was irrational, for theirs was a rational age. To be sure, Judaism comprises many rational and irrational commandments, ranging from prohibitions on theft to affixing a *mezuzah* (parchment with biblical texts) on one's door. The Maimonidean generation was prepared to preserve the rational commandments but wished to discard the irrational. To combat this, and to reaffirm the place of Judaism in the hearts, minds and actions of the Jewish nation, Maimonides fathered the first school of Jewish rationalism, best embodied in his celebrated philosophical work *A Guide of the Perplexed*, which gave a rational justification for many of the most difficult commandments. This alarmed much of the population of the time, especially those purists who felt there was no need for such a rationalization and considered Maimonides was bringing foreign criteria and influences into Judaism, particularly of Greek philosophers such as Aristotle who seemed to be a greater influence in his work than Moses.

So why did Maimonides do this and risk vitriolic attacks and the tarnishing of his reputation? Not because he necessarily saw any particular advantage in a rational approach, as opposed to a mystical, or super-rational approach, but rather because he wanted Judaism to be able to compete in a world where people were studying philosophy and rejecting those things which seemed irrational. Maimonides wanted Judaism to be at the forefront of world civilization, and he believed emphatically that Judaism had an integral and irreplaceable contribution to make to the world. He was therefore prepared to clothe Judaism in a very rational guise, even to the scorn and ambivalence of his compatriots, and perhaps even where it appeared to deny or contradict the integrity and tradition of Judaism up to that time.

This is nowhere clearer than in his interpretation of the sacrifices: he gave them a rational explanation which supplanted the previous mystical explanation, rather than adding to it. Animal sacrifices, Maimonides maintained, essentially weaned people away from idolatry and were therefore a means to the higher goal of an abstract worship of God; he gave the Jews a way of worshipping in a more tangible way with which they could identify, rather than just asking them, after being immersed in the materialistic society of Egypt, suddenly to embrace abstract forms of worship such as prayer. Animal sacrifices served only as an intermediary step until the Jews were ready and prepared to accept the truly auspicious, intangible, proper modes of worship, which reflected God's incorporeality, such as prayer, meditation, withdrawal and introspection. He went further to claim, amazingly, that God chose specific animals to be permitted to be brought into the temple, which symbolized the slaughtering of the gods of the ancient pagan peoples, so that for example the sheep represented the god of Egypt, the goat the god of Chaldeans, and cattle the god of India.

He writes: 'The general mode of worship in biblical times consisted in sacrificing animals in temples. It was in accordance with the wisdom and plan of God that He did not command us to give up and discontinue all these manners of service. Man generally cleaves to that to which he is used, and for this reason God allowed these kinds of service to continue . . . By this Divine plan it was effected that the traces of idolatry were blotted out, and the truly great principle of our faith, the Existence and Unity of God, was firmly established; this result was thus obtained without deterring or confusing the minds of the people by the abolition of the service to which they were accustomed . . . It is not in God's will to change the nature of man (by way of miracle), hence the mission of the prophets and the giving of the law. Sacrifices are not the primary object of God's commandments as we are not commanded to sacrifice in every place and every time, and indeed there are many restrictions necessary to limit this kind of worship. Jeremiah says (in the name of God) that the primary object of the precepts is this, Know Me and serve no other being; "I will be your God, and ye shall be my people" (Leviticus 26:12).' (*Guide of the Perplexed*, chapter 32).

Rationalism as a Means Rather Than an End

There are many instances in Maimonides' writings, however, that suggest he felt the rational was only an antechamber for the super-rational. He writes in the Mishnah Torah, in the laws of *Meila*, that the laws of the sacrifice have no logical or rational explanation, and he criticizes those who try to apprehend certain commandments. Summoning the verse Exodus 19:24, when God tells Moses, 'Away, get thee down, and thou shalt come up, thou, and Aaron with thee: but let not the priests and the people break through to come up unto the Lord, lest he break forth upon them,' Maimonides transplants this to those people who attempt to offer a rational explanation for the commandments, saying that it could consume and destroy their minds. This seems to indicate that he saw it as a very arrogant attitude that mortal man, with his limited understanding and constrained intellectual capacity, should try to apprehend mysteries of creation which transcend his capabilities. Further, he states that the sacrifices are *chukim*; *chukim* being not irrational but super-rational (as opposed to irrational) commandments. He even goes so far as to say, in his introduction to his commentary on the Mishnah, that 'due to our great sins, the matter of the sacrifices has been lost in our days, and there are very few people who study it, and it is not remembered by even those who do, for there is no concrete explanation to establish these habits and there is none who ask, expound, or are interested.' In other words, because the sacrifices lack a sensible, rational explanation, people have discarded their study, which serves to reinforce the contradiction in Maimonides' attitude towards the super-rational commandments.

Einstein's Search for a Unified Field Theory

One of the problems with Jewish rationalism has been that it has tended not to be all-encompassing. To draw an analogy from the empirical forces, Einstein died a very broken man knowing full well that quantum mechanics and his novel Theory of Relativity contradicted each other. He searched in vain in the last years of his life, especially while he was at Princeton's Institute for Advanced Study, for a unified field theory, but never attained it.

Just as there is an inherent paradox in the empirical world as we understand it, between colossal systems such as planets, stars and galaxies, and tiny objects like subatomic particles, the same can be said of the rational and intelligible versus the super-rational and mystical. The above contradiction in Maimonides actually permeates much of Jewish thought. There exists an inherent paradox at the very heart of human life and intellectual endeavour between the rational and the mystical that seemingly cannot be reconciled.

It seems clear, then, that Maimonides deliberately set out to give rational reasons for the sacrificing of animals in the Temple, despite his going to great lengths to state there is no rational, logical explanation and that it does not behove us to seek one. As we have seen, this apparent contradiction is merely a small part of a far greater battle that has always existed between the rational and super-rational. What I perceive is that perhaps that tension is necessary, for it leads to creativity.

Tension Between Male and Female

For example, at work there is the conflict between promotion and negation of self; when to assert yourself and when to be subservient. Or in devotion to one's faith, at what point does one say, 'Yes, I will do what God asks', and when does one maintain, 'But I want to be an individual as well; I don't just want to read a standard prayer from a prayer book that was written two thousand years ago and doesn't accommodate my own personal aspirations'? There is this constant tension between the infinite and the finite, the super-rational and the rational, the submission and promotion of self.

This is described in the Kabbalah, Jewish mysticism, as the tension between male and female; women represent the passive, infinite dimension of God and can therefore give birth to children, and men represent the masculine, more finite element of God. These differences are said to be evidenced even in the anatomical make-up of men and women whereby males represent a line which has a beginning and end, thus finite, *kav* in the kabbalistic vernacular, and women represent a circle (or receptacle, which possesses no beginning or end, *igul* in the Kabbalah), the infinite. This conflict or discrepancy is what leads to their attraction and union.

The conflict is found throughout all the major world disciplines, whether it be called yin and yang, whether it is called in the Kabbalah *ilah v'alul*, or *ratzoh veshuv*, or whether it is the Greek concept of contraries. The point is that this tension is universal, and Judaism maintains that this is because it reflects a real and universal dialectic, one which originates in the Godhead itself. God has both finite and infinite characteristics, both transcendent and immanent features. Thus Descartes's notion of the transcendental God and Spinoza's arguments of the immanent God may both contain valid arguments.

Are these two strands irreconcilable? No, rather they are essential for human creativity and perhaps for life itself; life is a struggle amidst the tensions between self and what is beyond the self, between the microcosm and macrocosm. Seen in this context, the contradictions within Maimonidean thought and everywhere else between the rational and super-rational may, ultimately, be irreconcilable and a standard feature of human intellectual endeavour. Let's face it, even those of us who claim to be rational and logical people are still aware of the deep, dark mysterious forces operating within ourselves that often govern our actions.

Rationalism as Necessary

Earlier I mentioned that Maimonides fathered Jewish rationalism largely in order that Judaism could compete with the prevailing philosophical forces operating in the world at that time. In that respect, Maimonides may have considered the rational explanations he gave as necessary, but not essential, to the Jewish endeavour of bringing God to the world. He outlined this clearly in his introduction to the *Guide of the Perplexed* where he wrote that this book was only for those who in the field of Jewish practice and thought felt confused or bewildered. If someone was prepared to accept Judaism as a super-rational force, an act of special revelation by an intangible and immortal Creator, and relegate it to the realm of the transcendental, then that was far better. He largely viewed his rational explanations of the commandments as a concession to the faithless or confused masses. This is why he did not consider his most monumental work to be the *Guide of the Perplexed*, his work of philosophy, but rather the Mishnah Torah, which is a book of relegation to the sublime, a book of law in which he gives no reasons for the commandments, but just laws as to what was permitted and what was forbidden, and the obligations incumbent upon the Jew in everyday living. In fact, he did not even include footnotes to show from where in the Talmud he had collected his laws!

Earth as an Arena for the Unity of God

However, if it is true that this tension between the rational and super-rational emanates from God himself, then we are faced with a dilemma. According to our teaching, the whole historical endeavour is meant ultimately to culminate in a time when God will be unified, when there will be synthesis, an amalgamation, a marriage of heaven and earth, of the infinite and the finite, where the unity of God will be demonstrated throughout His world. Human history in general and our individual lives in particular are meant to be the arena for that manifestation of Divine unity. For example, every time a man and woman marry, unite, and have children, they display the unity of God. Although as above they both may emanate from two distinct aspects of the Godhead, they show, by creating a single life together, that ultimately those two sources are one. (Hence the centrality of marriage within Jewish thought comes into sharp focus.)

This unity of God will ultimately be revealed to the naked eye in the epoch of the Messiah. At that time there will no longer be Godly truths that are spoken from the heavens, but from worldly experience we will be able to understand these truths without hindrance. There will be an interlinking of Torah knowledge, revelation and human experience, what we call wisdom. People will be able to look at everyday experience and discern truths revealed to humankind only thousands of years ago at Sinai.

I believe we are quickly approaching that time.

The only way forward for religion in this day and age is Jewish rationalism; however, this is not only for Maimonides' reason, that people are not prepared to hear anything else, and thus rationalism is a concession, a necessary evil, for the faithless masses. Indeed, it could easily be claimed that this is an irrational age on the evidence of the rise of cults and mystical groups since the 1960s which demonstrate that people are fed up with the superficiality of society and are looking for something lofty that transcends their ordinary lives, because they have found that life is largely unliveable without something of major significance above them. So why is rationalism so important for our times?

Should a Jewish Group Host Mikhail Gorbachev?

Many people told us that we should not host Mikhail Gorbachev, including Orthodox Jews at a lecture in Manchester which I delivered: they said we should not host him because he was a secularist. They claimed he brought about religious freedom not out of an active choice and pursuit of personal liberties but because the Soviet system was crumbling and political and social pressures dictated this course of action. On this line of thinking, the only thing he should be credited for is the fact that he did not send tanks rolling in to crush the people once this quiet and largely passive revolution began.

However, I disagree totally with this view. On the contrary, I believe that the beauty of Gorbachev is that he *was* a secularist. If Billy Graham or the Pope had to go to the Soviet Union and preach that God would overcome the destructive and Godless forces of Communism, the message would have been purely external; ignorant people could embrace Divine truth. It would have meant that once again Divine truths superseded human truths, and people were forced to look to the heavens for wisdom and teaching. Had the Soviet Union changed as the result of a religious revival or awakening, then the world would not have changed. Rather, it would have been said that the heavens had superimposed its values upon humanity. The only credit humankind could have taken was that they were wise and courageous enough to embrace these revealed truths.

Gorbachev the Secularist

But Gorbachev as a secularist understood that truth has a way of outlasting falsehood and of vindicating itself. He saw that the truths of religion – freedom of choice, freedom of worship and the freedom for people to be themselves – which had been established on Mount Sinai thousands of years ago, could be deduced by people directly. Here there occurred a marriage of the rational and the super-rational; truths which Communism had tried to destroy outlived their oppression, because ultimately there is one thing which cannot be destroyed, that is, being people, and there are certain truths so evident that they can be gathered from human life and earthly experience.

The only way forward for religion today is this same marriage between heaven and earth. The religious agenda preached by rabbis and priests must not be foreign. Their message must not be truths culled from the heavens but rather one which relates directly to people, regardless of how much or how little previous exposure they have had to religion. When modern individuals sit in seats at synagogue or in a pew in church, listening to a clerical sermon, they must feel that every word being uttered is totally consonant and synonymous with their own experiences and is in no way alien to their own experiences. The greatest form of religious truth today is when a once far-off truth is preached to people who can already identify with its message. In this way, God can speak to us from human experience, rather than from a far removed position which is extraneous to our lives.

Judaism Addressing Love Relationships

It is common knowledge that Jewish religious organizations which are successful today in bringing people back are those which speak to people specifically about issues that were not previously touched on, but are very human. I would say that half of the rabbis I know deal extensively and sometimes exclusively with issues of relationships, marriage, sex, or children – and with drugs and medical ethics – because these are the issues central to today's society and they display the orchestration of Judaism with life. Where in the Talmud are there long passages about how to have a successful marriage, for example? There is much advice to be found, but it cannot be said that these passages are central to the Talmudic endeavour. These are new agendas which religion has taken and they are necessary for they demonstrate, not just the continued relevance of religion to everyday life, but the synthesis between the message of God at Sinai and the realities of everyday living.

Pre-marital Sex and Adultery

Imagine a rabbi coming to speak to university students on the subject of pre-marital sex. There are two ways he could go about this. The first is to lay down the law on the matter, explaining that it is forbidden and a sin. This, however, means nothing to the students he is addressing; it is totally foreign to their experiences. The second, and I believe much more proper and effective method, is to say, 'I know that the propensity for pre-marital sex is great. So why oppose a natural human condition? For the betterment of the human condition; if you are prepared to make the sacrifices necessary in waiting, then later within your marriage that intimacy we call sex will not only be unique and memorable, but it will bind you together with your spouse for the rest of your life. Sex with your partner will have remained an exclusive practice only the two of you shared, which is what makes it special for you.' Couched in these terms, the message is essentially the same, but will be more readily accepted. But it must be said in this way not only for reasons of expediency, but because if Judaism doesn't make sense to the masses then it has defeated its essential purpose of bringing unity between the heavens and the earth. Similarly, if instead of lecturing about the evils of adultery, rabbis advocate methods by which to retain passion in monogamous relationships, then our message becomes not only more accessible, but more natural.

Heavenly Truths and Earthly Experience

I am therefore opposed to any form of religious proselytizing whereby one religious exponent seeks to impose his values on a recipient. Rather, we must go beyond this: we must deliver heavenly truths which corroborate earthly experience. If one seeks to impose one's own religious views on a non-accepting community then one is essentially telling people somehow to incorporate religion as an added, and sometimes foreign, feature into their existing lives. The message is, 'You live in an un-Godly world and must somehow make room for Godliness.' A positive message which encourages people to develop what they already are is far better. By telling people what they can do to make themselves better, the negative things will fall away. Rather than 'becoming' religious, we must seek to allow our natural religiosity, the fact that we are all part of God already, to express itself. This is why I am convinced that the best way of encouraging Jewish students to develop their religion is in a totally natural way, and why many of them become more religious without realizing it, by starting to come to Friday-night meals and ending up at classes without a conscious decision to 'be more religious'. In fact they would probably be shocked if it were pointed out to them.

In conclusion, therefore, it becomes clear that our aim must be to arrive at a point where what appears to be super-rational commands are obeyed on a rational understanding, and where Godly truths can be understood directly from human experience. We must marry the rational and super-rational; we must synthesize our religious and natural selves. At this point there will exist a harmony, which Buddhists perhaps call *nirvana*, and Thomas Moore called *utopia*. The Jews call it a Messianic era. A perfect world. Perfect not only because in that time the world will be free of death, disease, jealousy and contention, but because we will be free of the terrible inner tension which eats away at our very being, the tension between the active and the passive, between the finite and the infinite, whence we are derived and which we all incorporate. Without this harmony the result, as is already too evident, is broken people, with some idea that harmony might be possible if only they had the means to achieve it. It is no wonder that when people die we use the epitaph, 'Rest in Peace'. But this is a lie. Inner peace is not only attainable in death, and this should never be our goal. We must never dignify death.

With harmony on this planet and in our inner lives, the paradox of the rational and the super-rational may finally be resolved and the result will be a world where people are whole and nations are at peace.

Chapter Forty-six

EVOLUTIONARY ETHICS AND MORALITY

To a university, the quest for truth is paramount, and supersedes all other goals. If a truth is universally recognized, then the learning process is the simple one of acquiring the necessary knowledge. However, there are far more unanswered questions than answered ones, even in the rarefied atmosphere of academia, and it can be difficult for students to wean themselves from the expectation that there is *somewhere* a completely correct explanation, if only they could find it in the library or their tutor would tell them. For some arts students this is a reasonably simple process to grasp: after all, teachers and tutors have always said there are no right answers in the interpretation of texts or history, only more or less plausible hypotheses. For those coming from a philosophical or scientific background, though, uncertainty can be profoundly disconcerting. What are we to make of Heisenberg's Uncertainty Principle when the whole of our academic career to date has concentrated on finding more and more accurate ways of quantifying the world?

For some, it is tempting to abandon the search for truth altogether: they treat the academic roller-coaster as a mere game to play until they can get that upper second degree and leave for the 'real' world of the city. However, this is not the point of the exercise and must leave those who do so feeling they missed out somewhat on the main opportunity of three or four years' study, which is, after all, to spend time thinking and exploring the world without being too involved on a day-to-day level.

A Cracked Ivory Tower

University is a wonderful opportunity to explore ideas without having to make up your mind, to reach maturity without being told what to do and think every day. This surely must be the origin of the disparaging term 'ivory tower' – an isolated world of privilege where the everyday problems can be ignored. However, this is also precisely the first attraction of university, the reason why so many people look back on their university days with such affection. That is also the reason why we should not give our allegiance to dogma until we are convinced for ourselves that it is correct, until we have internalized it as a truth that we can be proud to say we have considered in depth.

The Evolution of Darwinism

In the autumn of 1992, a science reporter, Richard Milton, published a book entitled *The Facts of Life: Shattering the Myth of Darwinism*. The immense media interest and controversy surrounding the book, and it truly generated a storm in Britain, has cast the spotlight on the scientific validity of Darwin's theory of the evolution of life. As Jews, our principal interest should be the promotion of truth, regardless of its consequences. When I say this, I mean even religious consequences. This was the position always adopted by a name I continually return to throughout this work, and one of our greatest thinkers, Maimonides, who wrote, 'Accept truth regardless of its source.' I sincerely believe we have no interest in perpetuating Judaism, or even the notion of God, if it is contrary to the truth. Judaism is not merely a culture or way of life that was practised by our ancestors. It is either truth or it is nothing. I personally have no interest in merely perpetuating an ethnicity, and neither do the intelligent young minds I encounter every day. Ethnic origins lack passion and cannot inspire the way a personal God and His revealed creed can.

As a Jew, I am watching this debate on Darwinian evolution very closely, and encourage others to do the same. It is for this reason, for instance, that the Oxford University L'Chaim Society have sponsored numerous debates on Darwinism, which featured scientists of international renown. All too often in the past, 'scientific' positions (which are contrary to Judaism) have been adopted without delving into the validity of those scientific assertions: this is bad for the truth if the theories are wrong, and the situation is worsened if Jewish faith is weakened because of belief in false or inaccurate scientific dogma. Another, perhaps more important, reason to intensify the debate on this issue in particular is the way in which Darwinism can sometimes be manipulated to promote dangerous morals and ethics.

When Theories Are Treated as Fact

The theory of evolution, unlike almost any other single theory in science, has had a profound influence on moral and religious development in the short space of just 130 years. Evolution, far from being just another single theory, is a total statement of what man and nature are, what history signifies, and what the basic laws of the world are. Although the religions still survive, all, even Judaism, have become deeply penetrated by the attitudes and ideas generated by evolution. Their foundations have been gnawed away and the faith of the believer is now overcast with doubt. The doctrines of evolution continue to dominate the philosophy of the western world. Few members of western society exist whose very thought and speech are immune to the assumptions and doctrines of evolution. Upon it have been built ideologies, philosophies, and even the everyday behaviour of ordinary people.

In a relatively short amount of time, evolution has become scientific dogma. Although religionists continue to fight, virtually all formal secular opposition has stopped. Evolution is now so indoctrinated everywhere that it is difficult for a scientist to question it without risking the loss of respect.

Sadly, most people, including many of the theory's leading exponents, are blind to its universal implications and ramifications for humanity. We conveniently ignore the question of what kind of world, and what hope for mankind, the theory of evolution can leave us. My purpose in the following lines is to examine the theory of evolution's *weltanschauung*, its holistic world view leaving it to the reader to draw the conclusions.

Domination of the Master Race

'The more civilized so-called Caucasian races have beaten the Turkish hollow in the struggle for existence. Looking to the world at no very distant date, what an endless number of the lower races will have been eliminated by the higher civilized races throughout the world.'

Compare the above quoted statement with the following rationale for euthanasia: 'In nature there is no pity for the lesser creatures when they are destroyed so that the fittest may survive. Going against nature brings ruin to man . . . and is a sin against the will of the eternal Creator. It is only Jewish impudence to demand that we overcome nature.'

These statements express such similar sentiments that the reader may initially suppose they were written by the same author. However, the author of the former was a scientist, Charles Darwin, and the author of the latter statement was a political leader who lived by Darwin's evolutionary ideology. His name: Adolf Hitler. Hitler was a spiritual and ideological student of Darwin and evolution. His entire concept of the Aryan master race evolved in response to the ethical implications of the theory of evolution.

Sir Arthur Keith, one of Britain's leading evolutionists before the Second World War, lived through that war and endured with others the awful suffering visited by Hitler on Britain and the world. He did not write the following statements out of any feeling of sympathy for Hitler and his cause. Rather, his honest understanding of the real nature of evolution, in which he firmly and fully believed, impelled him to say:

> To see evolutionary measures and tribal morality being applied vigorously to the affairs of a great modern nation, we must turn again to Germany of 1942. We see Hitler devoutly convinced that evolution produced the only real basis for a national policy . . . The means he adopted to secure the

> destiny of his race and people [were] organized slaughter . . . Such conduct is highly immoral . . . Yet Germany justifies it; it is consonant with tribal or evolutionary morality. Germany has reverted to the tribal past, and is demonstrating to the world . . . the methods of evolution . . . The German Führer, as I have consistently maintained, is an evolutionist; he has consciously sought to make the practice of Germany conform to the theory of evolution . . . It was often said in 1914 that Darwin's doctrine of evolution has bred war in Europe, particularly in Germany . . . In 1935, a committee of psychologists, representing thirty nations, issued a manifesto in which it was stated that 'war is the necessary outcome of Darwin's theory' . . .
>
> (*Essays on Human Evolution*, page 26.)

Reaching Toward Homo Supremus

If his views still seem extreme, it should be pointed out that the ideology of conflict and struggle for survival is not only in accordance with evolution, it is its most rudimentary tenet. In dealing with a concept of humans strictly as biological organisms in a 'great chain of being' with all other organisms, many evolutionary biologists have divided homo sapiens into various 'subspecies,' or races, in the same way that other species are subdivided.

In evolutionary terminology, a race is an incipient species. If racial development is progressive and beneficial in the 'struggle for existence', then that race will be preserved and others may die out: the surviving group eventually becomes a new and 'better' (in the sense of more adapted to its environment) species. The ape-like homo erectus may have evolved into homo sapiens, and some day a particularly superior race among the latter may evolve into, say, homo supremus, superman.

The ordinary human of today in relation to the 'superman' of tomorrow may be labelled 'subhuman', and subsequently unnecessary to be preserved, or worse, befitting removal and annihilation. Just as the majority of today's humans feel it moral to experiment with apes for the benefit of their own higher species, homo supremus may deem it necessary to experiment with homo sapiens for their benefit. Thus, in the diseased minds of the Mengeles and Eichmanns of the past, they only implemented experimentation on what was, to them, a lower species for the benefit of the higher species, namely the Aryan race.

Philosophically, there is no moral justification for our present use of other species (especially the higher mammals and of course the primates) unless somewhere we posit a quantifiable difference between humans and other animals. To say that we are more intelligent is not enough to tip the balance in our favour; the difference must be a whole order of degree, otherwise we must fall back on the weak arguments of 'we do this to animals because we have the power to, and of course we wish to help our own species'. Such thinking exonerates the National Socialists from all their atrocities because they were thinking logically on the basis of the theory of evolution, and they had the power to preserve their own race at the expense of others. While their thinking may, of course, be warped, it still exemplifies the extent to which these hypotheses can be carried.

Different Orders in Creation

The analogy is very frightening and real. According to the creation model of the world's origin, God created four orders: mineral, vegetable, animal and intellectual. These classifications instilled within the creation are immutable. Nothing within the creation can ever, or will ever, transcend its classification and evolve into a higher order. All that now exists has always existed in its present state. In sharp contrast, evolution sees all living things as being in a potential state and never culminating. Organisms continually climb the evolutionary ladder.

Charles Darwin gave his major work on evolution, *The Origin of Species by Natural Selection*, the provocative subtitle, 'The Preservation of Favoured Races in the Struggle for Life'. Though in this book the discussion centred on races of plants and animals, it was clear that he also included the various human races in the same concept. If the criterion is mere power, we may eat animals because we have gained power by accidental evolution. Extending this concept to people, the theory could easily be manipulated into meaning that the murder of weak innocents in the struggle for life is but a logical result of the theory of evolution. No distinction is recognized between cattle abattoirs and the German murder factories, except the degree of 'accidental evolutionary development' between empowered and powerless.

Inter-human Competition

Consider the following statement made by a former president of the National Academy of Sciences: 'We can, of course, be grateful to nature for the highly remarkable genetic gifts which we have inherited as a result of the very complex process of selection which our ancestors experienced. We must also keep in mind, however, that many of our most valued characteristics probably emerged out of inter-human competition.'

Thomas Huxley, the man most responsible for the widespread acceptance of evolutionary doctrine remarked, 'No rational man cognizant of the facts believes that the average Negro is the equal, still less the superior, of the white man.' In fact, after the evolutionary theory erupted in 1859, questions of whether blacks were of the same species as whites extended to questions of whether or not Afro-Americans could survive competition with their white relations. The momentous answer was a resounding 'No!'

The African was inferior because he represented the 'missing link' between ape and man. Of course, considerations of modern political correctness may have altered these beliefs, but the underlying premise often still remains.

I am in no way insinuating that such is the necessary, logical outcome of the theory of evolution, or that any of its founding fathers or leading lights believe or seek willingly to promote these offensive thoughts. What I am saying is that evolution lends itself to being misconstrued or misrepresented by those who would actively seek to promote such warped and base views.

The Image of God and the Shadow of an Ape

Judaism, by contrast, could never be manipulated to promote this kind of racism because the Torah teaches that humans were created 'in the image of God', not in the shadow of an ape. This is the sole criterion by which Judaism insists on the equality of all people. Superficially, in fact, egalitarian ideas are supported by no evidence. Inequality amongst humans is blatantly apparent. The only way one can find any support for the idea of equality is in the religious teaching that all people are born in the image of God, and are therefore equal. Thus quantitative differences, such as amount of intelligence, wealth, ability to love, are all subordinated to the qualitative definition of the universal equality of all humans by virtue of being a Homo Spiritus, a God-like being. There can be absolutely no value differences between humans.

A Case for Higher Human Species

With this kind of evolutionary thinking essentially universal, it is no wonder that the concepts of evolution were so important in the development of the master-race idea. George Gaylord Simpson, a leading evolutionist, writes: 'Evolution does not necessarily proceed at the same rate in different populations, so that among many groups of animals it is possible to find some species that have evolved more slowly, hence are now more primitive, as regards some particular trait or even overall. It is natural to ask – as many have asked – whether among human races there may not similarly be some that are more primitive in one way or another or in general. It is indeed possible to find single characteristics that are probably more advanced or more primitive in one race than in another.'

Thus, according to Sir Arthur Keith, what Hitler simply did, using the unpreventable ramifications of evolutionary thought, was to identify who these 'more primitive' races were, and put the Jew at the head of this list. Thus he used the Jew for scientific experiments, just as the Homo Sapiens use apes in laboratories.

Let me make it clear that it is preposterous to hold the theory or its proponents responsible, even partially, for Nazi horrors. Just as many historians, particularly Robert Wistrich in his book *Anti-Semitism: The Longest Hatred*, have pointed out how various traditional Christian dogmas have led to atrocities against the Jewish people, the same may be said of evolution. Still, this does not directly fault Christianity or its adherent, so much as indicate its susceptibility to abuse and manipulation. However, the theory of evolution provided for many racists a ready-made justification of their denegration of other people. My purpose in this chapter is not to make subjective arguments against evolution based on an examination of its morality. Rather, it is to draw attention to the fact that evolution is not merely a scientific theory, but a comprehensive view of the quality and meaning of life. As such, it must be scrutinized with the same moral and ethical standards that have always been applied to religious and political doctrine.

Connecting with Nazism and Communism

Evolution may be said to have had a determinative influence not just on Nazism, but also on similar collectivisms such as Fascism, Marxism and modern Communism. All such ideologies, built up as they are on the concept of statist totalitarian control, are influenced by the Darwinian doctrines of struggle for existence and survival of the fittest. Friedrich Nietzsche, the indirect and unwitting philosophical father of these systems, was an ardent evolutionist, as were his prize ideological disciples, Hitler and Mussolini.

The Politics and Science of Evolution

Social Darwinism, the general term used to label the many collectivist systems resulting from evolutionary thought, has often been understood in the sense of a philosophy exalting competition, power and violence over convention, ethics and religion. Thus it has become the basis for nationalism, imperialism, militarism and dictatorship, and of the cults of the hero, the superman and the master race. Commonly used expressions, such as 'might makes right' and 'dog eat dog', have come into general use and been justified by evolutionary thought. From the 'Preservation of Favoured Races in the Struggle for Life' it was a short step to the preservation of favoured individuals, classes or nations – and from their preservation to their glorification.

Fascism is generally perceived first and foremost as a right-wing movement, and Communism as left-wing. Both, however, are variants of the same species: evolutionistic, totalitarian collectivism. That there were many similarities between Fascist Germany and Communist Russia can be documented quite easily by tracing the acceptance of Marxism by Lenin and the eventual development of Bolshevism and Leninism. The thinking of the leaders of the former USSR was rooted deeply in an evolutionary outlook.

Evolution and Class Warfare

Karl Marx, amongst the leading intelligentsia of the world, was a prime devotee of Darwin's concept of 'natural selection', or 'struggle for existence'. Marx wrote to his associate Friedrich Engels that he considered Darwin's ideas about competition of living things in a natural environment to be relevant to what Marx reasoned was a warfare or struggle of classes of human beings. Marx and Engels wrote most explicitly of competition between the working class and the bourgeoisie. For Marx, the concept of 'struggle for existence' became translated into 'class warfare'. One author expresses this idea succinctly: 'In an age of social Darwinism, the combination of the ideas of struggle, of historical evolution, and of progress proved irresistible. The Marxists became merely a sect in the larger church . . . In urging these lessons, Marx and Engels set the pattern of all subsequent Marxist polemics by using what may be called the evolutionists' double standard: "When you do it, it's wrong, because you are the past; when we do it it's right, for we are the future." '

Belief in Manifest Destiny

In fact, dictatorial actions by Hitler, Mussolini, Lenin, Stalin, Khruschev and current Marxist leaders as well, have all been supposedly sanctioned by Darwin's theory of natural selection through the struggle for existence and the survival of the fittest. The Fascist Axis nations were believed by their leaders to be most worthy of survival. Similarly, the Communist nations, either the former USSR and its satellites of the 1970s, or China, Vietnam and other Communist Asian nations, are claimed by their own theoreticians to be most worthy of survival. Empirical evidence is abundant that other states and ideologies cannot co-exist with Communist nations, that the 'dog-eat-dog' mentality encourages the devouring of other peoples or ideologies.

Evolution's Impact on Psychology

Evolution has also strongly influenced the social sciences, most of all psychology. Psychology, the study of the mind, is in modern times almost entirely based on the assumption that humankind are only animals, derived by evolutionary descent from ape-like ancestors. This, of course, was the view of Sigmund Freud, who has exerted probably the greatest single influence on the structure of modern psychology. Freud utilized the Lamarckian concept of 'inheritance of acquired characteristics', which was never entirely relinquished by Darwin himself, whereby characteristics acquired during the lifetime of an individual were somehow transmitted to offspring. Though this idea is now fully discredited – no evidence having ever been found that after thousands of years of binding the feet of Chinese girls, they were at all more likely to have ready-deformed feet at birth – when Freud accepted the idea, he gave significant importance to the assumption that the individual's behaviour is the consequence of the environment in which growth and development have occurred.

Where Can Evolutionary Ethics Lead Us?

Once a man has replaced God with a slime-cell origin, there is no more Divine constraint towards honesty, purity, charity or any other ethical values associated with Divine revelation. What we are left with is secular humanism and arguments for goodness that only work if man is the ultimate beneficiary of his own goodness. The Mishnah states, 'Know that which is above you; an Eye that sees, an Ear that hears, and all your deeds are recorded.' Rabbi Menachem Schneerson, the Lubavitcher Rebbe has repeatedly emphasized that if man removes the 'Eye that sees and the Ear that hears', and thus denies the ultimate arbiter of right and wrong, then there is no telling what atrocities will take place within an individual or collective framework. Without a Supreme Judge, man is free to act according to animalistic whims, and the world becomes a jungle in which 'right' and 'wrong' are determined by 'like' and 'dislike', impulse and repulse.

Desirable Behaviour

If there is no God, then good and evil simply do not exist. There are only subjective opinions regarding desired and undesired behaviour. If there is no God, what we call good and evil or right and wrong are merely euphemisms for personal taste. You don't like stealing, so you label it 'wrong'. Another person may enjoy stealing, and labels it 'right'. If you dislike an action intensely you may even go so far as to call it 'evil', but without God this judgement can never get beyond the process of attaching labels to actions.

Eichmann's Evil

Gideon Hausner, the chief prosecutor in the Eichmann trial in Jerusalem, wrote of how often he was asked which of Eichmann's characteristics he found the most reprehensible and frightening. He said it was unquestionably the fact that Eichmann was a completely rational and sane man. That a human being who is mentally balanced, and has a deep revulsion for the murder of other human beings, can suddenly relegate an entire people to the standing of 'subhuman' and 'fit for extermination' should be incomprehensible, but the implications of the theory of evolution can make it in some horrible way 'logical'.

When God's law of 'do not murder' is removed and we rely on man's or society's law of 'do not murder', the foundation of which is secular humanism, then people have the right to interpret it as they see fit, because it was invented by them in the first place. 'Do not murder another human being', we humans say, but in the Nazi vernacular 'human' did not include the Jews. However, when God says, 'Thou shalt not murder', it is not man's law and it is also not subject to man's interpretation and rests outside his right to tamper with it. It includes all human beings, because all were created by Him and all are protected by the law.

Ethics for the Scientific Age

Since science has removed our former guide for goodness, many scientists feel constrained to provide, in substitution, new 'scientific ethics'. Of course, the basis of these scientific ethics has to be evolution itself.

Unfortunately this approach makes nonsense of the whole anti-utilitarian drive of human culture: we know that we humans can choose to be altruistic, and that is what separates us from the rest of creation. Professor Bently Glass suggested a more 'natural' definition of the concepts of 'good' and 'evil', whereby they would be completely divorced from their moral connotations. In his opinion the concepts of morality and ethics are illusory. His 'natural' guidelines would define 'good' as what is good for the development of the species; what is not good for the development of the species would, by definition, be 'evil'.

Compare the idea proposed by Nobel Medicine Prize winner, Francis Crick, who suggested that it may be a good idea to redefine the concepts of 'birth' and 'death'. He recommended that the time of birth of an infant be redefined as two days after parturition so that there would be time to examine it for defects. If its defects were sufficiently deleterious, the infant could presumably be eliminated with impunity because it had not yet become alive. Similarly, Crick proposed redefining death as occurring when a pre-determined age, such as eighty or eight-five, were achieved. At that time the person automatically would be declared dead and all his or her property would pass on to the heirs. Here, too, the aged human could be eliminated with impunity, because he or she was already legally 'dead'.

A Means of Escape

I leave the last word on the topic of evolutionary ethics to Aldous Huxley, who came from a family of avid supporters of the theory of evolution. He wrote the following towards the end of his life:

> I had reasons not to want the world to have meaning, and as a result I assumed the world had no meaning, and I was readily able to find satisfactory grounds for this assumption . . . For me, as it undoubtedly was for most of my generation, the philosophy of meaninglessness was an instrument of liberation . . . from a certain moral system. We were opposed to morality because it interfered with our sexual freedom.

Chapter Forty-seven

DREAMS OF THE MENTAL EYE

Perhaps one of the more perplexing aspects of living at college for the students is that the usual routines of life are eroded so quickly. The weekend, sacred to those at school or in nine-to-five jobs as the only time for relaxation, is either transformed into the end of one long party, or used for just as much work as the weekdays. It is so easy to consider a day as just a part of the fifth week of term, or, more excitingly, Eighth Week, the last of the term, rather than in the more usual way of 30th March and so on. Everyone who has had an 'essay crisis' (last-minute attempt to do the week's work overnight before the weekly tutorial) knows how disruptive working all night can be to 'normal' sleep patterns. Towards the end of three or four years it seems increasingly unlikely that an Oxford student will ever be able to achieve the routine other people seem to find so easy: getting out of bed at seven and going to sleep around midnight, not at four in the morning after yet another profound debate. In this context, it is not surprising that discussions about sleep (or the lack of it), and dreams in particular, feature heavily in those brunch-time conversations when students have just emerged from bed, or the late-night talk-in hosted in a student's room.

While studying as a rabbinical student in Sydney, I came into contact with many Jewish psychoanalysts who were eager to discover the Jewish perspective on dreams. I would lead a weekly class on Judaism in one of their offices, and was forced to undertake extensive research into the Jewish attitude toward dreams and rabbinic dream psychology in order to satisfy their desire for knowledge. Subsequent research on the subject resulted in the full-length book, *Dreams*, which I published in 1990 (Bash Publications, New York), and a weekly class on the subject given to residents of Sydney. After its publication, I was invited to speak in cities around the world on the subject, because previously there had not been any book in English that served as a comprehensive guide to Judaism and dreams. Thus I visited Hong Kong, Montreal, Rome, Los Angeles and Melbourne, all to lecture on dreams. I also received letters from around the world with people writing to me of their dreams and asking for an interpretation or explanation. The subject still holds many fascinations, for the lay reader as well as the 'expert', partly because the world of dreams is so difficult to rationalize.

Oxford's Love of Dreams

To my great surprise, the interest among Oxford students and academics in dreams is immense. One might expect that in this, the world's illustrious intellectual crossroads, scholars might not have the time or interest to investigate the realm of the subconscious and would rather devote all time and energy into mastering the conscious realm. But such is not the case.

A City of Dreaming Spires

Oxford has always been 'the city of dreaming spires'. From Oxford's outlying hills two or three miles away, what strikes the observer as he looks down into the city centre is a vista of spires and towers, creating a picturesque and breathtaking skyline. There is no other town in Britain that possesses such a prominent collection of steeples and spires.

This panorama has been immortalized in the poem of Matthew Arnold, which relates, 'And that sweet City with her dreaming spires, She needs not June for beauty's heightening' (*Thyrsis*, 1867). Ever since the publication of the poem, 'the city of dreaming spires' has described Oxford.

The students, however, cynical as ever, and under incessant academic pressure, have rephrased the poem to read, 'Oxford, that city of *perspiring dreams*'.

Welcome the Dream Interpreter

When I arrived in Oxford and word got out that I had written a book on dreams, I received many visitors, both Jewish and non-Jewish, primarily young students, who asked me to interpret their dreams. To date, the stream of people has not stopped and I find that even those students who have no great interest in becoming involved with our activities will drop by in my office to discuss their dreams. They feel a bit disappointed when I tell them that just because I researched the subject and wrote a book on dreams does not mean I have any mastery in interpreting them. Indeed, the great majority of the time I am completely in the dark about a dream which someone will tell me, unless I know the person very well. What I did start to do in order to assuage people's curiosity was to deliver a lecture once-a-term on the subject, which is, thank God, always well attended, even by those who heard aspects of the dream earlier.

The following thoughts encompass points which were not included in the original book, and offer a considered and mystical approach to dreams and their interpretation.

Alternative Dream Psychologies

In just this last century, the significance attributed to dreams and their interpretation has waxed large in the intellectual world, primarily in the field of psychology. Thanks to this recent surge of interest, those who have been either intrigued, inspired, alarmed or frightened by the dreams which they have experienced have turned to dream psychologists in an attempt to alleviate their anxiety and appease their curiosity. Whereas before dreams were largely believed to be nothing more than nonsensical visions of night, they have suddenly emerged as 'the royal road' to understanding the human subconscious and the agent by which to unravel the mind's inner workings.

In my opinion, an unfortunate outcome of this otherwise beneficial trend has been the forsaking of ancient Talmudic dream dogma. In extrapolating from the many biblical accounts of prophetically inspired dreams, secularists have overlooked rabbinic dream psychology in the false assumption that it would only accept dreams as instruments for supernatural communication, and not as the material for subliminal mental activity. While a dream of prophetic import is, of course, a bona fide reality in Jewish doctrine, the Talmud was nevertheless one of the earliest sources to distinguish between dreams of a clairvoyant nature, and the far more common dreams of the mental eye, resulting from unworked mental activity. No individual before the time of the Talmud save the Greek philosopher Aristotle believed that dreams were a result of the mind's distortions of the day's events, external stimuli and reflections of waking experiences and emotions. In his work, *Parva Naturalia*, Aristotle attributed dreams to 'sensory impressions from external objects . . . pauses within the body . . . eddies . . . of sensory movement often remaining as they were when they first started, but often too broken into their forms by collision with obstacles'. All other religious and even philosophical schools of the day believed that dreams could only be caused by supernatural means and were messages sent by the various gods.

The early psychoanalysts confined their interpretation of the purpose of dreams to satisfying a single desire: sexual wish-fulfilment, according to Freud; power, according to Adler; cosmic and transcendental inspiration, according to Carl Gustav Jung. The talmudic rabbis did not take this restrictive outlook; rather they viewed dreams as expressive of a whole range of ideas, from unworked daily thoughts to profound symbolism; from irrational strivings to reason; from morality to unconscious wisdom. Moreover, they viewed dreams as an important function of our mental processes as well as a potential source of Divine inspiration.

If we are to criticize any one party for a constrained view of dream phenomena, it would be Freud and the psychoanalytic school who considered all symbols to be but a representation of a single feeling, born of a single cause. Whereas people had begun to recognize the multifariousness of dreams in general, Freud forced all the incongruent parts back into a single uneven structure, and unwittingly propelled the study of dreams back to its infancy. As a result, even today, the study of dreams is cluttered in confusion and tainted with the unproven dogma of modern psychology.

In sharp contrast, Jewish sources provide a coherent understanding for the common, everyday dream in clear and broad terms with which the reader can identify. It would be a pity not to acknowledge the richness and diversity in our subconscious lives.

Dreams in the Talmud

The Talmud relates, 'The Emperor of Rome said to Rabbi Yehoshua the son of Rabbi Chananya, "You [Jews] profess to be very clever. Tell me what I shall see in my dream [tonight]." Rabbi Yehoshua said to him, "You will see the Persians making you do forced labour, and despoiling you and making you feed unclean animals with a golden crook." He thought about it all day and in the night he saw it in his dream.'

Our memory, to adapt what the Talmud and its commentators explain, can be compared to a glass plate which instantly registers the impression of an image projected onto it by the lens of a camera. As long as the instrument is functioning properly and the image was clearly focused, the plate will provide clear and precise pictures whenever it is required to do so. But suppose the opposite is true: the image was vague to start with, or it was captured under unfavourable lighting conditions or from too great a distance. We would then obtain from the plate only a vague silhouette, or a series of ambiguous shadows and unclear outlines.

Compared with the camera, the human memory is remarkably superior, given its capacity to renew itself as it operates. Its photographic plate is always ready to register whatever is projected onto it. For each of us, memory is a vast storehouse of images, much like the large cabinets in which a photographer keeps her collection of photographic plates. Yet even in a photographer's cabinet, there may be some plates we can show her that she will fail to recognize as her own, given that she has seen thousands of others over the years since she took them. Imagine, then, how much more difficult it is for us to plumb the fathomless depths of images stored in our memory. These images are being taken every moment of our lives, mostly without our being aware of them. It is these 'photographs', says the Talmud, of everyday experience, which are responsible for all dream imagery.

Of course, the degree of clarity of the images we see in our dreams depends on the degree of perfection with which the memory-images were originally perceived. Thus when we dream about people or things we think have never seen before, this may be nothing more than the fact that we have lost any direct recollection of the circumstances under which the memory-images were formed. We may also fail to recognize their original form, because they have been distorted by the action of the imagination. In this respect, we resemble a photographer who possesses a picture without realizing it.

Nothing New Appears in Dreams

It is therefore possible to conclude that we see nothing in dreams that we have not seen before. The Talmud itself goes to great lengths to establish this point by reiterating, '*Ein marin lo le'odom ela mei-hirhurei libo*' – 'There is not shown to one [in a dream] but from the thoughts of his heart.' Here is a vital recognition of the role of 'day residue' in a dream. As Maimonides explains, 'That which greatly encompasses man's attention while he is awake and in full possession of his senses forms during his sleep the object of his imagination.' Thus the proper talmudic definition of dreams would be the representation in the mind's eye of the objects that occupy our thoughts. The nature of our memory-images will have an enormous influence on our dreams. The people we meet, the surroundings we live in, the shows we see, the paintings and albums we look at and even the books we read all provide a multiplicity of images which are duly stored away in our memories. In a dream, what was originally the work of an artist may take on the solidity and appearance of reality, so that we can effectively dream of imaginary people.

It may be argued that this is exactly what happens in waking life, when we let our imaginations roam freely in search of new ideas. After all, human creativity, invention in painting, in literature and in science are all surely the combination in a novel way of the various elements already present in the human mind, based on the prompting of the memory. The story of the discovery of the structure of benzene illustrates this point: the great scientist Friedrich August Kekulé had for weeks pondered the way in which the chemical could be constructed, but the insight only came to him at last in a dream when he was freed from his usual logical constraints. In his dreams, circles and snakes writhed and twisted, dancing before his eyes: in the dance, snakes placed their tails into their mouths, forming rings. It was only when he awoke that he realized that his dream mimicked the structure he had been trying to discover mathematically: only a ring-shaped benzene molecule satisfied all his equations for the structure of compounds.

There is, however, an enormous difference between thinking and dreaming, since in waking life the world about us prevents our imaginative ideas from assuming a clearly defined form: they remain largely non-visual.

What Determines the Train of Ideas in Dreaming?

What we refer to as an 'association of ideas' may be defined as the affinity which causes one idea to bring forth another, whether the connection between them be obvious or otherwise. We will use the term in this accepted sense, while establishing two basic principles: (1) that the images of a dream are the representation in the mind's eye of the objects occupying a person's thoughts, and (2) the image, or images, connected with a specific idea appear as soon as the idea arises.

The vision we see in our dream is only the accessory to the principal factor which calls it forth, the idea itself. The vision is to the idea exactly what a projected picture is to the lighted glass-plate of the slide projector.

While awake and preoccupied with real life, people generally guide their ideas along a chosen path, not allowing the mind to wander off in other directions. But there are moments of passivity, which are often referred to as day-dreaming. Everyone has had the experience of sitting idly, thoughts wandering, and then being suddenly brought back to reality. For example, on a long bus trip, an announcement by the driver about a particular stop can bring one back to the real world with such a jolt that one can catch the working of one's mind. These experiences vouchsafe us a view of the dreaming state where ideas are free to roam, unconstrained.

The Imaginative Faculty

Maimonides explains that this free roaming of the mind is caused by the 'imaginative faculty' or *koach hamedame*, the primary function of which in humans is to act upon impressions received by the senses, combine them, and then transmit their impression to the mind. The impressions are then preserved and stored within the mind's memory. This storage begins on a temporary scale in the active, conscious mind and eventually becomes more permanent in the mind's subconscious. The input of images is a continuous process as long as the body's senses are active: the mind is therefore continually gaining added information via these probes into the outside world.

While fully awake, this imaginative faculty, which constitutes the lowest element of human intellect because it is shared by animals too, is regulated by the higher 'objective intellect'. One's thinking and the recurrence of memory patterns are in logically formed sequences. The mind naturally and intuitively connects images and events which are indeed similar and related through its 'imaginative faculty'. The imaginative faculty is subject to the regulation and jurisdiction of the active, rational intellect, so its conjugation of images must be logical and coherent, in accordance with the logical trend of thoughts of the active intellect itself.

It is only while we are asleep or thoughtlessly passive, when the objective intellect is caught off guard, that the imaginative faculty is free to connect completely unrelated images and impressions. This is due to the fact that its subjugation to the active intellect has stopped, and the 'imaginative faculty' is not being coerced into meeting the logical norms demanded of it when the mind's intellect is active.

The Objective Intellect Sleeps

The active and objective element of the human mind is only operative when one is in a conscious frame of mind. Upon going to sleep, the objective faculty of the brain becomes inoperative: the mind descends from its lofty plane of objectivity to that of subjectivity. So, without the objective intellect governing it, the 'imaginative faculty' connects diverse thoughts and events which not only have no connection between each other, but which may even be completely contradictory.

This unregulated conversion and configuration of impressions by the imaginative faculty is comparable to a ball which one throws and subsequently allows to roll on its own. Eventually, the ball will roll even into areas which the thrower had never originally intended it to go, and could never have predicted. So too, one contemplates diverse thoughts throughout the day, and inevitably, at night, when uncontrolled, the thoughts begin to enter realms which they were never consciously designed to inhabit.

How One Thought Leads to Another

For instance, travelling by plane to Israel I day-dreamed vividly, making wild connections that would, literally, have been unthinkable while fully awake. The last thought which came into my mind before falling into this reverie aboard the plane was of a friend who had recently phoned me from Israel, and whom I was about to see. His phone call reminded me of the time I stayed in Jerusalem, and as a result a memory of the Kotel, the Wailing Wall, immediately came to me. At the Kotel I had met a well-known author. I thought of a book he had written about children, and this thought took me back to a long forgotten time in my childhood when I used to play with my friends in the lovely park next to my home. A flood of childhood memories carried me further still . . . Coupled with the images, this reverie or day-dream would have become an actual dream.

Dreams of the Impossible

But how to account for the truly incredible dreams? The great majority of dreams incorporate visions of the impossible, images which one will claim never to have seen and never to have experienced. This is so to the extent that even those things which are seemingly inconceivable are seen by a great many people within their dreams. I'm sure that the reader too, more often than not, has experienced such occurrences in a dream.

Only while dreaming may one experience true opposites which are humanly impossible, such as seeing oneself experiencing antithetical emotions of great joy and sadness simultaneously, or being in two distant geographic locations at once. This is possible because the imaginative faculty is ungoverned during sleep. Humans are swayed by their emotions and one of the laws of emotions is that people are so limited by emotions they can generally experience only one at a time. One may be either ecstatic or depressed, angry or at peace, agitated or calm, but never both at once. On the other hand, in a dream, when conscious thought departs from the mind, there are no rules or restrictions and one begins to experience antithetical emotions simultaneously.

Similarly, in a dream one may see oneself transported from one place to a distant area almost instantaneously, for the restrictions of time and place do not apply in the free world of the dream. One may see those who are dead appearing as if alive, or a person who is recognizable as one individual suddenly becoming another. In a dream, there are no rules.

Is there any explanation for these incoherent dreams in which monstrous, bizarre and misshapen images appear before us, images that not only have we never seen in real life, but are far removed from any natural train of ideas?

Juxtaposition of Possibilities

In a Chasidic discourse of the year 5562 (1801), the Alter Rebbe, Rabbi Shneur Zalman of Liadi, raised a strong protest against the notion of dreams resulting from the interplay of memories and images by the mind's imaginative faculty. He asked how, if indeed dreams are caused by the mind's imaginative faculty, one can conceive images which one has never seen or experienced before. If it is true that a dream results from the interaction of previously stored images and impressions within the mental eye, how then may one see phenomena the likes of which one has never experienced, or which do not even exist, and have never existed?

To answer this we must begin with the words of the Middle Rebbe, Rabbi DovBer of Lubavitch, who in his magnum opus, *Toras Chaim*, stipulates an important premise in the understanding of each individual dream image, when viewed as an entity unto itself.

As has already been mentioned, the images experienced in a dream are merely previous thoughts encountered over a recent period of time which have been engraved within the mind's memory. The only real difference between the mental recall of those same thoughts while in a waking state and a dreaming state is that a dream places those images outside their original configuration. The thoughts themselves are not distorted or perverse, but rather the correlation between their original configuration, with regard to time and place, and the very context by which they were originally obtained, becomes distorted.

From this we derive the premise that the visions and images which one experiences in a dream are all, by themselves, authentic. For instance, if one sees a boat flying in the air, both individual elements of the dream are true. In reality, there does exist something known as a boat, and there do exist objects which fly in the air. Yet, notwithstanding these truths, the correlation between these two images, when synthesized, is incorrect, because boats are not among the list of entities which take to the air and fly. Each idea in itself is true: it is only that the juxtaposition of the two together comprises a misrepresentation of reality.

In essence, this is saying that the images and circumstances in a dream are not, as separate entities, false or incorrect; rather, because unrelated, and often contradictory, phenomena are integrated as one, their order and sequence is erroneous.

Resurrection within a Dream

This, then, is the inconsistency of dreams. They are inconsistent in their interplay of images, people, places and events. Therefore, one may dream about an individual being dead at one instant, and the very next moment being alive. The dreamer has in the past experienced both of these phenomena: she has seen life and she has seen death. The only thing which she has not seen in waking life is both these contradictory phenomena occurring together within the same time-frame. In a dream, the limitations of time and place are negligible: life and subsequent death may be synthesized as one, and their logical sequence may even be reversed.

This same principle applies to a dream of being in different geographic locations at once. One perhaps dreams about being both at home with family and yet being on the dead surface of the moon. As separate entities, these locations are each a reality unto themselves. Yet, when harmonized together as one, which, of course, entails divorcing each location of its inherent limitation to the confines of space, the vision is false, or unrealistic.

Even the simple day-dreams that we have while dozing already contain an element of incoherence, revealed in a dislocation of time and place. The memory of an event, person or object that has made an impression on us at some period of our lives carries with it as a background the image of the house, the garden, the street: in a word, the location in which the original impression occurred. As long as we are only thinking, this background remains in shadow, but as we begin to day-dream, it also appears, emerging clearly when we are completely asleep. Often it happens that this picture fades more slowly than the thought with which it was associated, and succeeding episodes unrelated in time or location may replace the original thought, leaving the picture much like a piece of theatre scenery left over from the previous act of a play.

Backdrops Which Refuse to Fade

What occurs with the background may also occur with any number of its details, or with any clearly defined image which stays in the mind after the first idea has been replaced by another. For example, a woman may dream that she is present at a bullfight in which the matador is mortally wounded by the furious bull, and she finds the sight distressing. Next, through an association of ideas, she finds herself transported to a zoo where once she saw a furious bull. Because the sight of the wounded toreador affected her so strongly it takes longer to fade from her mind than the image of the arena and the spectators, and she may dream that she sees the fighter's bloodstained body in the middle of a peaceful country scene. She awakens in a cold sweat and says she had a nightmare.

The same principle lies behind another remarkable phenomenon which we have all experienced on numerous occasions. To draw an analogy from a slide projector, if we place a second slide in the slide projector before removing the first, they will become superimposed. Thus a memory image of a man superimposed with the image of a chimpanzee would yield a single image of a hideous ape-man, whereas the case mentioned above will show us the body of the bullfighter lying unnoticed amid a family picnicking at the zoo. Both of these could constitute a frightening nightmare, but the frightening thing is the disjunction of the thoughts, not each element itself. The range of possible variations is of course infinite.

Two ideas, with their accompanying images, can also sometimes appear, as it were, in confrontation, conjured up simultaneously before the slide projector. Recalling ideas simultaneously produces a simultaneous projection of images. For instance, I may be thinking of a model of the Holy Temple in Jerusalem, Beis Hamikdosh, paying special attention to the beautifully designed columns which decorated its magnificent structure. By association, there immediately comes to mind a friend who was killed in the Six-Day War, the war in which the last vestige of the Beis Hamikdosh, the Kotel (Wailing Wall), was captured. From these thoughts my mind wanders to Rome where I have also seen beautiful columns and arches. Suddenly,

I see my friend, who has been dead several years, and we are in Rome, visiting the sites of antiquity.

Another cause of the bizarre in our dreams is the mind's tendency during sleep to proceed by abstraction when it envisages various subjects drawn from memory. The mind transfers the qualities or mode of being of one subject on to another, which for some reason it prefers. Let us suppose that while dreaming dreams of an emaciated horse drawing a broken-down cart, I notice in particular the thinness of the animal; if the cart then reminds me of some poor farmer with a like wagon, I may transfer the idea of thinness and dilapidation onto the farmer, who may then appear in the middle of the dream looking as if about to draw his last breath. Alternatively, it may be the idea of the harness that the mind seizes upon, and with the greatest ease it will then picture the farmer himself in harness.

We see, then, that the mere evocation of the images stored in the memory is sufficient to produce what are the most astonishing dreams, arising out of the different ways in which they are brought forth and combined.

Intervening External Stimuli

We have spoken so far only of those dreams in which ideas follow one another of their own accord, without their course being complicated, interrupted or modified by any internal or external physical cause. This 'pure' state of dreaming occurs only seldom; usually there are innumerable little incidents arising either outside ourselves (noises, warmth, contact, and so on) or within the organism (difficulty in breathing, nervous movements, and the like) that give rise to ideas associated with the impressions they make on the mind. The prophet Isaiah's reference to dreaming of drinking yet waking up thirsty prompts Rashi and the *Aruch* to conclude, 'All dreams have value, but that which one sees [in a dream] when one is thirsty has absolutely no value.' Similarly, rabbinic writings attribute a large percentage of dream imagery to the effects of somatic stimuli. Of course all these new ideas bring their own images into the dream, leaving the mind to make what it can of the resulting mixture. In fact we may expect to meet any number of complications, superimpositions and incongruities without having cause for surprise.

The Language of the Imagination

Another interesting consideration in the evolution of distorted dream images, and here we begin to enter the esoteric realm of dreams, is raised by Rabbi DovBer of Lubavitch, who points a fundamental difference between dreams and the normal mental processes of waking life. Whereas one's waking thoughts consist primarily of mental speech

– 'one thinks to oneself in terms of words and sentences' – dreams consist almost entirely of pictures and images. It will be appreciated, therefore, that as sleep supervenes, the mind begins to transform, or literally, translate, verbal thinking into visions often comprising stunning images.

The conscious mind thinks in terms of mental letters, which become words and subsequently build entire thoughts and thought patterns. From everyday experience we observe how, in the mind, the individual actually talks to himself in words and sentences. This is the nature of the great majority of thoughts experienced during one's waking version of reality.

Translating Verbal Messages into Visions

It can be appreciated, therefore, that upon going to sleep, the mind begins to transform its verbal thoughts into mental visions. Verbal messages must be translated into visual effects. While asleep, the letters and words which comprise a single thought may become integrated with the logical and coherent assemblage of letters in other thoughts as well. It would follow, then, that in a dream, the actual letters comprising one thought will intermix with the letters of other thoughts which one has recently contemplated. (This follows the principle of dreams in general, that even though a dream is comprised of one's recent thoughts, seen because they are still fresh in the mind and have not sunk too deeply into the abyss of the subconscious, nevertheless the thoughts are jumbled and unclear.) A combination of words and ideas may arise which has no real equivalent in the waking world. Consequently, these verbal thoughts, when transposed to form images and pictures, assume the form which their verbal equivalent dictates. One can thus dream not only about contradictory matter, but of things which have never been and have no equal in the waking realm. Completely new entities can be concocted in a dream as a result of the letters of names of different objects blending together to form a new entity, and a visual equivalent.

Amalgamation as a Creative Dream Factor

In the process of losing their proper spatial-temporal correlation, each element in a dream begins to intermix with thoughts of a completely different nature. As a result of this, one image or thought may incorporate within itself fragments and pieces of other thoughts which the dreamer has contemplated over a recent, or even an extended, period of time. When the different thoughts amalgamate, their order interchanges. Instead of events being envisioned in the logical sequence in which they actually transpired, they are disorderly and variant. Therefore, events which have absolutely nothing in common, and that are often contradictory, can apparently occur at the same time.

So, the principle that the mind's stored images return in a chaotic pattern when going to sleep applies not only to the complete thoughts and images which one envisions, but also to the building blocks of thoughts themselves, that is, the words and even the letters which constitute those same thoughts. Thus, since the human brain thinks in patterns of words and letters, and the thoughts which one experiences are composed of words and letters, these can be orchestrated and integrated with the thoughts and letters of other, non-related experiences, and return to us during sleep in a jumbled manner and pattern.

The thoughts are the same, which is logical, since these are the thoughts which one pondered throughout the day. It is only that these same thoughts, and their component words and letters, now return in an anarchic and chaotic manner without the individual and original thoughts distinguishable from one another. They are all mixed together.

Since in sleep the letters and words which comprise a single thought may become intermingled with letters of other thoughts, this can lead to a connection of words and ideas having no real equivalent in the waking world. Consequently, these verbal thoughts, when translated into images and pictures, assume the very same form. Thus we are able to conjure up often contradictory and impossible phenomena via the 'letters' of different objects blending together to form a correspondingly new visual equivalent. This, briefly stated, is one of the ways in which Jewish mysticism accounts for the truly impossible visions of night.

We can now understand that dreams, although resulting from previous impressions encountered during one's waking experiences, and the interplay of those impressions by the imaginative faculty, may nevertheless envision inconceivable and impossible phenomena, the likes of which have truly never existed. The objection of Rabbi Schneur Zalman of Liadi can be successfully countered and answered.

Deciphering Coded Dreams

It would follow from the above that the secret to interpreting a dream is to decipher the new configuration of transformed mental letters. Through this decoding process, one may come to understand what the original, elemental thoughts consisted of. Then, by studying the manner in which the mind synthesized these seemingly unrelated images, one may illuminate the pathways of the mind discerning what internally connects two thoughts which are rationally unrelated.

According to Abravanel, the great fifteenth-century Spanish exegete, this method of interpretation was used by the sorcerers of Pharaoh in their attempt to unravel his mysterious dream of the lean and the healthy cows. They understood that a dream is only an analogy or allegory of a concept hidden within: by examining the final imagery, one may regress by association to the original seminal input.

Pharaoh's sorcerers, therefore, sought to understand the content of his dream by applying this method, but met with no success because they mistakenly assumed that Pharaoh's dream was void of any prophetic content. As it was indeed clairvoyant, they could never return to the original image since its input was not on the part of Pharaoh's own memory bank and thought process. Rather, images had been planted into his dream reverie by supernatural forces.

Dreams as a Release of Unworked Mental Phenomena

While other, indeed most, dreams may not be prophetic, Rabbi Menachem Mendel of Lubavitch, the famous Tzemach Tzedek, mentions that they nevertheless serve a very necessary psychological function. Composed, as it is, of mental residue, the dream becomes in effect an 'exhaust pipe', a device whereby the mind rids itself of worthless mental film. Hence we observe that when awakening the intellect is fresh. One is more ready for study and intellectual exertion in the morning than at any other time of day. Rabbi Menachem Mendel comments that just as when sediment is removed from wine, the wine becomes sweeter and tastier, so too by releasing the blockage of unworked mental sediment from the mind, the dreamer awakens refreshed and clear.

With this explanation we may understand the Talmud's assertion that 'All who sleep seven nights without dreams are considered evil.' The statement, far from connoting a moral wickedness, refers to the fact that someone who does not dream is polluted with an excess of mental residue, and it is the state of dreaming which can rinse one of that confounding waste.

Chapter Forty-eight

THE PHANTOM OF FREUD'S JEWISHNESS

Unlike other world-renowned universities, Oxford is perceived to be essentially irrational in its approach to administration and the like. This belief in chaos in administrative affairs has noteworthy repercussions. Taking a trip to the university's sporting complex, down Iffley Road, is like entering the third world. I shall always remember when I attended my first basketball game to watch some of my student friends on the varsity team. There was a female student with a pin-up board sticking up hand-coloured numbers, made from oak tag, to keep the score of the game. If she paused to drink from her can of Pepsi, which she did intermittently, the score was lost, which wasn't all that bad since Oxford was losing. And as I was the only spectator, no one seemed to mind much either. Yet there is a current, probably apocryphal, tale that the university refused an endowment from the Rhodes Trust – yes, the same one the scholars are named after – to build a sports complex for the whole university. The reason given was that it might make sport here *too professional*! Whether this is true or not, the very fact that this tale is believed by those to whom it is told signifies something about this institution.

Oxford is justifiably proud of its long-standing tradition of excellence, but it also tends to be proud of its tendency to archaism. There are still no serious moves to establish a Student Union Centre for all junior members to enjoy: the Oxford Union, although with approximately three quarters of undergraduates as members, is in effect a debating society and one of the expensive clubs rather than a meeting place for all: membership currently costs £94.72 ($150). Few arts students have to go near a computer during their first degree, so computer skills are seen as a bonus rather than assumed to be standard, which also surprised me. The American universities I was exposed to demanded that every academic paper submitted by a student be typed. At Oxford, when students search through their pockets for £3.50 to pay us for Shabbat dinner, or entry to an event, they often pull out a crumpled piece of paper stuffed into their pockets with the words, 'Better not lose that. It took me a whole night to write that essay which I'll submit tomorrow.' Undergraduates are still impressed when a tutor uses word-processed notes, rather than regarding them as entirely normal.

Similarly, Oxford's libraries, although amongst the best in the world, are only slowly being computer-indexed to facilitate access to texts, so finding books is often a frustratingly long process.

There is indeed a sense of irony in the fact that although the great Bodleian Library is one of the best-stocked in the world, with over six million volumes, these, I have found, can be extremely difficult to get to because of the waiting time.

However, the complicated reasons for the development of the Oxford attitude to life and change are probably as difficult to analyse as the reasons individual humans behave as they do.

Student Psychoanalysts

Students in Oxford, like all people, love to indulge in analysis of their peers: 'She's a flirt because she's basically insecure and needs to feel loved by everyone' and 'He's paranoid that everyone is getting at him because he's never learned to cope with people disagreeing with him' are comments I've heard in the recent past. Oxford people love to scrutinize the reasons for people's behaviour, firstly because reasons can absolve the analysts from recognizing the failings in themselves: for example, taking the first comment, the speaker was hoping to go out with the young woman involved, but thought she did not like him, so he turned the rejection he felt back onto her. Secondly, people are just plain curious about what makes other people tick, particularly the opposite sex. Students and others are perennially fascinated with the topic of how relationships work.

Of course, when the process of analysis is turned upon the analyser, they are often not so pleased. It appears that while we want to be able to explain the behaviour of others in objective terms, we also need to feel that we ourselves are in control of our own lives, able to make important decisions without being conditioned by our environment. Rather than accept that people do things because they 'just happen', we need to exert some control over them by understanding and perhaps being able to predict what they do. But when the process is reversed and it is we who are psychoanalysed by our peers, we resist vigorously.

The verbal and mental tools used for such analysis owe more to Sigmund Freud than any other person. Although his approach is officially largely ignored in Oxford (psychoanalytic psychology is not an academic option here), he lives on in other ways. His ideas and terminology have so pervaded our language that it is difficult to attempt to understand others without resorting to words such as 'subconscious', 'repressed' or 'complex'.

Because of my interest in dreams, I became part of a circle of Freudians which included students, tutors and professors, many of whom attended my lectures and discourses on Rabbinic Dream Psychology, as well as the similarities, if any, between Freudian psychoanalysis and Chasidism. As I had encountered in Australia, there was fierce resistance by the Freudians even to the lightest criticism of Freud. But fascinatingly, they were always anxious to hear more about Freud and his Jewish identity. For this reason, I became a serious student of Freud's Jewishness, though admittedly I was completely unprepared for the almost schizophrenic contradictions in his relationship with his Judaism. So amazing is the story of how Freud's Jewishness pursued him like an unrelenting phantom that I used his example as an archetype of the general confusion which has reigned, specifically among the most educated Jews, ever since Jewish emancipation. Though the conflict between Judaism and modernity has since significantly diminished, there is still much that young Jewish students entering the world of academia can learn from an exploration and analysis of the life and contribution of one of our most illustrious and influential sons.

Freud and the Modern World

Few people, if any, are apathetic about the contribution to science made by Sigmund Freud. After Darwin had shaken mankind's self-esteem by proposing a theory demonstrating human kinship with other animals, Freud shattered it still further by asserting that people were far less master in their own mental house than they had always supposed. While Freud's ideas and terminology have rapidly pervaded the whole of western society, argument is still rife about the validity of his whole approach to the human psyche.

Many people regard Freud's theories as absurd conjecture, having no scientific foundation whatsoever. It is even questionable whether the psychoanalysis actually helped his patients: after a long study of Freud's analysis and the progress of his patients, Fisher and Greenberg conclude that: 'Freud never presented any data, in statistical or case-study form, that demonstrated that his treatment was of benefit to a significant number of the patients he himself saw.' (Assertions such as the one found in *The Taboo of Virginity*, describing the 'subconscious' wish on the part of a newly married woman to castrate her husband so as to retain his manhood, have been met with moral reprehension and even astonishment.)

Women who Attack Freud

Feminists are among Freud's strongest critics, employing both logical and moral critiques of his work. Essentially, Freud denied women any intrinsic identity within his theoretical framework. In his history of childhood development, he describes how a young boy has an innate desire to lie with his mother, but feels threatened in the execution of these desires by the father, who seems to have prior rights to the mother. The boy's fear makes him give up and 'repress' all these unseemly desires, which live on as the famous Oedipus complex in the subconscious, promoting all sorts of neurotic symptoms in later life. This Oedipus complex assumes the central role in Freudian speculations.

Yet in Freud's female version of the Oedipus complex, a little girl's discovery of her lack of male qualities leads her to believe that she is an inferior being. She becomes disillusioned with her mother, whom she blames for her condition. This turns her towards her father as a love-object, and she desires to bear his child. The resulting child, Freud supposes, will compensate the girl for her lack of male organs. This stage of emotional development is brought to a conclusion by the girl's growing perception of other men as potential impregnators who will enable her to have a baby, and so overcome her continued sense of being an inferior kind of human being. Thus a woman to Freud is totally dependent on a male for fulfilment and development.

Another feminist gripe is that the mother plays a secondary role in the male and female version of the Oedipus complex. In both children it is the father, either as an object of fear in the male, or as an object of desire and jealousy in the female, who plays the fundamental role in the development of the Oedipus complex.

It was Sir Peter Medawar, winner of the Nobel Prize for Medicine, who offered, 'Freud's theories will remain for ever one of the saddest and strangest of all landmarks in the history of twentieth-century thought.'

Psychoanalysis Carries Religious Fervour

However, Freud's teachings are still carried by a devoutly loyal movement of psychoanalysts. Their uncompromising approach to his original theories and sharp emotional defences to all attacks against Freud strongly resemble religious zealotry. Psychoanalysis has often been referred to as a religion because of the intensity of the disputes within the movement that so often led to rebels leaving it and setting up rival schools or splinter groups, in a manner reminiscent of religious sects.

The resemblance to religion does not end there. Virtually everyone except for a few fundamentalist Freudians agrees that psychoanalysis is very far from being a science, since its theories are not open to refutation and cannot be used for prediction. In his last introductory lecture on psychoanalysis, Freud wrote that 'Marxism has acquired the energy and the self-contained exclusive character of *weltanschauung* . . . Any critical examination of Marxist theory is forbidden, doubts of its correctness are punished in the same way as heresy was punished by the Catholic Church.' Yet exactly the same was true of psychoanalysis in its early days. Although its heretics, Adler, Stekel, Jung, Rank, and many others were not subjected to torture and execution, their characters were assassinated by being labelled neurotic or psychotic. Some of the language used to describe such heretics is quite intemperate.

Of this attitude, Hans Eysenck wrote in *Decline and Fall of the Freudian Empire*: 'It seems to me to partake more of a religious conversion than of a scientific persuasion, to be based on faith and belief rather than fact and experiment, and to rely on suggestion and propaganda rather than proof and verification.'

It is even reasonable to suggest that Freud himself was blinded to the religious overtones of his new 'science'. In *Freud and Religious Belief*, Philip argues that 'Science became Freud's faith, psychoanalysis his sect. Whatever illusions other men might or might not possess, his illusion was science.' At the end of *Totem and Taboo*, Freud refers to his imaginary adversary's God as 'your God', the God of conventional religious belief, and opposes to it what he calls ironically 'our God', *logos*, the voice of reason. Freud's use of this verbal device reveals more about himself than he admitted. Exclusive belief in Reason or Science can be as irrational as belief in God. Certainly, Freud's belief in psychoanalysis went far beyond any evidence of its truth which could possibly be called scientific. Freud's own emphasis on the importance of 'Freudian slips' for revealing true ideas and feelings would of course preclude us from seeing his reference to God as merely metaphorical and symbolic.

Modern-day Moses

The whole drive of psychoanalysis was towards creating a *weltanschauung* rather than a specific and strictly limited theory of the diseased human mind. Even in its earliest days, Freud did not confine himself to an explanation of neurotic symptoms but strove to create a coherent system of ideas which would not only explain all forms of mental illness, but also religion, art, literature, humour, the descent of humankind, and human social organization. He seemed to wish to replace religion with a science that was capable of explaining the sum of human experience. In this capacity, Freud was the law-giver of the new discipline and it is interesting to note that a great deal of psychoanalytic wisdom seems to have depended upon oral transmissions rather than writings, much in the same way that Moses had instructed the Jewish people.

Freud asserted, 'My illusions . . . are not incorrigible, like the religious ones, and do not have a delusional character. If experience should show – not to me but to others after me, who think the same way – that we have been mistaken, then we will renounce our expectations.' But the historical facts are different. Andreas-Salome asserted, 'It is clear that any independence around Freud . . . worries him . . . quite automatically in his noble egoism as an investigator.' Similarly, Estelle Roth says that Freud was prone 'to cry resistance at all such opposition . . .'; this clearly reduces psychoanalysis to the level of dogma.

Psychoanalysis lacks many of the features associated with religion, but in a secular age in which those who could not subscribe to the old faiths often felt rootless and insecure, psychoanalysis offered an explanatory system that could be eagerly embraced as a substitute. Psychoanalysis, at least in its earlier days, seemed to proffer a secular form of salvation. This insight may partially account for the disproportionately high percentage of secular Jews, most of whom emanated from observant households just one generation previously, who became the principal devotees and evangelists of the Freudian school.

Problems with Freud's Science

The truth the poet writes and recognizes as akin to beauty is not the truth the scientist recognizes. The poetic identification of truth with beauty is essentially meaningless to a scientist. There may be some connection between this truth and hermeneutics, but for the scientist truth is the statement of generalizations of universal validity subject to proof and experiment. This is far removed from poetic truth, or the truth of music, painting and drama. It was with scientific truth that Freud claimed to be concerned, and it is by its criteria that he must be judged.

One of Freud's most telling remarks was, 'If I think I see something new I am uncertain whether I can wait for it to be confirmed.' Throughout his career, he fluctuated between tolerance of empirical research into his new science and hostility to objective investigation.

Aversion to Refutation

Freud's apparent approval of direct investigation, along factual lines, of the behaviours he postulated was often ambiguous. If the clinical reconstructions of early life experiences were genuine and if the children being analysed had been threatened with castration, with being seduced, or had been traumatized by seeing their parents engaged in sexual intercourse, the accuracy of these recollections could surely be tested directly by suitable investigations. Freud did not agree, and not in order to protect the vulnerable patient from intrusion: 'It may be tempting to take the easy course of filling in the gaps in a patient's memory by making inquiries from the older members of the family. But I cannot advise too strongly against such a technique. One invariably regrets having made oneself dependent on such information. At the same time, confidence in the analysis is shaken and a court-of-appeal is set up over it. Whatever can be remembered at all will anyhow come to light in the course of further analysis.'

In other words, interpretation of doubtful symbolic meanings of dreams and everyday behaviour is to be preferred as evidence to direct observational reports by actual witnesses, because these would constitute a 'court of appeal' which Freud was keen to avoid. There must be no external source of evidence against which his interpretations can be tested.

In a reply to Rosenzweig on his attempts to study repression experimentally, Freud stated, 'I cannot put much value on these confirmations because the wealth of reliable observations on which these assertions rest make them independent of experimental verification. Still, it can do no harm.' Nothing could demonstrate more clearly the non-scientific side of Freud's thinking: in his view, experiments were not needed to confirm his hypotheses, nor could they influence him. No other discipline claiming attention has so clearly and decisively cut itself off from experimental testing of its theories.

When Freud engaged in psychoanalysis or interpreted dreams, if the patient agreed with the analysis, then Freud's theory was obviously correct. If the patient disagreed, Freud was also correct because of the patient's subconscious 'resistance': the analyst's interpretation was made unacceptable to the patient precisely because it was correct. Clearly, then, there is no way to disprove such a theory.

Wooing the Wolfman

For instance, the patient Freud referred to as 'the wolfman' had experienced a powerful vision in a dream of white wolves, and Freud interpreted it as a reference to the primal scene of watching his parents in intercourse, the white being their nightshirts (what were his parents doing wearing nightshirts during intercourse?). At the time, the wolfman seems to have agreed with Freud, but in an interview conducted years later when he was eighty-seven years old, he said of Freud, 'When he interprets the white wolves as nightshirts . . . that's somehow far-fetched, I think. That scene in the dream where the windows open and so on and the wolves are sitting there, and his interpretation, I don't know, these things are miles apart, it's terribly far-fetched.' The only differences between this and his prior acceptance of the interpretation seems to be that the patient had grown older and that Freud had previously been there to convince him.

Freud was so dogmatic on the subject of 'female castration' as the sole motive for development as a woman that it has been suggested he had a strong emotional interest in his theory. He desperately defended it against any opposing views, whether plausible or not.

Freud's patient was a young woman who first came to him at the age of eighteen suffering from a dragging leg and fainting fits with convulsions and delirium. Although the symptoms suggested an organic syndrome (indeed Dora had grown up with a tubercular father who had contracted syphilis before her conception, and both father and daughter manifested virtually identical asthmatic troubles), Freud characteristically described her as a neurotic. According to Freud, she was a weak-willed woman who was repressing her subconscious wish to sleep with her father. Freud did not apparently give Dora a routine physical examination, but rather subjected her to an extraordinary campaign of mental harassment.

When Dora said she had recently suffered an attack of appendicitis, Freud decided that the appendicitis had really been a hysterical pregnancy expressing her unconscious sexual fantasies. Her coughing, according to Freud, was just another timid female love-song. He finally diagnosed her painful asthmatic symptoms as a reaction to hearing her father wheeze while copulating. Reading the whole case history of Dora without prejudice, it is hard to avoid the conclusion that once Freud had made up his mind about a point, he would not take no for an answer, using all his ingenuity and his considerable powers of persuasion to compel his patient to admit that he was right.

Despite Freud's frequent claim that psychoanalysis was a treatment in which influence and suggestion played no part, he often allowed treatment to be considered as complete only when the patient finally agreed with him. He said that psychoanalysis should be used to treat young people since 'old people are no longer educable', whilst persons under the age of adolescence 'are often exceedingly amenable to influence'. This reveals that suggestion plays a far greater role in psychoanalysis than he generally admitted.

Hans is Herbert, Herbert is Hans

Before turning to the famous case of little Hans, it may be interesting to contrast Freud's accounts of two four-year-old children, little Hans himself who was almost five, and little Herbert, some months younger. Herbert is described as the product of enlightened child rearing, 'a splendid boy whose intelligent parents abstained from forcibly suppressing one side of the child's development'. Apparently, little Herbert displayed 'the liveliest interest in that part of his body which he calls his wee-wee maker . . . because . . . he has never been frightened or oppressed with a sense of guilt, he gives expression quite ingenuously to what he thinks.' According to Freud, the little boy brought up so well by psychoanalytically oriented parents is likely to become one of the great non-neurotic personalities of our time.

Contrast this with the unfortunate Hans, who, according to Freud, was a paragon 'of all the vices'. Before he was four years old, his mother had threatened him with castration and the birth of a younger sister had confronted him with the great riddle of where babies come from, as 'his father had told him the lie about the stork' which made it 'impossible for him to ask for enlightenment upon such things'. Partly because of the perplexity in which his 'infantile sexual theories' left him, he succumbed to an animal phobia shortly before his fifth birthday.

Just as we are about to indulge in that old-time Freudian heritage of blaming the parents for the child's illness, we find out from Ernest Jones's definitive biography of Freud that Hans and Herbert are the same child. The account of Herbert was written some months before, and the account of Hans some months after, the boy had succumbed to his animal phobia (but not before the events which Freud was later to consider as pathogenic). Indeed, Freud even suggested that Hans–Herbert suffered more strongly in the development of his phobia because of his 'enlightened' upbringing.

The symptoms reported of Hans were fear of going outdoors, depression in the evening, and a fear that a horse would bite him in the street. Freud suggested that 'the ground was prepared by sexual over-excitation due to his mother's tenderness' and that the reason he was afraid of horses now was that 'he had taken so much interest in their widdlers'.

Later, Freud interpreted the boy's repeated emphasis on being frightened by 'what horses wear in front of their eyes and the black around their mouths' as meaning fear of his father, who wore a moustache. The father said the whole anxiety began when Hans witnessed an accident involving a horse-drawn omnibus, in which one of the horses thunderously fell down: apparently, the 'black thing round their mouths' referred literally to the horses' muzzle. Yet all the while Freud continued to intimidate the child into believing the horse represented his father whom the child would like to see fall and die so that he might conquer his mother. Of the incident, Freud said, 'Hans had to be told many things which he could not say for himself . . . his attention had to be turned in the direction from which something was expected to come.' One can only wonder what Freud's analysis did for the young Hans and what his methods have in common with science or objective observation. Freud displayed a naive reliance on interpretation of a highly speculative nature, a seemingly blatant disregard for facts and a failure to consider other theories, an almost messianic belief in his own infallibility.

As Frederick Crews puts it, 'In Freud's now prurient mind, steaming erotic speculations were of greater diagnostic interest than manifest signs of disease.'

Lamarck and the Original Patricide

In his classic assault on religion and its origins, *Totem and Taboo*, Freud speculated that early humans lived in paternal hordes, family groups dominated by a single male who fathered most of the offspring. One day, the sons killed their father, but the guilt caused them to forbid any more killing of fathers and also to impose restrictions on taking for themselves the wives their father had had, giving rise to the two repressed wishes of the male version of the Oedipus complex. Freud thought that this primal slaughter of the father was a real event that was so catastrophic that it left 'ineradicable traces in the history of humanity'. In other words, Freud believed in the long discredited Lamarckian hypothesis of the inheritance of environmentally (as opposed to genetically) acquired characteristics. Until his death, Freud obstinately maintained that acquired characteristics could be inherited and that the origins of religion and morality could indeed be traced back to this specific event. In any case such an event would have only initiated guilt amongst the males of the species, since presumably the females in the primal horde had neither been jealous of their father/husband, nor wished to kill him, but Freud does not address this issue. There is no evidence from anthropology that a 'primal horde' dominated by a single male ever existed in early human history. Darwin had derived the notion from hearsay reports about the organization of gorilla troupes which have since been shown to be false.

The Right to Psychoanalyse the Psychoanalyst

Since there is so much to contend with in Freud's theories and methods, it seems only fair to psychoanalyse the first psychoanalyst. I do so not for the purpose of waging battle with a theory which seems so hostile to theistic belief, because indeed Freudian mechanisms seem to have much in common with Judaism in general, and Chasidism in particular. A particularly powerful case in point is the similarity between Freud's ideas on the most basic motivating drives in man, namely the id and ego, and the Chasidic notion of an animal and Godly soul. The former is governed by innate primitive lusts and uncultivated desires, while the latter stands for enlightenment, culture and functional productivity. Rather, I choose to analyse Freud precisely because of these similarities and the way in which he grappled with his Jewishness throughout his life. Freud's adoption of his world-view, and the fervour with which he defended it, must have been, as they say, in character. Freud himself acknowledges that the events of his life had a direct bearing on the foundation of psychoanalysis, stating, '. . . the story of my life and the history of psychoanalysis, they are intimately interwoven.' Can we then identify any motivations within Freud's personality which might have inspired some of his theories?

W.W. Meissner, Jesuit and psychoanalyst, writes: 'It seems clear that Freud's religious views perhaps reflect underlying and unresolved ambivalences and conflicts stemming from the earliest psychic strata. Behind the Freudian argument about religion stands Freud the man, and behind Freud the man, with his prejudices, beliefs, and convictions, lurks the shadow of Freud the child.'

Freud's ongoing struggle to reconcile his Jewish origins and his place in the Jewish faith served in no small measure to inspire many of his theories. Freud seems to have employed a dual ethic of Jewish affiliation of almost schizophrenic proportions. In 1899, Freud referred to the 'religion of science which is supposed to have superseded the old religion'. There can be no doubt that by the old religion he meant Judaism. For him it had become old, and yet he could never discard it, as we shall see.

Militant Atheism

On the one hand, Freud advertised his atheism at every possible opportunity. He had taken some pride in his claim that psychoanalysis had made the most recent contribution to the critique of the religious world-view. He was no Marxist, but he agreed with the young Marx that 'criticism of religion is the premise of all criticism'.

Freud seemed to feel, perhaps with some justification, that religion was the only serious rival to science. Freud seems often to have felt he was such an essential part of 'scientific progress' that any attack on science was a personal attack on him. He described religion as a real threat to science because it was 'prodigious power disposing over mankind's strongest emotions'. He was also quick to recognize that science and religion fought over the same material: 'Of the three powers (art, philosophy and religion) that may contest the soil of science, religion alone is the serious enemy.' We may assume that Freud saw religion as a personal enemy as much as the enemy of science, but he could never vanquish it completely.

His desire to assert and substantiate his aggressive atheism seems to have governed Freud's entire adult life. While still a student, he had come across the writings of an unusual man, an ex-priest who respected Darwin while he retained his belief in God, Franz Brentano. Freud toyed with the temptations of theism under Brentano's influence, but in the end his encounter with Brentano's powerful arguments was used to test the strength of his non-belief rather than to convert him to religion. Freud protested that he would sell his atheism at a high price: 'I have no intention of surrendering so quickly and so completely.' Indeed Freud remained embattled with the Deity until his dying days. Only one year before his death he wrote in a letter to Charles Singer, 'Neither in my private life nor in my writings have I ever made a secret of being an out-and-out unbeliever.'

Freud's atheism was repeatedly described by his contemporary and rival psychoanalysts, Jung, Adler, Buber, Fromm et al., as 'aggressive atheism'. In October 1927 he wrote to Pastor Pfister of his 'absolutely negative attitude toward religion, in every form and dilution'. Rather than being content to believe religion was an adult extension of the fears and complexes all children develop while growing up, he constantly had to reiterate his opposition to it. 'Methinks the atheist protesteth too much': Freud's aggression was clearly fighting an enemy that he did not yet feel he had defeated.

Seeking Legitimacy Outside Jewish Culture and Religion

At times Freud expressed deep shame for his Jewish heritage, seeing it as barbaric and uncultured. This rejection of his Jewishness often centred on his father, and at times on his people and his inherited religion. In essence it was an expression of Freud's deep need to be accepted by secular western society. A lonely, outcast Jew seeking legitimacy in the only civilization that could offer it.

Freud's fantasies allowed him to escape from the father whom he viewed as a mediocrity who had done nothing to overcome the confinement of his existence within the intolerable limits of his inferior birth. He would not assimilate and he would not fight for his Jewishness, he just was. Freud's disdain for his identity preceded his concern with civilization and its discontents. Numerous instances express Freud's disgust for his 'primitive' ancestry. In *The Interpretation of Dreams*, Freud recounted an early dream about his father, who by all accounts was far more observant than Sigmund and is said to have studied the Talmud almost daily. In the dream, Jacob Freud handed his children a secular book for them to destroy. Martha Robert, author of *From Oedipus to Moses*, says correctly of this incident that there must be a serious moral trauma involved for, at the age of forty, Freud could still not bring himself to disclose the meaning of the dream. She suggests that the scene might have indicated to Freud a pseudo-assimilated, still barbarous father, one who truly revered only the Book of Books.

Another revealing tale is the famous 'hat in the gutter' episode. Freud's father Jacob had encountered an anti-Semite who had, in the middle of the street, knocked his hat from his head into the gutter, but he had felt powerless to resist. He merely picked up the hat and continued. Freud later remarked on this, 'This struck me as unheroic conduct on the part of the big, strong man who was holding the little boy by the hand. I contrasted this situation with another which fitted my feelings better; the scene in which Hannibal's father, Hamilcar Barca, made his boy swear before the household altar to take vengeance on the Romans. Ever since that time

Hannibal has had a place in my fantasies.' Freud needed a hero, but as his Jewish father could not match his expectations he turned to another role model. So infatuated was Freud throughout his life with the Carthaginian general that he could not bring himself to visit Rome, the arch-enemy of Hannibal, much as Hannibal himself had never entered the city.

But Freud did attempt to replace his despised Jewish heritage with the revered heritage of Rome and the European culture it had given rise to. Freud had a continuing fascination with Rome and all that it stood for, both in his waking life and in his recurrent dreams. He wanted to embrace Rome but he could not: he thought of what it had done to his people and felt alienated from the cradle of western culture, from the very non-Jewish legitimacy he craved.

Denial of Professional Status

Freud also had a dream in which he saw himself as the anti-Semitic minister, Count von Hartel. This seems to signify a subconscious desire to break once and for all with his Jewishness, with all its perils of hereditary diseases and outward disadvantages for an ambitious person determined to rise in the world. The anti-Semitic university in Vienna had repeatedly denied him the title of Professorus Maximus, which he so obviously deserved. It seemed that all the achievement in the world still could not undo the curse of Jewishness imposed by unlucky birth.

Freud and his family seem to have employed the standards of western acceptability when referring to their people. At the funeral of a family friend, Sigmund wrote that the eulogizing rabbi 'spoke with the powerful voice of the fanatic, with the ardour of the savage, merciless Jew'. Freud wished to distance himself from some of the predominant characteristics of Jews which he thought were degrading. During the rise of Nazism, a story went out that the Jews of Berlin had paraded through the streets carrying banners with the device 'Throw us out!' Believing it had happened, Freud gave vent to his indignation by saying to his friend Zweig in a letter that 'such undignified behaviour was typical of the Jewish character and my only consolation is that these people are half German.' According to Freud's son, Martin, the women amongst the Galician Jews 'were certainly not what we should call "ladies" . . . Galician Jews had little grace and no manners.'

Freud's mother, Amalie, was described by his children as a 'tornado'. Estelle Roth, a London-based psychoanalyst, even maintains that Freud's opinions of women 'might well have been compounded by later "probably repressed" embarrassment at the volatile Yiddish-accented Amalie Freud.'

Freud wished to distance himself from all religions, but especially from the methods of one particular type of religion, Judaism. He even delayed publishing his speculative thesis on the origins of Judaism, *Moses and Monotheism*, because 'it did not seem attractive to find oneself classed with the schoolmen and Talmudists who delight in exhibiting their ingenuity without regard to how remote from reality their thesis may be.'

His close confidante, Sarah Deutsch, writes that Freud was 'very happy' at any recognition from officialdom, or when a colleague of acknowledged scientific rank joined the new movement of psychoanalysis, despite his own disdain for official position. However, even his success could not free him from what he saw as the chains of his Jewishness. Freud tells us that he was made unhappy by his father's lack of western culture, so much so that for many years the intellectual attainments he won inspired him with a sense of guilt.

Within the movement of psychoanalysis, there were tensions between Jew and Gentile, and Freud often championed the cause of the Gentile. When Karl Abraham expressed reservations about the sincerity of the new convert to psychoanalysis, C.G. Jung, Freud begged Abraham to be patient since 'only his appearance has saved psychoanalysis from becoming a Jewish national concern'. Freud pleaded to Abraham, 'Please be tolerant and do not forget that it is really easier for you than it is for Jung to follow my ideas . . . for you are closer to my intellectual constitution because of racial kinship, while he as a Christian and pastor's son binds himself to me only against great inner resistance. His association with us is the more valuable for that.'

When Freud slapped the Viennese Jewish psychoanalysts in the face by making Jung president of the International Association of Psychoanalysts, they convened a meeting of protest. Freud walked in on this meeting and, in a highly uncharacteristic display of emotion, with tears in his eyes, he pleaded with them to grasp the inconvenient truth that it was the Gentiles who would rescue them from their isolation and guarantee the survival of the movement.

Jewish Affirmation

At the same time, Freud went to great lengths to emphasize his pride in being Jewish. In a letter written in January 1935 he claims that it is only the Jewish religion that he is at odds with: 'I can say that I am as remote from the Jewish religion as from all others . . . on the other hand, I have always had a strong feeling of solidarity with my people and have also fostered it in my children. We have all remained in the Jewish confession.'

In one of the most extraordinary testaments to the mysterious and elusive nature of Jewish identity, which is so analogous to the Chasidic definition that when I first read it it shocked me utterly, Freud writes with great eloquence of his Jewishness in the introduction to the Hebrew translation of *Totem and Taboo*:

> No reader of the Hebrew version of this book will find it easy to put himself into the emotional position of an author who is ignorant of the language of holy writ, who is completely estranged from the religion of his fathers, as well as from every other religion, and who cannot take a share in nationalist ideas, but who has yet never repudiated his people, who feels that he is, in his essential nature, a Jew, and who has no desire to alter that nature. If the question were put to him: 'Since you have abandoned all these common characteristics of your countrymen, what is there left to you that is Jewish?' he would reply: 'A very great deal, and probably its essence.' He could not now express that essence clearly in words. But someday, no doubt, it will become accessible to the scientific mind.

It is incredible that a man of such profound eloquence, who was able to express man's deepest psychological impulses, and influence a century of psychological thought, could still not find words to express what it meant to be Jewish. He endowed the quality of Jewishness with something miraculous, mysterious and indefinable. Shortly after the English psychoanalyst David Eder had died, Freud wrote of him, 'We were both Jews and knew of each other that we carried this miraculous thing in common, which, inaccessible to psychoanalysis so far, makes the Jew.'

In an address to the B'nai B'rith Society, Freud, again speaking in strange mystical overtones, defined Judaism as being 'not the faith, not even the national pride . . . but many dark emotional powers, all the stronger the less they could be expressed in words, as well as the clear consciousness of an inner identity, the familiarity of the same psychological structure.' The man who postulated the inner identities of so many thousands could not even find the adjectives to express his own most intrinsic identity.

Freud was keen to bring this 'inner identity' into his family, too. In a classic example of his inability to reconcile the antithetical emotions of dismissal and affirmation of his Jewishness, he wrote in a letter to his fiancée, 'something of the core, of the essence of this meaningful and life-affirming Judaism will not be absent from our home' (E. L. Freud, 1975, pages 18–22). But his future wife came from a devout and committed background. It was Freud who brought about the complete disintegration of her observance, even refusing to permit her to light the Sabbath candles.

Psychoanalysis as a Jewish Science

At other times Freud appeared to be fascinated, and rather pleased, by the relationship between his psyche and his Jewishness. A letter written in 1926 to Morselli reads, 'I do not know if you are right in your judgement which wants to see psychoanalysis as a direct product of the Jewish spirit, but if it were so, I would not feel ashamed.' In 1922 he mused to Ferenczi about 'strange secret longings' rising up within him, 'perhaps from the heritage of my ancestors – for the Orient and the Mediterranean and a life of quite another kind: wishes from late childhood ill-adapted to reality'.

In later years he even felt able to acknowledge that there were positive aspects to the faith of his ancestors. He repeatedly expressed his regret for not having been taught the 'holy language' by his own father. Sigmund's son, Martin, was cautious of informing his father that he had joined a Zionist Youth group, since most 'leading Jewish German figures were hostile', and Freud had been waging war on religion and its attendant ideologies all his life. However, Freud wrote to his son that he consented: 'Zionism awakened my strongest sympathies, which are faithfully attached to it today.' Freud even enjoyed the company of a young talmudic student he had met, remarking, 'He really is a sage, I enjoyed him very much.' This tolerance is very far removed from his commitment to science as the great enemy of religion, battling for the souls and minds of the people.

Freud's articulation of his Jewishness gained strength with the rise of anti-Semitism in Germany. While most German Jews reacted to prejudice by affirming their German identity to the detriment of their Jewish side, Freud preferred to reject such behaviour outright: as he asserted in an interview, 'My language is German. My culture, my attainments, are German. I considered myself German intellectually, until I noticed the growth of anti-Semitic prejudice in Germany and German Austria. Since then I prefer to call myself a Jew.'

By 1932 he had begun to articulate his inner yearning for religious understanding and fulfilment. He had attacked religion as a neurosis, useless, even counter-productive, and outdated. Yet, he remarked to his friend Arnold Zweig about Palestine, 'It is impossible to say what we have taken along in blood and heritage from life in that country. Oh, life would be very interesting if one only knew and understood more about it.' Yet only an examination of the religion itself could have told him what he needed to know.

Finally, on his eightieth birthday, he was greeted by the Hebrew University in Jerusalem, and he responded with the confession, 'I am one of yours.'

Reconciling the Contradictory Nature of Freud's Jewishness

How is it possible to reconcile Freud the progressive, enlightened Jewish atheist who had shed all the backward characteristics of his father's Judaism with Freud the affirmed and proud Jew? *It is my belief that they never were reconciled.* The dynamics of this inner tension, Freud's willingness yet inability to discard his Judaism, served as the motivating force for some of the major elements of the new science of psychoanalysis.

Freud was the victim of a severe complex. A complex very different from the one he called Oedipus, but nevertheless rooted in the same cause: the anxiety he felt towards his father and his Jewish heritage. Despite some waning observance, Jacob Freud served as the symbol of the Judaism that Sigmund himself should have been practising.

Himself a product of the German-Jewish enlightenment and who had experienced first-hand the ambivalence felt by young Jewish intellectuals to their ancestral faith, the Czech Jewish author Franz Kafka was in a unique position to comment on the inner workings of Freud's theories. After being exposed to them for the first time, Kafka wrote to his intimate friend Max Brod, 'What appeals to me [of Freudian psychoanalysis] is the observation that the father complex from which more than one Jew draws his spiritual nourishment relates not to the innocent father but to the father's *Judaism*. What most of those who began to write in German wanted was to break with Judaism, generally with the vague approval of their fathers. That is what they wanted, but their hind legs were bogged down in their father's Judaism, and their front legs could find no ground. The resulting despair was their inspiration.'

In fact, Freud himself might have showered the same reproach on Jacob Freud that Kafka did on his father, Herman. Jacob was by no means as innocent as the father the Greek Oedipus was destined to kill. On the contrary, he was doubly culpable: guilty of being too much a Jew and at the same time guilty of being too little Jewish. Neither Jacob nor Herman could completely break with tradition and allow their sons to be fully acceptable to secular society, but at the same time they lost the respect of their sons since there was nothing for the children to see but an empty shell of ritual, not enough of a Jew to hand down the possibility of authentically self-contained and self-justifying existence.

Kafka never got along with his father. In an attempt at reconciliation, he wrote the following letter, which his father never read:

> It would have been thinkable . . . that we might both have found each other in Judaism or that we might have begun from there in harmony. But what sort of Judaism was it that I got from you? . . . It was also impossible to make a child, over acutely observant from sheer nervousness, understand that the few flimsy gestures you performed in the name of Judaism, and with an indifference in keeping with their flimsiness, could have any higher meaning. For you they had meaning as little souvenirs of earlier times, and that is why you wanted to pass them on to me. But since they no longer had any intrinsic value, even for you, you could do this only through persuasion or threat. On the one hand, this could not be successful, and on the other, it had to make you angry with me on account of my apparent obstinacy.

The Herman Kafkas of the world have brought little authentic Judaism with them from the ghetto, and yet demand of their children a vague fidelity to Judaism, while at the same time consenting equally vaguely to break with tradition. Their sons, whatever they may do, are unhappy animals, doomed to live between two worlds and to be taken in by their own duplicity. In her famous text on this very subject, *From Oedipus to Moses*, Martha Robert contends that 'Psychoanalysis deals precisely with this father and its first task, quite apart from its more general message, was to explain their very definite conflict to a whole generation of spiritually and socially uprooted Jews' (page 111).

Unable to Break with Tradition

Freud, like many of his enlightened contemporaries, wished to divorce himself once and for all from what he saw as an outdated heritage which hindered his progress and acceptance in Gentile eyes. To Freud his Judaism did nothing for him except to retard his academic work, having it branded as yet another Jewish science. Notwithstanding his effort, the ghost of his father's Judaism tormented him and he could never completely rid himself of it. Thus his theory embodies the ambivalence felt by a son to his ever-pursuing fatherly image, either literally in the form of Jacob Freud or metaphorically in the form of Judaism and the Jewish people.

In the words of John Morris Cuddihy, 'Freud's life work was to make sense out of the trauma experienced by Jewish intellectuals in the process of emancipation who found themselves increasingly involved in Gentile society, in political, economic, and cultural spheres while remaining excluded from the social sphere.' Cuddihy believes that Freudianism, like Marxism and Reform Judaism, another post-emancipation ideology, was designed to transform the 'normative social conflicts' of the awkward, modernizing, East European Jew into 'cognitive scientific problems'. Psychoanalysis was concerned to show that behind the civility required by the rules of Gentile society, all men, like the uncouth upstart Jew, were pariahs since all were motivated by the untamed forces of the id.

We may postulate that herein lies the reason behind Freud's not attributing to women an intrinsic identity. Freud's model of woman is essentially a caricature of a castrated man and, as such, closely resembles one of the caricatures of the exilic Jew which both the Gentile and, to a certain crucial extent, the enlightened Jews themselves internalized. It is a parody of a man who is castrated politically, socially and sexually. It involves at once a denial and a projection of the unacceptable feelings of envy for the phallic qualities of the Gentile. A deep feeling of shame for their lack and, as an important adjunct, the opportunity of channelling a certain amount of anti-Semitic aggression toward a weaker target.

Freud had some inkling of this when he wrote in a letter to Pastor Pfister of an insight into his own work, 'Why did none of the devout create psychoanalysis? Why did one have to wait for a completely Godless Jew?' Yale historian Peter Gay, the author of a critically acclaimed biography of Freud, asserts, 'It was as a particular kind of atheist, a Jewish atheist, that Freud was enabled to make his momentous discoveries.' No other atheist would have cause to experience such immense inner tension over renouncing his heritage.

Freud's Life Comes Full Circle

Thus Freud's work does not develop along a straight line, but rather in an enormous circle around one and the same motif which is constantly reconsidered. Beginning with *The Interpretation of Dreams*, where the real person of Jacob Freud scarcely figures in the Oedipal drama inspired by his recent death but is conceived as the guilty father, the constitutive factor of the human psyche at all times and places, the circle closes in *Moses and Monotheism* with a grandiose vision of the Jew as essentially a parricide. Freud desperately attempted to put to rest the phantom that had pursued him his entire life – the Jewish faith. The first psychoanalyst returned to the very act which he had long ago tried to surmount, and re-embraced it on the eve of his death and at last called it by its right name, considering it the act that initiated his entire civilization.

In *Moses and Monotheism*, his last published work, Freud adopted the premise of Ernst Sellin, which when first announced was rejected by all other Jewish scholars. It should be noted that *Moses and Monotheism* is universally accepted to be Freud's least impressive work, with many critics wondering aloud why he had written it at all. Freud controversially suggested that Moses was not in fact a Jew, but an Egyptian prince who, having pity on the injustices perpetrated against the Jews, rescued them from Egypt, and whom they subsequently killed after he had led them forth from Egyptian bondage. Although *Moses and Monotheism* has been rejected as the least convincing of all Freud's works because it has no factual basis whatsoever, Freud was obsessed with its publication. In a comment about the book he cries, '*Moses* torments me like an unlaid ghost.' He wrote to Zweig, '*Moses* will not let go of my imagination . . . I picture myself reading it aloud to you when you come to Vienna, despite my defective speech. In an account of Tel el Amarna, which had not yet been fully excavated, I noticed a comment on a certain Prince Thotmes, of whom nothing is further known. If I were a millionaire I would finance the continuation of the excavations, this Thotmes could be my Moses and I would be able to boast that my guess had been right.' That is, he would have been finally able to put the ghost of Moses, the Jewish lawgiver which persecuted him from within throughout his life, to rest by proving that in fact he was not Jewish at all, but Egyptian.

Freud finally confronted his guilt about Judaism by declaring outright war. He attempted to prove that it was untruthful. His lifelong work and impetus was about to climax in the confrontation he had been stalling with his other theories.

The Spirit Breaks Forth

In his final days, Freud was still trying to do what for every Jew throughout the ages has proven an impossible feat: to quell the irrepressible Jewish spirit that yearns to break free and find expression in the life of a Jew. Freud must have known that to publish a book with no scientific basis would merely offend the Jews, especially at a time when Nazi persecution had engulfed all of Germany and Austria. Central to any true reading of *Moses* must be an understanding of why Freud was desperate to publish this work when its foundations rested on 'clay', so that the culmination of his life's work ultimately reduced itself to a few interesting conjectures rather than an explanation of major world religions. This book did not even advance the central theories of *Totem and Taboo*, but went against them. If Moses was an Egyptian he was only the father of the Jewish people in a figurative sense, and his murder ceased to be the archetypal parricide by which Freud explained the genesis of the most highly developed religions. There must have been some underlying cause, of which Freud seems oblivious or which he actively seeks to repress, to make him unwilling to accept the more probable thesis that Moses was a Jew and was killed by the Jews.

Moses and Monotheism represents Freud's final stirring of revolt against the inexorable fatality of affiliation, which so narrowly limits every human being by forcing upon each one of us an origin, a race and a name. Frightened by his increasingly marked resemblance to Jacob Freud, Sigmund fought with all his strength against this 'return of the repressed'. We read in *Moses*, 'In his old age even the great Goethe, who in his years of storm and stress had undoubtedly looked down upon his unbending and pedantic father, developed traits that had formed part of his father's character.' Freud's last novel can therefore be interpreted as a brilliant expedient of a mind confronted by ultimate necessity. It was the son's last bulwark and protest against the inevitable return of the father: he attempted to deny that the man called his spiritual father, Moses, was related to him at all. Freud could thus identify with Moses, not as an Israelite, and not even as an Egyptian, but because he had renounced the backward ideas of his time. He wished to be like the murdered prophet, the product of his life's work, but through choice and not because his heritage made it necessary.

The Lesson Today

The lesson for Jewish students at a place like Oxford is obvious. Oxford commendably has none of the institutionalized anti-Semitism experienced by Freud himself, which would stunt the natural progress a Jewish intellectual should achieve as he climbs through the ranks. What Oxford does have, however, is a tradition of doing things in a certain way, which goes back almost a millennium. The pressure to conform to the status quo is not inconsiderable. Faced with this subconscious pressure to abandon some of his identifying Jewish marks, what a Jewish intellectual can often be persuaded to do is find academic and scientific arguments to buttress his rejection or outright denial of his Jewish heritage. Of course these arguments can take and have taken various forms: the theory of evolution, biblical criticism, archaeological digs, or even psychoanalysis itself. Living here in Oxford I have come against all these disciplines, which no doubt deserve careful scrutiny and the full attention of today's serious Jewish scholars who strive to make Judaism live again in the minds of our talented young.

At the same time, it behoves the student to be honest enough with him or herself to decide whether or not these 'proofs' against Judaism were present before or after his rejection. Were they the cause of his disillusionment – which I would find fair enough if he had investigated the matter, spoken seriously with rabbis on the subject, and still emerged dissatisfied – or were they merely supports for his lack of pride in what he saw as an archaic tradition.

Biblical Criticism Claims a Victim

In my third year at Oxford, I became very friendly with a student from a completely non-observant background. He enjoyed studying Judaism immensely, and it became his passion. He studied with me as well as anyone else who was prepared to teach, and read a lot of books on Judaism. After one year at Oxford, he went to yeshivah for the summer, where he became completely observant. He was looked up to by all the students who frequent our centre because of his conviction, sacrifice, and how knowledgeable he had become in such a short period of time. Now he desired to extend his Jewish studies more formally. So he transferred from English, his original course, to study Hebrew at the university. The Hebrew curriculum at the university revolves around classical biblical criticism, and within a few months this student had become an expert in that as well. He began to feel that his entire Jewish observance conflicted with the new truths he had acquired through the university curriculum. He discussed the matter with me and others umpteen times. The problem was that neither I nor the rabbis I sent him to were well versed in biblical criticism, and thus proved of little assistance. After a while, however, he told me he had concluded that his continued strict observance of Halakha was intellectually dishonest since he no longer believed any of it. He told me that within a few weeks his beard would come off and he would gradually phase out his observance. This last conversation took place just before the summer break. He was going to Israel to take a course at the Hebrew University in Jerusalem. I pleaded with him to visit some leading Orthodox Jewish scholars who had worked for years on traditional responses to biblical criticism, but he refused. It was too late. When he returned to visit me six weeks later, he was barely recognizable.

My attitude to the abandonment of everything he had gained was philosophical. I felt that the most important thing was our friendship, which was real. As a Chasidic Jew I had always been taught that *Ahavas Yisroel*, disinterested love for my co-religionists, was paramount, and nothing else was nearly as important. We were real friends, and we both agreed that we would preserve our friendship. But after a while he became very hostile to my lifestyle. He became almost a missionary for his new-found beliefs and was very cynical and openly critical of any of the students who sought to advance their Jewish observance. Suddenly, anything and everything connected with Judaism began to bother him. It reached crisis point. We could no longer be friends. He harboured an inner hostility that was irrational and affected all of his relationships with his Jewish friends. When it was no longer tolerable, I approached him and told him how hurt I was that religion of all things had come between us. I spoke of how I always believed that friendship was something that must last for ever, regardless of changing lifestyles or systems of belief, and was impervious to the changes of circumstance. If this was not true, then we had never been friends. Finally I told him the following story.

For the Atheist There are No Answers

In the famous Volozhin Yeshivah in Poland, one of the *iluyim*, protégés, of the academy, was so brilliant that he was embraced by the secular intellectual establishment of his city. After some time had elapsed he became so ingrained in his secular circle that he left the yeshivah for an altogether better material life, and eventually abandoned Judaism altogether. His departure caused great grief to the head of the yeshivah, the acclaimed sage, Rabbi Chaim Vollozhener. After all, this was one of his greatest and most celebrated disciples.

Years later he chanced upon his former student, who was barely recognizable from his yeshivah years. The student, obviously uncomfortable with the confrontation, continued to walk past his former master. But Reb Chaim would not allow him and embraced him warmly. The student began to fire off deep intellectual objections as to the validity of the rabbinic tradition, offering this as a rationalization for the momentous changes in his life.

Reb Chaim looked at him and said, 'Perhaps you can tell me one thing, my son. Did you have these questions before you left the yeshivah, or only after?' He concluded by asserting that in the final analysis, for he who chooses to believe there are no questions, and for he who chooses not to believe there are no answers.

So too, I told my friend, all these insignificant details which now so irked him are completely unrelated to biblical scholarship, and if the cause of his leaving Judaism was the pursuit of intellectual honesty, then he must now be honest as well. Was he really finding everything about Judaism evil and irksome, or was the real truth that he was seeking rationalizations for his dismissal of Judaism? And how could he possibly justify having alienated all of his former friends, all of whom were tolerant and good people? He left that conversation angry.

Three days later he turned up at my home on Shabbat afternoon and told my wife to wake me up, because it was an emergency. When I came downstairs, he had tears in his eyes. He apologized for how he had behaved and agreed with me that real friendship was so rare, and so valuable, that it must be preserved at all costs. 'Where should I go from here?' he asked.

I responded that Judaism is not an all or nothing game. Because he found contradictions between the biblical account of the history of the Jewish people and archaeological digs, this did not mean that Judaism contains nothing which is valuable or relevant to the enhancement of his life. 'You cannot be a fanatic either way,' I told him. 'Don't be fanatically religious, but also don't discard the entire corpus of Judaism when there is so much of it which is life-affirming and conducive to a goodly life.'

Since then we have re-established our relationship to its former glory. And while he has not re-embraced Jewish observance, he now comes to all the Shabbat and festive meals, and many of the lectures. He extracts from that what he feels comfortable with, and I am once again proud of his example and encourage other students to emulate it.

Chapter Forty-nine

DARWIN AND MOSES: THE CHALLENGE OF EVOLUTION

Arriving at a university can only be with the purpose of seeking knowledge. This, of course, is just the culmination of a long and ongoing process which begins with the earliest infantile stage. But there are also some questions which are acknowledged as being more important, hence more central to our being, than others. Many parents, upon their children reaching an age of reasonable understanding, experience a dilemma when confronted with *the* question, the most feared, and the most profound, 'Mummy/Daddy, where do I come from?' This question, which is often brushed aside by the embarrassed parent with amusing stories pertaining to biological origin, or the age-old tale of the stork, is in truth a deep philosophical inquiry. The child realizes that he or she hasn't always existed, and therefore asks, 'What preceded me? Whence does everything, including me, spring forth?'

Origins in 'The Beginning'

This question of origin, which confounds all individuals at one time or another, has traditionally never confused the Jew. For him or her, the beginning of all existence was summed up in the first verse of the Torah: 'In the Beginning God created the heavens and the earth.' In his monumental philosophical work, *Guide of the Perplexed*, Maimonides teaches: 'Those who follow the law of Moses hold that the whole Universe has been brought by God into existence out of non-existence. This theory is undoubtedly a fundamental principle of the law of Moses; it is next in importance to the principle of God's unity. Do not follow any other theory!'

Yet this is precisely what has happened. Credence and acceptability have been given to an alternative, scientific explanation as to the origin of life and all existence, which claims libraries of proof, and is popularly known as 'evolution'. There can be no question, at least in my mind, that evolution has served over the past hundred and fifty years as *the* greatest challenge to traditional Judaism and biblical claims. Ever since it was first systematized and offered by its founder Charles Darwin, it has gnawed away at the faith of the believer, which now, at the very best, will always be cast with some degree, however small, of doubt.

The most direct result of the surge in the respectability of the Theory of Evolution has been a discrediting of the biblical narrative of creation. It has suddenly been labelled as primitive, mythological and simplistic.

I hope that this chapter on evolution will serve as a catalyst for the reader's further quest for knowledge of 'The Beginning', the fabulous creation which traditional Jewish thought asserts is constantly being re-enacted by a benevolent Creator, Lord of heaven and earth.

If there is one matter which I am constantly questioned about in Oxford, and indeed which has posed the greatest challenge to my work over the past five years, it is the spectre of science and evolution having supplanted religion and the need for a Divine origin for human existence. If God created us, then it makes sense to assume this was for a purpose. If life, however, sprang up by chance, then it follows that we owe no homage to a Creator or a tradition, both of whose validity are shaky at best.

This challenge is especially great at Oxford because of its formidable scientific reputation. The sciences and humanities are the leading disciplines in this university, and Oxford has given the world some of its most important scientific discoveries.

Coupled with this, of course, is a student's natural tendency to challenge authority. There can be nothing more authoritative than a Creator who called your being into existence, and thus deserves complete jurisdiction, and demands accountability, over how one leads one's life.

Opening the Floor to Real Debate

I must say now that I have never shied away from debate on these subjects. Any religion purporting to preach truths which refuses to debate the major issues of the era betrays a deep fear of being exposed. On the contrary, these lines which I write on evolution, culled from many different respected scientific sources, are not intended to oppose debate, they are meant to open it up again from what I believe is an unhealthy stagnation into unquestioningly accepting all mechanisms and propositions necessitated by the Theory of Evolution. If it is unhealthy for an individual to jump blindly into religious doctrines and belief, and I have constantly told my students that it is, then the same is true of scientific theory as well. Judaism has a very proud intellectual tradition which should continue to govern all aspects of our life.

Importance of Critical Debate

Critical debate is a central part of the learning process. In past times, the principal method of learning for English lawyers was to debate and discuss points of law in the Inns of Court. Similarly, in Oxford and Cambridge the famous and much approved tutorial system rests on the idea that the student contributes at least as much to the discussion as the supposed teacher. It is therefore surprising, particularly in our supposedly sceptical and enlightened age, to hear students and others accept theories as facts without really thinking about them. This is particularly so in the case of Jewish students, who show a marked enthusiasm for intellectual stimulation and also have the weight of a tradition of searching for the truth that is more than three millennia old.

What is central to understanding my following points, and the way in which I deal with the challenge of science in Oxford when its claims directly contradict Jewish teaching, is not that I attack science, but that I refuse to alter my traditional Jewish teaching until such time as the theories being proffered by science are as close to fact as possible. So long as they remain conjecture, or so long as they are riddled with major gaps and inconsistencies, then it is ludicrous to discard so ancient a tradition for a theory which itself is still in a state of flux and may indeed undergo severe modification, before it is promoted as fact and incontrovertibly true.

This was the approach of the great Jewish thinker and scientist, Maimonides. He taught that one should not accept any refutation of the words of the Bible until that refutation has been proved to be absolutely and unarguably true, within reason. The Torah needs no apology. It has soundly withstood the many attacks launched against it from time immemorial. I would contend, along with the many knowledgeable people whose ideas and scholarship have contributed to this work, that whereas admittedly there are important issues relating to the story of creation which must be elucidated and explained, the biblical account of creation has yet to be conclusively refuted by any scientific theory.

A Quest for the Truth

We have no business embracing Judaism unless it is true. Belief in the tenets of Judaism is worthless if they are not facts: there is no separation in our religion between the empirical world and the world of theology. Neither can the preservation of Judaism as an ethnicity or empty tradition alone inspire the passion or commitment to ensure its flourishing and survival. At the same time, opinions that are in direct contradiction with the Torah must be subjected to the greatest level of rational scrutiny before we attempt to substitute their truth for that of the word of God.

Refuting the Theory of the Eternity of Matter

Maimonides himself came up against such a dialectic between Scripture and secular thinking when he refuted Aristotle's almost universally accepted 'Theory of the Eternity of Matter'. Writing in *Guide of the Perplexed*, Maimonides expressly emphasized that his reaction to Aristotle's assertions was not merely moulded by the literal meaning of the text of Genesis, which proved incompatible with Aristotle's theory. 'We do not reject the eternity of the universe, because certain passages seem to contradict this premise, for such passages are not more numerous than those in which God is represented as a corporeal being [which Maimonides went to great lengths in the first section of the *Guide* to refute]; nor is it impossible or difficult to find some suitable interpretation for them. We should perhaps have had an easier task in showing that the scriptural passages referred to are in harmony with the theory of the eternity of the universe if we accepted the latter, than we had in explaining anthropomorphism in the Bible, when we rejected the idea that God is corporeal.'

Instead, Maimonides subjected the proofs of Aristotle to critical investigation, and reached the conclusion that the philosophers had *failed to prove* the eternity of the universe. Hence, he accepted the Scripture's account of creation literally, especially since this interpretation was properly consistent with what is taught in all other sections of the Written and Oral Torah concerning the Divine rule of the world, miracles, the age of the earth, and so on.

If the philosophers or scientists propose a 'law' which is proven beyond the shadow of a doubt, by some infallible means, to be true, then we will attempt to reconcile it with our Torah to the extent that we might even be forced to diverge from the literal and accepted traditional interpretation of the Scriptures in order to account for this inconsistency. Now, this is far from blind faith. Rather, we accept our traditional interpretation until proven otherwise. While evolutionary theory of course has many learned and respected adherents, it also possesses many holes and gaps, which we shall investigate shortly.

I must reiterate. *The purpose of my writing on this subject is not to refute evolution.* I am not a scientist, and am therefore incapable of such an endeavour, particularly because I surely have an agenda which I seek to promote, largely in contradiction to evolution, which may cause my arguments to be rather subjective.

Rather, my purpose, as a rabbi, is to investigate and discover the truth. That is my role and purpose as a Jew, and especially one with communal and leadership responsibilities, however lacking my qualifications may be. It happens to be that, from my experience, when one does undertake a thorough study of evolution one sees not only its astounding ingenuity and brilliance, but also some of its major shortcomings and inconsistencies which, curiously, seem to be overlooked by many scientists.

Officially Sponsored Debates

In our ongoing quest to ascertain the truth, and project ourselves as genuinely concerned with not shying away from the pressing questions which affect modern-day religions, but rather engaging momentous theories, the L'Chaim Society here in Oxford has sponsored major debates on the issue of Darwinism and Creation as well as debates on the broader struggle between science and religious belief. These have always been remarkably well attended, and have acted as stimulants for more private debate and thought, as well.

History of Scientific Debate at Oxford

In 1860 Oxford was the venue of the first great debate between science and religion. At a historic confrontation in the newly built edifice to science, the university museum, Bishop Wilberforce defended religion and creation against Thomas Huxley, the representative of that spearhead of agnostic scientific reduction, Darwin's theory of evolution.

History tells us that on this occasion religion lost the debate to science, but the question was not settled by any means: it is still arguably a leading question as we accelerate into the twenty-first century.

Because the proof of evolution has, in many people's minds, by no means been achieved, I decided to restage the debate within its original 'home' in the prestigious University of Oxford, one hundred and thirty-one years later. To argue the case for and against, we assembled some of the most eminent names in the field of science. We invited scientists who express a faith in God, as well as those who vehemently maintain that religion must have no place walking hand in hand with science on the path to knowledge.

Panel of Religious Scientists

I decided to stage the debate because I see that the main bar to many students affirming religious belief and practice is an uncritical conviction that science has somehow invalidated religion. Therefore, the objective of the debate was to allow the experts on both sides of the divide to present their views so that all might make a more informed judgement on the matter.

The scientists on the side of religion were Professor Herman Branover and Professor Velvl Greene. Professor Branover is the world leader in his specialist field, magneto-hydrodynamics, as well as a foremost researcher for the NASA space programme, and the 'Star Wars' defence project. Originally he was a Soviet citizen and scientist, and later a high-profile 'refusenik'. As a 'refusenik' he did much to promote Jewish education and culture despite harassment and persecution. He was finally released from the Soviet Union through the direct intervention of President Carter.

Professor Greene is a noted epidemiologist and is a former Director of the NASA Life-Science Research Centre. While he was brought up in a secular environment he found his religious life through the Lubavitch movement twenty-five years ago, which did much to change his life and outlook on the question of religion and science.

Joining the panel of religious scientists and the only woman in the debate, was Danah Zohar, an Oxford-based physicist. Danah, who is a close friend and very kindly wrote the introduction to Volume II of this book, achieved world acclaim for her trilogy of books on the subject of quantum physics and human consciousness: *The Quantum Self, The Quantum Society* and the forthcoming *The Quantum Spirit.*

On the side opposing religion were the very distinguished figures of Dr Richard Dawkins, Professor Colin Blakemore, and Dr Peter Atkins, all of whom are noted for their scientific achievement and their committed belief that science has indeed replaced religion and is the only means by which to apprehend the truth. Dr Dawkins is Reader in Zoology in the University of Oxford and published the enormously popular expositions of evolution, *The Selfish Gene* and *The Blind Watchmaker.*

Professor Colin Blakemore is Professor of Physiology in the University of Oxford. He was a BBC Reith Lecturer and the author of *Mechanics of Mind* and *Mindwaves.* His particular interest is neuroscience, and he hosted his own television series on the BBC called *The Mind Machine.*

Finally on the scientists' side was Dr Peter Atkins. He is Lecturer in Physical Chemistry at the University of Oxford. He has written twenty-four books, including the world-famous attack on creationism, *The Creation*, some concentrating on promoting strict reductionism, and he lectures widely on the relationship of science and religion, claiming that science is the only way to truth.

The two sides faced each other and presented their cases in Oxford's Gulbenkian theatre. The large auditorium packed in over seven hundred people who represented a complete cross-section of the university, many of whom had travelled to Oxford just to attend the debate. So did religion carry the day on this occasion, or did the forces of scientific reductionism prevail?

Theories which cannot be Refuted

Speaking first were Professor Greene and Professor Branover. Professor Greene argued that there is no essential contradiction between science and religion. He said that theories such as that of evolution which contradict religion are not the challenge to religion we may assume them to be. This is because these theories are only quasi-scientific; they are not amenable to strict refutation as are other scientific theories. He added that when scientists attack the 'unscientific' cosmology of the Bible, and its account of the origins of man, they are assailing a 'straw man', in that they mistake the intentions of Genesis, particularly assuming it to be cosmological when the purpose of it is to provide a setting for the real purpose of the Bible which is to declare what God requires of the human race. Greene also emphasized the deficiency of the theory of evolution by indicating the great division among scientists as to the actual mechanism of evolution, which is by no means clear.

Professor Branover assented to the general theme presented by Professor Greene and added his own criticisms of another key area of evolutionary science which is very commonly used to 'reduce' religion. Many evolutionists and scientists have an axiomatic belief in the ancientness of the universe and of the earth itself. They maintain that the world is millions of years old, and point to the 'evidence' of the fossil record. This is said by the evolutionists to contradict the Bible and religion as the biblical chronology puts the creation of the world back to *c.* 4000 BC.

Role of the Observer

Professor Branover said that this objection is not self-critical and is superficial if seen in the light of the implications of quantum mechanics for our understanding of time. Citing the work of Nobel laureate Eugene Vigner, Branover said that until the advent of the first observer the world was unactualized and merely formed a pool of probabilities, since according to quantum mechanics 'events' only actualize or occur from the pool of probability when they are observed. Therefore he argued that only with the emergence or creation of the first individual can the universe be said to have its beginning and creation. So it does not make ready sense to talk of millions of years of pre-existence before humans were on the face of the earth.

After the case for religion had been stated, the scientists for evolution presented their arguments. Dr Dawkins firmly believed that there was no contest between science and religion. He said that religion never openly addressed the problems of science. He claimed that religion instead occupied one of three invalid positions against science according to circumstances. He said that religion either claimed to know it all, or that it knew nothing or that it simply declared 'no contest'. He went on to say that religion itself did not present itself to question, which is the contrary of real science.

Dr Atkins took a similar position. He said that science is the only path to truth and that he shunned religion because he thinks it implausible and partly because it does nothing for man. In summation he said that religion is ultimately the enemy of truth and only science may suffice.

Professor Blakemore concluded on behalf of reductionism. His position was simply to dismiss religion *per se*. He claimed he could not understand the motivation of religion, nor could he make any sense of religious practice. One need only look at the empirical achievements of science to corroborate its truths.

In summary, both sides gave strong polemical defences of their positions before an enthusiastic and receptive audience. Professor Greene and Professor Dawkins were considered to have given the strongest arguments for their respective positions. When at the end I brought the matter to a vote, I asked if anyone present had changed their mind as a result of what they had heard. A few hands went up three said they were swayed from religion to science, two said they were swayed to religion. Thus the position of religion lost by a single vote, not the foregone overwhelming conclusion in favour of science that most people would assume it had to be.

Time for a Rematch

The event as a whole made a great impression on the university. Nearly a tenth of the university were actually present. It was widely talked about by the students the next week and also some of Oxford's best-known scientists were heard to debate the issue in Broad Street. Subsequently I was asked to reconvene the debate in the future and a number of leading academics volunteered to debate.

Difficulty in Finding Panelists

For a while we had tremendous difficulty getting all the panelists we wanted to turn up. The problem was not that they did not feel it worth their while to come to Oxford for a student society's debate; on the contrary, they felt the issue was so important that deep rivalry sprang up between two participants. This was reported in the famous 'Peterborough' column of Britain's *Daily Telegraph* newspaper:

> Originally the Darwinist team was to feature Richard Dawkins, scientist and author of *The Blind Watchmaker*. But when he discovered that Richard Milton, a journalist and science writer, was to take part, he decided to withdraw. The pair came to verbal blows recently over a review in the *New Statesman* of Milton's book, *The Facts of Life: Shattering the Myth of Darwinism*. Dawkins dismissed Milton's effort as 'twaddle that betrays, on almost every page, complete and total ignorance of the subject at hand'. Milton, peeved, promptly fired off a letter to the magazine's editor arguing that Dawkins 'seems to have mistaken fundamentally the nature and intent of the book'. What's more, he decided to withdraw from the debate. 'Darwinists have a religious attachment to their evidence,' he

> said yesterday. 'Rather than accept any new scientific evidence they try to portray their critics as nuts.' On hearing that Milton had withdrawn, Dawkins changed his mind and decided to take part. Boteach, who has kept his cool with commendable spirit, says: 'All we are concerned with is discovering the truth.'

In the end, this second debate was staged in November 1992 and involved Dr Dawkins again as well as Professor John Maynard-Smith, Professor of Evolutionary Biology, University of Sussex, and Professor Sir Herman Bondi, President of the British Humanist Society and formerly chief scientist to the British government. These were the pro-Darwinism panelists, and once again we had a strong debating opposition for them. Dennis Prager, Dr Arthur Peacocke, a distinguished biochemist and Warden of the Society of Ordained Scientists since 1987, and Professor Robert Winston, Professor of Fertility Studies, University College, London, were advertised in advance, but perhaps the most interesting panelist as it turned out was the presence on the pro-religion side of the debate of Professor David Berlinski. David Berlinski is the author of *Black Mischief*, a detailed and scientific critique of modern evolutionary theory. In the debate he used Dr Dawkins's and Professor Maynard-Smith's own arguments against them, pointing to holes in the supposedly perfect cloth of the theory of evolution. He stressed the bizarre (to an evolutionist) gaps in the fossil record, the mainstay of the scientific establishment's belief in evolution. By the end of the debate, Dr Dawkins and Professor Maynard-Smith were visibly frustrated by the combination of his grasp of the scientific facts and his logical refusal to interpret them in their way. Still they asserted vociferously and many evolutionary students maintained thereafter that he has manipulative evidence and fact to his advantage.

Certainly if one thing became clear from these debates it was that science cannot blithely claim it has displaced religion. Religion still has strong claims to dealing with the eternal verities and our existence in God, and as such it is by no means incompatible with the search for scientific knowledge. For science may supply us with the 'how', but to religion and God we must look to the 'thence' of existence. And to the students of Oxford who witnessed some of the world's greatest scientists unable to refute the validity or usefulness of religion in an academic debate, this message came to life as never before.

The Second Debate in Greater Detail

This most recent debate was attended by upwards of a thousand people. This second debate was initially suggested by the recent publication of a book claiming to refute Darwinism by Richard Milton, *The Facts of Life*: this book had been given wide publicity, but this did not at first stimulate staunch evolutionists to discuss the issues it raised. Rather, Dr Richard Dawkins was extremely reluctant to stand on the same platform as Milton, and refused to take part in the debate if Milton were present. His reasoning was that Mr Milton, as a science reporter, was not a serious scientist, and I must admit that this was a sentiment we heard quite a bit about from others whom we approached to participate.

An Appeal to Dawkins

The withdrawal of Dr Dawkins, so popular among Oxford students, threatened the whole of the debate with cancellation. This, then, was my appeal to him to rejoin.

'Dear Dr Dawkins,
Thank you for your letter of 29 August which was indeed written in an extremely courteous and friendly manner, despite your firmness not to debate Richard Milton. Before I say anything else, I sincerely thank you for the friendship and assistance that you have always shown me, despite our differences. You are a man of dignity and honour and I value your acquaintance.

'In the first instance, my invitation to Richard Milton was predicated on your reviewing his book in the *New Statesman*. I felt sure that if you were willing to review the book, you would also appear on the same platform as him. More importantly, however, is your objection to his participation on the grounds that as he purports not to be religious, there should be no interest to our organization in a debate between yourself and Milton. When I first mentioned to you that Dennis Prager would argue in the debate that an irreligious or Godless world would lead to atrocious crimes, your response was that your interest is promoting truth, regardless of its consequences. This was a position that I entirely concur with and I have no interest in perpetuating Judaism, or even the notion of God, if it is contrary to the truth. Judaism to me is not a culture or something practised by my ancestors. It is either true or it is nothing.

'But your position also led to the possibility of a non-debate. You will be arguing how science has refuted religious teachings on the origin of life and the world, and Prager will be arguing that we need religion to be moral. It was thus imperative that Sir Herman Bondi focus on that matter with Prager in the debate, and someone take issue with you on the validity of your assertions. This would make for a real debate.

'My firmness in having you participate in this debate is quite simply due to the fact that you are the best-known exponent of evolution in the entire country and stood as the best speaker in our last debate. This was the consensus of virtually all those in attendance. I hope you appreciate that the same must be true of the other side. We want to have the best possible speakers on both sides. Richard Milton's book is the only one in objection to evolution that has ever been taken seriously by the media.

'Which brings us to the next point. I fully understand your unwillingness to give his book publicity. Yet, the simple fact remains that it is getting a tremendous amount of publicity anyway. In this respect, I believe that the advice of Stephen Jay Gould [he advised that Dawkins refrain from being dragged into a situation where his presence would lend much coveted interest in quirky Creationist causes] which you quote in your letter, does not pertain to this particular matter. To my knowledge, none of the books by Henry Morris, for example, whom you cite in your review, were ever given serious attention, much less credence, by the media. This book has. And a lot of it. The *Sunday Times* last week (first section) and this week (Julia Neuberger's book review), BBC *Newsnight* (who interviewed him), Channel 4 yesterday (a full documentary about the book and scientists' reaction to it), and these are just the programmes which I have seen. Surely there is a lot more coverage of which I am not even aware.

'Your insistence that I choose between you and Milton puts me in a very difficult position. On the one hand, the debate without you, in my opinion, is a waste of time. You are certainly the most articulate and best known of all the scientists who could do this debate. I have read both *The Selfish Gene* and *The Blind Watchmaker* and notwithstanding my religious convictions, was deeply impressed with both works. You are a serious force to be reckoned with, and without you the debate loses its quality. On the other hand, there simply is no one at all besides Milton whose objections to evolution have been given a microphone to the world.

'I think the question that must be asked is this: If Thomas Huxley were alive today, would he still have debated with Bishop Wilberforce? I believe he would. Because he would have seen it as a further opportunity to prove the validity of his position to those who have not yet accepted it. With or without Milton there are still many sceptics of evolution, including myself, who are extremely eager to see an event like this take place.

'If it makes it any easier, I shall refrain from making any mention of Milton's book in the advance publicity. We will advertise him as a science reporter and nothing else. Based on conversations that I have had with people on the subject thus far, I believe that this will be one of the most significant events to have taken place in Oxford in recent memory.

'Based on the above, it is my sincere hope that you reconsider.'

Success at Last

Fortunately, a man of his word, Dr Dawkins, to whom I continue to be indebted for his warm friendship and gentlemanliness, agreed to come and amidst its turbulent beginnings and organizational nightmare the debate went ahead, leading to a fascinating discussion of the issues. As I have written above, however, Richard Milton then declined participation, citing the impossibility of being given a fair hearing as the reason for his withdrawal. We are currently preparing the texts of the speeches for publication, and they will be well worth the wait. This was a fiery debate, with no holds barred. Dr Berlinsky, who savagely attacked the validity of evolution, was equally vociferously opposed by Dr Dawkins and Professor Maynard-Smith. At times the arguments became personal and cut-throat. But then, it served for greater entertainment, and also, who can blame the participants when it comes to debating so emotive and controversial a subject?

Everyone who attended was highly impressed by the quality of the arguments and the ferocity with which they were delivered.

After this lengthy introduction, the following few pages are presented in all humility as an exposition of the concerns and questions that important scientists, many of them devout evolutionists, have themselves raised about the theory of evolution. As I stated earlier, I cannot claim to be a scientist. But I also recognize that these issues affect everyone, not just those involved in scientific research into the origins of life, and everyone has a right to try to understand them. The arguments are presented here for the purpose of enabling those interested to take both sides of the debate rationally, rather than leaving those who have belief in the special creation of God floundering on the rocks of scientific opacity. After all, we do not all have the knowledge or the time to go through specialist books on geology or biology, but the implications found by others can be relevant to the ordinary person interested in knowing the truth. What I can assure the reader is this: in the five years since I have been here, and since I published these remarks in 1989 as part of the first specialist occasion which we devoted to the issue of evolution, entitled 'The 2001 Principle', many students have at least come to understand that just as Judaism today does not have all the answers to the most difficult challenges posed against it, neither does science. Evolution has at least as many serious obstacles as Judaism that it must overcome before it can be embraced as fact. Let us examine what they are.

Part One

Evolution vs Accountability

The human body is a highly complex, integrated system. Building blocks in the form of limbs, organs, veins and blood combine together to form the select being of each person. These features are all visible and to an extent definable; we share these characteristics with other animals. The feature that does distinguish us from all other living systems is not discernible as these constituent parts are; it is our conscience.

Inherent character dispositions and attributes enable each human to interact with other humans, and the other inhabitants of the world. It is an integral part of the human system to be born with certain tendencies to feel love and hate, pride and shame, contempt and compassion. Though these tendencies vary greatly amongst individuals, at a certain point they converge to a level at which all people are equal. It is therefore inescapable that humans, from the beginning of time to the present, have all had a number of common tendencies, some positive and others negative.

Some of the negative tendencies, such as the disposition towards laziness, we have partly overcome by redirecting our natural tendency towards inactivity so that it may be used productively. Others we have universally failed to develop.

A Dislike for Accountability

One of the most common elements of the human organism is the tendency to resist authority, responsibility and accountability. From childhood to old age, the human nature actively repels responsibility.

The material composition of the complete human, in similarity to the physical matter he or she is composed of, desires to exist in its lowest, its most undeveloped, state. When someone defies responsibility, they are simply expressing the natural state of humankind. For this reason, there are only a few people – the great leaders of the past, either spiritual, political, or military – who have distinguished themselves from the rest by resisting this human tendency and developing a second nature of responsible discipline. A small minority has been able to become accountable not only for themselves, but for others as well.

The great majority, on the other hand, instead of cultivating and nurturing this human disposition have looked for an easier escape in the form of excuses of mitigating circumstances designed to relieve them from responsibility. These excuses have been developed in a hierarchy ranging from the most immature in human existence, to those used by the most educated. The excuses we gave our teachers as young pupils in school are still fresh in many people's minds as a faintly embarrassing or amusing memory: 'the dog bit me', or, 'I was kidnapped', the youngster tells the teacher, only half expecting to be believed. For many children, these excuses form a challenge to society and authority almost as much as they are an excuse.

Responsibility Haunts Us Throughout Life

Later, when the totalitarian rule of the teacher is ended, we rejoice. The human bias to resist authority is then met with an even greater challenge: when we begin working for an employer, the authority to which we were subjected in childhood grows in power, and the need to avoid such responsibility grows commensurately. The solution is either to get promoted or to get rid of the whole hierarchy of bosses and go into business for oneself.

If we enter into our own business enterprise, we come into contact with even greater authority: the government dips deep into our pockets and drives us silly with taxes, rules and regulations. Our impulse to escape this authority, again, could be enacted in the form of building a wooden raft to float to a deserted island where formal government has not yet reached. So it goes on, human creativity always finding ways to escape authority, and the possibilities seemingly endless.

No Escape from the Creator

Yet, amidst all the escape routes, there will always remain one authority which is ineludible. For no matter where we turn, He is there. The authority of which we speak is of course that of the Creator. It is unbearable for many humans, for if the demand for responsibility increased commensurately with increasing authority (as we have all experienced with our parents, teachers, bosses, governments etc., in succession), the degree of responsibility and accountability demanded by a Creator, a God, would be unfathomable. He would most certainly ask us to adhere to a certain moral code of ethics, Divine commands – no, our entire lives would have to be devoted to Him.

Divine Graffiti

For centuries, this was unavoidable: there was always the One Authority that even human ingenuity could not overcome. We tried closing our minds and denying His existence, but that was impossible. Every time one merely took a walk outside, the world shouted, 'Purpose!' Everywhere we looked, intention and design expressed themselves and a master artisan must have been the cause. God's graffiti were found in every corner of the universe, proclaiming, 'I am here!' The great oceans and the solid earth needed a Forger; the miracle of organic life needed a Miracle-Worker; the great variety and diversity among living organisms demanded an Originator; the biological complexity of the organisms signified a Designer. God was not seen, but His *effects* were seen and felt and His denial seemed absurd, unless these effects could be explained in a different light.

Earliest Origins of Evolution

The Greek philosophers were the first to develop theories in which it was implied that the variety of living organisms was not an act of special creation of individual species, but rather that the divergent species on the face of the earth had somehow evolved from a common ancestor. This was the first step to diminishing the recognition of the interaction and necessity of a Creator, but it could not exclude Him from the totality of existence.

In later generations, theories suggesting the ultimate supplantation for Divine creation began to develop. These theories sought to explain the origin, development and meaning of all things in terms of natural laws and processes which are said to operate today as they have in the past. No extraneous processes, requiring the special activity of an external agent, or Creator, would be necessary in such a scenario. Rather, the universe, and all its aspects, evolve into higher levels of order, from particles to people, by means of the innate properties of matter. Thus the naturalistic, self-contained and continuous process of evolution would eliminate the necessity of special creation, and subsequently a personal Creator.

What Evolution Has to Prove

The first obstacle to accepting evolution was the universal belief in the relative youth of the earth. Proponents of evolution recognized that the 'human history' of the world was available for only the past few thousand years. The beginning of written records, with anything approaching a verifiable chronology, dates from about the first dynasty in Egypt (between 2500 and 3500 BC). Such a short time span obviously ruled out the possibility of gradual change leading to the diversity of species. Unless scientists assumed that the age of the earth was to be reckoned in billions of years, evolutionary thought had no chance of gaining a foothold.

Mutability of Species

For evolution to be accepted, proof would also have to be brought that plants, animals and even people undergo biological modifications, from pre-existing primitive forms to highly complex organisms. The theory would have to demonstrate that they do not breed true to type, remaining unchanged and identical with their inaugural forms. This transformation of living things from one form to another would also have to be proved to be the result of purely accidental events, and not the result of deliberate purpose on the part of a Divine Power.

The modern earth was at that time by consensus viewed as the result of two factors: (a) the shape God had given it in the beginning; (b) the damage He inflicted upon it when He punished Man with a flood (scientifically known as catastrophism). Consequently, the globe had not changed its basic structure since the deluge had left the face of the earth. In a scene of such changeless monotony, there was no need for living things to alter. Evolutionary development was therefore unthinkable. Evolution had to prove a changing environment.

Overcoming the Argument from Design

Perhaps the great obstacle that evolutionary thought had to overcome was the argument from design. The empirical world testified to intelligent, providential design. As biological research developed, scientists were more and more struck by the fitness and efficiency of living things. Fins, feathers, hearts, lungs and eyes were so admirably adapted to the functions they served, it seemed inconceivable they could have arisen spontaneously – much less by chance. They must have been deliberately designed.

The apparent resolution of these problems was the beginning of modern-day evolutionary thinking and, more properly, Darwinism. Charles Darwin did not wholly invent evolution. As mentioned previously, the germs of the idea existed long before his time. In fact, a generation before him, detailed theories of evolutionary development had been proposed by Buffon, Lamarck and Charles's own grandfather, Erasmus Darwin. The significance of Darwin's contribution, so much so that the world dates evolution from him, was that he proposed a 'theory' that bestowed on the Doctrine of Evolution a certain measure of reasonableness, which made it acceptable.

Influence of Lyell

Darwin was greatly influenced by the research and theory of geologist Charles Lyell, who stated that instead of viewing the globe as being defaced by universal cataclysms such as floods (catastrophism), the earth had rather undergone continuous physical change. The natural forces now at work were the ones that had always been shaping its physical features. The terrestrial globe was and always had been the province of terrestrial processes – wind, rain, flood, erosion, subsidence, sedimentation, and above all the titanic and unceasing cookery of volcanic heat. This theory, known as 'uniformitarianism', assumes that fossils, rocks and other features of the earth's crust formed slowly over vast aeons of time by the same processes that can now be seen at work on the earth.

Lyell's 'mobilization' of the history of the globe set the stage for the possibility of continuous biological change. Based on this theory, Darwin began to appreciate that if the globe had undergone such far-reaching changes, it was reasonable to assume that life had undergone a comparable transformation. If not, the passage of time would have brought about a lethal maladjustment between living things and their environment, and in the long run the earth would have depopulated itself. Therefore, those species which had been outmoded by geological change would have to be replaced by new, freshly adapted ones.

'Descent with Modification'

He then proposed that these new species had evolved from their outdated predecessors by 'descent with modification'. He stated that varieties of life branched out of a common stem, and therefore even divergent species shared a common ancestor. Primitive organisms slowly developed into more and more complex ones with the progress of time.

This theory of 'descent with modification' did not answer the two most pressing questions. How did these new species emerge, and what guaranteed their adaptation? To answer these two questions, Darwin suggested the twofold processes of random variation and natural selection.

Mutation and the Mechanics of Change

Modern science interprets Darwin's proposal of random variation to be 'random mutations in the hereditary information store (the DNA molecule) that go on to be preserved in future generations'. A mutation is assumed to be a structural change in a gene, of such character that something novel is produced. In some way, the linkages in a segment of the DNA molecule are changed. This change is inherited by the next generation so that different 'information' is passed on via the mutated genetic code and the structure of the descendant is therefore different. These mutations in their turn produce 'novelties' in the descendant, previously unpossessed by the parent, as will be explained in detail later on. In spite of the fact that each novelty is more or less negligible, their successive accumulation from one generation to the next will lead to the establishment of changes which are highly significant.

The phenomenon of mutation, therefore, is an important component of the evolutionary model. The model most postulate some mechanism to produce the required upward progress in complexity which characterizes it. Evolution, then, predicts that mutations must be potentially beneficial, generating a 'vertical change' upwards toward higher degrees of order. To explain the survival of the more complex descendant, Darwin proposed what he called the 'survival of the fittest'.

Only the Fittest Survive

He reasoned that if these changes and mutations should have a beneficial effect, then they would give their host organism a better chance of survival.

For nature only produces a modest amount of resources of food, air and water, as a result of which there is a ferocious struggle for existence. In each struggle, individuals endowed with favourable novelties will survive whereas the less fortunate individuals will perish. The less fortunate are those with unfavourable mutations or those that have not adapted at all. In turn, the fortunate individuals will pass the new beneficial feature to their descendants. In this manner, Darwin suggested that the form which possesses this hereditary advantage will eventually become the majority in the population. When this happens one could say that the population itself has changed.

After a sufficient number of such changes the new population will eventually be recognizable as a new species. Moreover, this process continues to operate at higher and higher levels. Gradually mutations in populations give rise to a new genus, a new family, a new order, a new class, and eventually to a new phylum. In this fashion, Darwin suggested that life started from the simplest of forms and developed into a multi-celled organism from which the invertebrates and then the vertebrates arose. Of the vertebrates, first there were the fish, then the amphibian, the reptiles, the birds, and the mammals. From a small carnivorous mammal all the mammals including the apes developed, and from the apes there arose humans. Thus Darwin's theory explained the Doctrine of Evolution.

The Effect of Evolution

Unlike almost any other theory in science, this theory of evolution has had a profound influence on moral and religious development in a short space of time. In just 130 years, evolution, far from being 'just another theory', has become a total statement of what humankind and nature are, what history signifies, and what the basic laws of the world are.

Although the religions still survive, all, even Judaism, have become deeply penetrated by the attitudes and ideas generated by evolution. Their foundations have been gnawed away and the faith of the believer is now overcast with doubt and confusion. The doctrines of evolution continue to dominate the philosophy of the western world. There exist few members of western society whose very thought and speech is immune to the assumptions and doctrines of evolution. Upon it have been built ideologies, philosophies, and even the everyday behaviour of ordinary men and women. Evolution can be said to have become scientific dogma.

Even though religionists continue to fight, virtually all formal opposition has stopped. Evolution is now indoctrinated everywhere. No scientist dares question it without losing his standing. Naturally one would expect that a theory so hailed by brilliant scientists and accepted by millions of people the world over is supported by an overwhelming mass of impressive proofs. Critical investigation would suggest that it is not.

Rabbi Menachem M. Schneerson, the Lubavitcher rebbe, in a letter describing the inaccuracy of scientific dating systems, has stated, 'If [people] are still bothered by the theory of evolution I can tell them without fear of contradiction that it has not a shred of evidence to support it.' The accuracy of this pronouncement is supported not only by the lack of scientific proof for evolution, but also because evolution has constructed a framework in which it cannot be disproved.

A leading modern biologist has pointed out, 'Our theory of evolution has become . . . one which cannot be refuted by any possible observations. It is thus outside of empirical science but not necessarily false. No one can think of ways in which to test it . . . evolutionary ideas have become part of an evolutionary dogma accepted by most of us as part of our training.' The noted evolutionist, Arthur Keith, stated in a similar manner, 'Evolution is unproved and unprovable. We believe it only because the only alternative is special creation, and that is unthinkable.'

Why Evolution?

Yet before we begin to analyse the shortcomings of evolution, I feel it imperative to address the question of why the idea of evolution may have been advanced in the first place, if the theory is weak and there is truly 'not a shred of evidence' to support it. The Lubavitcher rebbe, Rabbi Menachem Schneerson, writes: 'The answer, again, is to be found in human nature. It is a natural human ambition to be inventive and original. To accept the biblical account deprives one of the opportunity to show one's analytic and inductive ingenuity. Hence, disregarding the biblical account, the scientist must devise reasons to "justify" his doing so, and he takes refuge in classifying it with ancient and primitive mythology and the like, since he cannot really argue against it on scientific grounds.'

Taking this a step further, we may add that in the process of deriving their own hypothesis for the origin of life and thus being inventive and original, the scientists have gone to great pains to postulate a theory that would completely remove the necessity for any outside agent, namely God. By believing that life arose and developed by chance alone, extreme comfort is offered to those who find a natural resistance to being subjects to a higher Cause or Ruler. If life arose by chance, then there is no Creator. If there is no Creator, then there is no Divine Ruler. Humankind then achieves a significant degree of freedom.

Evolution as Escape?

Professor Weisman proposed the following argument: 'We must accept the principle of natural selection because it offers the only explanation of the purposefulness of the natural world without our having to assume that it was created by a force that desired it and created it intentionally.' Similarly, Dr M.S. Watson made the following observation: 'The theory of evolution itself [is] a theory accepted not because it can be proved by logically coherent evidence to be true, but because the only alternative, special creation, is clearly incredible.' Clearly, these pronouncements have little to say in the way of the scientific method, and support the point set out above.

A support for the previously mentioned explanation that evolution is a theory which scientists have an active purpose in promoting can be observed from a statement by the eminent palaeontologist, D. Dwight Davis: 'The facts of palaeontology [fossil study] conform equally well with other interpretations . . . e.g., Divine Creation etc., and palaeontology by itself can neither prove nor refute such ideas.' One of the main causes and evidence for the emergence of the evolutionary theory was the fossil record: Darwin himself writes in his introduction to *The Origin of Species*: 'I was struck with certain facts . . . in the geological relations of the present to the past inhabitants of [South America]. These facts seemed to throw some light on the origin of species.' What, then, was the compulsion to devise a new theory based on facts that were explanatory in accordance with an already accepted theory? One reason may be, as above, 'It is a natural human ambition to be inventive and original.'

To Question the Validity of an Accepted Theory

Another important consideration to remember before addressing the difficulties of evolutionary theory is that it is not unreasonable to question the validity of a theory, even when it is widely and firmly held by many knowledgeable professionals. For tens of centuries, knowledgeable astronomers and geographers thought that the earth was a flat disc. This idea did not appear foolish during those times because the objective and scientific evidence available then made such a hypothesis very reasonable indeed. When more information was accumulated and more accurate measurements were made, these ancient theories turned out to be false. The mere fact that many people believe in a particular hypothesis does not automatically make it true.

Keeping the above in mind we may now begin an investigation into the feasibility of, and proof for, evolution. Much has been written by many leading scientists with the purpose of refuting evolution. Many of these works, although brilliant in scientific scope and overall thoroughness, are exhaustive and extremely detailed, not designed for the lay reader. My purpose in the following remarks is to summarize and simplify the arguments, adding a few insights as we go along.

We will deal primarily with the major evidence brought in favour of evolution and explore the validity of the evidence and its accompanying arguments. In doing so, we follow the dictum taught in the Talmud: 'Rabbi Simlaài said: Every place from which the atheists may prove [the non-existence of a Creator], the refutation is found near at hand.' Thus, from the proofs themselves, we intend to demonstrate evolution's shortcomings. Furthermore, as mentioned earlier, although labelled a scientific theory, evolution has completely changed humanity's view of itself, of the world and history. In the light of this fact, it is inevitable that the theory should have philosophical, moral, and indeed religious overtones whose significance cannot be overlooked. We will explore the consequences of evolution in each of the above-mentioned fields, and because the theory's implications are more general than most scientific theories, we will begin by examining evolution in a philosophical light.

Part Two

Philosophical Analysis of Evolution

One of the most accepted principles of philosophy, a principle that has become law in every field of science, is the law of cause and effect. This states that every phenomenon is only an 'effect' of a 'cause' and no effect is ever quantitatively 'greater' or qualitatively 'superior' to the thing that caused it. An effect can be lower than or almost equal to its cause, but never higher, never more logical or more perfect.

Evolution would state that the universe is its own cause. There was no designer who fashioned the universe, but rather through random motion of primeval particles all the great complexity, energy and intelligence of the universe came about by mere chance. Philosophically, this negates the basic premise of the law of cause and effect. If everything is the result of a previous cause, and all causes relate back to an original first cause, then rational logic dictates that the original first cause must be an 'uncaused first cause'. This is an argument used by Maimonides at the very beginning of the 'Laws Foundation Principles of the Torah'. He writes that if there does not exist a first cause that had no cause of its own, then the causal chain would continue ad infinitum and no result or conclusion, hence no explanation, will have been reached. Therefore using 'causal' reasoning we note that the First Cause of limitless space must itself be infinite; the First Cause of endless time must itself be eternal; the First Cause of infinite complexity must be omniscient, and so on.

While explaining how from matter all existence emerged, the theory of evolution is admitting that something must have preceded the matter.

Although matter itself is clearly mutable and finite, it must ultimately have been caused by something eternal and infinite. We are forced to ask what made matter, and we answer, 'God'.

The most common retort by an evolutionist to this is the question, 'Well, who made God?' By asking, 'Who made God?' one is asking, 'Where does God begin?' The most essential intimation of a God is infinity, that He is a primal cause, and nothing precedes a first cause. God has neither a beginning nor an end. Therefore this question as to the origin of God is being addressed to the wrong party. It is just as illogical as asking, 'What is the final number in an infinite number line?' One cannot request an explanation for the beginning of an infinite Being!

While this question cannot be asked in relation to God, since by definition He is infinite, it can be asked in relation to matter, which is finite. One may of course imagine matter as existing eternally, in one form or another, as great philosophers did such as Plato, and Aristotle in his *Theory of the Eternity of the Universe*. Yet if one is to accept that matter is the origin of the universe, space, time, complexity, etc., then this primeval matter will (aside from being eternal) have to be omnipotent, omniscient and infinite, based on the law of cause and effect. If an individual is ready to believe in eternal, omnipotent, omniscient and infinite matter, one may as well just shift one's vocabulary and call that 'God' or 'Creator', because in essence they imply the same thing.

Contradictions with General Relativity

Another grave difficulty with evolution in a 'conceptual system' of science has arisen as a logical result of Einstein's revolutionary 'theory of relativity'. Einstein emphasized that all frames of reference as to size, position, time and motion in the world are relative, not absolute. This argues that the universe cannot be an absolute in itself, and therefore can have no independent or absolute existence. Since it could not produce itself, it must be in existence due to the omnipotence of an external Creator, who is Himself its absolute standard. No wonder then, that Einstein himself affirmed a powerful belief in the deity, remarking that 'God does not play dice with the Universe' and also that 'Science without religion is blind; religion without science is lame.'

Another fact worth noting from a conceptual system of science comes from the study of forces and fields. Interactions in nature depend on three types of force and the 'fields' associated with them: namely, electromagnetic, gravitational and nuclear forces. All three have apparently always acted as they do now, since the beginning of the universe. There is no evidence that these entities have ever 'evolved' into their present form. The field action is propagated through free space in the form of wave action (electromagnetic waves, gravitational waves, etc.) at the same speed as that of light, 300,000,000 metres per second. There is real mystery in this wave phenomenon because it takes place in the 'nothingness' of free space – a vacuum. What vibrates in this wave motion? No one has been able to answer this question. However, it is a doubly puzzling problem for evolution. It is unlikely that wave phenomena could evolve in the void of a vacuum where there is nothing to evolve from.

Part Three

Scientific Questions on Evolution

As previously mentioned, before the theory of evolution could be found acceptable, major obstacles had to be overcome. Although there are many others, the fundamental arguments against evolution were: (1) the immutability of species; (2) the seemingly young age of the earth; (3) the permanence of the earth's physical structure; (4) the argument from design.

To solve each of these difficulties, and to provide a workable theory for evolution, Darwin and fellow proponents of evolution (both earlier and later) proposed theories and solutions the accuracy of which we shall now examine. For reasons of clarity, we shall classify the various propositions pertaining to each individual argument in its own category.

1: The Immutability of Species

Pre-evolutionary thought conceived of all living species as existing continually in the same unaltered form in which they had been created. Evolution therefore had to prove that living organisms have undergone development from the simple to the complex. In addition to this, an extraordinary mechanism had to be found for this purpose. If it was really true that random matter had evolved through successive stages into elements, stars, living cells and even complex humankind, then there had to be a powerful and persuasive principle which impelled systems to higher and higher levels of complexity. The mechanism proposed was genetic mutation, complemented by natural selection.

Random Order and the laws of Entropy

A basic law of increasing organization which introduces new systems into nature and which develops existing systems into higher systems is surely the most fundamental and important prediction of the evolution model.

Therefore, the evolution model can only be valid if there is such a principle of increasing order operating in nature. This, however, is not the case. Here the theory of evolution comes into direct conflict with the two laws which govern all natural processes. These are the First and Second Laws of Thermodynamics. It should be stressed that these two laws are proven scientific laws. They have been experimentally tested, measured and confirmed, many times, and no scientist today doubts their full applicability in the space co-ordinates accessible to us. Therefore the cosmic implications of the two laws are profound.

The late great scientist writer, Isaac Asimov, writes that 'This law is considered the most powerful and most fundamental generalization about the universe that scientists have ever been able to make.' Yet another scientist states regarding these laws: 'The two laws of thermodynamics are . . . accepted by physicists as perhaps the most secure generalizations from experience that we have.'

The First Law, the Law of Conservation of Energy, states that although energy can be transferred from one place to another, it can neither be created nor destroyed. Thus the total quantity of energy in the universe is constant. The First Law itself is a strong challenge to evolution since it implies a basic condition of stability in the universe. The fundamental structure of the cosmos is one of conservation, not innovation!

From Order to Disorder

It is the Second Law, however, that poses an even greater challenge to evolutionary theory. There is a universal process of change, and it is a directional change, but it is not an upward change. The Second Law (Law of Energy Decay) states that every system left to its own devices always tends to move from order to disorder, its energy tending to be transformed into lower levels of availability, finally reaching the state of complete randomness and unavailability for further work. This energy transformation into lower levels of availability is known as 'entropy'. Each quantity of energy has a quality of entropy associated with it: the entropy measures the degree of disorder associated with it. Energy must always flow in such a direction that the entropy increases, and the final stage will be one in which no energy is available.

Inefficiency of Physical Processes

For this reason, no process can be a hundred per cent efficient, with all the available energy converted into useful work. Although the First Law of Thermodynamics states that energy cannot be destroyed, yet in each reaction some must be deployed to overcome friction and this energy will be degraded to non-recoverable heat energy, which will finally radiate into space and disperse. Isaac Asimov, himself a professed evolutionist, expresses this concept simply as follows: 'The universe is constantly getting more disorderly. Viewed that way, we can see the Second Law all about us. We have to work hard to straighten a room, but left to itself, it becomes a mess again very quickly and very easily. Even if we never enter it, it becomes dusty and musty. How difficult to maintain houses, and machinery, and our own bodies in perfect working order, how easy to let them deteriorate. In fact, all we have to do is nothing, and everything deteriorates, collapses, breaks down, wears out, all by itself, and that is what the Second Law is all about.'

The tendency to regress from order to disorder includes biological and geological processes. How is it then that living organisms which naturally go from order to disorder are governed by evolution which generates order from disorder? Remember, the theory will not allow the existence of an external force to steer evolution in the right direction. All evolutionary changes are subject to random chance. For the gradual evolution of a more advanced organism, energy and order, instead of being lost, must somehow be gained. The Second Law says that this will not happen in any natural process *unless external factors enter* to make it happen. This remains one of the fundamental obstacles which evolution must surmount to be viable.

Systems which Transcend the Law of Entropy Increase

To be sure, there do exist a few types of systems in the universe where one sees an apparent increase in order, superficially offsetting the decay tendency specified by the Second Law. Examples are the growth of a seed into a tree, the growth of a foetus into an adult animal, and the growth of a pile of bricks and girders into a building. Now if we closely examine all such systems to see what it is that enables them to supersede the Second Law locally and temporarily (in each case, of course, the phenomenon is only ephemeral, since the organism eventually dies and the building eventually collapses), we will find in every case at least two essential criteria that must be satisfied.

Firstly, there must be a programme to direct the growth. A growth process which proceeds by random accumulation will not lead to an ordered structure, but merely to a heterogeneous blob. Some kind of pattern, blueprint or code must be there to begin with, or no ordered growth can take place. In the case of an organism, this is the intricately complex genetic programme, structured as an information system into the DNA molecule for the particular organism. In the case of the building, it is the set of plans prepared by the architects and engineers.

Secondly, there must be a 'power converter' to energize the growth. The available environmental energy is of no avail unless it can be converted into the specific forms needed to organize and bond the separate components into the complex and ordered structure of a completed system. This point is best illustrated in a statement made by a leading evolutionist: 'We have seen that organization requires work for its maintenance and that the universal quest for food is in part to provide the energy needed for the work. But the simple expenditure of energy is not sufficient to develop and maintain order. A bull in a china shop performs work, but he neither creates nor maintains organization. The work needed is particular work; it must follow specifications; it requires information on how to proceed.'

Photosynthesis

In the case of a seed, one of the required energy conversion mechanisms is the marvellous process called photosynthesis, which by some incompletely understood complex series of reactions converts sunlight into the building of the plant's structure. In an animal, numerous complex mechanisms – digestion, blood circulation, respiration, etc. – combine to transform food into body structure. In the case of a building, fossil fuels and human labour operate numerous complex electrical and mechanical devices to erect the structure, and so on.

Yet where in all the universe does one find a plan which sets forth how to organize random particles into people? Where does one see a marvellous motor which converts the continual flow of solar radiant energy bathing the earth into the work of building chemical elements and into replicating cellular systems, or of organizing populations of worms into populations of humans, over vast spans of time?

What we must examine is whether or not the random phenomena postulated by evolution, such as mutation and natural selection, are an adequate code for such a gigantic task. Can they assimilate energy into a more highly organized form of the structure it affects? Natural selection is not a code to direct the production of anything new; it serves merely as a screen which sifts out unfit variants and defective mutants. It certainly does not appear to be an anti-entropy energy-conversion device.

Noting the great difficulty inherent in random development into complex, orderly life, we now move on to explore the process through which this order is said to have come about, namely mutation.

2: Mutation: Mistakes Make Perfect

Mutation is the modern means by which evolutionary development is said to take place. It appears to this author that mutation was not selected because it offered a good logical possibility, but rather because those means which had seemed to offer really good possibilities, such as Lamarck's 'Theory of Acquired Characteristics', and Darwin's own 'adaptation' theory, were rapidly disproved.

The theory runs as follows: contained in the nucleus of every cell are spiral strands formed like twisted ladders made of DNA (deoxyribonucleic acid). These strands are located in the chromosomes and contain the genes which chemically control the processes in the cell. Occasionally, a small accidental change occurs in the chemical structure of the gene. New 'information' is thus conferred to the descendant and new physical and physiological changes are produced. The new organism after many generations will 'evolve away' from its ancestral mode to a higher and more complex system of life. In order for this to happen, the mutations must be beneficial, propelling the organism to a higher degree of order. They must, of course, also be very common.

One author, admittedly not a friend of evolution or objective about the subject, puts it in this manner: 'Supposing typists kept typing out copies of a book on the "Mechanics and Construction of an Outboard Motorboat", the evolutionist wants us to believe that as the typists go on repeatedly recopying, their selected errors would gradually change the book into increasingly high technical instructions for building, say, a nuclear submarine . . . instead of the book developing into complete nonsense as one might have supposed.'

Mutations are Harmful and Usually Lethal

More seriously, some of the hurdles which mutation must first overcome to be deemed viable are these: Firstly, the probability of a mutation occurring in an organism has been measured at one in ten thousand. Out of these very rare occurrences, almost every one is harmful, many even lethal. H. J. Muller, the man who devoted more study than any other individual to experimental observation of mutations, said, 'Mutations are of random nature . . . accordingly the great majority of mutations, certainly well over 99%, are harmful . . . as is to be expected of the effect of accidental occurrences.'

It is an undeniable fact that mutations are practically universally harmful. Crow states, '. . . we could still be sure on theoretical grounds that mutants would usually be detrimental. For a mutation is a random change of a highly organized, reasonably smoothly functioning human body. A random change in the highly integrated system of chemical processes which constitute life is certain to impair – just as a random interchange of connections in a television set is not likely to improve the picture.'

Ernst Mayr wrote, '. . . it is a considerable strain on one's credulity to assume that finely balanced systems such as certain sense organs (the eye of vertebrates, or the bird's feather) could be improved by random mutations . . . However, the objectors to random mutations have so far been unable to advance any alternative explanation that was supported by substantial evidence.'

Julian Huxley remarks: 'One would expect that any interference with such a complicated piece of chemical machinery as the genetic constitution would result in damage. And, in fact, this is so: the great majority of mutant genes are harmful in their effects on the organism.'

Tests that Show Mutation is Destructive

Muller, the winner of the Nobel Prize for his work with mutations, corroborates this view: 'It is entirely in line with the accidental nature of mutations that extensive tests have agreed in showing the vast majority of them detrimental to the organism in its job of surviving and reproducing, just as changes accidentally introduced into any artificial mechanism are predominantly harmful to its useful operation . . . good ones are so rare that we can consider them all bad.'

Theodosius Dobzhansky, a staunch evolutionist, draws the conclusion from his research: 'Most mutants which arise in any organism are more or less disadvantageous to their possessors. The classical mutants obtained in Drosophila (the fruit fly) show deterioration, breakdown, and disappearance of some organs.'

The author of *The Mystery of Heredity* concludes: 'We have to face one particular fact, one so peculiar that in the opinion of some people it makes nonsense of the whole theory of evolution: although the biological theory calls for incorporation of beneficial variants in the living populations, a vast majority of the mutants observed in any organism are detrimental to welfare. Some are lethal, causing incurable diseases or fatal deaths; others are sub-lethal, killing off or incapacitating most of the carriers but allowing some to escape; still others are sub-vital, damaging health, resistance or vigour in a variety of ways.'

'All known mutations are unmistakably pathological'

C. P. Martin of McGill University adds: 'The mass of evidence shows that all, or almost all, known mutations are unmistakably pathological and the few remaining ones are highly suspect . . . all mutations seem to be of the nature of injuries that, to some extent, impair the fertility and viability of the affected organisms . . . The impaired stamina of present-day domestic breeds is shown by their inability to survive in natural environments . . . Resistance to disease conferred by some mutations in an unusual environment is no evidence that they are not injuries, for injured organisms are sometimes more viable than normal ones in exceptional environments.'

Thompson stated, regarding mutations, in the introduction to *The Origin of Species*: 'If we say that it is only by chance that they are useful, we are still speaking too leniently. In general, they are useless, detrimental or lethal.'

Finally, to demonstrate this point we will quote Heribert Nilsson who made the following comment about organisms with mutated genes: 'A review of known facts about their ability to survive has led to no other conclusion than that they are always constitutionally weaker than their parent form or species, and in a population with free competition they are eliminated . . . Therefore they are never found in nature (e.g. not a single one of the several hundreds of Drosophila mutations), and therefore, they are able to appear only in the favourable environment of the experimental field or laboratory . . .'

Thousands of Mutational Steps Necessary

The same Julian Huxley quoted above, who is one of the individuals most responsible for our modern view of evolution, stated the following with regard to the necessary mutational steps for evolution to produce, say, a horse: 'A proportion of favourable mutations of one in a thousand does not sound much, but is probably generous . . . and a total of a million mutational steps sounds a great deal, but is probably an understatement . . . With this proportion, we should clearly have to breed a million strains (a thousand squared) to get one containing two favourable mutations, and so on, up to a thousand to the millionth power to get one containing a million . . . a thousand to the millionth power when written out, becomes the figure 1 with three million noughts after it; and that would take three large volumes of about 500 pages each, just to print! . . . No one would bet on anything so improbable happening. And yet it has happened!'

Drosophila Experiments

More than the mind is boggled by the enormity of the number Huxley mentions, the mind is boggled by how Huxley, after making this statement, can end with just an uncritical, matter-of-fact statement of support for evolution. Surely even he recognized the kind of obstacle a figure of such magnitude poses to evolutionary progress. Organisms such as fruit flies and bacteria have been studied in the laboratory. Thousands of generations have been bred and even forced to induce and speed up mutations by using X-rays, irradiation and chemicals. After nine hundred generations, the fruit fly did not develop a single new organ. All mutations were harmful, causing lost wings and eyes. In fact, the number of beneficial mutations that have ever been observed is suspect.

The attitude of scientists towards radiation supports this view of mutation. Radiation has been proved to increase the frequency of mutations, and nuclear explosions are an obvious cause of this radiation. Scientists do not support the idea of nuclear bombs being exploded in the atmosphere in order that the radiation should speed up evolution by inducing mutation, thereby furthering the development of humanity.

A Monkey Typing Shakespeare's Hamlet

Even if we assume that mutations have a one out of two chance of being beneficial (though the calculation by Professor A. M. Hasofer of the University of New South Wales in Sydney, is that the likelihood of any beneficial mutations having occurred during geological times is far less than ·0048), and then we assume that a million mutational steps are needed for the evolution of a horse (although this is probably also an understatement), still the probability will be only one out of 10 to the 300,000th power (10 with 300,000 zeros after it) that this horse will evolve! In addition to this, the chance of the evolution of just the first molecule of life has been calculated at 10 to the 242nd power (10 with 242 zeros after it). If we add the other figures as well, such as the possibility of a beneficial mutation and the number of mutational steps needed, to this figure, the product becomes a staggering number. As one statistician put it, it is equal to the possibility of a monkey, randomly hitting the keys on a typewriter, typing Shakespeare's *Hamlet*. Not just once, but 4 quadrillion times!

The World's Wastebasket is not Big Enough

Britain's leading astronomer, Sir Fred Hoyle, put it this way: 'No matter how large the environment one considers, life cannot have had a random beginning. Troops of monkeys thundering away at random typewriters could not produce the works of Shakespeare, for the practical reason that the whole observable universe is not large enough to contain the necessary monkey hordes, the necessary typewriters, and certainly the waste-paper baskets required for the deposition of wrong attempts. The same is true for living material.'

Infinite Time

If this is so, why is evolution taken seriously by the scientific community? The answer is provided by no less a personage than a Harvard professor: 'The important point is that since the origin of life belongs in the category of at-least-once phenomena, time is on its side. However impossible we regard this event, . . . given enough time it will almost certainly happen at least once . . . Time is in fact the hero of the plot . . . Given so much time, the impossible becomes possible, the possible probable, and the probable virtually certain. One only has to wait: time itself performs miracles.' There appears to me to be an almost Divine quality associated in this statement with time, according to this scientist possessing the ability to convert impossibility into inevitability. What we therefore must question is why a belief in a miracle-working time is any different from a miracle-working

Creator, and is evolution, which attributes such incredible feats to time alone, suggesting it as a replacement for the need of a deity?

Uncritical Support

Nobel prize winner Dr Ernst Chain had this to say about mutation: 'To postulate that the development and survival of the fittest is entirely a consequence of chance mutations seems to me a hypothesis based on no evidence and irreconcilable with the facts. These classical evolutionary theories are a gross over-simplication of an immensely complex and intricate mass of facts, and it amazes me that they are swallowed so uncritically and readily, and for such a long time, by so many scientists without a murmur of protest.'

3: Fossils: Proof of a Quantum Leap

Fossils are the history book of nature. The fossil record shows us what plants and creatures lived on earth long ago. In fact, evolution owes its origin to the fossil record. For even before it is a scientific theory, evolution is a conceptual scheme for interpreting the fossil record.

The fossils are the only potential source for real evidence that life has evolved, changing from one form to another, over many millions of years. Without the fossil record, there would be no grounds for introducing the evolutionary theory or believing in it. Yet, as we shall soon see, whatever the fossil record conveys, it seems that evolution is not one of the possibilities.

Evolutionists say that the fossil record tells a story of slow change, from very simple sea creatures in the 'oldest' rocks to very advanced animals in the 'youngest' rocks. (How young and old are distinguished will be discussed later.) Imagine that we take a geological journey up through the layers of the earth's crust: as we pass each layer, evolution tries to explain what has happened. The theory says that although some creatures get left by the wayside as evolution progresses, such as the dinosaurs and the dodo, basically simple invertebrate sea creatures change into fish, fish into amphibians, amphibians into reptiles, reptiles into birds, and birds into mammals. At the top of the pile sits homo sapiens.

Absent Intermediate Links

One would expect, therefore, to find intermediate links, that is, transitional stages between the different categories. The problem is that they simply do not exist. As a leading evolutionist has remarked, every palaeontologist knows that most new species . . . and nearly all categories above the level of families, appear in the record suddenly and are not led up to by known, gradual, completely continuous, transitional sequences. Yet another scientist states, 'So far as we can judge from the geologic record, large changes seem usually to have risen rather suddenly . . . fossil forms intermediate between large sub-divisions of classification were not found.'

The missing transitional links actually emerged as a major point of contention between Dr Berlinski and Dr Dawkins and Professor Maynard-Smith in our last evolution debate, with the latter two doing their utmost to fend off Berlinski's vicious attacks.

Research Would Expose the Missing Links

It must be remembered that evolution is based on the premise that there is a gradual change of the simplest forms into more and more complex forms. Therefore if there are no transitional links, only systematic gaps in the fossil record, then this constitutes a significant challenge to the premise that life evolved gradually. Darwin himself recognized these gaps as the strongest disproof against his theory. He explained these by assuming that the intermediate stages had been destroyed, an assumption based on pure speculation. He was confident that subsequent research would restore these lost chapters, and the continuity of the record would eventually be recognized. In the *Origin of Species* he writes: 'The number of intermediate varieties which have formerly existed must be truly enormous. Why then is not every geological formation and every stratum full of such intermediate links? . . . This is the most obvious and serious objection which can be urged against the theory. The explanation lies, as I believe, in the extreme imperfection of the geological record.'

Invertebrates to Vertebrates

Yet it is more than one hundred and thirty years since then, archaeological exploration has dug up almost every corner of the earth, and still none of these intermediate stages have yet been found. It seems fair to question whether indeed they ever did exist. To give the reader a brief idea of how great some of these gaps really are, take for example the transition from invertebrates to vertebrates. The notion that the vertebrates are derived from the invertebrates is an assumption based purely on the theory of evolution. Vertebrates have soft outer parts and hard inner parts, that is, skeletons, an example being homo sapiens. Invertebrates do not have an inner skeleton, but have either no hard parts, like jelly fish, or an 'exoskeleton' like crabs. Clearly, the differences are profound: the evolutionary transition from invertebrates to vertebrates must have involved billions of animals, but no one has yet found a fossil of one of them. Furthermore, this transitional change in evolutionary terms would take a huge amount of time. Most evolutionists estimate this to be at least a hundred million years. Incredible! One hundred million years of evolution and no transitional forms. All hypotheses combined, no matter how ingeniously, could never pretend, on the basis of evolutionary theory, to account for a gap of such magnitude in the fossil record.

T. George wrote: 'There is, however, one gigantic gap in the record that is of a different kind – the gap of Pre-Cambrian times. About two-thirds of the earth's geological record, the Pre-Cambrian period, does not contain any significant quantities of indisputable fossils, and some contend it contains absolutely none.'

Axelrod, of the University of California, confessed: 'One of the major unsolved problems of geology and evolution is the occurrence of diversified, multicellular marine invertebrates in lower Cambrian rocks on all the continents, and their absence in rocks of greater age . . . These sediments apparently were suitable for the preservation of fossils, because they are often identical with overlying rocks which are fossiliferous, yet no fossils are found in them.'

No Satisfactory Answer Yet Found

Despite intensified search by hundreds of geologists, the rocks older than the oldest fossiliferous Cambrian sediments remain almost as barren of fossils as when they were first studied one hundred and fifty years ago. Some of them are displayed in thicknesses of thousands of feet; they may be as unaltered and as undeformed as many fossiliferous rocks of later ages; they provide clear indications of having accumulated in environments, lacustrine and marine, apparently wholly favourable to both plant and animal life; and they sometimes underlie fossiliferous Cambrian rocks in a unitary suite of strata little affected by changing geography. Yet they have yielded few fossils that are recognizable as plants, and none that are certainly animals. One scientist states the problem thus: 'On the other hand, the earliest Cambrian rocks, formed about 500 million years ago, are relatively richly fossiliferous and contain a fauna already highly diversified . . . Moreover, the major phyla when they first appear display an evolutionary differentation that implies a complex phyletic history in pre-Cambrian times . . . Granted an evolutionary origin of the main groups of animals, and not an act of special creation, the absence of any record whatsoever of a single member of any of the phyla in the Pre-Cambrian rocks remains as inexplicable on orthodox grounds as it was to Darwin ("To the question why we do not find rich fossiliferous deposits . . . prior to the Cambrian system, I can give no satisfactory answer").'

Harland and Rudwick wrote in *Scientific American* about the sudden proliferation of fossils with no transitional links leading up to them, at the Cambrian stage: '. . . they were complex organisms that clearly belonged to the various distinct phyla, or major groups of animals, now classified as metazoan. In fact, they are now known to include representatives of nearly every major phylum that possessed skeletal structure capable of fossilisation . . . yet before the Lower Cambrian there is scarcely a trace of them. The appearance of the Lower Cambrian fauna . . . can reasonably be called a sudden event . . . One can no longer dismiss this event by assuming that all Pre-Cambrian rocks have been too greatly altered by time to allow the fossils ancestral to the Cambrian metazoans to be preserved . . . even if all the Pre-Cambrian ancestors of the Cambrian metazoans were similarly soft bodied and therefore rarely preserved, far more abundant traces of their activities should have been found in the Pre-Cambrian strata than has proved to be the case. Neither can the general failure to find Pre-Cambrian animal fossils be charged to any lack of looking.' Kay and Colbert query: 'Why should such complex organic forms be in rocks about six hundred million years old and be absent or unrecognized in the records of the preceding two billion years? If there has been evolution of life, the absence of the requisite fossils in the rocks older than the Cambrian is puzzling.'

These facts and the general lack of transitional fossils has led to much upheaval in the scientific world. Many evolutionists modified the theory in an attempt to account for such 'quantum leaps' in the fossil record, the most famous of which are Richard Goldschmidt's Hopeful Monster Theory and Stephen Jay Gould's Punctuated Equilibrium Theory. Alternatively, what the fossil record may be telling us, apart from professing evolutionary development, is that the fossils in the deepest rocks are sea creatures, that is, those we would expect to find on the sea floor. Swimming sea creatures come next, followed by those equally at home in sea or on land (reptiles and amphibians). Finally, land creatures and birds are found at the top of the geological column. If this is true, then it would not necessarily indicate evolutionary development at all.

4: The Age of the Earth and Faulty Clocks?

As mentioned earlier, Darwin and his contemporaries realized that an evolutionary theory based on the slow accumulation of small invisible 'novelties' presupposes huge lengths of time. If the earth was viewed as being relatively young, evolutionary thought would not stand a chance. Thus, through modern dating systems, science has pushed back the age of the earth at least a few billion years.

Real (that is, chronicled by humans) history that has been recorded from earlier times extends back just a few thousand years. Any events that took place before that must be deduced indirectly by extrapolating some present-day process (e.g., radioactive decay of uranium into lead, soil erosion, canyon cutting, delta deposition, etc.) back into the distant past, to arrive at an approximate date when those events took place.

Because deductions can only be reached by means of extrapolation, as Rabbi Menachem Schneerson, the Lubavitcher rebbe, points out in a famous letter sent to a university student on the subject, these deductions are fairly weak for the following reasons: (a) they have been advanced on the basis of observable data obtained during a very short time period; (b) on the basis of this small range of known data, theories are conjectured by means of the weak scientific method of extrapolation; (c) the theories advanced by scientists to date the world disregard important factors which existed at the birth of the universe such as the fact that temperature, atmosphere and many other factors were totally different from their present state; (d) there must have been many radioactive elements in the initial stages of the universe which now no longer exist.

If we deal with the two most popular modern scientific dating systems, they are, respectively, index-fossil dating and radioactive dating. These two dating systems, more than any others, are responsible for the age of the earth being reckoned in the billions of years. The first method is said to be the most accurate and most respected. Proof to this effect comes from a notable geologist: 'The only chronometric scale applicable in geologic history for the stratigraphic classification of rocks and for dating geologic events exactly is furnished by fossils. Owing to the irresponsibility of evolution, they offer an unambiguous time scale for relative age determination and for worldwide correlations of rocks.'

Index-fossil Dating

In terms of the evolution model, fossils would of course be the best way to determine geologic age. If we really knew evolution was true by some infallible means, then the 'stage-of-evolution' that the fossils were holding at would definitely be the best way to date rocks. Therefore, in order to date rocks, science often uses what are known as 'index fossils'. Hence, if certain fossil remains which are assumed to be of a very great age are found in a rock, that rock is in turn assumed to be of parallel age. But how is the age of the index fossils determined? The answer, however paradoxical, is by assuming evolutionary ascent. By supposing that all life has undergone a steady transformation from the simple to the complex, we conclude that fossils of simpler animals are older, and fossils of more complex animals are considered younger. As we noted before, the only way of proving that evolution does indeed operate is the fossil record. Carl Dunbar has stated, 'Fossils provide the only historical, documentary evidence that life has evolved from simpler to more and more complex forms.'

A Circular Argument

This is clearly a circular argument. Fossils are used to date rocks. Fossils themselves are dated by assuming evolutionary progression. Evolutionary progression is based on fossils. Hence the main evidence for evolution is the assumption of evolution. With this method of dating, scientists and evolution can never be disproved, because there is no room for objective verification outside the given system. The logical outcome of this system would be that rocks set their watches by the fossils, and the fossils know what time it is from the rocks!

Radioactive Decay

The second dating system, and the one most responsible for reckoning the age of the universe in the billions, is measured by means of radioactive decay. Whether the radioactive decay material be carbon, potassium, uranium, or some other substance, the general method is the same. The materials change from their original substance by shooting off atomic particles through long decay processes, finally becoming a new substance as the atomic balance amongst particles is altered. The substances which break down by emitting atomic particles must be accurately measured, and the products of this breakdown must also be accurately measured. Then, by knowing the rate of disintegration and assuming it to have been constant throughout the ages, calculations are made to determine the age.

It is much like determining how long a candle has been burning by measuring what is left of the candle, and calculating the rate at which it presently burns. If the candle has always burned at that speed, and you guess right as to its original length, you can be quite accurate. You can never know for sure, however, that these assumptions of speed and length were correct. Radioactive dating is therefore only accurate if two conditions are satisfied. Firstly, the process rate must have remained the same (which it is quite unlikely to do, for every process in nature operates at a rate that is influenced by many different factors which vary greatly with the passage of time). Secondly, the system must have initially contained none of its daughter components.

The Existence of a Daughter Component

The importance of this second assumption cannot be underestimated. If any of the daughter components were present in the sample at the beginning of time, then the entire dating process is completely inaccurate. For example, Uranium 238 decays into Lead 206 with a 'half life' of 4·5 billion years, that is, after that time has passed, exactly half of a sample of originally pure Uranium 238 will have decayed into Lead 206. Based on the lead content found within the uranium, we would proceed to calculate the age of the radioactive substance in which it was found. But if the lead were already present when the system first formed, that is, if at the creation of the system the daughter component was initially created in combination with the 'parent' component, then the calculations will be completely misleading. This is a possibility that no one can doubt, since no one was there when the rock or earth strata first formed.

Faulty Dating of Volcanic Eruptions

This is not a response to evolution spawned out of desperation. The following examples adequately demonstrate this possibility. A few years ago the uranium ages of some lava from recent volcanoes was dated by the radioactive clock. Samples of lava were taken from different parts of the world. All were from volcanoes which had erupted during the past two hundred years. That is, all samples were known to be less than two hundred years old. Yet radioactive dating said that several of the samples were between a hundred million years and ten billion years old. Basaltic rocks which were formed from an eruption of a Hawaiian volcano into the deep ocean were radioactively tested for age. These rocks were known to be less than two hundred years old. The radioactive dating listed them as being 22 million years old. Similar modern rocks formed in 1801 near Hualalei, Hawaii, were found to give potassium-argon (radioactive) ages ranging from 160 million years to 3 billion years.

Aside from demonstrating the possible inaccuracy of radioactive dating, these extremely erroneous dates might be easily explained by attributing the high ages of the lava rocks to the incorporation of the daughter component from the time of formation, not coming about as a result of decay only after the volcano's eruption. As the radioactive decay was present well before the eruption, therefore the dating, which is measured by the content of decay present in the lava, registered much higher than its formation date. Indeed modern experiments have shown that rocks, formed by lava flows from the earth's interior mantle, commonly contain uranium minerals and these, more often than not, are found to have radiogenic substances as well as leads within them when the lava first cools and the minerals crystallize. Such rocks, if animals were entombed in them and were later fossilized, would be dated as being far older than the age of the fossils themselves: imagine the remains of those suffocated in the lava of the eruption of Pompeii being dated as millions of years old!

Richard Milton, whom I mentioned earlier, has this to say about radio-carbon dating in his book *The Facts of Life*:

> It is perfectly true that radio-carbon dating has been tried on objects whose age is independently known from archaeological sources and scored some impressive early successes. One of the very first artifacts to be tested was a wooden boat from an Egyptian pharaonic tomb whose age was independently known to be 3,750 years before the present. Radio-carbon

> assays produced the date of between 3,441 and 3,801 years, a minimum error of only 51 years. But after this promising start, the method quickly ran into difficulties. Anomalous dates were produced from successive assays, including the discovery that some living shellfish had very little radio-carbon in their shells and so had been theoretically dead for up to 2,300 years. This made chemists look again at the technique and made them realize that some creatures may interact with parts of the reservoir that are deficient in carbon 14.
>
> In one of the most recent cases of anomalous dating, rock paintings found in the South African bush in 1991 were analysed by Oxford University's radio-carbon accelerator unit who dated them as being around 1,200 years old. This finding was significant because it meant the paintings would have been the first bushman painting found in open country. However, publicity of the find attracted the attention of Mrs Joan Ahrens, a Cape Town resident, who recognized the paintings as being produced by her at art classes and later stolen from her garden by vandals. The significance of incidents such as this is that mistakes can be uncovered only in those rare cases where chance grants us some external method of checking the date technique. Where no such independent verification exists, we simply have to accept the verdict of carbon dating.

The position resulting from these anomalous discoveries was summarized by Hole and Heizer in their *Introduction to Prehistoric Archaeology*: 'For a number of years it was thought that the possible errors . . . were of relatively minor consequence, but more recent intensive research into radio-carbon dates, compared with calendar dates, shows that the natural concentration of Carbon 14 in the atmosphere has varied sufficiently to affect dates significantly for certain periods. Because scientists have not been able to predict the amount of variation theoretically, it has been necessary to find a parallel dating method of absolute accuracy to assess the correlation between Carbon 14 dates and the calendar.'

Can the World Have Been Created Already Aged?

This is also an important general consideration when discussing the age of the earth. Even if contemporary methods for the age of the world could actually prove, with substantial evidence, that the earth indeed is at least a few billion years old, this would not necessarily refute the fact that Judaism maintains that the world was created only 5,753 years ago (at the time of this writing). For just as when God created Adam, the first man, he did not create him in his infant stages but rather as a mature adult, likewise it is possible that God did not create the globe in its infant stages but rather as an aged or adult world. I realize that this argument can seem a bit far-fetched, but it remains a possibility. Just as it would be mistaken, had we bumped into Adam moments after his creation, to assume that the world was at least twenty or thirty years old in accordance with how old Adam was, so too is it mistaken to base the amount of time the world has been in existence upon the apparent age displayed by the earth.

Dating the Universe by the Light of the Stars

Similarly, this argument applies to the age of the universe. There are those who have suggested a hypothesis to the effect that the universe is billions of years old from the evidence of the stars. There are many stars which are billions of light years away from the earth, yet their light reaches us. If it takes that light billions of years to reach us, and now it is reaching us, we must conclude that these stars have existed for a parallel amount of time. Who is to say that immediately at their creation the light of these stars was not reaching earth? The stars could have been created with their light already radiating. The Torah relates that the primary purpose for the creation of the stars was to illuminate the world. I do not offer these arguments as definitive, nor in an effort to be totally convincing. I do think, however, they should be considered.

5: The Interior Decorator

The most forceful argument against evolution and in favour of Special Creation is the intelligent design displayed by all aspects of the world. All mineral, plant, animal and of course human specimens bear witness to providential design and the activity of a super-intelligent designer. The strength of this argument, in my opinion, can in no way be understated. How could such a highly complex, symmetrically balanced, wonderfully ordered world have come into existence by mere chance and accident via the random formation of simple matter?

Darwin and the Human Eye

Darwin himself wrote that he became sick when he thought of how the complexity of the human eye could have evolved by mere chance. The evolutionists realized that the strength of the argument from design was overwhelming and incapable of being overcome. Yet if no solution were offered, evolution could only be laughed at as an amusing but absurd theory. To a large extent, instead of offering an explanation for how such purpose and plan could have been generated by chance or accident (the chances of which are so astounding that they can be said to be negligible), they offered a counter-argument, attempting to prove that the world is not as purposive as everyone seems to think.

Before we discuss this counter-argument let us briefly consider the great design of the universe. I wish to mention that had every person who ever lived, since the beginning of time, written a book describing the purposive design of creation, that would still be quite far from doing justice to the subject; how much more so the few lines I now write.

The Earth on Its Axis

Beginning with the order of earth itself, if the earth were an inch closer or further from the sun, human life as we know it would be impossible. If it were not tilted on its axis 23 degrees, huge mountains of ice would pile up from the water vapour of the oceans. The earth revolves at a speed of 1,000 miles per hour: if it were to revolve at only 100 miles per hour, night and day would increase ten times in duration, plants would be scorched in the day and seedlings would be frozen to death at night. If the moon were a bit closer to the earth, the tide would flood all lands including the high mountains. If the oceans were deeper, carbon dioxide and oxygen would all be absorbed and no plants could exist. If the atmosphere were thinner than at present, millions of meteors which are burned up in the air would fall to the earth and cause terrible fires. While most substances contract when they freeze, water miraculously expands by about one-eleventh of its volume. This makes ice float on top of a lake, preventing the lake from freezing all the way through and killing all the fish. The cause for this expansion still perplexes scientists.

Rattlesnakes, Beetles and Bats

Moving on to the extraordinary design in living things, the rattlesnake discovers food among stones because it has a sensitive mechanism which enables it to sense differences in temperature between living and mineral substances. A beetle judges speed and direction by gathering light signals on the facets of its retina, correlating their arrival time in its brain and combining this information. In a flash, these complicated processes inform the beetle how fast its prey is moving and in which direction. This is as 'accidental' as a speed-altitude indicator on an aeroplane. Flies have a superb flight-stabilizer which engineers are attempting to copy for use in aeroplanes. The larynx of a bat is a sonar device of magnificent efficiency. In order to detect a mosquito in the dark, the bat's sonar picks up echoes rebounding from the mosquito's body out of background noises 2,000 times more powerful than the signal of the mosquito. The body of an electric-eel is an electric powerhouse having more than 5,000 batteries and turning out, at the eel's command, 500 volt high-power shocks. That is more than twice as strong as the electricity that lights the human home. By means of this electric shock, the eel goes fishing by paralysing the fish.

Flies and Spiders

A spider has a tiny gland which is a mini-laboratory capable of synthesizing a substance which is so chemically planned that it is a liquid when inside the gland, but when expelled and coming in contact with the air it instantaneously congeals into the precise consistency of a flexible rope. In addition to this open miracle, the spider's tiny brain possesses a built-in control-system which causes her to suspend the threads of her web in precise mathematical patterns better than any skilled engineer. The fly struggles when caught in the web, and the flimsy gossamer ought to snap, but the threads are so cunningly spaced and balanced, according to the best principles of architectural engineering, that despite their extreme weakness they are able to withstand the struggles of the trapped insect. Even an orphan baby spider knows how to make this web because she is born with the ingenuity to do so. In the utriculus and sacculus chambers of the inner ear, crystals of calcium carbonate rest on beds of sensory 'hair cells'. When the head changes position, the crystals shift and excite the hair cells to send signals to the brain; and thus the miraculous system of equilibrium is maintained. This phenomenon is found in everything, from humans all the way down to crayfish and lobsters. These are just some of the examples of the unfathomable design of creation.

Complexity of the Human Brain and Foetus

As for the evidence for superior design in humans, a useful insight may be gained from this simple statement from Isaac Asimov: 'In man is a three-pound brain which, as far as we know, is the most complex and orderly arrangement of matter in the universe.' An embryology textbook, *From Conception to Birth*, asks honest questions about the human brain and its nervous system. How do the billions of cells which comprise this system come into being in the first place, and how do they attach themselves together to form a network connecting the brain to every muscle, organ and gland in the entire body? How is it possible that without a designer, there came into being microscopic chromosomes each containing all the coded information necessary to produce and 'wire' an entire human being? The book points out: 'It would be relatively easy to understand if the neurons were connected to the brain like spokes of a wheel, but they are not. Most of these neurons are connected to a great many other neurons; one estimate is that on the average, each neuron is cross-connected with 1000 others. This means a total of 10 trillion connections. A complete wiring diagram of this network would stagger the imagination. All of the telephone cables of the world would comprise no more than a small fraction of it . . . The neuron, like any other cell, contains a nucleus in which lie chromosomes that are identical to those in the original fertilized egg. Thus the nucleus of each neuron contains a catalogue of potentiality inherited from both mother and father. How can a collection of genes possibly account for the multifarious connections between neurons and the human nervous system? Or for the relationship between neurons and the muscles and organs of the body? There are only some 40,000 genes in all the chromosomes, seemingly not enough to encode instructions for performing 10 trillion connections.

'But if every last interconnection is not spelled out in the chromosomes, how do the neurons get connected? Do they just reach out for one another haphazardly? Obviously not, since all neurons fulfil definite, specialized functions, not random ones. Connections between the nerves associated with hearing and those controlling, say, the biceps muscles wouldn't be logical or effective, and above all the nervous system effectively co-ordinates whatever the person does or thinks . . . 'The eyes, for example, are formed on the sides of the head and are ready for connection to the optic nerves growing out independently from the brain. The forces that ensure this integration have thus far not been discovered, but they must be formidable indeed, since more than one million optic nerve fibres must mesh with each eye. Think for a moment about what is considered to be a feat of human engineering: the drilling of tunnels from both sides of the Alps that must somehow meet precisely and merge into one continuous highway. Yet any one of the thousands of things the foetus must do as part of the routine of development is far more wondrous . . .'

The Nervous System

'The nervous system eventually comprises the most efficient cable system in the world for the transmission of messages. Ultimately each nerve fibre will be covered by a sheath of protective cells (sometimes 5,000 per fibre), and each will be able to carry messages at a speed of 150 yards per second, or 300 miles per hour. From these primitive cells, first distinguishable at 18 days after conception, the embryo will form more than 10,000 taste buds in its mouth . . . Some 12 million nerve endings will form in the baby's nose to help it to detect fragrances or odours in the air. More than 100,000 nerve cells will be devoted to reacting to Beethoven's Fifth Symphony or the ticking of a Swiss watch. The piano has only 240 strings, but the baby's ears will have more than 240,000 hearing units to detect the smallest variations in sound. The baby's eyes, which begin to form at 19 days, will have more than 12 million screen points per square centimetre; the retina, or light-sensitive portion of its eye, will have more than 50 billion such points. The composite picture the eyes record is homogeneous because these light-sensitive points blend into a whole. Take a hand lens and examine any picture in any daily newspaper. You will find it made up of hundreds of points each, light or dark, which together make up the picture as you look at it from a greater distance. This is exactly what the eye does only in much finer detail.

'Where do these billions of cells in the nervous system come from? From the original fertilized ovum which is still dividing after one month to form the tissues and organs that the child requires. It has been estimated that all two billion of the specific nerve cells which make any individual educable are located in the outer covering of his brain, its cortex, and that these 2 billion cells could be stored in a thimble . . . Development continues even after birth in certain parts of the brain. By the end of the first month of embryonic development none of these parts of the brain, spinal cord, nervous, or sense organs is completely formed but the foundation for all of them has been laid.'

The embryo is but one example of the high level of structured complexity which is manifest in nature. Even in the simple everyday occurrences we overlook, design perpetuates itself. Did you ever wonder why all fruits change their dull greenish colour to a bright and attractive one just as they ripen on the tree? And subsequently they even release themselves from the tree once they are edible but not sooner in order that they do not make someone sick.

Bionics

There is even a field of science, known as bionics, which in designing machinery emulates the intelligent design found in nature. Bionics is a relatively new scientific discipline which is based on mimicry. Bionics practitioners closely examine the design of live objects, hoping to employ the designs as models for tools and machinery which will be useful to humanity. Hearing devices are patterned after the ear; seeing devices after the eyes. According to bionics, anyone building a ship should first look at the design of a fish. Builders of aeroplanes should study birds.

Intuitive Design

In fact, this principle of design as indicative of intelligent planning is already operative in the minds of astronomers. The following is their line of thinking: if somewhere in the universe there is non-human intelligent life, perhaps there are non-human civilizations which are capable of space travel. If so, maybe non-human creatures will some day approach the earth in spaceships. Now, if these non-human space travellers enter our solar system and glance at planet earth, if they are too far away, they will not be able to pick out anything on the earth's surface which would indicate that there is intelligent life here. According to Carl Sagan, a noted astronomer, however, if the aliens came sufficiently close, they would find 'unambiguous' and 'convincing' evidence of intelligent life on earth, 'as soon as they sighted things such as city crossroads, neat suburb housing, or contour ploughing and planting'. Sagan writes 'that without ever having seen the streets paved, the suburbs being built, or the fields being ploughed and planted, the aliens would infer that intelligent life exists here.' Direct experience of the designing would not be necessary.

Rabbi Akiva's Challenge

This scientific approach to design is remarkably similar to the understanding of those who believe that God created the universe. According to the *midrash*, a disbeliever once approached the great sage, Rabbi Akiva and asked him, 'Who created the world?' 'The world was created by the Lord, blessed be He,' answered Rabbi Akiva. 'Prove it!' the disbeliever countered. 'Who wove your garment?' asked Rabbi Akiva. 'A weaver, of course.' 'Prove it!' demanded Rabbi Akiva. He then turned to his students and said, 'Just as the garment testifies to the weaver, the door to the carpenter, and the house to the builder, so the entire world testifies to the Holy One, blessed be He who created it.'

Rabbi Akiva's objection remains. As Dr Lee Spetner notes, 'The theory that seemed to be able to overcome the objection raised by Rabbi Akiva was received into the body of science without verifying that it in fact could overcome this objection . . . That the Doctrine of Evolution was accepted on this basis is the shame of science.' Nobel Prize-winning chemist, Dr Harold Urey, had this to say about design: 'All of us who study the origin of life find that the more we look into it, the more we feel that it is too complex to have evolved anywhere.' However, Urey adds an incredible 'but': 'We believe as an article of faith that life evolved from dead matter on this planet. It is just that its complexity is so great, it is hard for us to imagine that it did.'

Blueprint of a Living Organism

One of the oldest and most prestigious scientific associations is Great Britain's Royal Society. Recently, members of the society were asked to list the five most 'sensational' scientific advances of the 1970s. The most frequently mentioned paper in the biological sciences was that by Fred Sanger and his colleagues at Cambridge (England) in which they described the entire sequence of nucleotides, or 'words', in the DNA of a virus, PhiX-174 (*Nature*, Volume 265, 1977, page 687). This achievement marked the first time that the complete chemical 'blueprint' of a living organism had been unravelled and followed shortly after Dr Sanger's group and a second team working under Dr Walter Gilbert had improved methods for reading DNA sequences. Although it is certainly an extremely simple life form, PhiX-174 proved to contain 5,375 nucleotide words. Grouped into sentences, 'genes', they specify the composition of a virus particle when it replicates. And indeed they control all its functions. A perplexing revelation from this work was that the genes overlap. Like a telegram with no spacing, the coded message read entirely differently, depending upon whether one began with the first, second or third letter.

DNA Results from Intelligence

The fact that three messages were contained within one seemed to some researchers artificial or contrived, prompting Drs Hiromitsu Yokoo and Iairo Oshima to revive the theory, first suggested by Dr Francis Crick and Leslie Orgel (*Icarus*, Volume 19, 1973, page 341) that life on earth began from organisms sent here billions of years ago by extra-terrestrial civilizations that decided to 'seed' other planets. The Japanese scientists suggested that the gene sequence PhiX-174 might contain messages, or signals, as yet encoded. In their reasoning, such overlapping messages would be a highly economical way to send information through vast tracts of space. In other words, the most sensational biological discovery of the 1970s was that DNA, the 'chemical blueprint' of a live form, was so 'contrived', that is, it exhibited such a high level of design and complexity, that scientists were forced to conclude the DNA had to have been produced by intelligence. The design compelled an intuitive appreciation which led not to God, however, but to a mysterious space civilization.

Vestigial Organs

As mentioned earlier, evolution has never fully explained how such intricate order could come about by accident. Rather, one of the ways in which science dealt with the problem of design was to suggest that living organisms are not as well arranged as is thought. One of these counter-arguments took the form of pointing out the existence of vestigial organs, that is, parts of the body which are useless vestiges of past evolutionary forms. Evolution's argument with regard to rudimentary or vestigial organs is that the existence of certain organs which have no function shows that they are evolutionary leftovers; that is, organs which did have a function somewhere down the evolutionary line, but which are no longer useful to the organism, though still present in it. These vestigial remnants of assumed former evolutionary changes can apparently still be seen in the structures of organisms living today.

Ignorance of an Organ's Function

Evolutionists pointed to a number of 'useless' organs in the human body and decided, as one evolutionist writes, that 'Such facts make nonsense of the argument from design.' On the basis of this reckless attitude in the past, they declared the tonsils a useless vestigial organ, to be removed on the slightest pretext. It then became practice to make two million unnecessary tonsillectomies every year in the USA alone. However, as medical knowledge progressed, the list of vestigial folly began not to grow but to shrink. It was learned that the tonsils, as a vent for the lymph system, only inflamed in order to rid the body of infectious material. Likewise, the pituitary gland, a supposedly useless vestige of some former state of existence, was found to be the master regulator of the entire body. The 'useless' thymus gland was discovered to be a vital guardian of the body's health. And the appendix, which has been most commonly slandered as the best example of a vestigial organ, has now been proven to be an immunologic organ whose removal permits the development of leukaemia and related forms of cancer. In view of the history of this subject, it would seem wise not to claim any organs at all as vestigial. Ignorance about the specific functions of such organs clearly does not prove that they have no useful function.

Coca-Cola on the Moon

Aside from the flaws of this argument, I fail to understand what the existence of vestigial organs would have proved in the first place. Even if there were to exist vestigial organs, would that actually prove that the world did not display high technological design and was not crafted by a master craftsman? Suppose one leaves the earth in a spaceship and visits a distant planet where no life is known to have existed before. Suppose further that all the highly advanced, onboard instruments indicate that indeed no life form has ever put foot on the planet. Suddenly, on disembarking from the spaceship and surveying the alien terrain, the traveller finds a digital watch: it cannot be used by anyone, it just exists, mysteriously on this planet. Now, would it be reasonable for the traveller to insist on retaining the original premise that no one has ever before visited this planet? True, all markings and symptoms indicate that no life form has been there, and yet here is this watch. How could one explain its existence? Would one, because of loyalty to the original premise, develop a hypothesis attributing the efficiency of its mechanism and numerical digital display to a freak chance development from the planet's surface, chemicals which, via electrical storms over millions of years, gave rise to this watch?

Most individuals using their deductive processes would be forced to conclude that it had been deliberately designed, and that would automatically imply the existence of an intelligent designer. Would not this argument apply equally as well to the traveller finding something as simple as a can of Coca-Cola? Applying this principle to the eye, the transparency of the cornea, the precision of the lens, and the adjustability of the pupil all co-operate to serve vision. The marks of design are too strong to be overcome. Design must have a designer. Even if useless vestigial organs did also exist, none the less the fact that just one feature of this universe displays design would force us to conclude the latent presence of a designer.

This was the meaning of King David when he wrote in Psalms: 'From my flesh I perceive God.' The complexity of human life causes our eyes to be lifted heavenward and embrace a benevolent creator.

Chapter Fifty

IF GOD IS GOOD, WHY DO PEOPLE SUFFER?

The chancellorship of Oxford University is a largely ceremonial post but of enormous prestige. It is currently held by Lord Jenkins of Hillhead, a former British Foreign Minister. The chancellor is in Oxford only on special occasions, such as to host a dignitary, or attend a special ceremony or lecture.

Having said this, imagine, then, the uproar if an undergraduate went to the chancellor of the university and piped up with a serious complaint: 'I don't think things have been done very well in Oxford recently; the teaching seems to be doing more harm than good, and I feel that the standards in this university have rapidly deteriorated.' Effectively, this does happen every year in a less outrageous way: some of the young people who have come up to Oxford decide that this university is too old-fashioned or involves too much regular work for their liking, so they drop out, are 'rusticated' or 'sent down', that is, sent away for a time or permanently expelled.

Now, this is a very different scenario from a member of the public approaching the current Prime Minister, John Major, and telling him that things are going pitifully badly with Britain. The latter is much more plausible for these two reasons: Firstly, the university has been around for much longer than any government or political theory, and can perhaps afford a little complacency about its methods and their success. Secondly, and perhaps more importantly, the Prime Minister is elected by the people, and dissent is a natural part of the democratic process, allowing politicians to refine their ideas until they match what the people want as closely as possible. Criticizing the chancellor of Oxford is a different matter: in the eyes of the university, the student is there on the university's sufferance, not the other way round. The reply to the person who complains that Oxford is doing no good will surely be a dry and laconic, 'There must be another institution which might meet your expectations more exactly. Perhaps you should go there instead?'

Of course, the university sees little need to change its ways to suit these dissenters. The university has for centuries been accountable to no earthly power but itself, although sometimes protests have a greater impact on Oxford than one would think possible.

Deciding to Opt Out

One young biology undergraduate had a very strong idea that the university's emphasis on mathematics and physics was too great in his subject, and showed this by conspicuously failing his prelims (first year examinations), although he was a reasonable student in those subjects. When the time came for him to sit his second and last attempt to pass those same papers, he failed again, making his views on the overemphasis on mathematics and physics known both to his subject tutor and the college authorities. He left, of course, when the dismal results of his re-sits were published, but the next few years saw a steady improvement in the relevance of the Oxford biology prelims; his career was not blighted, either. He found a course at another university that allowed him to pursue his varied interests in biology and anthropology; he managed to retain his government grant; he is being sponsored to study the tribes of Nias Island off the coast of Sumatra, and is thoroughly enjoying himself. Others, however, and I have known a few, would have been completely demoralized, even destroyed, by an Oxford dismissal.

A little more of the democratic process could probably be infused into Oxford with no harm done, but for the moment the commitment between those taught and the institution is largely one-way. Oxford has proved that it is not anything to be trifled with: even Lady Thatcher was denied the traditional honorary degree for a Prime Minister who once studied here, from a university deeply angered by her squeeze on higher (tertiary) education funding.

Unionizing the Oxford Scouts

Oxford students have a scout, or cleaning person, who comes to tidy their rooms. The scouts are paid pitifully little. A Canadian graduate student I came to know, because his parents sent him to speak to me before he got engaged to a non-Jewish girlfriend, was a great lover of humanity both in speech and action. He took up the cause of the scouts, having engineered a meeting between the college head and student representatives including himself. This particular college was headed by a world-famous social philosopher and advocate of human rights. At the meeting, he made the case that the scouts were treated as if they worked in the Third World. They deserved better pay and better working conditions. The college head, clearly never having been challenged before by a lowly student, stood up and told the student that students were there to study, not govern. If there was something the student did not like, he could always leave of his own accord. If not, the college head continued, the college itself might have to consider taking action against troublemakers. Noting the threat now being directed at him, the student then stood and read aloud an excerpt from a book which asserted that one must stand up for human rights even at the risk of great personal loss and misfortune. The college head stood up as well and yelled, 'Get that nonsense out of here. I have already made my position clear.' The student turned the book cover around. It was a book written by the head of the college. 'Yes, it is indeed nonsense,' the student responded. And with that he stormed out of the meeting. After this incident, he complained to me bitterly of how much he disliked Oxford, and was only too glad to leave when his M. Phil. was completed. Of course, this was just a one-off incident and the great majority of students who study here are happy and indeed feel privileged.

Nonetheless, to students who are somewhat upset and frustrated at the irresponsiveness of the university authorities to their plight, it is rather comforting to see that the greatest of all authorities, the Almighty, is shown in the Bible to be open to debate about His decisions and actions, with some very saintly individuals having been openly critical about the way in which God runs the world.

Part One

Immediately after his first encounter with Pharaoh to allow the Jews to leave Egypt, which ended in miserable failure, Moses, in his dialogue with God, offered a complaint that would be shocking even if it were said to any mere temporal power. It was doubly significant because it was also the very first challenge recorded in the Bible claiming a Divine miscarriage of justice. Moses had just been sent by the Almighty to demand the Jewish people's release from Pharaoh. The result of this first encounter was that Pharaoh refused to free them, and also gave orders that the Jewish slaves should not be given straw to build bricks, yet were required to fill the same quota every day. This invited a sharp response from the future law giver, a sharp and direct challenge to the existence of suffering: 'And Moses returned unto the Lord and he said, "Lord, why have You dealt ill with this people? Why is it that You have sent me? For since I came to Pharaoh to speak in Your name, he has dealt ill with this people; neither have you delivered at all Your people." '

Suffering is the Greatest Challenge

Among the various and difficult challenges posed to religion and the religious believer today, the most difficult, in my opinion, is that which is also the oldest: the problem of suffering. Darwinian evolution, biblical criticism and archaeological excavation or psychoanalysis may pose a seeming contradiction to specific claims in the Torah, which the devout Jew will no doubt seek to reconcile, but human suffering poses a threat to the overall and most important claim in religion. In all my time spent at Oxford and amidst the formidable challenges to my system of belief that I have sought to defend, none has ever been as troublesome or as persistent as that of suffering. In my experience at least a third of the people I meet who have rejected Judaism and its values have done so or at the very least find justification for their action due to their inability to cope with the problem of suffering. This has always been the principal issue I have dealt with as a rabbi in Oxford, with women's issues in Judaism being a distant second.

Religious faith says that there is a benevolent God who seeks a dialogue with every created being. He cares and listens, and is attentive to our prayers, and above all is a personal God. When someone is afflicted with an incurable illness, or when war snuffs out the life of the young, then one of the fundamentals of Jewish belief is seen to fall. When good or innocent people suffer it seems impossible to accept that God is all-powerful and causes everything that happens in the world, as well as that God is just and fair, rewarding the good people and punishing the wicked as they deserve.

Immanuel Kant pointed out that if it is arrogant to defend God, it is even more arrogant to assail Him. Yet the Jew in particular, amongst those who approach religion rationally in general, has always grappled with cosmic whys. It is in part this grappling for authenticity which distinguishes the religious person of reason from the religious fanatic, who is moved by intense and uncritical devotion, and who is untroubled by rational problems.

Of course, those who believe in a benevolent God have responded to this intellectual challenge throughout the ages. The traditional Jewish theodicies, or responses to suffering, are numerous and diverse. By dividing them into thematic groups it is hoped that their message can be more clearly analysed.

Ultimately, I believe that each of these answers is unsatisfactory. In response to this, we will attempt to offer a new perspective culled from Moses and our forefathers' various challenges to Divine justice. It is interesting to note that many of these theodicies appear in related form in non-Jewish traditions: rationalizing suffering and apparent injustice seem to be common preoccupations amongst many peoples. The following grouping of traditional theodicies is taken from the book *God and Evil*.

1: Finite Man Cannot Comprehend Infinite God's Ways

These theodicies argue that the whole of creation is working towards a good end: even in the midst of apparent disasters and unfairness, God is in control and not allowing any real evil to happen.

The unifying theme of this group is the implication that the universe is somehow better with *apparent evil* in it. The argument assumes that the things we automatically interpret as evil are actually for the greater good in the long run. The real problem lies with our human limits of perception: our finite minds cannot understand the infinite God, and so we misinterpret His actions for good as manifestations of evil.

Another aspect of this argument is the suggestion that a good person is punished in this world to increase his or her reward in the world-to-come. A painful life or death simply increases the infinite rewards in the hereafter, and is therefore actually to be desired because it is ultimately better.

According to this thinking, God's ways are inscrutable. God has His ultimate purposes known only to Him. We must overcome our misgivings and doubts and have implicit faith in God's justice.

For example, these theodicies might argue that in the next world the Holocaust will be seen as a good thing for the world: the Jews regained their homeland, western society began to find racism morally unacceptable . . . and so on. And those who suffered will find ample reward in the hereafter for their pain and affliction.

The logic and necessity of the things that we think are evil, but are in reality good, will eventually be revealed to us. God's ways will be made understandable to us in the next world.

2: We are Punished for Our Sins and Failings

This whole group of arguments rests on the idea that God does allow genuine evil and suffering, but that they are a part of His need for justice. In a sense, God is made subservient to His own perception of the need to punish evil; and since all the world is evil, even those we think are good or innocent could receive the punishments that God's justice rightly demands should be made. Hence the good and righteous God is said to be actually creating punishments that incorporate evil for His creatures because of their misdeeds.

The arguments take many forms, but include the following ideas: the iniquities of the fathers are visited upon the sons (this is sometimes called 'vertical responsibility'); there is no suffering without sin; all humans are imperfect and sin in some way; suffering is due to evil deeds or neglect of religious observance; Divine Providence is linked to piety and intellectual attainment, and the absence of either leaves humans vulnerable to evil.

In other words, humankind is responsible for sin and suffering, not God. The most direct expression of this idea seems to be the Christian doctrine of the Fall of Man. The sin of Adam brought suffering upon the world, for which we are all responsible because we are born human. For Adam's sin we are for ever liable to the punishments that God has a right to inflict on us, however young or innocent or good we may appear to be to the imperfect perception of human minds.

According to this way of thinking, the Holocaust would be seen as just retribution for the sins of those destroyed, or the sins of their ancestors for which they were being held responsible. Jews and gypsies, although put through unheard-of pain and suffering, were part of God's great need to plant justice on earth. Even the little children killed were part of the wickedness that was being destroyed, evil that God had a need and a right to punish and eliminate. This begs the question of why there are any people left on the earth at all: and if God is staying His hand from us, why did He not do so for the innocent children?

3: Hester Panim: Hiding of the Divine Face

This is a particularly specific argument, and refers to the idea of a temporary abandonment of the world, a suspension of God's active surveillance. This concept is rarely applied as a general response to theodicy, but is used rather as a response to a particular catastrophic series of events.

The argument runs that disasters and suffering on a huge scale can only happen if the presence for good in the world, God, has temporarily absented Himself from His creation.

Since God has chosen to remove His good presence from the world for a time, the natural tendency to evil manifests itself in full force. Taking the example of the Holocaust, this would mean that for a period of years God was absent from the world, and chose to ignore the pleas of the desperate millions, letting the evil ones triumph for some unknown purpose.

This implies that without God the creation is evil: there is no way that good people can overcome evil by their own efforts, there must be the hand of God to save us from destruction. This of course has grave implications for arguments attempting to reconcile God's foreknowledge with the free will of humans, since a world that needs God's *active* presence to keep it moving towards goodness seems to imply that in the normal state of affairs, there is no genuine free will. It is only during a period when we are left to our own evil devices that we truly enjoy free choice in our actions.

4: Traditional Responses to the Suffering of All People

These often centre on the concept of *yissurin shel ahavah* or 'tribulations of love', which are intended to purify, ennoble and chasten us. They raise us to a higher level and test us, because through suffering comes redemption. The problems we encounter serve to increase our reward in the world-to-come and provoke us to reflect on our inadequacies and propel us to develop our potential. The process of Divine justice takes time and we must have patience.

In contradiction of the above type of argument, some say that nature is 'morally neutral'. This implies a separation between God and nature, so that the good God has nothing to do with the indiscriminate ways of His creation. Similarly, some argue that *Hashgacha*, 'Providence', does not apply to acts of nature: there is no purpose in the world, only blind chance. This theory of the natural world is analogous to the theory of evolution. Elsewhere in this book we discuss the idea that a doctrine such as evolution that claims the world is 'morally neutral' must, if it is true, logically favour those who are amoral. When the fight for survival is on and there are no absolute values, those who refuse to take part in the struggle must go to the wall.

Some of these theodicies say that our present suffering is going to be more than rewarded when everything is finally taken into account. In recompense for pain, fear and anguish we will receive a reward in the world-to-come. This implies that we are basically good creatures, buffeted and manipulated by the will of our Creator so that He can be all the more generous to us at the end of the day. Suffering is interpreted as a form of discipline, warning us against sin. Suffering keeps one from committing the sin of hubris. Suffering lessens the physical pride and selfish nature of the individual. Amongst all this suffering, though, our best interests are at heart – but of course we have no choice in the matter.

In apparent direct contradiction of this, the same people often argue that sins are forgiven through suffering. Those who suffer in this world do so in order to be purified and to have the slate cleaned for the world to come. This argument implies that we are bad creatures whom the Creator lovingly chastises so that He can ultimately draw us, fully expiated of our many sins, to His gentle and forgiving breast. However, before He is willing to allow us into His presence, justice must be done and the wrongdoers must be punished in full for their wickedness.

This latter argument also contradicts the reality that we see so often in our world: the good often suffer much more than those who change with the world and avoid trouble by being flexible in their beliefs. Returning to the example of the Holocaust, this argument says that those who suffered the most were, just as the Nazis said, more deserving of punishment than the rest of humanity.

5: Why the Good Suffer When the Evil are Spared

Mainstream traditional responses often address the specific problem of the suffering of the *tzadik* (saintly individual).

A common answer is, 'When permission is given to the angel of destruction, no difference is made between the righteous and wicked.' This makes the servant of God into a crude instrument of destruction, an atom bomb that its Creator can set off but not control.

Another reply is, 'The righteous person should have acted more forcefully in promoting righteousness or interceding for the people.' A good person is apparently held to a much higher standard than other people, and a *tzadik*'s suffering is atonement for all the people.

If good does not seem to be rewarded in this world, the obvious reply is that the righteous will get their reward in the world-to-come. Some merits God acknowledges in this world, and some God rewards in the hereafter. In the end, the good people will receive justice, as will the bad.

Finally, it is argued that the *tzadik* is 'gathered in' prior to the appearance of great evil; he or she is really being favoured with God's selection when undergoing what seems to be suffering in the form of martyrdom or pain.

6: Freedom of Human Will

Adherents of this idea argue that there are self-willed constraints on God's intervention that are in place to protect freedom of choice for human beings. Our freedom must be protected, even at the expense of suffering. This of course implies that freedom is incompatible with happiness and joy, that the quest for perfection is a hopeless one because if it were ever achieved the thing that makes us uniquely human, our independent spirit, would be gone.

A related argument is that suffering is an indispensable spur to human aspiration and achievement. Without trials and challenges, the spirit of determination and curiosity would wither and die in us and we would lose some of our faculty for independent thought, just as the most abject slaves have done throughout history. Suffering pushes the human spirit over the brink to rise up against oppression, to demand freedom, and to reach for a higher way of life. Without opposition, we would endure a permanent and debilitating slavery, a slavery to the indolence of our unchallenged lives.

7: Kabbalistic Response

The complex Kabbalistic response to evil incorporates the following concepts in combination: *tzimtzum*; 'breaking of the vessels'; 'dualities'.

8: There Currently is No Answer

There is no answer. However, the lack of an answer is held not to be a fatal flaw in the overall theology. We have no answer at present, but the answer will be clarified in the messianic era. This differs from the first group in that there is no attempt made to interpret the evil we see in the world, it is merely to be accepted that we will later understand all.

Part Two

A Final Response to Suffering

The very fact that well over twenty major theodicies appear in various forms throughout Jewish literature reflects great dissatisfaction with any one existing response to the terrible pain we see all around us in the world. Clearly, each of the above responses has a gaping hole which offers the sufferer or those observing suffering little consolation. How then are we meant to respond as we bear witness to great suffering? If and when the Almighty, whom we believe actively controls our universe, visits calamity, death and destruction on ordinary people, how should we react?

The Torah is not a history book, but a book of instruction; a guide to life. When it recounts for all of eternity the disputes and dialogues between the Almighty and the giants of Jewish history like Abraham and Moses, it is instructing us to emulate their response, as we shall explore.

I believe the only authentic Jewish approach to suffering begins with the underlying premise that there is no comprehensive answer or reconciliation to the problem of why good people suffer and ache. There is, however, a *response*.

Firstly, Judaism recognizes the existence, even the need, for dual purposes which have the potential to clash. Take, for example, a little girl who constantly misbehaves, breaking everything in sight. Her mother is obviously cross and warns her throughout the day to behave herself. Yet, even while offering a reprimand, the mother fully understands that it is natural, even desirable, for her daughter to misbehave, as children do. In fact, if the child sat lifeless and still throughout the day she would be dragged to a psychiatrist! So the role of a child is to misbehave, and the job of a parent is to correct and maintain discipline. Each party carries out a legitimate role, although they conflict.

Leaving God's Affairs to God

As human beings, it is not our role to concern ourselves with God's affairs. Why God brings suffering upon mankind, especially to the righteous, is something we currently cannot comprehend. It is none of our business, even if our frail minds could comprehend it. The moral imperative when we witness the suffering of another individual is to *cause it to cease*, not to attempt to understand it ourselves or explain it to others. If it is something which we have no power to control, such as incurable illness, or a powerful aggressor such as the Nazis, our obligation is to lift our heads heavenwards to object, and launch vociferous protests against this miscarriage of justice, although it seems sanctioned by the Divine.

The real question which should be posed to God upon witnessing a child with leukaemia, or a collective Holocaust, is not, 'Please God, explain to us why this happens and how it fits into Your overall plan for creation,' but rather, 'Master of the universe, how could You *allow this to happen*?! We are not interested in any rationalizations. Was it not You who taught us in Your Torah that life is sacred and must be preserved at all costs? So where is that life now?! Was it not You who also promised that the good deserve goodness, and not pain? Where is Your promise now? By everything which is sacred to You, I demand that this cease, and that Justice be restored, now!'

This is not a challenge to Divine providence, because we are not contending that God does not know what He is enacting, or maintaining that nothing positive can result from suffering. Rather, our statement is this: 'We believe that somehow this must be to our benefit, and that You are a good and just Creator. But You are also all-powerful and would it not therefore be possible for You to bring about this desired end in a less painful pill?'

Whereas Christianity advocates faith and devotion to God above all else, and Islam actually translates as submission to the will of the Divine 'Yisrael', the name of the Jewish people, means 'wrestle with God'. A Jew is someone who is in constant dialogue with God, protesting vociferously against human suffering and perceived miscarriages of justice.

Paying for a Novocaine Injection

Take, for example, my visits to the dentist. I complain about the needle the dentist uses to inject the anaesthetic that will numb my tooth. Yet I am the one who has paid for the treatment in the first place! What I am really saying is this: 'I accept that your poking my gums with the needle is for my own good. But after all these years, has medical science, with all its impressive progress, not developed a means to numb a tooth without pain?' The same applies to a more general approach to suffering. Whatever good we might argue results from suffering can surely be brought about in a positive and joyful manner as well.

What follows from this is the general conviction that there is no intrinsic good to suffering at all. Every time a member of the clergy sits with parents who have just lost a child to leukemia and tells them that this is for the best and is ultimately good, he commits a travesty. Rather, he should raise his hand toward the heavens and shout, 'Why, God?' Better yet, let us applaud all those doctors and researchers who search for a cure, as well as offer our fervent prayers to the Almighty that no one ever die like this again.

Death is an Aberration

Judaism sees death, illness, pain and all forms of suffering as aberrations in creation which were brought about through the sin of Adam in Eden (this should not be confused with the Christian doctrine of original sin and the spiritual fall of humankind). The mission incumbent upon us ever since is to abolish suffering and death from the face of the earth for all eternity, never to make peace with them. By using physical tools such as studying medicine, giving charity, and being there in times of need; by using spiritual means such as protesting to God against injustice and demanding and praying that He correct the flaws of the world, we help usher in an era where only goodness will prevail over the earth.

Travesty in Giving Meaning to Suffering

Those who try to give meaning to the Holocaust miss the point. Our job as humans is not to give meaning to aberrations, unless that is a part of the more important process of abolishing them from our planet. Human beings are commanded by God to occupy themselves with life, not death. Our energy must be dedicated not to explaining hurt and pain, but fighting it.

However, we also refuse to embrace the fanaticism that refuses to look critically at the world and God's role in it. I believe that Judaism is best described as a force for active good.

The word suffering has another meaning that is rarely remembered in these modern times: it means not only pain, anguish and all those negative things we has been discussing, it also means 'allow'. If a subject is in front of a king 'on sufferance', then they are there only as long as the king tolerates their presence: they have no right to be there. Similarly with the other kind of suffering, that which is equated with pain: evil in the world does not arise spontaneously, but because people allow it to happen or actively promote it. Our task is to turn around to say, 'I will not allow this to happen. I will not suffer this suffering to exist', and to eliminate distress with our actions.

Refusing Reconciliation to Misery

From this perspective, there is no answer to the problem of the existence of pain and anguish, and the question of suffering. But there is a positive *response*. Positing an answer means being reconciled to the problem. Responding by never remaining passive, nor adopting a quiet religious obedience, but fighting with every fibre of our beings ensures that we shall be harbingers of redemption instead of prophets of doom. As long as we can explain why people should be gassed, or people die of miserable illness, and as long as we can find rationalizations and justifications for the problem of suffering, the pain associated with these losses will be dispersed and mitigated. And that is not meant to happen. Our responsibility is to demand that they be removed. In this respect, we must use our pain not to look for reasons, but to demand the messianic era. Our questions should not be, for example, why innocent Israelis die in bomb attacks: rather, we must search for peace. We do not seek to reconcile ourselves to such sad events, but to prevent them from ever happening again.

A Tradition in Challenging Heaven

For those who argue that challenging God is sacrilege and most un-Jewish, let them learn from the giants of Jewish history. Their response to witnessing injustice and suffering was to challenge the Almighty and attempt to contravene the evil decree. When God came to Abraham and informed him that He was about to crush Sodom and Gomorrah, cities which Abraham himself knew were deserving of punishment, Abraham refused to bow his head and accept Divine judgement. He pounded with his fist and demanded, 'Shall not the Judge of all the earth do right?' (Genesis 18:25.)

Moses' complaint to the Almighty, 'Lord, wherefore hast Thou so evil entreated these people? Why is it that Thou hast sent me?' (Exodus 5:22) shows clearly how we are to respond to suffering. He did not ask God to explain what good the Jews received from their enslavement in Egypt. Rather, he demanded that God stop it. Better still, Moses led the Jews out of Egypt.

When Moses was informed by the Almighty that He intended to devour the Jewish nation for their idolization of the golden calf, the leader of the Jews responded, 'Yet now, if Thou wilt forgive their sin – ; and if not, blot me, I pray Thee, out of Thy book which Thou hast written' (Exodus 32:32). According to Rashi's interpretation, Moses' words at this point indicate that he took the extraordinary step of admonishing the Master of the universe to remove his name from the Divine books, so that he would not have the terrible shame of failing to save his Master's victims.

Finally, after the debacle with the spies, God made the threat, 'I will smite [the Jewish people] with pestilence and root them out.' Moses again challenged the wrath of heaven and demanded clemency.

My argument is not simply that this response is proper because it was practised by Moses. Rather, it was the Almighty Himself who required this reaction, as is explained by the commentaries on His statement to Moses, 'Now therefore let me alone, that my wrath may wax hot against them and that I may consume them' (Exodus 32:10). Moses had not yet even begun to speak, yet the Almighty told him not to interfere: the explanation is that God was hinting to Moses to open his mouth to defend the Jews, not to accept the terrible fate that He had decreed for them.

As above in the example of the parent and child, the relationship between humans and God involves contradictory responses. God's job is to steer the world in the way that He sees fit, for whatever reason. Our role as humans is never to accept something that is, through God's own revealed truth, known to be evil simply because it exists. Our task is to promote those values which He conveyed to us as supreme.

Death Shall Be Defeated

It is in this way that we can appreciate the importance of demanding the Messiah and the final redemption. All those who refuse to clamour for the Messiah are, *de facto*, accepting the world for what it is. By not demanding from God that the world return to its original state of perfection we simultaneously embrace the world with all its ills and accept that 'such is life'. As Jews we retain an eternal belief that 'death shall be defeated'. Our first preoccupation must be, in the words of the '*Aleinu*' prayer which we recite thrice daily, 'to perfect the world under the sovereignty of the Almighty.'

Elie Wiesel at Oxford

One of the greatest contemporary examples of someone who challenges God and defies Him to bring justice, to live by His own principles of virtue, is Holocaust survivor and Nobel Peace Prize winner, Elie Wiesel. There is probably no writer alive today who better exemplifies the need humanity has to speak to and challenge God, and beseech Him to make the world better and cease visiting what appears as overt suffering upon humanity. His books, especially such classic works as *The Town Beyond the Wall*, explore a remarkable dialectic between humans and God that is resolved in terms beyond any mere intellectualization of suffering. At the heart of his understanding of the God-man relationship is his insistence on wrestling, like Jacob of old, 'with the Angel, with God himself, in a stirring, agonizing, moving encounter' (Norman Lamm, *Faith and Doubt*, page 315).

The Oxford University L'Chaim Society hosted Elie Wiesel and his wife Marion from New York in March 1990. It had been our largest event up to that time and we flooded Oxford with publicity weeks before. There was great excitement among the students to hear this living legend.

We had been inundated with calls from students who wanted to have lunch, dinner, tea, anything private with Mr Wiesel. An intimate lunch for about forty students, which included virtually every Jewish Rhodes and Marshall Scholar, was held at our home.

'Do You Still Believe in God?'

At the lunch Mr Wiesel did not speak, but rather fielded questions from the students. One of the questioners asked, 'After the Holocaust do you believe in God?' His response was this: 'Yes. After the Holocaust I must believe in God, I can't not believe in God. But I am angry with God and I feel that I have the right to express my anger. To demand of Him that He treat us better, that He prevent such evil occurrences from ever happening again.'

Indeed, every one of Professor Wiesel's books has been a long transition to this kind of thinking, beginning with his outright rage at God in his early books, *Night* and then *Dawn*, to his more recent works in which he seeks reconciliation between God and humankind. When I thanked Mr Wiesel before the crowd at the Oxford Union for his lecture, I mentioned, 'What Mr Wiesel has done is to effect a rapprochement with God after the Holocaust. He looked to the heavens and said, "We may have made mistakes to incur your wrath, but perhaps you have also allowed a lot of cruelty and suffering to be visited upon us unjustly; and for that we demand that, just as you will overlook our transgressions, we will overlook your transgressions, and we will somehow come closer together." ' In the wake of the Holocaust, there could not have been any better reconciliation. While many people see this as blasphemy, it is what Judaism was always meant to do; effect a dialogue between man and God.

People before Theodicies

Elie Wiesel's achievement has been brilliantly analysed in the final chapter of Norman Lamm's book, *Faith and Doubt*. Lamm suggests that Wiesel's *The Town Beyond the Wall* is the most theological of his works, confronting through the medium of fiction issues such as suffering, evil, rationality and indifference: 'According [to] the Sages, Michael, the Guardian Angel of Israel, performs the role of a high priest in heaven, who every day offers up a sacrifice consisting of the souls of the righteous. In Wiesel's story, it is Michael who protests the sacrifice of the innocents which it is his tragic role to behold.'

Conventionally, we think of God and humankind being vastly unequal in their dialogue, God being omnipotent and the human protestor merely His creature. But in Wiesel's *The Town Beyond the Wall* we find a significant inversion of this relationship: in Lamm's words, 'a keen awareness not only of man's power but also of his self-consciousness as an autonomous agent . . . It is not rational or even mystical explanations that Wiesel is seeking but rather human approaches and, even more, a confrontation with the God who permits suffering.'

This challenge to the Divine is perhaps best contained in the character Varady, who preaches a sermon to the town: ' "He emphasized the strength of man, who could bring the Messiah to obedience. He claimed that liberation from Time would be accomplished at the signal of man, and not of his Creator . . . each of you, the men and women who hear me, have God in his power, for each of you is capable of achieving a thing of which God is incapable! . . . [man] will conquer heaven, earth, sickness, and death if he will only raze the walls that imprison the Will! And I who speak to you announce my decision to deny death, to repel it, to ridicule it! He who stands before you will never die!" '

This dynamism in our relationship with God because of the existence of suffering is also extended to our relationships with others. One of Wiesel's main characters in *The Town Beyond the Wall*, Pedro, says, 'The dialogue – or . . . duel . . . between man and his God doesn't end in nothingness. Man may not have the last word, but he has the last cry. That moment marks the birth of art . . . and friendship is an art' (page 103). In other words, the meaning of suffering is discovered when we protest against it to God, and the most effective way of dealing with suffering is to extend ourselves to other humans in friendship, which is an art in the same way that Wiesel's book is. This is made even clearer a few pages later: 'To say "I suffer, therefore I am" is to become the enemy of man. What you must say is, "I suffer, therefore you are." Camus wrote somewhere that to protest against a universe of unhappiness, you had to create happiness. That's an arrow pointing the way; it leads to another human being. And not via absurdity' (*The Town Beyond the Wall*, page 127).

Elie Wiesel's message is an inspiring and humane one, and it was for this reason that so many students flocked to hear him; it was one of the largest events we ever staged, with over 1,200 students in attendance at the Oxford Union, both Jewish and non-Jewish. There were no seats unoccupied and many students had to sit on the floor and on the windowsills. Immediately before his lecture we held a spectacular dinner honouring Mr Wiesel in the Oxford Union's Macmillan Room. It was also a celebratory dinner in appreciation of forty years of leadership by the Lubavitcher rebbe. Some of Britain's leading personalities were there, including the chancellor of Oxford University, Lord Jenkins of Hillhead, the late publishing tycoon Mr Robert Maxwell, who has since become infamous, Sir Zelman Cowen, former Governor General of Australia and pro-vice-chancellor of the university, Sir Claus Moser, warden of Wadham College, Dr Baruch Blumberg, master of Balliol College, and Dr Jonathan Cohen, senior tutor of Queen's College and one of the world's best-known names in philosophy. Also present were many leading business figures from London who came to show their support for our activities.

Lord Jenkins, Ed Lazarus, the president of the Union, Brian Glasser, American Rhodes scholar and first president of the L'Chaim Society, Sir Zelman Cowen, myself, and Robert Maxwell were invited to speak at the dinner, and immediately after we transferred to the Union.

Mr Wiesel's speech, which was introduced by Brian Glasser, was entitled, 'The Story of Esther or God in Hiding'. It was a beautiful oration on the lessons that can be learnt from the story of Purim and how this pertains specifically to our post-Holocaust generation. Mr Wiesel spoke the entire time with a yarmulka on his head, a first for the Oxford Union.

His lecture was the most successful we had had so far. It had a lot to do with the fact that Elie Wiesel is someone who, more than anyone else, has made peace between heaven and earth. He has made God more accessible to human beings by showing that God is willing to listen. His speech was greeted with a five-minute standing ovation.

How Can One Not Believe in God after the Holocaust?

There were many questions after the speech: one student asked, 'Can you believe in God after the Holocaust?' Mr Wiesel told us a story from when he was a journalist working in Paris. He came for the first time to meet the Lubavitcher rebbe and said, 'How can I believe in God after what happened to my family, nearly everyone being murdered?' And the rebbe said to him, 'How could you *not* believe in God after the Holocaust?' Mr Wiesel said that he could not accept this from the rebbe as an answer. But he would accept it as a question and that is how he believed it was posed.

Stated in other words, what the rebbe was saying was this: What can we believe in after the Holocaust, besides God? There is nothing else. We can no longer believe in the power of humans alone to make the world better, we must demand things of God. Humanity proved itself utterly incapable as the custodian of life and goodness. This happened on two levels, actively on the part of the Nazi monsters who perpetrated the atrocity, and passively on the part of the nations of the world who stood by in silence.

Like a Child to a Father

I would venture to say that there has never been a more respected figure amongst all the celebrities we have brought who held his audience with such rapture; he makes his slow reconciliation with God a real issue to everyone who listens to him.

Whereas other Jewish thinkers and theologians speak of humanity's subservience to God and the need for human obedience in the face of the Divine, Elie Wiesel taught that we can approach God as a child to a father, not just as a servant to a master; questioning and asking for compassion and mercy; asking for a dialogue and a relationship. This is what the students want; a God they can relate to. They want a God they can speak to and feel that He listens; a two-way street, not just taking orders and taking commands. This is especially significant for Oxford students who have young, inquisitive and curious minds; they want religion to be open-ended so that they can participate in it and not just stand by as silent spectators. Elie Wiesel gave them the reassurance that it is OK to be actively involved, and this is his particular appeal. And of course his astounding contributions to the welfare of mankind, and his role in comforting the pain and bewilderment of an entire generation, are the results of his approach to suffering and God.

At the conclusion of his speech we invited everyone upstairs for drinks in the Union's Gladstone room and there was a line of about two hundred people waiting to get in. By all accounts this event served as an evening not to be missed, and the students felt privileged to have met Mr Wiesel. Elie Wiesel had proved to us that there is more to understanding suffering than many people suppose; nothing can stop us from taking to heart his message of hope and action.

Chapter Fifty-one

SEIZE THE DAY: TIME AND ITS DESTINATION

The Museum of Science on Broad Street, next door to the Sheldonian Theatre, makes it clear to a visitor that all modern science at bottom depends on measurement. The basic quantities that we measure are weight, dimensions, and of course time. It is only when we consider what our world would be like if we were unable consistently to deal with these quantities that we understand how much we depend on measurement. How could we eat if we kept on missing our mouths because we could not orient our bodies in space? If we did not sleep for a month because time somehow became unimportant to us, our bodies would be utterly exhausted. All living created entities need an awareness of time to survive: the plants need to correlate increases in light and warmth with the arrival of spring in order to put forth new leaves, and birds need to recognize the signs of autumn to migrate to warm climates before winter sets in.

A scientific reductionist could even say that the progress of science has been the story of attaining higher and higher degrees of accuracy in measurement. When the first attempts at measuring time were made, the instruments made were so crude that inventors would calibrate their machines using their own internal 'clocks', their awareness of the stars and the sun. These instruments preserved in the museum seem laughably crude to us, but they were the first steps to understanding the world around us in terms of measurement, measurement that is now so accurate that we think we have almost understood the universe itself. Nowadays, time for humans is determined by clocks, not the other way round. If I wake up with a start thinking it is seven in the morning, but the alarm clock says it is only 4 a.m., I roll over and go back to sleep rather than question the clock.

Time is to so many people the ultimate arbiter of modern life. We feel guilty if we 'waste' it, pleased when we have completed something with time in hand. If we are late, we apologize; if we leave two weeks before revising for our finals, we feel suicidal. Is time really so important? Philosophers certainly think so . . .

There is a great deal of discussion, both among Jewish and secular philosophers, about whether time at some time came into existence or whether it is eternal. If we say that time has been created, then there is an obvious question: 'Didn't God the Creator of time exist before He created time? If so, there was time (alongside of God) even before time's own existence. Therefore time existed before its own creation.' This is obviously a serious logical contradiction. Yet, if we are to say that God did not exist before time existed, heaven forbid, how then can we say that He was there in order to create time? In the same vein there is the question: 'If time is eternal and did not have a beginning, how and why did it come into existence at all?'

Time is Created

Jewish mystical thought is of the opinion that time was created and proves this point by means of the following analogy: 'One million dollars added to another million dollars equals two million dollars. Now, if two million plus a certain number, x, equalled an infinite amount, what would be the value of x? The answer is that x would have to be infinite. Should x be any finite number, as great as it may be, even a billion, or a trillion, ad infinitum, when added to two million, would total 1,002,000,000, or 1,000,002,000,000, etc. etc., for there is no limit to numbers, they can always go higher and higher. In other words, finite units cannot be added to, or subtracted from, infinite amounts. In comparison with the infinite, all finite units become negligible. Therefore, from one million to infinite is the same distance as from one to infinite. They both are infinitely removed from infinite.'

In truth there really cannot be an infinite composed of finite units (commonly referred to as objects). For example: 'Suppose we have an infinite amount of dollars and we add another five dollars to this infinite amount. Did the five dollars we added accumulate to the previous amount or not? According to our previous conclusion it should not be added to the infinite pile. For finite units are negligible when added to an infinite number. Now if we remove the five dollars from this infinite amount, will it subtract from the infinite? Most definitely it will. Because if this five dollars does not help to form the infinite series, how then can we discern that the five dollars does in fact exist within the infinite amount? Its existence should be negligible and completely unrecognizable within the infinite series, drowned within the all-encompassing uniformity which characterizes infinite. Yet, given that the five dollars does in fact exist within, and even comprises this infinite amount of dollars, if the five were subtracted, its void would be felt and would affect the infinite amount. For, notwithstanding the fact that this is an infinite series, it is composed of finite units (one, two, three, etc.). Given that this is the case, every finite unit, being an integral part of the constitution of the infinite, affects, and has significance with, the infinite series. This series, therefore, is not and cannot be a true infinite series, for real infinity, indicative of its most basic meaning, is something completely above and unlimited by any finite composition whatsoever.'

Therefore when we say that time is eternal, we are implying that time is unlimited. Put another way, until the present time, there has already been an infinite amount of hours. In reality, though, there could not have been an infinite amount of hours because hours are finite time units, and an infinite cannot consist of finite units.

Time in Existence Alongside the Creator?

We must therefore conclude that time is not infinite: it has been created and has had a beginning. It is intrinsically limited. This brings us back to our original question: Wasn't the Creator of time – God – in existence before the creation of time so that He might create time? If so, surely time existed alongside of Him, which means that just as God is eternal, so too is time eternal and has always existed? But this cannot be, as was previously explained!

To understand this paradoxical question, we must first understand the nature of time.

In essence, time is a measure of change. Defined and uniform units, such as seconds, minutes, hours etc., can be installed by an observer within the framework of time in order that it may be measured more accurately, but they are not themselves the essence of time. Created entities all change from one form to another; they may age, they may develop, they may decay, and so on. A measure of this transformation from one state to another is commonly known as time. Time exists only where these transformations and changes may take place. For example, even if I wished to deny the passage of time, and pretended that I did not age, I could not. No denial in the world would stop the sun from rising and setting, thus signifying that time indeed was elapsing. Similarly, I could not prevent or ignore the seasonal changes which would bring snow in winter and sunshine in summer, thus also indicating undeniable change. Most importantly, I could neither stop nor ignore the whitening of my hair, the wrinkling of my skin and all other physiological signs of aging. Something which does not, and cannot, change is not limited by time.

For instance, everyone knows with the greatest simplicity that $2 + 2 = 4$. Now, at what stage in time is it that $2 + 2 = 4$? Today? Tomorrow? Yesterday? Was it true of the era before the days of the flood as well? Of course! Maybe in the times of Adam and Eve, $2 + 2$ did not equal 4? How do we know that $2 + 2$ has always equalled 4? Because logical truths are not dependent on any time framework. Truth exists eternally. $2 + 2 = 4$ is a true statement. It cannot change. It is therefore not subjected to any time discrepancy. Thus all the time in the world will not change this in the slightest. For in the world of logic, time does not exist, because time and logic are independent of one another. Intellectual truths do not change and therefore their transformation cannot be measured. Similarly, intellectual truths are not subject to variations in space. The fact of 2 + 2 equalling four is just as true on Mars or Venus as it is on earth.

On the other hand, a physical object, by its very constitution, allows and requires transformation and change. It naturally changes, as we see by every physical measure we have at our disposal. Physical objects age and change their form. Today a tree is one year old and is one metre high, tomorrow at two years old it will be nearly two metres high, and so on. Its green leaves will change to brown in the autumn of the year, and new buds will emerge in the warmth of spring. This is also true in relation to humans who, when they age, experience transformations of the body and the mind. The list of transformations in the natural world goes on and on. In fact, everything in the empirical world changes and degrades itself constantly: this is not just known intuitively, it is proved from the laws of thermodynamics that there is a constant decay of energy in all physical objects.

This is manifested in the fact that after many years all created things decay and change their form. This is because a physical entity demands change. Therefore, physical entities are subject to the limitations of time, because time itself is a measure of change and it itself induces change.

God Cannot Change and is Thus Unaffected by Time

With the above explanation, we may answer the fundamental question. We inquired as to the nature of the Divinity before the advent of time. Did God exist before time, or did time exist before God? The answer is that God does not exist in a physical form which induces change, transformation, and He is therefore not subjected to the effects and measurement of time. Rather, He exists in a different dimension which excludes subjection to transformation and time. His existence is eternal: past, present and future are misnomers when used in reference to God's state of existence, as mentioned earlier. God is in fact identical with the world of logic and truth.

So, is time as important as the modern world seems to think? We certainly cannot decide that we are going to defy it, simply because logic and truth are outside of it. Even Oxford philosophers cannot decide that the category of time is irrelevant to their perfectly logical lives. On the other hand, the crude instruments which can be seen in Oxford's Museum of Science are not in fact that far different even from the atomic clocks and sub-molecular microscopes that are used today: we might think a candle clock is a pretty rough way of reckoning the hours, but then what does it actually mean that we can measure time to the nano-second? It means that we can measure time to the nano-second, that is all. We do not understand the whole world any better by being able to measure it so accurately: we just understand our categories of space and time better. A person is not a set of co-ordinates in space that has a certain time allotted in which to live, but a being who has relationships with other beings, including God. This is outside of and always will be beyond time and measurement. And it is specifically a connection and relationship with this Infinite Being which can bring a qualitative change to our lives by using Divine law as an immutable and absolute measurement of the progress we make in our lives.

Chapter Fifty-two

THE PASSION KILLER

The nation of Amalek waged a desperate battle with the Jewish people after their departure from Egypt. When the Jews emerged from Egypt, they were analogous, in the words of the Talmud, to 'a hot bath', which means to say that no nation dared confront them. They were scalding hot. Through God's intervention and the ten plagues which He inflicted upon Egypt, they had destroyed the mightiest kingdom on earth and its ruler, Pharaoh. Until this very day, museums around the world bear witness to the might, wealth and sophistication of ancient Egypt. The poor slave nation which had been dominated for two hundred years by the Egyptians emerged victorious and left only ruins behind for their former Egyptian masters.

It goes without saying that the entire civilized world was deeply impressed and awed by the Jewish people – protected by God they were no longer insignificant, they were invincible. Their fame had spread far and wide, and no one dared to attack them, because that would be waging war against God.

No one, that is, except for the nation of Amalek. Despite the fact that the Jews had vanquished the mightiest empire on earth, and the Amalek themselves had nowhere near the resources or military strength of Egypt, they still dared to attack the Jews as they left Egypt. To be sure, they paid a most terrible price and were largely annihilated in battle. Yet the Amalekites left a scar, too. The scar left by the Amalekites was the fact that they removed the sense of awe that was accorded to God through the Jewish people.

The Talmud says specifically that when the Jewish people were coming out of Egypt they were analogous to a hot bath. Every person points to the bath and says, 'There is no way you could put your hand in it. In fact, even getting close to it you will get burned.' Then along comes a man who decides to disregard this advice. Seeking to prove a point, he thrusts his hand into the bath, and he is scalded; his skin is badly burnt, and the wounds which he incurs will never heal. At the very same time, it is as if he has cooled down the bath. Not that it is any colder in reality; but now people can say to themselves, 'Look, he stuck his hand into the bath and survived, which means it probably was not that hot after all.'

The Contemporary, Internal Amalek

In every generation there is a battle with Amalek. There comes a time in a person's life when he or she begins studying religion, becoming involved in Jewish life, communal and religious, and the person feels on fire. The individual begins to feel engaged in something which they may have been deprived of for most of their lives, and become excited, enthusiastic and passionate, beginning to tell their friends of something new, exciting and holy that they have discovered. A man tells his friends of something which cures the suffocating selfishness and materialism of modern society. He is very enthusiastic about it, when suddenly a doubt comes into his mind and basically tells him, 'What you are studying is nice, but don't allow it to inflame you. Be more dispassionate about it.'

The modern Amalek is the intellectual fear of becoming emotionally attached to one's subject. Amalek represents our ability to study a subject and be very impressed intellectually, but to experience an emotional blockage. Amalek is the rubber stopper which separates our emotions from our intellect, and creates an insurmountable obstacle which renders our emotions completely unaffected by that which we study. Amalek is the ability for us to absorb a doubt, either from friends, colleagues or even ourselves, which means that although we continue to study Judaism and to be impressed with it, we are no longer impassioned about it. In fact, we fear becoming impassioned about it.

Living in Oxford, I have often noticed that the Oxford intellectual method involves always remaining completely detached from one's subject. In fact, Oxford would argue that becoming emotionally involved with your studies would necessarily infringe upon your ability to survey them objectively, honestly and sincerely. It is almost as if we believe that becoming emotionally involved in something will make us irrational, or at the very least, partial.

While this is often true, it is only true if you get emotionally involved before you study; and here, Chasidic teaching always distinguishes between emotions which are born of the intellect and emotions which, like weeds, grow on their own. The desirable emotions are those born of intellect, which means you begin with the mind studying, examining and scrutinizing a specific subject.

Intellectual Faculties as Mother and Father

The mind has the ability to be detached and objective. Since it is not modelled by emotional affiliation, it can examine a subject and then determine whether it is good or bad. In the way the human mind is constructed, what should happen next is that the intellect sends a message to the emotions, and dictates whether a person should develop a liking for that subject or a disliking. If it is good, a person should feel an attraction, a compulsion, towards the object; and if it is evil or harmful or dangerous, then the intellect should dictate to the heart the development of a sense of repulsion and distaste for that object.

On the other hand, emotion which is not born of intellect, which is just impulsive or intuitive, can of course be very dangerous. It can be like a wild growth, a weed in the middle of an uncultivated garden. It just grows, and indeed we find ourselves attracted to those things which are dangerous and harmful, such as drugs, or falling in love with someone you are not married to, or anything else for which we have a lustful desire but which, if we were to subject that desire to intellectual scrutiny, we would of course understand these feelings and how wrongful they really are.

Embracing what is Right

However, Amalek says that all emotion is bad, that we should only be cold and superficial about all subjects. Just as Amalek cooled down the awe of God as the Jewish people came out of Egypt, so Amalek seeks to cool our enthusiasm for life, for Judaism, for our spouse, for our children, for our study subjects. Amalek will even seek to prove that nothing is really so hot, nothing is really so special, and thereby it sucks out our vibrancy and enthusiasm for life. For this reason we were commanded to destroy Amalek, uproot it: life is not about subjecting everything to scrutiny and never becoming devoted to a cause. Life is about studying what is right and what is wrong, then firmly endorsing and pursuing that which is right instead of merely making moral statements about it. In fact, Judaism would argue it is imperative that we not only study what is right, but defend it to the death and seek to promote it, enhance it and cultivate it.

Laissez faire and indifference are crimes, sins, the arch-enemies of the Jewish people and everything that Judaism stands for. It is that blockage between the mind and the heart called Amalek which never allows our heart to become attached to anything. To live for nothing, to stand for nothing, to be blown by the wind, that is the *klippa* (the obstruction) which Amalek stands for, and what the Jews were meant to eradicate.

The Academic Approach to Judaism

Here in Oxford, Judaism is studied as intensely and as thoroughly as in yeshivahs throughout the world. Of course, anyone who comes to either of the two institutions, a higher academy of Jewish studies within the yeshivah framework, or a university teaching the same subjects, would find them very different. In the university you would find scholars who are looking not to ascertain whether something should be endorsed and promoted, but whether it is true or not true: they subject it to all kinds of academic scrutiny. Judaism advocates that we study not just to establish truth but to thereafter implement it; to bring thoughts to fruition in action.

The Talmud relates a story of a debate that took place between the houses of Hillel and the houses of Shammai, the two leading talmudic academies of the era, which were so important that they formulated Jewish law for all post-Talmudic generations. They debated which was greater, study or deed and action. As Judaism is an action-oriented religion it would make sense for us to assume that action won the day and carried the vote. The opposite is true. Both talmudic academies agreed that it was learning and study that was greater: 'Because it is study that brings to action.'

Action is the purpose of Jewish study, and this is why Judaism has always been so engaged in academic pursuits and intellectual scrutiny. Not just to make objective moral statements about specific subjects, but to pursue them based on intellectual guidelines and to develop an affinity, an attachment, a love for them. It behoves us to pursue this today as well. To study the Torah not just as a book of science but as a book of direction, a book of light, and a pathway of life.

Chapter Fifty-three

LESSONS FROM THE HEART

Everyone knows that Oxford is a romantic city. Not only is it extraordinarily beautiful, a circumstance that always seems to make people turn to matters of love, but a high proportion of the population has enough leisure time (students don't work continuously, whatever they may claim) to pursue romance almost as keenly as they pursue knowledge. In the summer, the Cherwell river is full of punts, each with a young couple doing nothing really active so much as enjoying each other's company, and the streets are crowded with similar people walking arm in arm.

It seems that everyone respects the law of the heart; undergraduates long since learned that if the week's essay is not completed, a sure way to elicit sympathy from even the crustiest old don is to claim that you have 'boy/girlfriend troubles'; and even more leniency is often available if a young man claims he has had a bad week with his boyfriend, or at least that is what I am told by the students.

Sometimes the pursuit of love has a less positive side; it is not unusual for bright young students to do badly in their examinations because of failed or unrequited love, and in recognition of this it is an unspoken rule that if a relationship is foundering in the run-up to exams or during them, one should do one's best to preserve the *status quo* until the academic pressure is off. Those who flout this rule of courtesy are not at all well looked upon in student circles.

Now of course the tradition of romantic love makes it clear that *true* love makes no room in the ardent young lover's heart for anything but the object of desire, and this inevitably means that other people may be neglected, including the lover him- or herself. It was the famous Oxford man, C. S. Lewis, who did more than anyone else to elaborate this theory of romantic love in the light of history: he claimed it was invented by the troubadours in the twelfth century and slowly made its way from a literary fashion for the nobility to an expectation held by the humblest swain and lass. The idea of romantic love took hold of western civilization very rapidly, and one of its most potent emblems was that of the heart. Without a heart, a person must die, and so the idea of 'giving your heart away' means that you cannot live without the presence of your lover. Such exclusive and also somewhat selfish love is of course foreign to Judaism; to love, you must remain aware, of yourself, the one you are in love with, and other people.

So, when the opportunity arose in February 1992 to host Dr Christiaan Barnard, the renowned surgeon who performed the world's first human heart transplant on 13 December 1967, we decided to delve more deeply into the meaning of this symbol of human emotions.

A Doctor of the Heart

Dr Barnard had primarily come here to debate under our auspices at the Oxford Union with the Emeritus Chief Rabbi of the United Kingdom and the Commonwealth, Lord Immanuel Jakobovits, on the subject of euthanasia. Dr Barnard is a world-famous proponent of active medical euthanasia, and has written several books on the subject, the most famous of which is *Good Life, Good Death*. In this he advocates that a patient whose quality of life has deteriorated to nothing but pain and a bleak future should have their life terminated, as a mercy killing.

We were privileged to have Dr Barnard with us for five days, in which time I and the officers of the society became quite friendly with him. He arrived on a Friday morning from South Africa, and we had the unique opportunity of hosting him for our Friday-night dinner at the L'Chaim Society. Now we knew that the Union event would attract hundreds of students (there were 950 students present), so on the Friday night we asked Dr Barnard to speak about performing the first heart transplant, and he did so very eloquently.

Toasting Shabbat and Friday Night

Before he did so, there is a custom at the L'Chaim Society every Friday night that we ask students around the table to say a toast to life, a *L'Chaim*. The purpose of this is twofold: first and foremost it is that once a week a student should lift a glass and toast to something positive, whether it be their friends, or the peace and serenity of Shabbat, or their Jewishness, or the state of Israel, or even something as universal as world peace, or their relatives. Shabbat should be our point of embarkation, the day on which we make wishes and express our hopes for the coming week. The second reason is that the students should be able to participate in the Friday night, and not just be passive recipients of my comments and remarks; I want them to feel actively involved, and to try to make their own statements about Shabbat. It has proved very successful and each week we have about sixty or seventy people who come to eat on Friday night with us, and everyone says the *L'Chaim*. Most of the toasts are very good because people prepare their *bons mots* beforehand.

L'Chaim to Little Girls

So we asked Dr Barnard to say a *L'Chaim*. He stood up, holding his glass and, sitting in front of him, was a student, the L'Chaim Society president, who was holding my three-year-old daughter, Mushkie, on his lap. Dr Barnard said, 'This *L'Chaim* is to little girls, who grow up to be such beautiful young ladies,' looking at my daughter. Then he told the story of why he had said this. He told us that after he had performed the first heart transplant, he became a world celebrity overnight. The first Christmas he was asked to go to one of the biggest shopping centres in Johannesburg so that children could have their pictures taken sitting on his lap. One particular three-year-old girl came to sit on his lap, and her photograph was taken. Later, when she was twenty-seven, she married him as his third wife. Everybody of course laughed at this; it was meant to be funny, and it was, although the student in question embarrassedly scrambled to remove Mushkie from his lap. After that we got on with the evening.

Dr Barnard then began to speak, giving a fascinating lecture about how he performed the world's first heart transplant, the complications involved, and the reaction of the world media. He said he had not been in the least prepared for the incredible exposure and world fame which was to inundate him overnight after the first heart transplant was performed.

He said there had been no great preparations for this operation. The facts were that there was a terminally ill patient, who was being operated on; without even a lot of help or explicit permission, Dr Barnard told his staff that he was going to perform a heart transplant that night; they got a donor, and then it was done. In the morning he announced to some of the staff what had happened; a newspaperman found out, and a few minutes later it was all around the world that the first heart transplant had been performed. He himself says it was only as he was driving back to the hospital after going home to sleep, a few hours later, that he heard on the radio his name being mentioned as being associated with the first heart transplant. That evening, journalists from all around the world arrived to interview him and take pictures. He described the scene as one of simple and tremendous adulation; the world's population was focusing its attention on just one man. His reaction was to say, 'After all, the heart is just a pump, so why do people see it as such a great seat of the emotions? It is just a pump which pumps blood.' Today he remains one of the world's most famous doctors, largely because of his successful heart transplant.

The Significance of the Heart

At this point, he was asked by one of the students why he felt that this indeed was such a great accomplishment in the eyes of the world, especially as many other organ transplants had already been performed. Why was the heart transplant so fantastic? In reply he said, 'The world has a fixation with the heart; it is perhaps the most important organ, the seat of the emotions, embracing feelings such as love and attraction. It represents and symbolizes so many things that people were amazed that it could be transplanted.' It was due to the importance of the organ that he in turn had all this honour bestowed upon him.

Then he endeavoured to explain why he thought people always see the heart as being the seat of the emotions. 'Basically, it is the only organ that we feel reacting to emotional situations. When someone falls in love they feel their heart pounding faster, when they are afraid they feel their heart pounding faster. The heart is the only organ that we can *feel* actually reacting to every human situation.'

On Sunday afternoon we arranged a dinner in honour of Dr Barnard which many of Oxford's leading medical names attended, including Oxford's Professor of Cardiology and heads of department from the John Radcliffe Hospital. There I gave a talk about Dr Barnard and his significance to our society. I mentioned his remarks, the heart being special to people because it reacts to emotion, and I said, 'In the Torah, everything has a superficial meaning, and then it has an inner, mystical, more profound meaning. Chasidism always dwells on this underlying meaning. The Lubavitcher rebbe has addressed the same issue that Dr Barnard did, but a bit differently.'

An Organ Dedicated Entirely to Others

The Lubavitcher rebbe said the heart is completely outwardly oriented. The idea of emotion is an outward effusion of one human being to another. Intellect is the exact opposite. Intellect is the ability to withdraw into oneself. Meditation, for instance, is the ability to withdraw from the world. When people wish to think, they can't be around other people. Thought thrives on pulling ourselves into ourselves, being reflective, being introspective. But emotion pulls us to other people. Even if we want to be alone we feel that we need others. We either hate them or love them but we have to react with everything around us. And that is what a pump is about. A pump works for other people, pumping the blood to all the other organs. This, the rebbe explained, is why traditionally humanity has associated the heart with the emotions. An emotion is something we feel for somebody or something else. So, too, the heart is entirely devoted to the other organs of the body. It exists and dedicates its entire existence merely to the other organs of the body. It does nothing for itself.

Lending itself to homiletics, the heart transplant, or homiletically transplanting one's heart, represents the ability for a human being to be devoted to others while alive, and not just to donate one's heart, enabling human life, only after one's demise. That is why the heart is the seat of the emotions.

Living Donors

This special significance of the heart reveals why Dr Barnard's visit to our society is relevant. The one message which we are trying to convey to the cream of Jewish youth who find themselves here in Oxford is that it is not enough to be only like the intellect, sitting here absorbing knowledge and information for your own personal development, even if this indeed is the principal reason one comes to Oxford. They should also strive to embody all those great characteristics and knowledge and culture which they can absorb at Oxford in order to give to others later, to be like the heart, to be like a pump, to dedicate their lives to the betterment of the world. A heart transplant homiletically means being devoted to other people whilst still alive. A high proportion of people in Europe and the USA have donor cards. A donor card means someone needs your ability to give life; since you don't need your heart, your kidneys or your corneas any more when you have died, why should you just allow them to rot when you can enhance someone else's life? We are used to this concept and the initial opposition to the idea of donating organs has slipped away, so that it is now entirely acceptable (although there are problems presented by Jewish law). But why are we only keen to make that sacrifice only after we are dead? What about dedicating our lives to others while we are alive? We all have to be heart transplant surgeons, we have to be donors while we are alive, living donors. We must emulate the heart in its selfless devotion to the welfare and sustenance of the body. We must see ourselves and our lives not just as independent, autonomous units, completely divorced from other people. Rather, humanity is one body, and it desperately needs a heart, as many hearts as possible, to ensure its health, well-being and continuity.

Ways in which to Express Love

This doesn't mean we have to give our lives and die for others, it just means we have to dedicate a part of our lives to others. Now people don't understand this message. They think that it is either an all-or-nothing game, they think about the heart being devoted entirely to someone, or not at all. I remember when I was visiting Miami in the summer of 1991, there was a story about a man who drove to Jackson Memorial hospital, the largest hospital in the area, and he was wearing a sign. He drove up to the hospital, put a gun to his head in the parking lot, and pulled the trigger, instantly killing himself. He was wearing a sign spattered with blood, which read, 'My brother is upstairs in the cardiac unit, he needs a heart donor otherwise he will die. He has been waiting and he has had no donor. Please take my heart and give it to him.' This is what we are used to seeing as a sacrifice, but this view is wrong. Such all-or-nothing sacrifices imply that if you are devoted to your brother you have either to give him your entire life or give him nothing. Because it is seen as so extreme, we often end up doing less than we could because a partial sacrifice is not seen as enough. In reality, we just have to dedicate a part of our lives. It is not all that hard, we shouldn't see it in such extreme terms. What God wants to see is that we dedicate our lives somewhat to others, like the pump we call a heart.

God Desires the Heart, Literally

There is a beautiful story the founder of the Chasidic movement, the Baal Shem Tov, used to teach about what was meant by saying that God wanted the heart. A Russian Jewish couple were peasants and uneducated. One Sabbath morning in the synagogue they heard the rabbi saying that God desires the heart. They went home and they discussed, 'What could this mean, that God desires the heart?' So the next Shabbat when they cooked a chicken, they took the chicken heart, and they salted and peppered it and roasted it and made it really delicious, and they brought it to the synagogue. They placed it in the holiest part of the synagogue, the *aron hakodesh*, the holy ark where the Torah scrolls are housed, and they left it there. As they left they felt happy that they had given God the heart.

Immediately after they had left, a beggar walked in before the Sabbath and said, 'God I have nothing to eat, I have nothing to give my children, nothing to give my family, I am hungry, please feed me.' At once he smelled a mouth-watering aroma coming from the *aron hakodesh*. He walked over, looked inside, and there was a heart. He said, 'Thank you God, thank you.' He took it home and his family ate it, and they were happy.

The next Friday the peasants again brought the chicken heart. And again the same scene happened, with the beggar coming and asking God for the food, and there it was. This went on for many, many weeks. After the first week, the peasants began to notice that the heart had been taken. They saw this as God having accepted their offering of the heart, and they were thrilled. The beggar on the other hand thought that God was giving him the heart, and he too was pleased. Each one thought that God was answering their prayers.

A few weeks later the rabbi happened to be in the synagogue praying; no one saw him, and he saw the young peasant couple bring in the heart and leave it in the *aron hakodesh*. A few minutes later he saw the beggar come in and beg God for food, and then take it thinking God had answered his prayers. He summoned them both into his study, and he said, 'You people are fools.' He turned to the peasants and said, 'Why do you put the heart there?' They said, 'Well you told us God desired the heart, and we gave Him the heart.' The rabbi said, 'And do you think that is what I meant?' They said, 'Of course that is what you meant. The proof is that God eats it, God takes it and it is not there.' So he turned to the beggar and said, 'That is because the beggar is taking it.' The beggar was startled to discover that in truth all of his food was coming from them, and not from God, and both felt very disappointed.

When the Baal Shem Tov heard this story he said the rabbi should never have said that. Who says that God wasn't taking the heart, and who says that God wasn't giving it to the beggar? God works in His own ways, this is how He fed the beggar, simultaneously accepting the offering of the poor couple, and made everybody happy. The rabbi was blind in his religious outlook because he failed to see it differently.

Selflessness of Student Officers

God wants the heart, just a bit of ourselves, to be dedicated to others, and to recognize that we have Divinely imposed obligations upon us to help our fellows. I can happily say that, thank God, we have cultivated an environment and a society which teaches this. More than anything else, our student officers dedicate themselves totally, with complete sincerity, to all of our activities. Here they are with essay crises, having to do exams, and still coming here for self-development and the acquisition of knowledge. They dedicate themselves to banal things like putting up posters, and exciting things like inviting speakers, and making sure that all goes well. Dr Barnard's entire visit was arranged by our two student presidents, Doron Junger of Green College, an aspiring medic, and Celia Rothenberg of St Antony's, an American Marshall Scholar. Both of them are extremely busy but they have dedicated a part of their lives here at Oxford to others, exemplifying this concept of a heart transplant while alive.

Incidentally, a lot of people told us when we first opened the society that we would breed insincerity. They said that people would come to our lectures and students would become attached to our organization because they wanted to hear and meet famous speakers, which is one of the exciting things the L'Chaim Society provides. What we discovered was the exact opposite. To put together one lecture by someone like Dr Christiaan Barnard, one debate in the Oxford Union, takes weeks of preparation. Doron sat on the phone making all the phone calls, also arguing with our suppliers about food for the dinner, and for the sound system, and for the video-taping, arguing for every penny, because he knows full well how hard we must work to raise charitable funds to stage these events. Celia, who was to take her M. Phil. exams at St Antony's just two weeks after the Barnard visit, helped my wife Deborah prepare the food for the dinner and everything else. These students, and so many others like them, exemplify what we are trying to do. Altruism means the ability at times to put other people's considerations before our own. This is what it means to give the heart while alive.

May God bless and reward Dr Barnard in merit of his fantastic contribution to the progress of civilization and human health that he may see many more healthy years and ultimately a time when all disease will be cured and removed from the earth.

Chapter Fifty-four

A JEWISH COSMOLOGY: THE ORIGIN OF LIGHT

How often do we come across the satisfying situation of our knowledge in one subject illuminating our conception of another area of thought or study? Cross-fertilization of ideas can be enormously helpful in overcoming the boundaries placed around disciplines from our early school days, to arrive at a synthesis of all our knowledge. The knowledge we have can then be used in far more flexible and creative ways. This wonderful process should not of course be confined to formal academic subjects. I am told that tutors at the university, as well of course as non-academic types, respond very positively to ideas and examples brought from the 'real' world, or from areas not always recognized for their intellectual content such as the worlds of faith or the media.

The purpose behind many of the expositions found in this book has been to approach age-old theological points with the illumination of modern science behind us. I sincerely believe that the disciplines have a great deal to offer each other in terms of intelligent discussion, and fresh viewpoints on interesting topics. The avoidance of simple reductionism can, paradoxical though it may seem to many scientists, lead to a more rational view of our world. To take one famous and delightful scientist as an example, the world-acclaimed physicist Richard Fienneman played bongo drums in his spare time and enjoyed an extremely spiritual approach to life. To exclude deliberately any one line of thinking from our intellectual armoury sounds, at best, irrational: it cannot promote us to the higher echelons of the world's mental élite.

I have tried as often as possible to make this point to my students. Ultimately, Judaism and the empirical sciences should be studied with an objective of synthesis, rather than callous compartmentalization. Of course, there is nothing as effective in demonstrating the complementary nature of science and religious studies as practical example. One of the seminars on this subject I once gave involved a comprehensive study of the origin of light from biblical narrative, *midrashic* anthology, and scientific inquiry. This particular class became famous, not so much for the content as for the one celebrated participant.

Stars Studying about Light

In November 1990 we hosted Jon Voight, the film actor who starred in *Midnight Cowboy* and who won the Academy Award for best actor for his portrayal of a paralysed Vietnam War veteran in the movie *Coming Home*, for which Jane Fonda won the award for best actress.

Jon is completely unlike the Hollywood stereotype. He is supremely and selflessly dedicated to loving and helping his fellow man, as well as enhancing the quality of life for all people. He is one of the most naturally spiritual people I ever met. It is not exaggerated to say that his career has been hurt in no small measure because of his humanitarian pursuits. His last great film was *Runaway Train* in 1985, for which he won the Golden Globe award for best actor. He came close to winning the Academy Award for a second time that year, but lost narrowly to William Hurt for *Kiss of the Spider Woman*. In his acceptance speech at the Golden Globe Awards, Jon spoke to a very surprised audience, and to national television, of the need for increased spiritual awareness and a nurturing of the soul. 'Boy, did they think I was weird,' he told me. From that time on, he put his flourishing career on ice and dedicated himself fully to simple gestures of goodness, such as helping deliver furniture to homeless people in Los Angeles. Having heard of his astonishing commitment to humanity through Chabad of the US West Coast, with whom he shares a close association, I invited him to give a series of lectures in Oxford on the subject of employing great material success and celebrity in the service of goodness.

Jon is not Jewish, neither does he aspire to become Jewish. But he derives his spiritual nourishment from Jewish teaching as well as that of the native Americans, especially the Hopi Indians. The days he spent with us were marvellous, and he insisted on studying Jewish thought with me every day. One day a reporter from the *Jewish Chronicle* came to my home to interview him, and found him participating eagerly in a seminar that I was leading together with ten students investigating the formation of light culled from Jewish and scientific findings. He insisted that the reporter participate, who was so impressed at the 'Torah-studying Gentile Hollywood Film Star' that he put a colour photo of the two of us studying on the cover of that week's *Jewish Chronicle*, the most circulated and read Jewish news publication in Britain.

I subsequently received many inquiries about the content of the lecture, which served as a model for science helping to explain difficult biblical narratives.

Illuminating Our Understanding of Creation

In a famous pronouncement that begins the tractate which deals with

Passover, the Talmud says, 'Light of the fourteenth [day of the month of Nissan] one is obligated to search [the house] for *chametz* [leaven]' (*Pesachim* 2a).

It is important to understand what is implied by the term 'light' in the context of this *Mishnah* in *Pesachim*: if 'light' means day, one is obligated to search the house during the day of the fourteenth. Very often in the Talmud, 'light' refers to night, and if this is the case here, then one is to search the house at nightfall of the fourteenth day of Nissan, the eve of Passover.

The Talmud begins an intensive analysis of the implications of the word in an attempt to solve this problem, quoting the fifth verse of the Torah, 'God called the light, Day' (Genesis 1:5), as implying quite clearly that 'light' is day!

The Talmud continues, though, that this verse offers no proof either way. For the Talmud renders the term *vayikra* not as 'He called', but rather 'He [God] summoned', and says, 'God summoned the light and appointed it for duty by day, and He summoned the darkness and appointed it for duty by night.' In other words, 'calling' does not refer here to giving a name but rather to 'summoning'.

We clearly see from the analysis of this passage that day is not synonymous with light, nor are darkness and night interpreted identically. Rather, day and night represent differing time intervals, and God instructed the light to function by the time interval termed 'day', and instructed darkness to function during the interval termed 'night'.

What is Light?

This, of course, raises the question of what light really is. Rashi, commenting on this talmudic passage, states: 'This calling [*vayikra*] was not the giving of a name, that one might infer that [God] named the light: day, rather [calling in this context refers to the fact that] He called the illuminating created matter [*briah hameirah*] which He created from the splendour of his garbed clothing, and commanded it to serve at day; and to the darkness at night, as a king who summons his servant to appear before him.'

Rashi thus defines light as being an illuminating created matter and says that this illuminating matter was created from the splendour of His garbed clothing (the implications of which will be fully explained later).

This definition presents numerous difficulties. Firstly, the word *barah* – created, a verb used in Scriptures exclusively with reference to Divine activity, is explained by the commentators as referring to 'producing something out of nothing' (*yesh meayin*), creation *ex nihilo*. As Maimonides comments, 'There is no expression in Hebrew for producing something from nothing other than the word *barah*, "created".'

Rashi, therefore, in using the word 'created' to explain the emergence of light on the first day of creation, seems to be of the opinion that the light was created from complete nothingness, *ex nihilo*.

The difficulty with this interpretation is that in describing the creation of light, the Torah states, 'And God said, (*vayomer*) Let there be light: and there was light.' Radak has proved that the term 'saying' or 'said' in the Bible never appears except in conjunction with 'one who is said to'. Nor do we find that 'saying' ever occurs in the self-reflective form of 'saying to oneself' – as is sometimes found to be the case for 'speaking' (*dibbur*). This eliminates the possibility that with this utterance of 'Let there be light' God was speaking to Himself. We must then conclude that God was speaking to a certain existent matter, and commanded that matter to radiate light. Not that He created, from nothingness, a new form of illuminating matter, but rather that He instructed some form of existing matter that previously had not radiated light, to add a new dimension to its composition, namely, the illumination of light. Were this not the case, and Rashi is correct in asserting that light was called forth from nothingness, who then was God addressing when He issued his command to radiate light?

Darkness which Radiates Light

It is for this reason that most of the classical commentators see the command being given to an already existent matter. Maimonides interprets this as intimating that the heavens, and all their potentials, are here being addressed by God. He willed that from their substance there should come forth a shining matter called *ohr*, 'light'.

In a similar vein, Rabbi Eli Munk notes that *ohr*, 'light', is derived from a basic root, *yar*, which signifies a downwardness or outwardness, the one referring to the emission of rays, the other to their absorption. Thus the Almighty was addressing an already existing but darkened substance, and commanding it to radiate light. This interpretation of light emerging from a previous darkness may be supported by Rabbeinu Bachya, who says that the original light of Day One emerged from the darkness described in the previous verse in Genesis, where it says: 'and darkness was upon the face of the deep'. With this he clarifies the intention of the Zohar with its famous, frequently quoted dictum: *butzeena dekardinusa* – 'the darkness which radiated light'. Accordingly, it would follow that darkness and light are essentially composed of the same substance, with the only difference being either an emission of rays, or their absorption (that is, lack of emission).

The Maharsha, too, seems to agree with the opinion of Maimonides. He writes (*Chagiga* 12b): 'Even before the luminaries [sun and moon] were set in the heavens on the fourth day [of creation] it is written,

"And there was day and there was night . . . ", for even without the luminaries the heavens themselves illuminated and radiated.' With these words the Maharsha postulates a light-source which, completely different from our sun and moon, preceded their creation.

Darkness as an Absence of Light

Subsequently, Maimonides continues to explain the next verse, '. . . and God separated between the light and the darkness', to mean, quite simply, that the distinction that was made was between light, the act of illumination by the heavens, and the ceasing of the heaven's radiation, and hence darkness, an absence of light. Maimonides explains that this darkness is an absence of light, in contra-distinction to the original darkness mentioned at creation's inception (verse 2), which could not have been an absence of light, for light had not yet been created, but rather 'the elementary fire which is dark, for were it red, it would redden the night for us'. Therefore, what emerges according to Maimonides is that there are two kinds of light, the one, elementary fire, being an independent entity which is intrinsically dark, and the other being merely a void of light.

Rashi rejects this explanation of Maimonides, probably because of his view of the nature of darkness. Whereas Maimonides primarily attributes the existence of darkness to be the absence of light, Rashi says in his commentary on the Torah (Genesis 1:14) that 'during the seven days of creation the primeval light and darkness served together both by day and by night'. It would follow that Rashi could not view darkness as the absence of light, since it coexisted with the light simultaneously. Rashi thus follows the majority opinion that darkness is a creation unto itself.

In addition to this, there is a serious difficulty with Maimonides' explanation which may also have led Rashi to reject this opinion because he writes (verse 15): 'In my opinion, the light mentioned here in the verse refers to day, and the word darkness refers to night, for these are their names, as it is written, "And God called the light day, and the darkness He called night." ' The difficulty with this passage is readily apparent. It directly contradicts the words of the Talmud quoted earlier, which specifically notes that these are not their names. Rather, 'called' refers to the fact that He summoned light to reign during the day hours, and darkness during the night hours.

When Were the Sun and Moon Created?

Another difficulty with Rashi's commentary is an inconsistency within the commentary itself, in alleviating a difficulty in the story of creation which all the major commentators confront.

On the first day of creation, as mentioned before, the Torah states,

'God said, "Let there be light", and there was light. And God saw that the light was good, and God separated between the light and the darkness. God called to the light: Day, and to the darkness He called: Night.' Later, on the fourth day, we read, 'God said: "Let there be luminaries in the firmament of the heaven to separate between the day and the night . . . and they shall serve as luminaries . . . to shine upon the earth . . ." And God made the two great luminaries, the greater luminary to illuminate the day, and the lesser luminary to illuminate the night, and the stars. And God set them in the firmament of the heaven to give light upon the earth . . . and to separate between the light and between the darkness' (verses 14–18).

The questions that immediately arise are: (1) If the luminaries (that is, the sun and the moon) were only created on Day Four, how was there light on Day One? (2) What is the difference between the light of Day One, and the light of the fourth day? (3) Concerning both Day One and Day Four it is stated that God separated between light and darkness and established the confines of day and night. In order for the verses not to appear repetitive, there must be some difference in these two seemingly identical acts. If so, what was the difference between the day and night of Day One and Day Four?

Spiritual Light Which Enables Visions

Commenting on these difficulties, the Talmud (*Chagiga* 12a) quotes two different systems of interpretation. The opinion of R. Elazar and R. Yaakov is that the light of Day One does not refer to an exclusively physical entity, but to a supremely lofty and sublime one, a light of spiritual transcendence, with which Adam was able to gaze from one end of the earth to the other. But when God looked upon the generation of the flood and the generation of the dispersion and saw the evil of their deeds, He withdrew it. In their opinion, the light of Day One was unique. Unlike the light we possess today, it was independent of a single, fixed source and was much superior to light as we know it. It was completely withdrawn and on the fourth day God created the sun, which emanated a totally new and far more inferior light of limited intensity and dependent on a single fixed source. There are many disadvantages associated with light emanating from a single source, the greatest of which, of course, is that any obstruction which comes between the light and its source destroys the light completely. Thus this was far inferior to the source-independent light which covered the earth at creation's inception.

But the Sages argue with R. Elazar, and deal with the contradictions very simply. The luminaries mentioned on the fourth day were created earlier, on Day One of creation, but were not set in the heavens in their orbit until the fourth day. Hence the light of the first and fourth day are identical – both having emanated from the sun, the only difference being the location of the light's source. It was not until the fourth day that the sun and moon were set in their current trajectory.

Rashi Embraces Opposing Views

Now Rashi, commenting about the light of Day One, writes (verse 4), 'He saw that it was not fitting that the wicked should use it. And so He set it aside for the righteous in the world to come.' Thus we see clearly that he rules according to the first opinion found in the Talmud, that of R. Elazar.

Yet later, while commenting about the light of the fourth day, Rashi writes (verse 14), 'On the first day they were created, but on the fourth day He commanded them to be suspended in the firmament.' This is of course the opinion of the opposing viewpoint, that of the Sages. Rashi is clearly embracing two alternative viewpoints.

The reason for Rashi choosing the opinion of the Sages regarding the creation of the luminaries on Day One is simple enough. When describing the formation of the luminaries on the fourth day, we observe the Torah's description of *vayiten osam* – 'and God set them in the firmament of the heaven'. Hence it does not say that they were now created, but rather implies that they had existed previously, and on the fourth day He merely placed them in the firmament of heaven.

Why then did Rashi not suffice himself with this second viewpoint, that of the Sages, and how could he quote and interpret the text of the Pentateuch according to two opposing viewpoints?

Moreover, if we are to accept the Sages' explanation and reason that the sun (luminary) was created on the first day of creation and set in position on the fourth day, we will have difficulty in contrasting the difference between day and night of the first day and day and night of the fourth day.

Night and Day in Different Hemispheres

With regard to Rashi's first explanation, the light of Day One was not radiating from a luminary, but rather was source-independent. Instead of darkness receding before oncoming light at dawn and light retreating at every sunset, in other words night and day alternately reigning on opposite hemispheres, another pattern prevailed. As it was not connected to the sun, the light of Day One was not constrained to one hemisphere at a time by the earth's shadow. It illuminated the whole globe continually for twelve hours – and then was completely absent for twelve hours, during which time darkness prevailed over the whole earth. At every point on earth, therefore, a finite time span separated the dark from the light periods.

It was unlike the present whereby at every moment both day and night are found on the globe of the earth, depending on a region's position in relation to the sun.

Later, when God withdrew this primordial light and once again darkness prevailed over the earth, He re-established the light in the form of luminaries, the sun and the moon, on the fourth day. Now that the light was emitted by a single radiating body acting upon the earth, day and night were constantly upon some point of the earth. 'Day' was a term referring to place as well as time, in other words the hemisphere upon which the sun was shining experienced 'day'. Alternatively, 'night' reigned over the hemisphere blocked from the sun's light by the opaque substance of the earth. When the earth later began rotating, a continued process of day and night began with each surface area of the earth experiencing a day and a night within a twenty-four hour period.

According to Rashi's explanation that the light of Day One also emanated from the luminaries, notwithstanding the fact that the location of the luminary was different on the first and fourth day, the nature of day and night would be the same. As the light emitted, in both instances, is from a single source, that would automatically cause light to appear on the hemisphere facing the sun, and simultaneously, night on the opposite hemisphere. If so, the question returns: What was the difference between the day and night of Day One and Day Four?

The Sun as a Focused Fragment of Previous Light

To account for these difficulties and inconsistencies in Rashi's commentary it is fair to reason that Rashi saw a medium between the two aforementioned explanations as to the origin of light. On the one hand, the Torah mentions that the luminaries were not *created* on the fourth day, but rather placed or set. Rashi therefore accepted the view of the Sages that the luminaries had already been in existence since Day One, albeit not in their current position. On the other hand, if they were existing in their present form, a focused luminous body such as the sun is, then there is difficulty understanding the contrast between the nature of 'day' on the first and fourth days. He therefore accepted the opinion of R. Elazar that the light of Day One was a lofty source, an independent light that spread throughout the globe. In accepting both views, Rashi reasoned that although the luminaries had been in existence since Day One, this must not necessarily mean that they were existent in their present form.

In fact, Rivosh comments that although the Torah states specifically that the luminaries were 'set in the heavens', this does not necessarily mean that their previous form of existence was similar to the way they appeared when set in the heavens. Rather, the term 'set' implies that the light, the radiation, already was, and the luminaries may have subsequently come about through a condensation of that original light.

Therefore we could reason that the lofty source-independent light of Day One was not retracted completely. Rather, it was contracted so that a fraction of it remained. That remaining fragment was condensed from being a widely dispersed layer of illumination, to the intensely potent fireball which we today call the sun.

With this interpretation, we can now revert to Rashi's explanation of light from Tractate *Pesachim*. From that explanation we may confirm, and elaborate upon, our conclusions thus far.

As mentioned earlier, Rashi referred to light as an 'illuminating matter which [God] created from the splendour of His garbed clothing'. This euphemism ('splendour of garbed clothing') is taken from a *midrash* found in Bereishis Rabbah. R. Shimon ben Yehotzadak asked R. Shmuel ben Nechman: 'Where did the light come from?' Answered he in a whisper: 'We are taught that the Holy One, blessed be He, wrapped himself in light as if it were a robe and flashed forth His splendour from one end of the world to the other.' Whereupon R. Shimon ben Yehotzadak asked: 'But why are you whispering when we have an explicit verse concerning this – "You covered Yourself with light as a garment!"' Replied the other: 'Since it was taught to me in a whisper, so too do I pass it on in a whisper.'

Now this question of where did the light come from is very much to the point. Earlier, in the name of the Radak, we noted that the term *vayomer*, 'he said', is used only in the event that someone or something has been addressed. In other words, it appears that in this context God was telling existing matter to change its form for another. What then was being addressed and from where did the light emerge?

Intellectual Light

The answer the *midrash* provides is that God 'wrapped Himself in a garment'. Now it should be understood that the absolute light and sublime essence of God is referred to in the Torah as 'light'. As in 'In Your light we see light', and in 'And the light of Israel shall be as fire'. The Sages of Kabbalah refer to it as the primal light – and that which is loftiest, they call the 'Infinite Light', or '*Ohr Ein Sof*'. God's essence, therefore, is the first source of light – the most primary source that is not itself illumined from any other light source since it is complete and absolute.

In Kabbalah and Chasidus it is explained that the mental lights were caused to descend successively from the loftiest intellect and primary light – through many filtering screens and concealing garments. This light was disseminated with the aid of these many screens and garments and windows until it materialized in constituting the lowest form of all forms of light, what we see as physical illumination. For the light of intellect is more complete, and the light of the angels (supernal intelligences) is still higher – and so on from rung to rung even higher and closer to the source of light. And the closer the recipient of light is to that first source, the fewer are the screens and garments that separate it from the first light.

It follows that the light which was created on Day One was the result of an emanation from His great light. He had taken from His glory and wrapped it in thick and screening garments which constrained it sufficiently to become light. Then it was further hidden in garments until it became the physical light of the sun and the stars. This *midrash* was therefore transmitted in a secretive whisper. For the real meaning of the statement that light was concealed by the screens is that the first wrapping of the light belonged to the lofty realms, esoteric and hidden from us; but that it descended stage after stage until the final wrapping which is the physical light of our universe. These things were passed on secretly on account of their connection with the hidden realms and disciplines.

Sparks of Light

Malbim, based on this *midrash*, explains that the light of Day One was a substance independent of, and unaffected by, a material source and consisted of sparks of light distributed throughout the cosmos. This, he notes, was 'pure light' which denotes sparks of light solely, in contra-distinction to a 'body of light' which is a luminous mass composed of matter which radiates light.

Malbim then lists three distinctions between this light of Day One, and the subsequent light that followed:

(1) This light was just below, in order of quality, mental light; there was only one screen separating them. It had a distinct preciousness because of its proximity to the mentalities. From one side it was light that is subject to being perceived, and from the other side it was mental light. This is the meaning of R. Elazar's statement quoted before, 'With this light, Adam was able to see [to perceive] from one end of the world to the other.' That mental aspect stemmed from its pointing to the source in the mental realm.

(2) The light of Day One was not localized, filling all space.

(3) The light of Day One enveloped the whole earth on all sides simultaneously and therefore there was uniform day and night over the entire earth at once. This is the meaning of the *midrash*'s statement that God 'flashed forth His splendour from one end of the earth to the other'.

Light Contracted to Form Our Sun

Later, however, when God realized that evil men would arise, He concealed this light for the distant future. This was done because individuals who are immersed in the material pursuits of this world, its folly and passions, cannot withstand such lofty mental light. So the Divine lofty light which illuminated the world in the initial period of creation was thereafter hidden away in a covering, in the sun. The light merged in the sun, which acted as a condensing agent and a screen which concealed this light of Day One and rendered it as physical sunlight. (After this condensation, which was made to form the sun itself, a filtering screen was added that further contracted the light.) The light then became (1) physical, tangible light, (2) localized and confined in one body, (3) radiated from a single source, hence causing day and night to exist upon the face of the earth simultaneously but in different locations.

Thus, the Malbim notes, the sun (or luminary) is referred to as *maor*. As a general rule, when the letter *mem* appears at the head of certain words, it signifies a specific location. Thus *mikdash*, the word connoting the Holy Temple in Jerusalem, means a particular place where *kedushah*, 'holiness', was to be found. Likewise *maor* means a specific location where light was to be found. In other words, the light of Day One was congregated from its expanse and contracted within the sun – hence it is named *maor*, a location for light.

As the sun's light originates from God's infinite, inexhaustible light, it too shines constantly without ever burning itself out or becoming invisible.

The Crown of Intellect

Malbim's definition of the light of Day One being a mental light may also be supported by Chasidus. For it is explained in Chasidic thought that Day One corresponds to the first of the heavenly spheres; *kesser* (the crown) which also represents absolute, divine will. That which was created on Day One corresponds to that which emanates from (is brought into being by) *kesser*, namely the sphere of *chochma* (wisdom, intellect) which represents Godly intellectual light. On Day One, Godliness was revealed in the form of intellectual or mental light.

This also seems to be the view of the Maharsha, who comments, 'Adam's ability to see from one end of the world to the other took place through his mental eye and intellectual faculties.' In other words, the light was a mental light that enabled him to perceive in the mind's eye from one end of the world to the other.

The Sky as a Curtain for Contraction

This explanation of the luminous body we refer to today as the sun, emerging from a contraction and condensation of the lofty primeval light of Day One, is also expressed by Aderes Elihayu, who similarly notes that *maor*, luminary, interpreted literally means 'from the light' (*me'or*). This signifies that the luminaries do not possess their own light, but rather receive their luminosity from the primal light that was obstructed by the firmament, which is what he identifies as the *tzimtzum* – the contraction which converted the spiritual light to physical sunlight. In this he understands the concept of *tzimtzum* quite literally.

This view of our firmament, the sky, acting as a literal, physical *tzimtzum* of the spiritual light, causing it to condense and descend in the form of physical sunlight, may also be the view of the Tosaphists in *Chagiga* 12b. The Talmud states that there exist seven heavens, and that the first and closest to earth is known as *Vilon* – literally a curtain. The purpose of this curtain, says the Talmud, is 'to enter by day, and exit by night': Rashi explains this to mean that the curtain 'exits or comes out of its casing by night and spreads out over the earth (below the sun), thus obstructing the sunlight and consequently bringing about darkness. By day it congregates and re-enters its casing, subsequently the light of the sun illuminates the world without obstruction.'

The Tosaphists disagree with Rashi's interpretation, for if the curtain spreads and obstructs the sunlight at night, the stars and their light would also be obstructed and would not be visible. Therefore the Tosaphists explain the Talmud's passage literally: 'By day the light enters the world and via the curtain the light vanishes.' The Maharsha objects to the Tosaphists' explanation because it seems so illogical that the sun's light is caused to shine and be seen by a curtain spreading over the world and obstructing the sun's light. An obstruction does not induce light to shine; on the contrary, it prevents the light from shining.

Therefore, in understanding the Tosaphists and explaining how a curtain could enhance the radiation of light instead of hindering it, we may postulate that the Tosaphists too understood the sun as being the congregation and condensation of the primeval light of Day One, which, when shone through the 'curtain' which acts as a contracting agent, is converted into tangible physical light. Tosaphos saw this *Vilon* as being that curtain which contracts the light.

An Infinitesimal Ray

That the sun as we know it is only a vestige of its former self, a contraction of a far more potent, intense and sublime primordial light, is a recurrent theme throughout rabbinic writings. Midrash Hane'elam, in a similar vein, states that the luminosity of the sun is only a *kav katon* – infinitesimal ray of the original intensity of the light of Day One. Midrash Rabbah too states that 'the ball of the sun is but a "shade" of the supernal light'. Likewise, Midrash Habahir states that the original light was contracted and only a seventh of that light remained.

Zohar Chaddash and Sefer Habahir call the light of Day One, 'The light which already was [even before the Divine command]', given that the light was contracted from God's primal light. With this, the great kabbalist Rabbi Menachem Rekanati notes the lexicographical similarity of the words and interprets the statement of the Talmud, 'The creation of light, *kadmah*, preceded the [subsequent creation of the] world', to mean that the light of Day One emanated from the *ohr hakadmon*, the primal light which preceded the world.

The Zohar states, in a similar fashion, that the sun resembles a glass which, when a source of light or fire is placed within, radiates light. This signifies that the sun itself does not possess any intrinsic illuminating property, but radiates the light of the primal [sparks of] light which was condensed and compacted into it.

Similarly, Mizrachi notes that the name *meorot* – luminaries – is also applied (at times) to the planets. This signifies that the sun was originally comparable to a dark non-luminous body such as the planets are now. Then on the fourth day, after the creation of vegetation that necessitated the radiation of sunlight, the luminous substance of Day One was gathered into it, making it a self-luminous body.

Rabbinical Postulates in the Light of Modern Science

Thus far this theory of the light of the sun is also accurate in the light of modern scientific thought. Einstein's General Relativity theory has led to the prediction of 'black holes' in space. These strange objects, which can arise from gravitational collapse of massive stars or galaxies, not only do not emit any matter or radiation – hence they are 'black', invisible to an outside observer – in contra-distinction to visible or 'white objects' which emit signals from their interior or reflect back signals hitting them, but are rather black holes which will absorb all matter and energy coming into their vicinity.

Therefore a model for the sun, consistent with our discussion thus far, would be that the sun was originally a 'black hole' which absorbed all the radiation in its vicinity. The sparks of the original primeval light were gathered into its interior, and subsequently the sun became 'white', eventually arriving at its present level of luminosity.

It is not at all far-fetched to say that Rashi postulated the existence of black holes nine hundred years before Einstein. In fact, the existence of black holes is something which the Talmud alludes to explicitly in Tractate *Pesachim*. Commenting on the verse from Psalm 148 which reads, 'Praise Him, all ye stars of light', the Talmud says that there are stars which radiate light, and then there are stars which do not (ibid., 2a).

The Maharal of Prague in his commentary on Rashi, Gur Aryeh, also

Chief Rabbi of the UK and Commonwealth, Dr Jonathan Sacks, himself a former Oxford graduate student, spoke for the L'Chaim Society at the Oxford Union, shortly after assuming office in September 1991.

Rabbi Menachem Schneerson, the Lubavitcher Rebbe, who founded the Chabad House of Oxford in 1988 and later sent Rabbi Boteach to be its director. Himself a graduate of the Sorbonne and the University of Berlin, he takes a very active interest in all of the L'Chaim Society's activities.

Double Pulitzer Prize winner and controversial investigative reporter Seymour Hersh debates with Professor Efraim Karsh, reader at the Department of War Studies at the University of London, on the morality of Israel's nuclear arsenal. The debate was chaired by Mr Ned Temko, editor of the *Jewish Chronicle.* Seymour Hersh wrote *The Samson Option* attacking Israel for its nuclear missiles.

Rabbi Faivish Vogel, director of Lubavitch UK, talking with Lord Jenkins, Chancellor of Oxford University and Sir Zelman Cowen, former Provost of Oriel College and founding senior member of the L'Chaim Society.

Sir Zelman Cowen, Provost of Oriel College and founding senior member of the L'Chaim Society, speaking to Dr Baruch Blumberg, winner of a Nobel Prize for medicine and master of Balliol College, at a L'Chaim Society dinner.

Mickey Duff, Britain's leading boxing promoter, defends the morality of boxing at a L'Chaim lecture.

John Patten, British Secretary of State for Education and Science, whose lecture at a L'Chaim Shabbat dinner provoked large demonstrations and death threats against him from some students because of government cuts to education grants.

Ambassador Morris Abram, a former Rhodes scholar and Permanent Representative of the US to the UN, attacked the United Nations for its bias and prejudice against Israel in a controversial ground-breaking speech at the first Elie Safra Memorial Lecture.

Former Oxford Rhodes scholar and Australian Prime Minister, Mr Bob Hawke addresses the L'Chaim Society at the Oxford Union. Mr Hawke made an eloquent defence of the State of Israel's historical record to a capacity student audience.

Rabbi Boteach presenting Bob Hawke with a koala teddy bear wearing a L'Chaim T-shirt, as a token of his Oxford lecture.

Gary Sinyor, director of the UK surprise hit *Leon the Pig Farmer,* lecturing to students about Jewish film-making.

Mikhail Gorbachev presents Mr and Mrs Edmond Safra with a plaque commemorating their support of the L'Chaim Society.

Professor Colin Blakemore, Professor of Physiology at Oxford and presenter of BBC Television's *The Mind Machine*, participated in the first Science vs. Religion Debate. One of the world's leading experts on the human brain, his laboratory at Oxford is protected by police because of the threats he receives from animal rights activists.

Dr David Berlinsky causes great angst among the evolutionary scientists to his left as he goes on the attack against Darwinism. This debate attracted well over 1,000 students and leading scientific figures such as Dr Richard Dawkins, Professor John Maynard Smith, the leading evolutionary biologist and Sir Hermann Bondi, President of the British Humanist Organisation.

Benjamin Netanyahu, leader of the Israeli opposition Likud party, at the Oxford Union where he brought 1,500 somewhat hostile students to their feet in a standing ovation.

The Rt. Rev. Kenneth Cragg, Anglican Archbishop of Jerusalem, debating the ethics of Christian evangelism against Rabbi Immanuel Shochet of Toronto and Richard Longley, Chief Religious Correspondent for *The Times* at the Gulbenkian Theatre, Oxford.

notes that the Sages, amidst their dispute with Rabbi Elazar, might still agree that the light of Day One was concealed, but not in its entirety. Rather a fraction was retained within the sun.

From all the above we may understand Rashi's view quite clearly, without difficulty or apparent contradiction. Rashi's reference in *Pesachim* to the 'illuminating matter created from the glory of God's donned garment' refers to the contraction of God's primal light to descend into the formation of lofty particles; the sparks of source-independent light which dispersed throughout the entire universe. This too is Rashi's intention at the beginning of Bereishis (1:4), when he speaks of the sublime primeval light which God contracted, since He deemed it improper for the wicked to benefit from such light. That light was therefore contracted and condensed into (the form of) the sun which became the centralized location for a lower level of source-dependent, tangible, physical light which was to radiate from a single source. When Rashi writes in verse 14, 'on the first day [the luminaries] were suspended in the firmament', his intention is not to say that they already existed in their present form. Rather the light which constitutes their make-up already existed, and later on Day Four was contracted into a single, luminous fire-ball that was suspended in heaven.

Stars and Types

One final interesting discussion can be derived from the Talmud's original discussion of light. Remember, an attempted proof is made in the Talmud to the effect that 'light' implies 'night' because it is stated in the Bible, 'Praise Him, all ye stars of light'. This is said to imply that light does in fact mean 'night'.

In fact, though, this is more complicated than it sounds: the verse does not mean that 'light' only exists at night (within the stars), but rather that all stars radiating with light must praise God.

Does this then imply that only those stars that radiate light must praise God, and those that do not radiate light must not? After all, the Bible elsewhere exhorts, 'Praise Him all His hosts'. Rather, this verse concerning the shining stars is teaching us that the light radiated by stars is also considered light. Thus far is the deliberation in the Talmud.

Stars which Give Off No Light

This leads to the interesting question of what is meant by the Talmud's statement concerning stars which do not radiate light. Is the Talmud implying that there are two types of stars: literally that there are stars which radiate light and those which do not? Are there then stars which do not radiate light?

From Rashi's commentary on this passage of the Talmud, it seems that although there are indeed two types of stars, they share a common characteristic. Rashi writes, 'That which the verse states, "shining stars", is not to exclude stars which do not radiate light (that they are not obligated to praise God) for all stars possess light. The verse therefore excludes nothing, but rather comes to teach us that the light of stars is also referred to as light.'

Rashi, then, implies that there are stars which shine and radiate light, and also stars which although they possess light, do not give out that illumination. However, all the stars that we can see in the night sky do indeed possess light. Are there then two types of stars?

Black Holes in the Talmud

One solution to this question would be that the Talmud's reference here is to 'black holes', which are indeed a second variety of star as discussed above. Although they arise from the gravitational collapse of sufficiently massive stars, they are unlike bright stars in that they do not emit any light or radiation (hence they are black to an outside observer). Not only this, but they actually absorb all energy coming into their vicinity. They possess energy and light; but they do not radiate that light. Still, it remains to be proven from a Torah context (or source) that these 'black holes' are indeed categorized and referred to as stars. Until such proof is brought, we may not infer, by assumption only, that the Talmudic reference to two differing types of stars is to black holes. We must therefore search for an alternative solution.

Three Interpretations of Starlight

In *Ohr Hatorah*, written by the third rebbe of Lubavitch, also known as the Tzemach Tzedeck, the statement is made that there are stars which are much larger and of greater mass than the sun, but due to their great distance away from the sun they appear much smaller.

This seems to be in direct contradiction to Maimonides, who wrote in his halakhic magnum opus, Mishnah Torah (Yesodei Hatorah 3:8), that although there exist stars that are manifold times larger than the earth, the largest of all stars is the sun.

The Zohar stated that stars do not possess their own light, rather *the six hundred thousand stars* receive their light from the sun when it submerges itself (at night) below the earth.

A number of difficulties arise as a result of this statement of the Zohar. Maimonides, as well as many other Torah authorities, refer to the sun as a star: for just as the sun is a self-luminous body, independent of any exterior light source, so too are the stars. On the other hand, the Zohar stated that the stars possess no light of their own and merely transmit the light of the sun. According to the opinion of Tzemach Tzedeck there exist stars of much greater size, at a very great distance from the sun. If their light is to be attributed only to the sun, a much smaller and weaker luminary, the light they receive after millions of miles through space would be diminished considerably. Furthermore it is written in *Raziel Hamalach*, an ancient Jewish mystical tract, and it has been confirmed by modern astronomy, that there exist literally billions upon billions of stars. Yet the Zohar referred to only 600,000 stars.

To investigate this, we must return to the biblical narrative of creation. Concerning the creation of the sun and the moon, the Torah relates a perplexing contradiction: God made the two great luminaries, and directly following this comes, 'the greater luminary to rule the day, and the lesser luminary to rule the night; and the stars'. First we are told that they were both great (of equal size), then we are told that one was greater than the other.

To resolve this discrepancy, the Talmud, along with a multitude of *midrashim*, explains that the sun and the moon were originally created of equal size, but the moon was diminished because it complained and said 'it is impossible for two kings to make use of the same crown'. Because the moon demanded greater power than the sun it was punished by being made smaller.

(In a more physical sense, this *midrash* signifies the fact that two great illuminating bodies make it impossible for night to exist. For day and night are results of the fact that a single luminary radiates light upon the face of one hemisphere: the opaque matter of the earth itself prevents the light from penetrating to the other hemisphere, and consequently on the other side of the globe darkness and night prevail. If there were two luminaries of identical luminosity shining upon the face of the earth, then on both hemispheres there would be constant bright light, and consequently night would be non-existent. Hence the complaint of the moon that 'it is impossible for two kings to make use of the same crown'.)

The Light Which Was Extinguished

The Tosaphos Harosh quotes a *midrash* which explains the origin, and meaning behind, the name of the stars. In the process of diminishing the moon, what the Almighty did was to blast it with a powerful force: sparks or chunks of the shattered moon dispersed throughout the heavens. The remaining moon contained only a fraction of its original size, with bits of the once enormous luminary scattered about in the form of small sparks. The moon lost its original luminosity and brightness with the loss of its mass, and subsequently became dark. Likewise, these small fragments do not radiate light as they once did when part of the huge luminary. These sparks thereby gained the name *kochavim*, translated as 'stars', but which literally means 'those which were extinguished', because their light was extinguished.

This *midrash* is fascinating in that it displays the knowledge of our Sages in matters which astronomers are corroborating in the present age. The Kesset Hasofer notes that the description above of the diminishing of the moon is in complete harmony with modern astronomy. Although I have not been able to corroborate this myself and have not found the source of the astronomy's observations which Kesset Hasofer quotes, he maintains that astronomers have recently discovered that there exist within our universe millions of solar systems, many of which possess two equal suns (or stars); the exceptional type of system is our own solar system, which possesses only a single sun. The astronomers have also discovered that there exists a tremendous gap between Mars and Jupiter: they suspect that this void was once filled by a huge star, possibly even what once was a second sun in our solar system. With the procession of time, astronomers, with the aid of high-powered telescopes, are discovering thousands of particle fragments which do not possess their own light but do in fact reflect the light which they receive from the sun. It is suspected that these fragments are remnants of this huge star/sun which, sometime in the distant past, must have exploded and distributed its residue throughout space. There are also astronomers who, on the basis of material structure similarities, reason that the moon as well is a proportional remnant of such an exploded star. If what Kesset Hasofer says can be corroborated, then this is indeed an amazing prediction by the Midrashim and the Zohar, although as I mentioned, I have been unable to corroborate this as of yet. I would be grateful to any of the readers of this book if they could either substantiate or even rebut this claim, based on further information.

Although the Kesset Hasofer made this brilliant parallel with regard to the origin of the moon, he was unaware of the *midrash* mentioned above which describes the origin of the 'stars' as also being remnants of the shattered luminary, the moon. This too is identical with the theory outlined by the astronomers whom he quotes concerning these star-fragments which reflect the light of the sun.

To explain: Torah Shleima takes the above explanation in the *midrash* concerning the origin of the stars a step further by clarifying that the *midrash* does not disclose the origin of all categories of stars, but only one category. Indeed, the Talmud in Brachos states explicitly that there certainly are different classes of stars.

New Types of Stars

With this we may conclude that there are indeed two general types of stars.

There are the prototype stars which (as Maimonides states) are similar to the sun in that they are source-independent, self-radiating, bodies of light. These stars exist in the billions and can be, as the Tzemach Tzedeck says, manifold times the size of the sun. Of course, this is the kind of star which is known to all of us as 'twinkling in the sky'.

Then there are those stars which are similar to the moon, both in composition as well as in that they are, like the moon, non-luminous, dark bodies which lack the potential and intrinsic property of radiating their own light, but rather receive and in turn reflect the light of the sun. So, too, these stars do not radiate their own light onto a particular portion of the earth, but rather channel the light of the sun, which shines upon them even when it is not observed from that hemisphere.

This is the type of star to which the *midrash* referred to as being caused by the explosion of the once awesome moon, and which modern astronomy has confirmed as being particle remnants of an exploded star of which, according to the Kesset Hasofer, the astronomers contend, the moon as well was once a part. Maimonides' comment that no stars are larger than the sun refers to this class of star. Thus Maimonides would not necessarily be said to contradict empirical astronomical observations in which there are many stars larger than the sun.

Indeed it is impossible for them to be larger since they are only fractions of the moon, which was only as large as, and not larger than, the sun even before it was diminished. Based on this premise we may reconcile that which is written in *Raziel Hamalach*, that there exist billions upon billions of stars, with the Zohar which recognizes only 600,000 stars. The *Raziel Hamalach* is referring to the common type of star (self-illuminating, source-independent) of which there exist billions, and the Zohar is referring to the second variety, the broken fragments of the smitten moon, of which, the Zohar tells us, there exist only 600,000.

With this interpretation, we may also clarify Rashi's classification in his commentary, in which he refers to stars which radiate light, and stars which possess but do not radiate their own light. The radiating stars belong to the first category: they radiate their own light without the assistance of an outside source. Then there are those stars which possess light, but this light is merely due to an outside agent for which they are merely a transmitting station. They therefore possess light, but do not intrinsically radiate their own light.

Chapter Fifty-five

DOES GOD'S FOREKNOWLEDGE VIOLATE OUR FREEDOM?

Students crave freedom. It is a very simple formula. There is nothing in life so liberating as leaving home for the first time, when society, friends and family all concur that you are now an adult. And the way in which one asserts and confirms one's adulthood is by making one's own decisions. For many setting out on an independent life of their own, there is a certain attraction in the idea of separation from parents and their values. There is the exciting feeling that the whole of one's life to date can be reassessed, and the next few years altered, by the mere assertion of will as much as by external circumstances. A few symbolize this change by choosing to be known by a new name, and some others feel it gives them the opportunity to reveal their true sexual identity for the first time. The entirely new environment forces young students to confront their attitudes toward personal relationships, ambition and self-motivation, as well as authority. Away from home, the choice to decide the everyday issues of where to eat and what to wear somehow leads to the feeling that more fundamental questions can also be explored independently.

Most students realize that the highly charged atmosphere of college or university is intended to arouse debate, questioning and speculation. The most basic assumptions are scrutinized and the students are encouraged to search for answers in their own minds as much as in the minds of those who have questioned before us: exhilarating as this process can be, it can pose problems.

It is not a secret here at Oxford that a high proportion of tutors delight in destroying a student's whole approach to life: the pupil may be left emptied of any firm basis for his or her being, aware of many contradictory impulses but unable to resolve them into a consistent pattern. Few tutors see the process of reconstructing a coherent ideology as a part of the curriculum. For some students, the convictions they have known since childhood are enhanced and confirmed by this period of exploration, and even gain strength from the exposure to rigorous inspection. Others are left on the wayside of academic debate, uncertain whether their previous trust and ignorance were not in some way more satisfying than their present informed scepticism. A third group bows out of the process, attempting to pretend that it never happened, and bury their unresolved doubts or questions without ever confronting them fully. The rest discover satisfaction in their new outlook on life.

Position of Authority

This is where I come in. In a sense, I serve in place of the student's parents. Mine is the position of authority. I have a title. I am an institution. This has both positive and negative consequences. Positive because the students see in me, and in an affiliation with the work that I do, a consistency with their life prior to university, almost a sense of stability. Many of them still long for their family atmosphere, or at least elements of it. We are the surrogate. But it can also be negative in that I also stand for the rule of law which infringes on the students' right to experiment. Thus my position among the students is a dual-edged sword and either appeals to them or turns them off. Usually, they pick and choose times in which to be close to us. On the one hand, the students crave the kind of beauty they found in their homes which is missing from Oxford, where achievement counts for everything and human closeness is the casualty. On the other hand, they want to choose their own way, and I am part of a long and accepted tradition.

But the students also recognize that Judaism can indeed be part of their experimentation, and to many it is absolutely new. Moreover, just as abandoning strict religious observance is a way in which the more Orthodox students rebel against their upbringing, embracing Judaism serves as the same kind of rebellion for those who come from completely secular homes. Thus I have noticed a phenomenon at Oxford which I have heard is quite common in other major universities: the Orthodox students become less Orthodox, while many of the wholly secular become more observant. There is a point at which they converge and can be constituted as the acceptable face of religious observance at university. Never too much, but not too little either.

The central theme behind all this is that it can never be coercive. So long as the students still feel that it is they who are choosing their own lifestyle, even if it is more restrictive, and life in accordance with Jewish law is necessarily so, the students define it as freedom, not bondage. Therefore the age-old theme of freedom of choice is something which I am questioned about by students on a recurring basis.

Committing Evil vs Being Evil

Every Friday night, after the synagogue service, there is a meal that we all enjoy together. Before we eat I deliver a short dissertation on the weekly

Torah reading (Parsha), but often these lectures open out into informal discussions that are just as fertile in content.

On the occasion of *Parshas Vaera*, which discusses the affliction of Egyptians with the ten plagues, I spoke on a classic problem which is raised in numerous commentaries on the Bible: if God 'hardened the heart of Pharaoh', as we are told in the Bible, then does this not make His subsequent punishment of Pharaoh unfair? In other words, God forced this mortal to behave in a certain pattern, and so was not allowing him genuinely to choose the mode of action for which he was punished, as we would expect from the just and noble God.

One of the solutions to this apparent problem is provided by Maimonides. The crux of his argument is that Pharaoh was not a blank page that God wrote on without his consent: he had already nearly covered the (initially blank) page of his life with the writing of cruelty and despotism. The Egyptian ruler had thereby shaped himself as a man with an intuitive propensity towards evil. He was no longer a man whose actions were wrong or evil, he had actually transformed himself into a person whose first characteristic was evil, much in the way that Hitler was to do thousands of years later. According to Maimonides, when a person such as Pharaoh (or Hitler) repeats evil actions so often, they become a part of their essence. Stated in other words, when a human being chooses the path of wickedness on repeated occasions, he is transformed from being a person who commits evil into an evil person. Such a being is suitable for God to use as an example to other people and nations; as a warning that such behaviour is unacceptable to the righteous God, and as a guide to better actions.

Now, Pharaoh's was a clear-cut case of evil, but there are of course many intermediate steps between being evil and being wrong-headed: our discussion then opened out to consider whether God's knowledge that one is about to perform a wrong or evil act in some way makes that action inevitable.

Maimonides Initiates the Question

In his famous *Laws of Repentance*, Maimonides devotes the whole of Chapter 5 to the topic of 'freedom of choice'. In an attempt to alleviate the difficulties of this obscure topic, Maimonides addresses what has now become the eternal question. He writes: 'If you shall inquire, Is it not so that the Almighty knows everything that happens even before it occurs? Does He know that a certain individual is to be either righteous or wicked, or does He not know? If you say that He does know that this individual is to be righteous, it is then impossible for him not to be so. For if you say that it is possible for the individual not to be righteous but wicked, then God's knowledge is impotent (instead of omnipotent).

'Know, therefore, that this answer's measure is longer than the span of the earth and wider than the sea, and many major principles and profound theological principles are instrumental in its understanding. But remember this foundation which I now lay before you: We have already explained in the second chapter of *Essential Foundations of the Torah* that the Almighty's knowledge is not acquired from something outside Himself, like human beings in which they and their knowledge are two separate entities. Rather, He and His knowledge are one. No man can properly apprehend this principle. For just as mortal man lacks the ability to comprehend the true being of the creator . . . so too can no one apprehend His knowledge (for they are one). We therefore cannot understand how the Almighty knows a person's actions (prior to their commitment).

'Still, it is guaranteed, beyond the shadow of a doubt, that a man's actions are subject to his own personal control, and the Almighty does not incline him, nor decree upon him, to perform a certain deed, or not to perform the deed . . . And this [right to freedom of choice] is the foundation upon which all words of the prophets are dependent.'

The highly critical commentator of Maimonides, Rabbi Abraham ibn David, also known as the Raavad, strongly protests against this statement of Maimonides. He objects that an author should not raise doubts in spiritual matters without being able to solve them properly and thus wear away the faith of the believer. In this context, the Raavad says that Maimonides has raised a serious question, but has left the reader with only sheer belief for an answer. Better not to ask, than to leave the multitude with unanswered questions pertaining to fundamental religious principles.

From this, we see that the Raavad saw no answer contained in Maimonides' statement, but rather a mere assertion that although God's knowledge seems to contradict man's freedom of choice, this is not so, although no explanation to alleviate the contradiction can be offered.

Raavad Attempts a Response

Having made his point, the Raavad runs to the rescue. His own answer to Maimonides' question is that God has intentionally removed from Himself the control of man's actions, and has placed the choice to be righteous or wicked in the hands of the people themselves. His knowledge, therefore, is not a decree upon the person to act in a preordained fashion. Rather, His knowledge of a person's actions is like that of 'astrologers who know of people's future actions by means of an outside force or cause'.

This obscure and somewhat controversial solution will be better understood by a similar solution proposed by Rabbi Moses Almushino, elaborated upon by Rabbi Menachem Schneerson, the Lubavitcher rebbe.

The rebbe explains that when a certain occurrence is known, it is not the knowledge of the occurrence which causes it to happen; rather, the reverse is true: the occurrence is the cause of the knowledge. For instance, if Abe throws a stone into the air with Dan watching, Dan knows that the stone was thrown. The stone was not thrown because Dan knew, but rather the opposite is true. Dan knows because he watched the occurrence. His knowledge is caused by the occurrence, the occurrence is not caused by his knowledge.

Taking this a step further, suppose Abe throws the stone into the air and is certain that sooner or later the stone will fall to the ground. Sure enough, he is right every time. Do we then say this his prediction or knowledge of the stone's eventual fall therefore precipitates or causes the occurrence? Of course not. His knowledge that the stone will fall is indeed prior to the occurrence, but this is not an effect brought about by his prediction. Rather this is due to his knowledge of an outside cause, namely, the forces of gravity. Therefore, even before the stone falls to the ground, he knows it will fall only because he is also aware of an outside effect, the forces of gravity. So again, in this instance his knowledge is not the *cause* of the occurrence, but rather is only the *result* of the outside force which actually caused the occurrence: gravity.

Enter the Fortune-Teller

We may take this yet further by the analogy of a fortune-teller, who predicts the actions and occurrences of a certain Abe who lives in a far-flung area of the world. The fortune-teller's prediction does not affect the free choice of Abe: rather, he knows that Abe, in exercising his freedom of choice, will choose to do such and such. This implies, once again, that the choice of actions which Abe embarks upon causes the knowledge of the fortune-teller, and not the reverse. The choice is the cause, and the knowledge is only the effect. As far as the mechanics of this phenomenon are concerned, it is just as if the fortune-teller gains his knowledge of the event only after the choice has been made. Abe's choice, therefore, is completely unaffected by the fortune-teller's knowledge. On the contrary, the fortune-teller's knowledge is dependent on the outcome of Abe's choice.

In the same vein, we could apply this argument to God's knowledge of human activity. His knowledge is not a decree or a cause for the actions of humans: rather, He knows only as a result of the outcome of our choice. The knowledge is only an outcome of the cause, this being what the person chose. It is as if He knows only after the choice has been made.

Moreover, with respect to God's knowledge, this answer would be more satisfactory than in the case of the fortune-teller. In the latter situation, the riddle is not completely solved. It is true that the fortune-teller's knowledge is only a product of the person's choice; but if so, how could he *know*, and not just guess, the outcome of Abe's choice before it has actually been made? In the circumstance mentioned before, of Abe throwing a stone into the air and knowing prior to the action that it will eventually fall to the ground, he can predict the fall because he is aware of the forces of gravity. But how does the fortune-teller predict the future?

It is quite clear that man is limited in time. For every mortal man there exists a past, a present and a future. Therefore we are right to ask how the fortune-teller, a mortal human living and limited by the present, can see visions of the future. But the same question cannot be asked of God who, by definition, is not constrained by time. Since He transcends any and all boundaries of time and space, in relation to God there can be no past, present or future. As the Midrash Shmuel states, 'Before the Almighty there is no before and after, for He is not within the confines of time.'

It is therefore logical to postulate that God knows what will occur in what we refer to as 'the future' since before Him the occurrence is as if it has already taken place. One must not think of God as existing in the present and looking at a future event as we suppose the fortune-teller is doing. In relation to God the event just is. Before Him, there is nothing which was in the past, or will be in the future. Rather, there is only that which is and has always been, divorced from any constraints or limitation. He therefore perceives all things in accordance with His own infinite existence.

This is therefore parallel to the knowledge which comes only after the happening has already taken place. We have already demonstrated that such knowledge does not affect one's choice since it is only a result of the choice that has already been exercised by God's creatures in what they refer to as their present, but what is to God a component of the eternal.

We now have an answer. God's knowledge of humanity's future actions does not contradict our choice, because God's knowledge even of future happenings is only an outcome of that which already is, and always was, in God's eyes. It is not the foreseeing of something that will be, but rather of something that has always been. For He knows all events constantly. Therefore, no fresh knowledge is ever acquired by Him.

If, then, this is the answer, a simple question arises, Why did Maimonides himself not answer so? Why does he state that the answer to this question is 'longer (more profound) than the span of the earth, wider than the sea . . . we therefore cannot understand how the Almighty knows a person's actions'?

God Cannot Be Said to Result from Any Preceding Cause

The answer above can only be correct if we assume that God's knowledge is comparable to humankind's in the sense that the knowledge is (only) a result of the occurrence. The event is the cause, and the knowledge is the effect.

(In truth, this in itself is a difficult position to maintain. If God knows only after the event, and His knowledge is therefore only an effect, then this implies that this event which He knows somehow preceded His existence. For there was never a time in which God did not know, and being that the cause of His knowledge is the event, then the event must have preceded Him. And being that God is the ultimate cause of all existence, nothing can precede Him.)

This notion was unacceptable to Maimonides, for this rule is dictated by human logic. Our entire argument until now has been that since all knowledge only results from the occurrence, therefore it can have no affect on the occurrence. The occurrence affects the knowledge and not vice versa. True, this rule applies to all human comprehension. But God has none of the limitations that man does. Before Him, knowledge is not the result of the occurrence.

Maimonides explains this concept at length in *Guide of the Perplexed*, Part 3, Chapter 21. In a profound and lucid explanation, befitting this most celebrated Jewish philosophical treatise, Maimonides illustrates the difference between God's knowledge and that of man:

> There is a great difference between the knowledge which the producer of a thing possesses concerning it, and the knowledge which other persons possess concerning the same thing. Suppose a thing is produced in accordance with the knowledge of the producer, the producer was then guided by his knowledge in the act of producing the thing. Other people, however, who examine this work and acquire a knowledge of the whole of it, depend for that knowledge on the work itself. E.g. an artisan makes a box [the clepsydra is meant] in which weights move with the running of the water, and thus indicate how many hours have passed of the day and of the night. The whole quantity of the water that is to run out, the different ways in which it runs, every thread that is drawn, and every little ball that descends – all this is fully perceived by him who makes the clock; and his knowledge is not the result of observing the movements as they are actually going on; but, on the contrary, the movements are produced in accordance with his knowledge. But another person who looks at that instrument will receive fresh knowledge at every movement he perceives; the longer he looks on, the more knowledge does he acquire; he will gradually increase his knowledge, until he fully understands the machinery . . . he cannot know any of the movements before they take place, since he only knows them from their actual occurrence. The same is the case with every object, and its relation to our knowledge and God's knowledge of it. Whatever we know of the things is derived from observation; it is therefore impossible for us to know that which will take place in the future.

> Our knowledge is acquired and increased in proportion to the things known by us. This is not the case with God. His knowledge of things is not derived from the things themselves . . . Those who seek the truth, and admit what is true, must believe that nothing is hidden from God; that everything is revealed to His knowledge, which is identical with His essence; that this kind of knowledge cannot be comprehended by us . . . Such intellect does not exist except in God, and is at the same time His essence.

God and his knowledge are one

This idea is further elaborated upon by Maimonides in his famous metaphysical treatise, *The Eight Chapters*. Maimonides states that where human beings are concerned, they and their knowledge are separate, divisible entities. The proof is that at one point they are void of a certain concept, and only after studying it does it unite with them. The Almighty is intrinsically unified, He and His attributes are one. In a similar pattern, Maimonides states in his halakhic compendium, Mishnah Torah, that one of the 'Essential Principles of the Torah' is to know that the Almighty

> does not know things by means of a knowledge outside Himself, as do we. For we are not one with our knowledge. But the Almighty, He is one with His knowledge from every side and angle . . . We therefore say of Him that He is the Knowledge, He is the Knower and He is the Known. This principle is inapprehensible by human intellect and faculties.
>
> He therefore does not recognize and know the created beings as a result of the beings themselves as we know them, but rather He knows them because of Himself. Therefore, given that he knows Himself, He automatically knows all of the created existence.

Maimonides continues this theme in the *Guide of the Perplexed* (Part 3, Chapter 20), where he explains as follows: '. . . Similarly we say that the various events are known to Him before they take place; He constantly knows them, and therefore no fresh knowledge is acquired by Him . . . His knowledge and His essence are one and the same thing; the [philosophers] likewise demonstrated, as we have shown, that our intellect and our knowledge are insufficient to comprehend the true idea of His essence. How then can they imagine that they comprehend His knowledge which is identical with his essence . . . ? The homonymity of the term 'knowledge' misled people; [they forgot that] only the words are the same, but the things designated by them are different; and therefore they came to the absurd conclusion that that which is required for our knowledge is also required for God's knowledge.'

From the above, the lengths to which Maimonides goes to stress that God's knowledge is by no means comparable with human knowledge are evident. That which we are able to know is only a product of observing that which has already taken place. This is due to the fact that humankind and their knowledge are not one. Our knowledge therefore results from something external.

But God's knowledge is intrinsically unified with His very being. 'His knowledge is identical with his essence.' In effect, He is the knowledge. Therefore everything He knows is due to, and results from, only Himself. He knows and perceives all because of His essence, not because of an outside occurrence or cause. His knowledge therefore is nowhere congruent with that of mankind's. For mankind's knowledge is produced by the occurrence of certain events, but God knows the occurrences *through a knowledge of Himself.*

The Raavad and Rav Moses Almushino's solution, therefore, is unacceptable to Maimonides, since it assumes that God's knowledge is comparable to that of humanity with respect to its acquisition. Maimonides, though, staunchly protests that this is not the case.

God's knowledge, therefore, is a truly profound and highly metaphysical concept, totally beyond human apprehension.

Question answered in a Question

We must conclude, therefore, that when the Raavad condemned Maimonides for raising a question but leaving it unanswered, he misunderstood Maimonides' intention. Maimonides did answer the question, and his answer is that since we, as humans, do not know the first thing about God's essential being, we cannot even dare to consider understanding the mechanics of His knowledge of the future, which is identical with God himself. He therefore writes, immediately after his question, that just as 'mortal man lacks the ability to comprehend the true being of the Creator . . . so too can no one apprehend His knowledge. We therefore cannot understand how the Almighty knows a person's actions.' Maimonides replies clearly that this riddle is not humanly solvable. For when we attempt to comprehend God's knowledge we automatically, subconsciously, apply to Him the same restrictions of our own, limited comprehension. So no human can present a proper solution.

This eternal paradox of God's knowledge versus man's freedom of choice was best summed up by the Ohr Someach who, after a rigorous attempt to resolve the question, admitted, 'Finally we must conclude that there is no answer to this deep perplexity. It is comparable to two individuals who, out in the cold, have but one blanket to cover themselves. When the one pulls, the other is left uncovered, and vice versa. So too, when we properly understand God's knowledge, the freedom of choice is contradicted. And when we understand man's free choice, God's knowledge is contradicted.

SECTION SIX

THE JEWISH YEAR: LESSONS IN IDENTITY

Chapter Fifty-six

IS JOY ELUSIVE?
THE MESSAGE OF SIMCHAS TORAH

If there is one problem which seems to affect all Oxford students on all levels, it is the elusive nature of happiness. From the experience of my five years here, I think it would be fair to generalize by saying that most of the students frequently experience depression. I cannot claim that they are all unhappy most of the time and there is a great number of students who always seem jovial. However, I know there certainly is a very significant number who are unhappy much of the time, and these are the ones who scamper in and out of my office, not really wanting to talk about why their lives are not what they want them to be.

Success Lends Identity

One of the reasons my students avoid conversation on this particular subject is that they feel discussion cannot positively help them. After all, most of the time, if a person is depressed, they are not sure of the causes. However, talking about it really can help, and in two ways: firstly, discussion can help to identify the source of their unhappiness; secondly, hearing that a friend feels for them, or encourages them to believe that they can surmount whatever obstacle is making them unhappy, nearly always cheers them up.

Unfortunately, in the end there is no getting over bouts of depression for an Oxford student, because everyone knows what the root of the problem is: Oxford itself. A young person, detached from home usually for the first time, suddenly finds him- or herself in an enormously pressurized environment. Oxford is a largely unemotional university, an institution which respects performance above all else. The pressure to succeed is immense, and there is no shortage of talent and success to challenge everyone still further. Many students who were shining stars at their secondary (high) schools or other universities are suddenly just another student in Oxford, someone who must work extremely hard in order to make the average grade. If any student comes up against a problem and needs counselling, this is as often as not seen as the next step to failure.

Suicides at Oxford

What this means is that students rarely, if ever, have a feeling of their own essential worth. Their perceived significance, indeed their very existence, lies in their potential to progress, and not in any existential mode of being. It is not enough that they just are. What is perceived as important is what they will be and what they will do. This kind of feeling is all-pervasive, to be found among tutors, parents, and fellow students. It means that Oxford has an inordinately high number of drop-outs and suicides. There is even a 'suicide staircase' at one of the colleges, and barely an academic term passes without us hearing how some forlorn student decided gruesomely to deal with the unbearable pressure.

A particularly sad case involved a young woman, just eighteen years old, who was extraordinarily gifted and bright. She arrived at Lady Margaret Hall in October 1992 from humble beginnings. Everyone had high expectations of her, especially since she had so excelled at an otherwise undistinguished secondary school, achieving the highest marks in the country on two A-levels. Within four days of arriving at the university, she was found hanging from the ceiling of her room at college. The many similar incidents, both 'successful' and unsuccessful suicides, are usually not publicized, partly because they are seen to reflect badly on the university.

It comes as no surprise, then, that I spend so much of my time encouraging the students, and myself I should add, to be happier. Every Friday night without fail, I devote at least one of my short speeches at the table, accompanied by a *L'Chaim*, to pointing out that Judaism is a celebration of life and calls for constant joy. As their rabbi, I am in a unique position to make this point to the students. Firstly, they can speak to me because I am not in competition with them, and they know it. I am not a fellow student, and the perspective of an outsider at Oxford can be most welcome. To an extent, my position outside the academic maelstrom enables them to express to me what bothers them within the university, without them feeling that I too am part of the problem in the way that some of the tutors, or even other students, might be. This is particularly important because for many students the only form of counselling that is known to be readily available is that given by a 'moral tutor', who is often also their subject tutor and may be perceived as the root cause of their problems in the first place.

Secondly and equally importantly, they feel that because I am married with children and have a job, I possess the one thing which they lack, and that is stability. The constant feeling of having to make the grade in order to achieve some lasting significance leads many of the students to feel rather lost. The warm environment of the family is what they seek most.

A Warm Family Atmosphere

For the first three years our activities in Oxford were run from our home, but we outgrew our accommodation there and started to lease our present place in the city centre. While I thought the students would appreciate the luxury and added space, especially on Friday nights, since in our house many had been forced to sit and eat in the kitchen because there was so little room, the students almost universally complain that they miss the family environment present at the house, but which has been lost to an extent at our new, large and office-like premises.

To make up for this, we are particularly keen to celebrate to the full the more joyous Jewish festivals when they come around. Even if the students do not absorb Jewish observance, they will at the very least learn that the essence of Judaism is: that God desires *simcha*, true joy, from His creation. There is always much dancing, singing and *L'Chaim* saying. Invariably, I will tell the students what has become one of my favourite contemporary tales.

Recently I heard a story said to have originated from the outstanding Chief Rabbi of the UK, Dr Jonathan Sacks, and it goes like this. In the process of the Israeli Chief Rabbinate's screening of recently arrived Russian immigrants (to ascertain whether they are truly Jewish), the examiners came across an elderly woman who seemed out of place in Jewish company. They asked her if she had a Jewish name, and she did not. What Shabbat was, but she did not know. 'What then,' they asked her, 'makes you think that you are Jewish?' She replied, 'Well the only thing I can think of is that when I was a child, periodically, my maternal grandfather, who had a flowing white beard and long black coat, would come over to our home, very tipsy, singing these special melodies without words, and bringing a general air of glee into our otherwise dull abode. When my father or mother would try to stop him from dancing on the table, he would shout, "*Kush in tochas!* [Yiddish expletive]." ' There was no answering this, of course. 'Yes,' the rabbis said, 'you must be Jewish, because your grandfather was a Chasid.'

This indeed is the joyful essence of Judaism. The rabbis were prepared to confirm her Jewishness based on the story of her jovial, Chasidic, grandfather although I cannot vouch for the veracity of the story.

The Festival of Joy

Every Jewish festival has its own specific nature and obligation upon the Jewish people. For example, the themes and obligations behind festivals such as Passover, Shavuot and Rosh Hashanah are extremely straightforward. On Passover, we celebrate the exodus of the Jews from Egypt from the bonds of their Egyptian oppressors. The themes of that festival are liberty and freedom, and the obligation is to eat the matza as a reminder that God took the Jews quickly out of Egypt, and also to make a *seder* in which we re-enact, as it were, the exodus from biblical times. With the festival of Shavuot we celebrate the giving of the Torah at Sinai, remembering to give thanks that God chose us as His people and gave us specific laws, religious laws and the Code of Ethics by which to lead our lives. The obligation associated with that holiday is to study the Torah since it was given on that day. Rosh Hashanah, celebrated as the first day of the year because it was the day humankind was created, on the sixth day of creation, 5,750 years ago, therefore serves as a time for us to think through our actions in terms of a day of judgement every year. The obligations associated with Rosh Hashanah are to pray, asking God for another year of life since it is the birthday of all humanity, and also to blow the *shofar*, which Maimonides understands to be, among other things, an alarm clock – a sound of a trumpet blast reminding us that on this most auspicious day we must behave appropriately, adopting resolutions for the coming year and rethinking our direction in life.

One of the festivals whose theme seems at once the most unambiguous and yet the most challenging is that of Simchas Torah. We complete the reading of the Torah, and we celebrate this completion by starting to read it over again. The theme of the day is merriment and the only obligation associated with that day is '*Mitzvat hayom b'simcha*' – to rejoice. Indeed, some of the most beautiful and memorable occasions at Oxford are our Simchas Torah celebrations, which invariably draw approximately two hundred students and continue throughout the night with non-stop dancing. Perhaps I should not mention that we also finish perhaps forty bottles of spirit in one evening, but then our name is the L'Chaim Society.

Commanding our Emotions

Now in the times of the Temple there were two kinds of sacrifices related to sin. One was a guilt offering for a person's sin or mistake, known as a sacrifice for a sin of commission. Then there was a sacrifice for a sin of omission. If it was incumbent upon believers to execute a specific duty (*mitzvah*) and they omitted it, they had to bring a sacrifice to the town. For example, if a man was obligated to put on *tefillin* and did not, he would have to bring a sacrifice. If a Jew was obligated to eat matza on Passover and he did not he would have to bring a sacrifice. The same applies to Simchas Torah: if you are not happy on Simchas Torah, it is analogous to having omitted to eat matza at Passover. For the only obligation upon the day is to rejoice with the Torah and dance with it, to do the *hakafot*, the seven circlings around the synagogue dancing and singing with the Torah.

In everyday life, we accept the need for obligations. If we are tired, we still have to wake up in the morning and go to work. Students still have to study most evenings, even though they would rather socialize with friends. Most people agree that even secular action is not purely associated with what we want to do: it is too important to be left to our selfish natures. So surely it is right and sensible for God to give us religious obligations. No one need consider that unfair. However, the obligation on Simchas Torah is a very special command from God. Many commentaries ask how God could command us to have this specific emotion – to be happy on a particular day. Is God justified in demanding of us that we are joyful, even if we may have no good reason to be? Particularly as not one of us is able to predict the events preceding Simchas Torah, and how we will feel about them. Emotional obligations are apparently more difficult to fulfil than those involving actions.

For example, elsewhere in this book I have made mention of the fact that in October 1991 the former American President Ronald Reagan was due to speak in Oxford. He was going to open our new Oxford University L'Chaim Society Jewish student centre in Oxford city centre, at Carfax. Just seventeen days before his lecture, after six months of preparation and approximately £10,000 of expenses, we were dancing at my house at Simchas Beis Hashoeiva (the intermediate festival of rejoicing, also a good holiday) when I had a phone call from his office in Los Angeles. It was a presidential aide with whom I was co-ordinating the visit. I thought they were confirming some details. Instead, it was the bombshell that the President was cancelling his lecture – he was unable to make it. Three days later, it was Simchas Torah. After six months of my life had been poured into this project of President Reagan's visit, all our finances were in tatters because we had aimed at raising approximately £80,000 in sponsorship; I really was not in the mood to dance. To say I was upset is an understatement.

Nevertheless, Jewish law commanded me to be happy on Simchas Torah and I did my utmost to comply. I had to purge myself of the earlier criticism I lodged against the students. I told myself that my own self-worth is not dependent on whether or not I host an American President. Needless to say, many empty vodka bottles were strewn over the floor that night . . . but I honoured the law. However, the question about the perceived conflict between God's law and our emotions still remains. Is there an answer to it? Is it justified, for example, for the Almighty to demand that we harbour a specific emotion at a specific time?

An Obligation to Love God

A similar question is asked in the commentaries concerning one of the most important obligations which we recite in the Shemah, the most fundamental statement of Jewish belief, on a daily basis: this is the obligation to love God (*ve'ahavta* – the Lord our God). It is readily comprehended that we can be commanded to obey God, to respect Him, to take His words seriously and not to be apathetic to His call, but it may seem inappropriate for the Torah to give commandments concerning human emotions.

Emotions are fine and delicate matters. Our emotional responses are built up not only over years, but over our lifetimes. For instance, even in the Jewish communities where arranged marriages continue to be common, parents may tell their boy to marry a certain girl, or a girl to marry a certain boy, yet they will never tell their child to love their betrothed. That would be unfair. You cannot expect a young person to heed even the call of their parents where love is concerned. Love cannot be manufactured; it can only be freely given. A parent can, however, direct their son or daughter to marry the person they have chosen because they have the interests of their offspring at heart (whether this is an appropriate form of marriage is a separate debate, of course). Clearly, no one expects their son or daughter to give unconditional love – not even in ancient times.

Interestingly, it was also for this reason that the fifth of the commandments – 'Thou shalt honour thy father and mother' – says nothing about love. The obligation is only to honour one's parents, but not necessarily to love them. The Torah understands that often, because of the intensity of feeling that exists in families, a child may not necessarily love his or her parents at all times. Often the child feels anger and frustration, perhaps even hatred. This is the nature of the human condition and perhaps is unavoidable in a relationship predicated on authority and a generation gap. The Torah is saying that although one may feel such things, one must still honour one's parents; they cannot be dismissed. It would be unfair to demand love at all times in this circumstance, and virtually all humanity would be faced with a possibly unavoidable transgression.

Yet having said all this, and made allowances for our human frailty, we are still commanded to love God. Likewise, the Torah commands, 'You shalt love a convert in your midst.' These emotions are apparently so important that they cannot be left to human choice; God has decided for us what we should feel. Still, these are particularly formidable obligations to fulfil: are they fair demands?

Are Human Beings Naturally Happy?

The questions that we have raised are all predicated on a specific philosophy. This philosophy is that human beings are not naturally happy, and that commanding them to feel joy on Simchas Torah or love for God or a co-religionist is unnatural and artificial. How can we expect people to respond to something which may be almost impossible for them on that specific day? How can we ask them to essentially transform their inner selves and experience joy when they just don't feel it? The reason the Torah can command us and is yet scrupulously fair in the matter is that it regards the common philosophy that people are unhappy as misleading. The Torah says that the congenital state of humankind, even from earliest infancy, is joy.

Empirical observation suggests that children naturally play and are joyous. Instead of requiring a reason to be happy, they need a reason not to be happy. Deny them chocolate and they may cry; but otherwise they will frolic very happily. It is a commonplace to say that adults envy the joy and innocence of the child. Indeed, joy and innocence are seen as intrinsically one. One of the reasons we adults envy the state of childhood is not only because it precedes any mistakes which we may have committed in our adult lives where we are responsible for our actions, but because childhood is filled with memories of constant joy and running amok, rather than worry and anxiety.

A child knows of no hurt, no responsibility, no obligations or duties, and therefore the child is purely and naturally happy. All of us grow up in a state of joy and happiness: it is because of the pressures and oppositions of life which descend upon us as we grow older – going to school, facing homework deadlines – that we suddenly discover there are reasons not to be happy. Then greater responsibilities come upon us: we get married, we have children; we have to support families and face all the bills that come flooding in. The anxiety caused by such responsibility is considerable and sometimes enough to suck the life out of any human. We must face being subservient to bosses, tax inspectors, and governments.

It is as if we can suddenly give ourselves myriad reasons not to be happy. But if those harsh lessons could be removed, I believe we would be happy. The biggest question that affects every single one of us as we grow up is what happened to the happiness of our youth? Why has it suddenly waned and disappeared – can't we reverse the unhappiness which we feel? By the time we reach adulthood, it seems as though emotionally we are the exact opposite of children. Adults seem fated to be unhappy, and need reasons to be joyful. A recent psychology poll in the United States, published in the *International Herald Tribune*, found that 67 per cent of all Americans admitted that they were 'unhappy' much of the time, and some 30 per cent admitted being 'significantly unhappy' more than half the time. People say, 'I will be happy if I only pass my exams; if I get that job; if I get engaged to the wonderful person I am seeing; if I get a raise,' and for a while this indeed works. But as soon as our expectations are fulfilled, we need other reasons to make us happy. We are addicted to happiness like a drug, experiencing one brief high followed by a period of depression waiting for the next 'fix'. An even more astounding figure produced by this poll was the fact that the number one way in which people rid themselves of depression is by going to the store and buying something, like purchasing oneself a gift. Can there be any greater indication of how we search for things to make us happy since we do not feel so naturally?

The Torah says that our obligation on Simchas Torah is wholly within our ability, for to be happy is our natural state. Focus on our blessings and not our tribulations: that is the way to contentment and joy. This, then, is the reason why it is totally justifiable for the Almighty to demand joy on Simchas Torah. He is not demanding that we generate a non-existent emotion, which indeed might not have been fair. What the Almighty demands is that we merely bring our innate, latent happiness to the fore. This is one of the reasons we toast *L'Chaims*. The purpose is not to induce an artificial state of happiness through drink. Rather, we seek, by blessing our anxieties and lowering our defences, to allow our true selves to be manifest: a happier, more joyous self.

Recommendation to Achieve Happiness

I would recommend to whoever has reasons to be sad on Simchas Torah – or any other day of the year for that matter – that they list ten principal reasons for their unhappiness, and then sum up the courage to show this to their best friends, people whose respect they desire. Few of us would be brave enough to reveal that list full of petty gripes and grievances. Would we dare to show our list to a survivor of the Holocaust, or to someone who has experienced tremendous tragedy in life? Thank God, life nowadays is not as bad as it used to be. Whenever we speak about the 'Good Old Days', we know in our hearts that they never existed. The 'Good Old Days' are now, when we can feed our children and clothe them, even though we are often under pressure to spend more than we earn on things we do not really need.

Let us, instead, focus our attention on those areas of life which bring joy to our hearts, that replenish our natural state of happiness. The Torah is not asking the impossible: it is not demanding that we entertain an emotion which is not congenital or fundamental to our existence.

A Natural Attraction to God

The same applies to the commandment to love God. Judaism believes that every created being has a natural disposition towards affection and attraction to their Creator. We observe how children naturally cling to their mother's dress and skirt. Everything pays homage to its origin, so surely we are disposed to love God. The problem is that all too often petty concerns and trivial pursuits cast a shadow over our hearts. We chase the phantoms of material success and wonder why we are not fulfilled. But Judaism, when it says we should love the Lord our God, is reawakening the natural congenital love that every Jew harbours for his or her Creator.

That the Jew does possess this love is amply demonstrated by the martyrs we have had through the generations. The greatness of the Jewish martyrs was not their number, the quantitative edge that we have over other religions; on the contrary, the greatness of the Jewish martyr was the qualitative edge, in other words the type of person who was willing to sacrifice all for their faith. In every religion, one would normally expect a martyr to be a teacher of religion, a priest, or a saintly individual, but the great majority of the Jewish martyrs in all ages were not part of the formal hierarchy of their religion. Most were uneducated, and many were completely estranged from their religion, yet they would not allow themselves to forsake their God and their religion for the promise of material or even spiritual advantage. The Jews who appeared to convert to Catholicism in the Spanish Inquisition proved to be fake converts; although they knew they were forfeiting a tremendous amount, they were willing to die for their religion. They were not rabbis: on the contrary, they were people who were originally willing to feign conversion in order to preserve their social status and wealth, but they finally chose to preserve their heritage instead. The same applies to the Jews of the Holocaust: although Hitler killed six million Jews, no Jews stood up at Auschwitz to curse their Jewishness. They were going to die for no other reason than that they were Jewish, they were given no way out, and the only thing they were given was a choice to at least curse their Jewishness and damn the fact that they were Jewish and had to die because of it. Yet in all the different histories we have of the Holocaust, there is no record of any significant number of Jews damning themselves and their Jewishness just before death.

Appreciating the Whole Picture

The easiest way to summon up the happiness or joy which Judaism believes to be natural is to accept our trials and tribulations. Instead of expecting life to be 'heavenly' we must embrace our problems as they occur, and rise to meet them. We should see them as an integral part of our lives. For example, a parent who has a child who is crippled may rage against fate. 'My child should have been able to walk. Why did this happen to me?' Yet a more positive approach is to see the child in all his or her life and wonder, not merely as a disability incarnate. If the parents were to focus on how fortunate they are to have a child in the first place, instead of having a crippled child, they would be infinitely happy. How many people try unsuccessfully for years to bear children? Stated in other words, the attitude of the parents should be, 'I am blessed with a child, but he has a disability.' Not the other way around, which is, 'I have a disabled child.' The disability poses no contradiction to the blessing of having a child. It is something external which must be dealt with in a manner that does not cause us to lose sight of the essential blessing inherent in having a child in the first place.

The same rule can be applied to life. Instead of complaining that our destiny should have been otherwise, and expecting our lives to be smooth rides without bumps, we must see the whole picture – just as the parent comes to appreciate their whole child, and not only the problem of disability. Our life is a great journey. Sometimes the road is smooth, and sometimes it is annoyingly bumpy – and we deal with it in as happy a way as we possibly can and allow joy and enthusiasm to dictate all of our actions. We cannot let the pitfalls hold up our journey. The road lies ahead and we must follow it, whatever we encounter.

What It Means to Be Happy

In my opinion, the basic definition of happiness is to look forward to the next hour, the next day, with enthusiasm and tremendous energy. The will to live and look forward to every moment of life is true joy. By contrast, depression is when we dread having to confront or endure any additional experience. We just want to be left alone.

Cast off depression by looking ahead to tomorrow, when we will wake invigorated and ready for new challenges. This is what we should aspire to, especially on Simchas Torah. And let us hope that the joy we achieve on this one day will also permeate our entire year ahead.

Chapter Fifty-seven

RESOURCES, RESPONSIBILITY AND THE REASONS FOR ANTI-SEMITISM

As discussed elsewhere in this book, every Sunday night we stage a Point-Counter-Point session in which a student volunteers to debate with me on a topical issue. Often these debates see me cast in the role of defending highly unpopular traditional Jewish positions on social concerns, such as pre-marital sex, Jewish women's issues, and the role of religion in Israeli politics.

One of the most difficult topics ever debated against a most worthy opponent was that of whether Jewish money and resources should be spent on non-Jewish charities. My opponent was a highly intelligent Jewish Rhodes Scholar from Harvard, who has one of the most methodical and analytical minds I have ever encountered. This debate was of such great interest to so many students that we decided to move it to Friday night, after the Shabbat meal. In the final analysis, I was surprised that the students found my arguments more convincing. My surprise was largely due to the fact that I myself began with very mixed feelings about the subject, and thus feared I would not passionately affirm a focused and coherent argument.

A History of Philanthropy

One of the reasons for the considerable student interest is the fact of Oxford itself. Oxford is a city with a proud heritage of innovation and philanthropism. There are hundreds of voluntary organizations and charities, and of course there is the international work of Oxfam, based in Oxford; all these testify to a desire to go out into the world and do something to make it better. This is not confined to a concern for foreign parts: in recent county council elections, Oxford returned the first ever Green councillor in the country, a remarkable achievement considering that Britain's electoral system is that of 'first past the post', and automatically favours the long-established larger parties. Although her election has been interpreted as an expression of the country's dissatisfaction with the Conservative and Labour Parties as much as anything else, it is also an indication that this city is willing to be different and say that the traditional parties are not doing enough to address issues which are increasingly seen as important. I can certainly not agree with all the politics of the Green Party, which is radically socialist and many of whose policies have been interpreted as being extremely hostile toward Israel. I do, however, feel that Oxford's willingness to be different and to address the really pressing social concerns is something to be applauded.

Responding to Holocaust Revisionists

The monies which make our work in Oxford possible are comprised entirely of private donations. It is I who must produce the funds, and as a result I have learned a great deal about fund raising. The very first rule one learns is that of the limited availability of resources. It would be wonderful to have enough funds to stage all the events which one has planned, but it completely defies reality. Thus choices must be made and it is always difficult to choose where resources are best employed. For example, a recent meeting of the Oxford Anti-Nazi League had as its speaker Esther Brunstein, a survivor of the Lodz Ghetto, Auschwitz, and Bergen Belsen. It may come as a surprise that I was not interested in attending this meeting to 'Stop the Nazi Lie of Holocaust Denial'. Attempting to stop people from saying that the Nazi atrocities never happened seems pointless: of course they happened, everyone knows they did, and there seems little purpose in fighting a lie that no one believes anyway thus lending credence and respectability to those who seek to promote these views. Perhaps the best response that I have ever seen to Holocaust denial was that of Professor Alan Dershowitz of Harvard. When challenged to take part in a debate against Holocaust deniers, he insisted he would only do so if they would also agree to debate the existence of the tooth fairy and Tom Thumb.

There is hardly a lecture or publication about the Holocaust today that does not give two kinds of culprits the responsibility for the terrible darkness that fell upon the world during the Hitler era. Of course there were the direct assailants, but there were also the passive bystanders: their inactivity allowed the atrocities to begin and to continue.

We speak of the Nazis who perpetrated the killings, but we speak with equal horror of those who must have known what was going on but did nothing to prevent it. We condemn 'the silence of the nations'. Most people barely uttered a protest when the terrible Nuremberg laws were passed, or even when it became known that there was an active programme of liquidation against the Jews and other unwanted peoples of Europe. We speak of President Roosevelt who refused to bomb the train lines which linked Auschwitz with the ghettos of Europe, without which the 'Final Solution' could not have been executed. We speak of British White Papers which curbed Jewish immigration in Palestine, ensuring that Jewish refugees from Europe would be forced to return to the Nazi ovens. And we speak of the citizens of all nations who went about their daily lives while the world Jewish population was halved.

Some see this silence as a world conspiracy against the Jews, and there are many commentators who perceive a bit more than a hint of anti-Semitism in the supposed stone-walling of the Allies and other nations. It is implied that while these people would never have actually *aided* the Nazis in ridding the world of the Jews, they would not actively intervene either. The world's indifference to the plight of the Jews is taken as an indication of lack of interest in a world with Jews.

Are Jews Equally Guilty of Silence?

If indifference is to be interpreted as a mild form of malice, it should be remembered that there was no great outcry from the world Jewish community when Pol Pot destroyed three million of his people in the killing fields of Cambodia; when Mao wiped out twenty million Chinese peasants; or when Stalin starved twenty million peasants to death. Nor, for that matter, does one hear any vociferous Jewish condemnation of the slaughter of *ninety-five per cent* of Europe's Romany (gypsy) population at the hands of Hitler.

Now of course, any analogy between the Nazi persecution of the Jews and Khmer Rouge or Stalinist/Maoist victimization of their own people is misguided and untruthful. In the case of the former it was a clear and unprecedented programme of genocide, while in the latter case there was no specific target for victimization, other than a supposed desire to establish new economic norms. None the less, the fact that in both cases millions of people suffered and died cannot be overlooked, and the lack of sufficient intervention and response on the part of the world Jewish community and its representative bodies is troubling.

Passive Indifference and Active Hatred

I do not agree that the world's unconcern for the gassing of the Jews during the Hitler regime was motivated by anti-Semitism. Rather, it was straightforward and simple indifference. The same indifference which leads us to turn to the next page of the newspaper on reading that a small child has been run over by a car is the indifference which leads us to ignore the plight of whole nations other than our own. In both cases it is not we, or one of our own, who is suffering, and so the pain does not strike very deep into our hearts. Upon reading that an innocent man has been shot dead in his store by armed robbers, we may indeed sigh while we turn the pages of the newspaper and mutter something about how sick the world has become, but our day is hardly affected. On the other hand, if we discover that this was someone whom we knew; or a co-religionist; or, much worse, a close relative, then we are deeply affected and the degree of pain is exactly related to the degree of our attachment to the victim.

As human beings, we are first and foremost sensitive to the suffering of ourselves and those we love and cherish, with everyone else taking a very distant second place. Thus during the Holocaust the only reliable ally which the Jews of Europe had were their fellow Jews in other countries. The same has been true throughout history. The Talmud states that, although the exile of the Jews from the land of Israel, and their subsequent dispersion throughout the Gentile lands, seems a curse, there is also an inherent blessing in it. This way, when one Jewish community is being persecuted by a wicked ruler or regime, their brethren from another country can step in to assist and apply pressure for the assertion of their rights. In recent years there has been tremendous political, economic and social pressure exerted by the United States upon the former Soviet Union because of its ill-treatment of Soviet Jewish dissidents. This pressure in its turn was due almost entirely to American Jews demonstrating and actively lobbying Congress and their senators.

An Enviable Spirit of Togetherness

Jews throughout the ages have had an enviable spirit of togetherness and community that has operated on many different levels. Almost all established Jewish communities, from the distant past to the present, had and continue to have a form of social security: a community chest for the poor, a free-loan society for those who have fallen upon bad times, a poor brides' fund, various educational funds, rabbinical courts to try their own constituents and ensure that there is justice available to all, and finally warm and open homes to guests and strangers. It is no exaggeration to state that hospitality is a central tenet of Jewish home living. Jewish communities throughout the world are famous for their hospitality to co-religionists, and one of the oldest Jewish customs is to scramble at the conclusion of synagogue services on the Sabbath to invite home as many guests as possible, before the other householders beat you to it.

In the medieval world, and later for hundreds of years in Russia, ruthless highwaymen and pirates kidnapped Jewish people knowing full well that they were more valuable for gold than other victims. This was because they would always be ransomed and redeemed by their concerned fellow Jews.

Is Jewish Togetherness Exclusionary?

The question that arises from all of the above is whether or not this community loyalty is proper. Perhaps Jews are devoted to their own people and causes to the *exclusion* of other peoples? It seems fair that Jews, by virtue of their own suffering, should have an even greater obligation of care towards other oppressed minorities.

I believe passionately that the global Jewish community should first and foremost be committed to themselves, but by no means exclusively so. The great majority of available resources must first be allocated to Jewish concerns. I maintain this position for two reasons which I shall discuss below, but briefly they are as follows: without a concern for oneself and those dearest to one, it is impossible to care for others; secondly, the world needs the Jewish people, the contributions which we have made and continue to make to civilization, the values which we have transmitted to the world, and that which they symbolize.

Caring for Family Before Others

Imagine a wealthy businessman who is stingy and uncharitable. He buys himself the cheapest clothing and spends nothing on his own family. They live in a small house bursting at the seams, and his children wear second-hand clothes that never fit. One day, a man knocks on the door. He tells the businessman that he is collecting for a family which has fallen on hard times. The bank is threatening to foreclose on their house. If they do, they will be forced to move to a tiny apartment. Also, the man has a daughter who must be given a respectable wedding. He is asked to help. Can you imagine that his response will be anything but 'What's wrong with them living in an apartment? If he can't afford luxury, then let him not have it! And if he doesn't have the money to give his daughter a proper wedding, let her get married in a Registry Office.' If he doesn't spend money on himself, will this man spend it on anyone else?

When the world Jewish community spends money on itself, by emphasizing the importance of Jewish education, and lobbying politicians to alleviate the plight of Jews in places such as Syria, we ensure that by extension we remain sensitive to the plight of others in general.

Human and Divine Goodness

Judaism accepts that there are two levels of ethics operating in our world. The first are humanly instituted and may even have been instituted without a Divine command from Sinai. This may be referred to as plain human goodness. The second category is that of divinely revealed ethics, rules for living which no human would have instituted alone: this is what we refer to as 'altruism', the ability for human beings to transcend their natural limitations and put the needs of their fellows first.

An example of the former ethical consideration is the prohibition against theft and murder. Human logic dictates that if we all steal from each other, or murder each other, the world will descend to a state of anarchy and chaos; it would be uninhabitable. The very fact that humans exist necessitates the institution of laws preventing such crimes.

An example of the divinely inspired type of ethics is the biblical command to send away a mother bird from her nest when taking the eggs. Human logic would not have dictated that human beings must display that degree of sensitivity toward an animal, but God demands consideration even for those beings with which we do not have emotional connections. What is even more surprising is that this is one of two commandments for the fulfilment of which one is promised long life in this world.

The other commandment is that of honouring one's parents. The human intellect might naturally accept that one must respect elders because without authority in the world civilization must descend into a state of dark lawlessness. This is a common-sense ethic. However, Judaism maintains that even if a parent unfairly abuses or severely humiliates him or her, the child dare not be abusive in return. Normal logic would be understanding of a child who rejected parents who insulted or abused, but Jewish law would condemn them and hold them accountable for their actions.

It is this lower level, the specifically humanly espoused ethics, which we were discussing above. Even without a God, and even if a person rejects the existence of God, each individual understands that it is wrong to injure another person merely because everyone can comprehend his or her own pain. Even if God had omitted the command not to steal, we would still know how upset and hurt we are when we are stolen from, and be wary of inflicting such hurt on other people. Had God not commanded us to avoid embarrassing each other in public, we would still understand how much we hate being humiliated. And even if God had not commanded us to feed the hungry, we would still understand how badly we want others to help us if we are in need.

By extrapolating beyond our own hurt and pain and applying it to others, we come to understand that we have a moral imperative to fulfil the words of the great Sage, Hillel the Elder, who proclaimed, 'That which you hate, do not do unto others.'

Transcending Differences to Achieve Harmony

This ability to extrapolate is the reason that although there are so many different religions, cultures and governments on this earth, we are all able to live together in harmony. Since we are all human, there is a certain level at which we are all the same and are motivated and hurt by the same occurrences. At some level we can all agree that murder, war and aggression are wrong, except in certain very limited circumstances.

If a person has lost the ability to extrapolate, or if a person does not feel for others because he or she simply cannot feel their own needs, then there is no hope for harmony in the world: civilization as we know it will be entirely lost.

Therefore, if Jews cannot first and foremost feel and care for themselves, there is little likelihood that they will truly feel for others. It is for this reason that our resources must first be spent on Jewish concerns. This should not of course lead to the exclusion of other ethnic minorities: a significant portion of our resources must be dedicated to others as well. However, there is no question that Jews must come first. We are a people and the same way in which a family has responsibilities first and foremost to each other, the same applies to the nation of Israel.

Arrogance which Masquerades as Goodness

I would even argue that there is a certain sense of falsity, even a lack of morality, in putting others before the ones you are responsible for.

A few years ago in Oxford there was a student who came from a very difficult family situation. His relationship with his father was terrible; he accused him of being a careless absentee parent. What seemed to bother this young man most was the fact that his father was interested in impressing and caring for the whole world, without first worrying about his immediate family. The student told me that his father was an immigrant to the United Kingdom, having come from an impoverished family background from the Middle East. Once a year, his father would go back to visit his brothers and sisters, now living in Israel, and would take away with him suitcases filled with gifts for his nephews and nieces.

'He never bought us anything,' the student told me, 'and if he didn't have the money it would never have bothered me. But once a year I watched him pack those suitcases, and as a child I wished that I had been given some of the things which he was taking to Israel. I would pick something up and say, "Dad, can I just keep this?" but he would stuff it back into his suitcase and brush me off. I hated him for that.'

There is a repellent, inhuman quality to the above story. A father must first care for his children, and only then can he begin to worry about all those who surround him. If you choose to bring a child into the world, that child becomes your first charge and responsibility.

Likewise, if Jewish people around the world were well fed, educated and successful, and if there indeed were tens of millions of us, then we would have an obligation, being secure ourselves, to help all those around us.

The present situation is nothing close to this comfortable ideal. Everywhere we turn we witness a global state of Jewish ignorance and non-commitment. Jews are disappearing at an increasingly alarming rate, victims both of persecution and intermarriage and assimilation. For every Jewish child who is receiving a Jewish education, there are ten who are not. For every Jewish adult who is growing in Jewish commitment, there are ten who are floundering. Predictions made by the Harvard Center for Semitic Studies are that by the year 2020 there will be less than three million Jews in the United States, from a current figure of nearly six million. Similarly the rise of the Zhironovskys of this world in places with large Jewish populations like Russia is extremely worrying and people living there are far from secure. How can we possibly dedicate the bulk of our resources to others when we are sinking ourselves?

A Ship that is Sinking Cannot Save Another

A close friend of mine from Spain comes from a difficult background. His parents had an awful marriage, which drove his mother to suicide when he was twenty. The tragedy left him terribly confused. In quick succession he lost his job and broke up with his long-standing girlfriend. Then he was unemployed for years, doing nothing but go to nightclubs with a terrible group of friends and burning his life away. Something needed to change in his life, he needed a fresh start. At last he was offered a job and a new way of life by his uncle, who lived in a different city. He phoned to tell me he had turned it down. The reason he gave was his younger brother, only eight when his mother died. My friend felt he had to look after the youngster, and said that if he left he would be abandoning his brother.

That is true, I told him, but what possible life can you offer him in your present state? As he grows up, will you show him round nightclubs and make him a witness to the steady stream of one-night stands passing through your apartment? Better to first establish even a limited degree of permanence and stability in your own life so that you will have something worthwhile to impart to your brother. One ship that is sinking cannot save another.

Rabbis Who are Politicians

It is for this reason that I am most perplexed by the actions of the large number of Reform and Liberal rabbis who are actively involved in various political campaigns. The causes they espouse are laudatory and necessary. They campaign for human and civil rights on behalf of blacks and native Americans, people for whom the American system clearly does not work. Can anyone fault them? Yes, because they are rabbis who are meant to be teaching Judaism. If their political activities do not conflict with their rabbinical duties, then we must applaud and emulate their examples. However, if they do, then they have a misguided understanding of their responsibilities.

It is specifically Reform rabbis and the other clergy members, those who minister to the less committed Jewish denominations, who should be the most dedicated first to their work as rabbis. These communities are the ones most in need of the contribution of a Jewish teacher. They have the highest rates of intermarriage and assimilation. Will no one curb it?

Commitment to Judaism should not just be seen in those areas of our lives which are obviously Jewish. It should be part of a holistic Jewish attitude to our lives and those things which inspire and motivate us. A Jewish student at Oxford who was applying for entry to the Stanford Business School in California called me up with a question. As part of his application, he had to write eight essays, one of which went something like this, 'If you could meet any four figures in history, who would they be and for what reason?' The student wanted to know what I would respond to the question.

I answered that I would be most interested to meet the four different people who best exemplified the specific character traits which I maintain are the most precious in humanity, for the purpose of discovering their secrets, and how they lived by these tenets. I listed Moses, for his humility (after all it is quite impressive that a man who used to communicate with God 'face to face', as the Torah says, can also be described as being 'the most humble human upon the face of the earth'); Hannibal, the great Carthaginian general, for his tenacity and determination (imagine leading ninety thousand men with food and supplies, horses and elephants in tow across the ice-capped Alps, losing half your number en route, and then, on descending, immediately launching a successful attack against the Romans!); Abraham Lincoln for human kindness and goodness and indefatigable leadership (he freed the slaves, although admittedly there was also a political consideration, and generally provided the will for the Union to remain together when most felt it was a lost cause); and finally Maimonides for the most incredible breadth and depth of knowledge, and being so prolific, amidst the most difficult circumstances (he wrote the first codification of Jewish law, which was so comprehensive that it has never been duplicated, also a commentary on the entire Mishnah, the definitive work of Jewish philosophy, and many other extraordinary works. Yet at thirteen he and his family were forced to flee Spain and its tyrannical Islamic regime, then lived briefly in Israel but had to leave because of the devastation wrought on the land by the Crusades, and finally settled in Egypt where most of his day was taken up serving as chief physician to the court of the Sultan Salachadin).

The student thanked me for my advice, but when I had put the phone down it occurred to me that I had made a mistake. Undoubtedly, there have been great non-Jewish personalities throughout the ages, and I had listed two of them, but surely there were Jews who would have exemplified these traits as well as they did. Why then did I not seek to derive inspiration first and foremost from my own people? Especially since my first priority is to give the modern Jewish student a sense of pride in the amazing tradition of which we are a part. Now, if a student's biggest heroes are Jewish, then that student will seek to preserve the memory and values of these extraordinary figures, and ensure that our people will never diminish.

To be sure, I believe the same is true for all nations and for all ethnicities. Because so many non-Jewish students frequent our events, I am often asked whether our society has a cohesive philosophy. My response is unequivocal: to inspire within all our members a sense of pride and elation in their own respective histories and traditions, within an overall universal and Godly framework.

Importance of Jewish Education

The argument that Jewish people should spend their resources first and foremost on themselves is similar to the argument for Jewish education preceding any other. If a child is not given a thorough grounding in his or her roots in the first stage of life, the chances are that they will retain very little of that identity later in life. That is why there is a need for *yeshivahs* and Jewish day schools. This is not to say that the child should not later study Greek philosophy, English literature, or Chinese history and culture. It is to say that in order for a Jewish child to develop and retain a Jewish identity, then Jewish education must be the first thing on the list of priorities. It is not even enough to have studies when he or she is young. A Jew must return to it over and over again throughout life.

If we do not allocate our resources first and foremost to ourselves, there is little hope that later in life there will be something of the Jewish nation left to preserve. And how can we dedicate ourselves to the advancement of other peoples if we cease to exist?

Judaism is Essential to Overall Human Goodness

This brings us to the second reason for spending our resources first and foremost on ourselves: because Jewish existence is central to the overall goodness of mankind.

Three thousand and three hundred years ago the Jews stood at Mt Sinai waiting to receive the Torah. That episode was to prove the greatest event – transformation even – in the history of humanity. For at Sinai, the Jews were charged with a Divine mission to bring the knowledge of God, and the accompanying laws which He commanded, to the nations of the world. They were chosen to be a light unto all peoples to cause the message of Godliness and goodness to permeate the earth. No longer would the world be run by force. No longer would 'might make right'. The earth's inhabitants were being informed that there is a Supreme Judge of the world, an arbiter of good and evil. He would exact punishment from those who deserved it, and bless those who led exemplary lives. He would reward, applaud and encourage acts of loving kindness while simultaneously rooting out real evil from the earth.

One of the immediate results of this event was that terrible, age-old curse which would for ever plague the Jews: anti-Semitism. Though the phenomenon of anti-Semitism has confounded the philosopher, historian and social anthropologist alike for centuries, the Talmud says that the reason for anti-Semitism began at Sinai, and it is for this reason that the mountain was called Sinai, which means 'hatred' in Hebrew.

Before the Torah was given at Sinai the world was, metaphorically, a jungle. Law was dictated by those people and nations who were the mightiest, and in the manner which they saw fit. Theft, murder, rape and general injustice were practised on a large scale. In addition to these crimes, humanity dedicated themselves to no higher purpose than to extract the greatest enjoyment from life and to live for nothing but self-interest.

A Light unto the Nations

Here the magnitude of what transpired at Sinai comes into perspective. Along comes the Almighty and gives the Jewish people an essential code by which to live which would transform them into a moral nation. Law was given and enforced by the ultimate judge who would ensure that there would be no injustice. Murder and theft were out. Just because one man was more powerful than the next did not give him a licence to oppress. God would always be watching, and no one is more powerful than He. In addition to leading lives of ethical excellence, God also demanded that the Jewish people should dedicate their lives to a higher moral purpose. They could not live for pleasure and self-gratification. They were beckoned by a sublime calling: to serve and worship the Supreme King of kings.

Not even this was enough. The Jews were also charged with spreading this new message to all the people of the world. In their capacity as a 'light unto the nations', they were responsible for disseminating God-given ethics to all corners of the globe. Seen from a different perspective, they were considered a nuisance to the people whose desire it was to dominate those weaker than themselves. So began the hatred for the Jew, whose principal purpose for existence was to bring the knowledge of God, and the obligations which He made incumbent upon all people, closer to the world.

The Class Goody-Two-Shoes

Imagine a classroom in which the children misbehave. They shoot spit-balls, pick on the smaller kids, and constantly insult the teacher. Along comes a new child, transferred from another school. He's the type of student who not only does all his homework, but even brings the teacher shiny red apples. As if it's not enough that he himself is a model student, he even begins to preach to the other kids. He tells them that their behaviour is totally out of line, that they have obligations which they just cannot shirk. What is the popularity rating of the new child going to be? How long before the other students in the classroom begin to conspire against him?

The new mission given to the Jews made them easy targets for abuse. When confronted with the message of Godliness and goodness which the Jews bore, the other nations had to choose one of two options. The first was to act in accordance with Godly morality. The second was to ignore the message, and the best way of doing this was to kill the messenger. In many cases they chose the latter option.

That this is true can be ascertained from an interesting fact about anti-Semitism. It is no coincidence that it is specifically the most barbaric and evil rulers and regimes who always identify the Jews as their Number One enemy. It is as if they understand, feel it in their very gut, that in order to spread their evil regime the main obstacle standing in their way is the Jews.

Jews are the Enemy

Witness therefore how the most evil regime of all time, the Nazis, always portrayed the Jew as the enemy of National Socialism. Through Hitler's rhetoric it becomes obvious he felt that so long as he could put an end to the Jew, his Reich could last the full thousand years that he predicted.

Hitler is just one example among many. Stalin hated the Jews no less, as did Chmielniki, and Torquemada. There have been many evil people on earth since time began, but those who represent evil incarnate, whose souls have descended to the most abysmal depths, have hated the Jews more than anyone else.

The world needs the Jews. They are its moral standard-bearer. If the Jewish people decline, if their numbers are again cut significantly, then not only do they suffer but everyone suffers alongside us.

It is not a coincidence that the world has a fascination with the Jews. That preoccupation has extended for thousands of years. It seems as though the world can love or hate us, but it cannot ignore us.

Working with the World's Inhabitants as Equals

Returning to the analogy of the 'goody-two-shoes' who moves into a classroom of misbehaved children and incurs the wrath of his peers, there are two possible outcomes. The first is that the other children will naturally hate him because he now sets a standard by which they will all be judged. But the other possibility is that instead of looking at the other children condescendingly from his high moral ground, he cares for them and endeavours to help them as well. He takes the naughtiest children over to a corner and speaks to them lovingly. He tells them that they have undeveloped inner potential which it would benefit them to use, and begins to help them do their homework to the point where they can stand on their own two feet. Additionally he explains to the children that he too experiences the same moral challenges as they, and can be just as lazy in doing his own homework. Essentially then what separates them is his greater exertion of effort and willingness to dedicate his life to a higher cause. By doing so he creates a classroom of equals. If instead of locking himself up in his own little corner where the errant behaviour of the classroom disrupts and affects him, he joins the mainstream of the classroom and tries to contribute to their welfare, he will be loved and not hated. The children will look up to him as a caring and decent human being and respect him. They will seek to emulate his example.

Breaking Down the Ghetto Wall

So, too, the Jews have two choices. They can lock themselves up in a corner, as they have done throughout history and continue to do, in self-imposed ghettos. This ensures that they will not be influenced by the evil of the world, but this will also serve to exacerbate the Gentile accusations against Jews, that they are élitist and think they are much better than anyone else. It will also cause the Jewish people to shirk their God-given responsibility of spreading a Godly message to all peoples. An age-old adage of the anti-Semites is, 'You Jews claim to be the chosen people. You think that you are so morally superior to us. You speak of an innate spirituality which you possess which we do not. Well, we will see how far this special quality gets you.' I do not seek, heaven forbid, to cast the victims of anti-Semitism as being responsible for their suffering. Rather, I wish to emphasize that Jewish insularity and Jewish withdrawal from mainstream society, the type of behaviour advocated primarily by more observant Jews, negates one of the central purposes of our existence to be a light unto the nations.

Although I have argued for the allocation of Jewish resources primarily for Jewish purposes and to ensure the religious, educational and cultural health of our nation, we should use this created vitality to contribute to our non-Jewish brethren in whose midst we live, to bring about a better, more Godly and ethical world.

Chapter Fifty-eight

IN SEARCH OF POSITIVE JEWISH AFFIRMATION

At Oxford, it is of course most important to try to remain in touch with Jewish life. Thus the L'Chaim Society keeps up, as much as possible, with the Jewish calendar and unfolding Jewish events. At times, this will mean convening a hastily organized debate such as that on the Israeli expulsion of 415 Hamas supporters in the wake of the kidnapping and murder of an Israeli policeman, to determine if this is within Jewish law, and what Judaism in general has to say about this. At other times, it can mean firing off an essay to the students to discuss whether or not women's only prayer groups are advisable, in the wake of the storm raised by British Chief Rabbi Jonathan Sacks's pronouncements on the same subject, which were essentially to allow women's *minyanim* but only off official synagogue premises. The real interest many students have in Judaism, particularly those who were not brought up within it, is not so much its ancient pronouncements, but their application to modern political, social and environmental concerns. Oxford is old enough, and the subjects taught, such as classics, ancient enough, to render students immune to being impressed by teachings just because they are ancient historically. What motivates the great majority of non-observant students to attend Jewish events is not a compulsion to preserve tradition: rather, they are impressed at the relevancy and wisdom which this ancient tradition holds for modern people, and find that aspect most interesting.

Tardy at the Seder

On a regular basis, keeping up with Jewish times at Oxford means organizing celebrations in accordance with the Jewish festivals. Interestingly, even students who do not come regularly for Shabbat and weekday events enjoy, and sometimes insist on, celebrating the festivals. I was once greatly moved by an English student with whom I was friendly: he had received a grant from the university to travel through Zimbabwe for the spring break, which coincided with Passover. On the last day of the festival, he came barging into our home, all excited that he was about to celebrate the *seder*. When I told him he had missed both *seders* by a week, and had obviously been confused about the times, he was so upset he could not compose himself. What was so amazing about this young man was that he was not at all observant, and rarely participated in our Friday-night Shabbat meals.

What we see in Oxford, however, is that the festival most celebrated by the students, and which they get most excited about greeting, is Purim. The first time I noticed this was in our second year at Oxford. The first year, Purim fell out of term time, and so we had a small crowd at the party we staged. The next year it fell on the last Saturday night of term, and we therefore decided to promote a large extravaganza at the Oxford Union. It was well advertised, and three hundred students attended: if the Union had not closed at 2 a.m. the party could have gone on all night. Everyone was adorned in fancy dress (the British way of saying costumes). There were students present whom we had never met before, dancing to the band's playing Chasidic rock, and others who were quite infrequent visitors. Yet everyone revelled together, and every year since then our Purim party is one of the largest and zaniest events held anywhere in the university. It is for this reason that we also receive large numbers of non-Jewish students who come to dance with us, and speak endlessly to their friends about it after.

But what is the secret of the attraction Purim holds for Jews, even for non-traditional types?

An Existential Celebration of Survival

Purim celebrates the triumph of the Jews over the evil designs of the conspirator Haman. Undoubtedly, Purim is the most joyous of all Jewish holidays: Jews are wont to frolic about, somewhat aimlessly, in fancy-dress costumes and saying more than enough *L'Chaims*. Although there are a number of religious obligations associated with the holiday, including the reading of the *megilla*, the exchange of food parcels between one person and another, and the distribution of charity, the essence of Purim transcends all these obligations. It is a celebration of our very being, not as members of a religion, not as a culture, not even as the chosen people. Rather it celebrates the mere fact that we are here. Notwithstanding the myriad attempts by people the likes of Haman to extinguish our presence, we still persevere. This is what gives us a sense of light-heartedness on Purim. Unlike any of the other festivals, in which we are engaged in a state of *becoming*, trying to reach the lofty ideals which constitute the reason for that festival, Purim celebrates our essential existence. We are not trying to be holy on Purim or serious, but we are trying to be ourselves: we celebrate in a way which declares that however we are, we are still worthy and acceptable.

Every Jewish festival is associated with a specific theme, and also engenders halakhic obligations which reflect that theme. Passover celebrates our freedom from bondage, and thus we eat matza, a slave's bread, but we also recline and drink wine like free people. Shavuot celebrates receiving the Torah at Sinai: we stay up studying Torah through the night and read the Ten Commandments in the morning. It is clear that each of these festivals celebrates a specific attribute of the Jewish people, be it their freedom, their chosenness, or the fact that they are possessors of the Torah. Since each of these festivals celebrates only a limited aspect of our 'peoplehood', the joy associated with them is equally limited. Purim, however, celebrates not just one detail of our existence, but our very being. Unlike Passover, before which our freedom was challenged, or Shavuot, before which our spirituality was challenged, or Chanuka, in which the continuity of our tradition was challenged, on Purim our whole continuity and existence was challenged – and successfully asserted. The joy and celebration associated with Purim cannot therefore be limited to a mere detail, because it is bound with our essence. And just as human essence is infinite, so too the celebrations of Purim know no bounds.

Perhaps this is the reason, as above, that in the post-Holocaust world Jews from all denominations and backgrounds love Purim and seek to celebrate it at any possible level. We who live just two generations after another attempted destruction, not of Jewish spirituality, but of the Jewish people as a whole, revel in Purim and what it represents. Not only does it symbolize Jewish survival, but Jewish *joy*. After so many persecutions in so many centuries, one might think that although the Jews have miraculously survived, the oppression must have taken a toll on their morale. Surely they are not keen to celebrate amidst the harsh reality of their history, and the continuance of anti-Semitism in modern times? Yet Purim disproves that assumption. It represents our will not merely to continue, but to flourish and prosper. Purim is our ability to laugh in the face of all those who hate us, and respond to them with our gaiety and life. Hence the centrality of the drinking and the *L'Chaim* toast to the Purim festivities.

The reasons for current hatred, and the reasons for Haman's particular hatred in the past, deserve closer scrutiny.

An Audacity to Defy Convention

Haman, arch-enemy of the Jews, came before Achashveirosh, King of Persia and its provinces, seething with anger. The king asked, 'What's bothering you? You are the most powerful man in the kingdom, save for myself. What irks you? What has the power to bedevil you so?'

He answered the king, 'There is a certain people scattered abroad and dispersed among the people in all the provinces of thy kingdom; and their laws are diverse from all people; neither keep they the king's laws: therefore it is not for the king's profit to suffer them . . . If it please the king, let it be written that they may be destroyed: and I will pay ten thousand talents of silver to the hands of . . . the king's treasuries' (Esther 3:8–9). Hands were shaken, the money was paid, and the dirty deed was done.

Polarizing Jewishness

What most bothers villains the likes of Haman is not the fact that the Jews exist; nor is it that the Jews live in their midst; nor is it that the Jewish people live by their own rules and traditions. Rather, it is the combination of all these three that irritates Haman and his successors.

In other words, Haman would have been willing to allow the Jews to live in their little ghettos, as the Jews supposed that Hitler would. He would allow them to maintain their different ways and rituals, if they would only do it where no one could see such goings-on. Alternatively, Haman would allow the Jews to live in the midst of the nations, living like all the other citizens in the king's realm, but only if they would discard their customs, their identity, and everything else about them that marked them as different. If they looked and behaved like everyone else, he was prepared to tolerate them. However, if they insisted upon living as part of mainstream Persian society, simultaneously clinging to their ancient beliefs which distinguish them from mainstream society, then he would annihilate them.

'Who is a Jew? That is for Me to Decide'

Stated in other words, and this is the key, Haman was willing to forgo his hatred toward the Jews as long as *he* was the supreme arbiter of Jewish identity. This is what he was trying to say: If you live in our land, then you must live by *our* rules. But you can't have both. We will decide what your name is, how you should dress, what festivals you should celebrate, where you should live, whom you shall marry, and finally what your children should be taught. But since the Jews were stubborn precisely about these things and insisted upon keeping separate Jewish names, dressing with yarmulka and *tzitzis*, celebrating Shabbat and the Jewish festivals, living in close-knit Jewish neighbourhoods, marrying Jewish partners, and educating their children in the traditions and rituals of the Jewish people, Haman was incensed. He wanted to slaughter them.

He could not believe the audacity of the Jews who, on the one hand, could live in a country that was not theirs, out of the benevolence of the Gentile rulers of the land, and yet also insisted upon being segregated culturally and spiritually. The modern equivalent of this thinking is the statement by the rabid anti-Semite, Karl Lueger, Mayor of Vienna: 'Who the Jew is? That is for me to decide.'

There can be nothing so humiliating as to have your entire identity dictated to you by an outside source, particularly one that hates you.

More than anything else, Haman was bothered by Jewish individualism and distinction. He would have allowed them to assimilate and acculturate into oblivion, or to live on their own. But he would never allow both.

Anti-Semitism Blocks the Way to Assimilation

Spinoza argued that the true reason for the longevity of the Jewish nation was anti-Semitism. He argued that '[the Jewish people] had continued to exist as a people only because anti-Semitism blocked the way to their assimilation.' He further predicted that 'if the foundations of religion have not emasculated their minds they might yet rebuild their nation in Israel and God may a second time elect them.'

The argument proposed by Spinoza was likewise advanced by the renowned French existentialist philosopher, Jean-Paul Sartre. Jews, argued Sartre, 'have neither community of interests nor community of beliefs. They do not have the same fatherland, they have no history.' What, then, do Jews have in common that constitutes their Jewishness, and by which they are bound to survive and live? Sartre argued that the sole tie that binds them together is the hostility and disdain of the societies which surround them. Thus the authentic Jew is the one who asserts his claim in the face of the disdain shown toward him.

Sartre and the Jews' Lack of Intrinsic Identity

For Sartre, to be Jewish is to be both the object of anti-Semitism and also to face this fact unflinchingly. However, as British Chief Rabbi, Dr Jonathan Sacks, has pointed out in his book *Traditional Alternatives*, Sartre's thinking contradicts itself. In Sartre's existentialist world, to be authentic is to 'let existence precede essence'; it is to make oneself, to be one's own author. Uniquely, though, according to Sartre, Jews do not make themselves. They are made by others. They exist as such only because they are singled out for hatred. As one commentator concluded on Sartre's analysis, 'The Jew is the fake being par excellence, essentially defined by the glance of the other.'

Furthermore, if we are to accept anti-Semitism as defining Jewish essence, then since Jews exist only by virtue of anti-Semitism, and since anti-Semitism would not exist in a society of authentic individuals, the Jewish identity is ideally self-liquidating.

But what is most troubling is that this is a philosophy that many Jews of late have entered. Today there exists a polarization in Judaism which is alarming for its similarity to Haman's plan. Dare I say it, it might even appear that Haman was the architect of this polarization.

Rejection of Modernity

On the one hand, we have Jewish communities who are extremely observant and overtly Jewish, proud of their tradition and identity, and eagerly imparting these to their children. But these are primarily insular communities who lead their lives in self-imposed ghettos. They eschew any secular knowledge or culture. Their children may indeed study English and mathematics, but they do so only in order to get a job and make a living. It is a necessity, not a life-affirming choice that brings benefit to its pursuer. They do not feel that there is any inherent value in Gentile culture: it is merely a necessity imposed on them by living in a secular world. Thus they learn to compartmentalise their Jewish and professional identities.

On the other hand, we have Jews who live in mainstream society, who are successful in fields as diverse as politics, academia, and the arts, but are largely secular and have abandoned tradition. We all know, for example, of the many Jewish movie stars in Hollywood, and as Jews we love playing trivial games and like to see if there are any we have not yet recognized. Thus one of the most startling things I revealed to the students in Oxford is that Harrison Ford, of *Raiders of the Lost Ark* fame, is Jewish, of which they had no idea. But notwithstanding our pride in their achievements, only a small minority openly affirm a Jewish identity or participate actively in Jewish communal life.

(I remember many years ago, the *Happy Days* TV cast was touring the United States playing softball games against American football teams for charity, and I went to see them play the Miami Dolphins. At the start of the game they went through the audience shaking hands and signing autographs, and when he reached me, Henry Winkler, who was immortalized through playing his character of Fonzie on the show, saw my yarmulka and lifted me up into the air – I was eleven years old at the time. He was so elated to see a yarmulka in the crowd. But incidents like these are few and far between.)

The type of Jew which so irritated Haman, whom he profoundly disapproved of, namely those who live mainstream lives yet are able to synthesize worldly achievements with a strong sense of identity and Jewishness, is increasingly uncommon. It seems that as Jews we are willing, even happy, to build thriving Jewish communities in places like New York and Jerusalem, but we feel utterly helpless in transporting that type of community beyond the borders of the Jewish ghetto.

The Ghetto Mentality

The biggest problem is that these Jewish ghettos are self-perpetuating. As soon as a family who lives in a non-observant community has children who grow old enough to necessitate a Jewish education, or if a family who lives outside mainstream Jewish communities suddenly becomes more observant, it insists on moving to a neighbourhood where there is an increased sense of education and identity. The family never insists on developing a Jewish presence in its own surroundings and transforming it into a more observant community.

Here, paradoxically, all our efforts in Oxford often work against us. If we are successful in cultivating a renewed and serious commitment to Judaism among the city's residents, students and academics, in virtually every instance they insist on moving out of Oxford to a place where their children can attend Jewish day schools, where students can attend regular *shiurim* in the stimulating company of other interested students, and where kosher food is readily available. By this process of withdrawal we have lost countless friends to London, Leeds and Manchester. I tell these Oxford expatriates that one more observant Jew in London will hardly scratch the surface, can make no visible contribution. On the other hand, one more observant Jew in Oxford can help transform an entire city. Together, we can build schools, establish weekly attended *shiurim* on Judaism, and inspire others to follow our lead.

Communal Obligations within Jewish Life

Recently, an entire family who became observant through an association with us told me they had decided to leave Oxford. I was very upset, especially since the father was a well-respected historian, and his new-found observance had been noted by all of his friends, sending ripples through them and his many Jewish students. 'But why should you go?' I asked them. 'There is so much to be done here!' They answered that I was the one who emphasized the importance of Jewish education, attending a synagogue daily, and bringing Judaism into every aspect of one's life. These things cannot be done in Oxford, they argued.

That may presently be the case, I countered. On the other hand, I emphasized equally that Judaism involves not only obligations between each person and God, but between each individual and everyone else. In other words, Judaism not only speaks of personal responsibility, but also of *communal* responsibility. I wanted them to consider the people who were benefiting from and being inspired by their presence, and indeed there were many. Miraculously, they decided to stay: they now host a weekly *shiur* in their home, which I deliver on the Parsha of the week. This has even involved many disgruntled Jewish academics from the university.

Compartmentalizing Jewishness

Then there is the other side of the coin. There are many Jews, especially in an academic centre like Oxford where there is great peer pressure to conform, who abandon a sense of identity in the presence of their non-Jewish, and even their secularly Jewish, colleagues.

To an extent, we feel that there is an element of our Judaism which at best is irrational, and at worst is embarrassing. Hence many Jews become uncomfortable when their non-Jewish colleagues witness 'odd' Jewish rituals: to counterbalance this, they try repeatedly to show them only those aspects of Judaism which are universally recognized as just, good and wise.

Disraeli's Defence of Jewishness

There is the famous story of Benjamin Disraeli who, although he had been converted to Christianity by his father in his youth, replied in Parliament to a member of the opposition who was making disparaging comments on his Jewishness, Yes, I'm Jewish, and while the right honourable gentleman's ancestors swung in trees, my ancestors served as priests in Solomon's Temple.

Now, Jews in England are fond of retelling this story, and I have seen the quotation in many published works. It clearly evokes a sense of pride in Jewish wit, but in fairness we should consider whether Disraeli would have bragged equally about our custom of twirling chickens over our heads before Yom Kippur. Or would he also have thrown in the face of the MP the details of the sacrificial service of the same Temple he so gallantly proclaimed, complete with the butchering of the limbs, and the sprinkling of the blood? I should think not.

Many years ago in Oxford there was a married Jewish student who became friendly with a highly prominent Jewish academic; they were almost like father and son. When the first son of the marriage was born, the student named the child after the academic, in his presence, at the circumcision ceremony. Naturally, he assumed the professor would be touched by this profound demonstration of love and affinity. But he seemed deeply perturbed. After the ceremony, the student asked him why he was upset: 'I thought you would be honoured.' 'Honoured!' the professor replied. 'I am furious. Why did you invite non-Jews to a ceremony that would only subject us Jews to ridicule?'

What he was referring to was one element of the Jewish practice at a *Bris Milah* (circumcision): the *mohel* bends over and extracts the blood of the wound with his mouth. Although according to Maimonides this is done for hygienic purposes, the professor maintained that this practice would appear barbaric to the non-Jews at the ceremony, and he was especially upset that other high-ranking Oxford intelligentsia were present.

Now, what is amazing about this story is that I know this professor to be a very proud Jew, lending very much support to worthy Jewish charities. So why should he be so displeased at non-Jews attending a circumcision? The answer is that his pride can be found specifically in those Jewish areas which are universally applauded, but not in those which can be derided as irrational. I was taken aback by how common this line of thinking was.

Compartmentalization of Jewish Life

As mentioned above, the compartmentalization of Jewish life was an ideal advocated by the enlightenment. The father of this kind of thinking was the celebrated Jewish philosopher, Moses Mendelssohn. Now Mendelssohn, history has forgotten, was a very committed and observant Jew. He once wrote that he even kept the Kaiser of Germany waiting for him for twenty minutes, because he had to pray the *mincha* (the afternoon Jewish prayer), not one of which he had ever missed, so he was not about to miss one now, even if that meant keeping the ruler of the country waiting.

Yet, what Mendelssohn did not foresee was that by advocating Jewish observance, but only in backwaters, by removing a sense of pride in their heritage from the Jewish youth, their faith could not be passionate or even sustained. If every time a non-Jew sneered they removed their yarmulkas or hid their *tzitzis*, then their observances could not have penetrated very deeply into them. If Jewish observance represents the soul of the Jewish people, and Jewish nationalism and pride represents the body, then the soul of Judaism will quickly expire when many Jews lose their sense of their intrinsic worth: a soul cannot exist without a body to sustain it.

That is exactly what did happen. Mendelssohn did not live to know that his own children and grandchildren would convert to Christianity: he would have been mortified had he known, but the system he advocated could yield little else.

Here we can see the point which Haman was making: the Jewish aspect he objected to most was the ultimate source of Jewish strength. Haman was extremely clever and understood that as long as Jews learned to retain their identity, even while immersed in secular culture, they were unbreakable and eternal: this was what he feared most.

The Sadism of the Nazis

Notice how the sadistic Nazis made a point of wasting their time cutting Jewish *peiot*, beards, *tzitzis*, and defiling countless other examples of Jewish spirituality. They felt menaced because the Jews bore their religious symbols proudly in the street. The ultimate defilement was to substitute Godly forms of identification – the yarmulka, *tzitzis*, and the Jewish beard – with a Nazi yellow star identification badge.

For this reason, we who have survived to tell the tale, who will read this Purim and every Purim of how an evil anti-Semite plotted to destroy the Jewish people, must increase our commitment to the observances which identify us as Jews in the street, or in public life.

The message and joy of Purim is the ability for us as Jews to counter established practices, and bring our Judaism to the fore. We can even be kings and queens, like Esther: nothing is stopping us from scaling the highest heights in terms of secular success. It should be remembered, though, that Esther remained a Jewish queen throughout, and because she was never lost to her people, in their greatest hour of need she was able to come through for them.

Whenever a student has finished their degree at Oxford and I am given the task of bidding them farewell, the words with which I leave them, and that I hope resonate in their ears for ever, are this: May you merit serving as a source of pride and inspiration to our people everywhere.

These words, spoken to me by the Lubavitcher rebbe at my first and only private audience with him in his office on the occasion of my Bar Mitzva, instilled within me an eternal sense of communal obligation and responsibility. And it is specifically that feeling of duty which has the power to sustain our observance at all times.

Chapter Fifty-nine

MISPLACED PREOCCUPATION WITH ANTI-SEMITISM

The sum total of my purpose at Oxford among the Jewish students and residents can be said to be the attempt to give people positive and life-affirming reasons to remain Jewish, and more fully develop their Jewish selves. At the same time, I recognize that the primary goal of students arriving in an institution like Oxford is to earn a degree, so that they can go out into the world and be something. For many, the desire to get a good job serves as the primary motivation, while for others, the priority is to make the right contacts for a future in politics or business. Still others seek culture and believe that one cannot properly enjoy life, money or power without a thorough grounding in art, theatre and the classics. Yet more students genuinely wish to pursue their chosen degree subject for the immense satisfaction it brings to them.

Very few students, however, come to Oxford seeking to be better Jews. In fact, they often argue that if that is what one is looking for, it is better to go to a yeshivah in Jerusalem or New York to find it. That is where I am meant to come in. I argue that one can be a *better* Jew by demonstrating the ability to thrive as a Jew at Oxford than by doing the same in an insular Jewish community, or a higher academy of Jewish studies.

Still, the most basic question that needs to be answered is this: What is so important about remaining Jewish in today's society?

In a previous essay we dealt with the issue of preserving tradition. The reasons given for bolstering Jewish commitment, while not in themselves negative, did draw upon negative experiences. A young student found renewed commitment through a terrible tragedy. His father passed away and he was left to come to terms with an untimely death. He found comfort and strength through embracing tradition and an ancient way of life.

Faith through Fear

Throughout history, it seems that Judaism becomes more fashionable in the face of adversity and tragedy. A mother comes to synagogue to pray for a child who is ill, a son comes to synagogue to recite *kaddish* for a beloved parent, and a girl lights Shabbat candles in the hope that they will shed light on a difficult relationship.

Perhaps the greatest historical example of Judaism thriving in the face of tragic circumstances is that of the Jewish community in Germany, after Hitler had come to power and introduced the Nuremberg laws. In his book *Holocaust*, Martin Gilbert writes of how synagogues in Berlin, sparsely populated in the years preceding Hitler, were now full to overflowing every Sabbath and at Jewish classes during the week.

Following the final *kaddish* of his *yahrtzeit* for his father, I approached the student mentioned in the aforementioned essay. I told him that, having said everything I did about the importance of keeping up his Jewish observance because of his parents, that still did not constitute the most fundamental reason for keeping up with tradition. To an extent, to advocate adherence to tradition because one fears it will be lost if it is not observed is still positive affirmation. It implies that one must always ensure that one never becomes a broken link, without considering what is important about the chain itself.

In reality, the reason that he had to keep the tradition was that he himself was Jewish. It was not only his father's soul that, according to our tradition, had heard God's voice resonate from Sinai, but also his own soul. Every rational reason that could be offered in terms of upholding tradition because of one's ancestors could never possibly equal the obligation which one has to oneself.

Generational Arguments for Preserving Judaism

In the years that I have been at my position in Oxford I have met many students who attend synagogue occasionally, or will even be fully observant, for no other reason than 'It was something which my father did, and his father, and his father before him, all the way back through the generations.' I have never found this reason to be seriously compelling: it leaves no one with a feeling of dedication or devotion to tradition beyond a fear of the unknown. It is an argument which states that 'I have always been *frum* [observant], and I don't know any other way.'

Similarly, many religiously observant students tell me that they have long since discarded a belief in the authenticity of Judaism because of historical, scientific or biblical contradiction, but they nevertheless sustain their observance because it has become ingrained in them from birth. Needless to say, there is very little passion in their observance. On the contrary, those with this attitude view observance as an encumbrance, a yoke, a needless burden. They are usually the first to make jokes about supra-rational Jewish traditions, unknowingly mocking themselves in the process. They do so to distance themselves from what they are doing, so that their own integrity not be sullied by strange and seemingly silly practices. They treat their Judaism as a burden which they would gladly cast off, but sadly cannot.

For some, the reason is fear of punishment. I have had exceptionally gifted and bright students argue to me that although they have no real interest in observing anything, they do so because at yeshivah or Jewish day school they were taught to fear Divine retribution. Better to be encumbered by Jewish practice, however tiresome, than to invoke Divine anger upon oneself. It sounds strange but this is still a motivating force in the lives of many serious young intellectuals.

Parental Coercion

Others come to us on Shabbat and other holidays because of tremendous parental coercion. There are parents who will spend hours on the phone coaxing their children to spend more time in Jewish company. When one speaks to these parents one discovers that their primary motivation is a somewhat belated attempt to scold their children into a Jewish environment, because they fear that their child might come home with a non-Jewish boyfriend or girlfriend, or even insist on marrying out. For some, the nightmare has already begun, and their prodding their children to come to see me or get involved with our activities is an attempt to reverse this. But for many others it is a fear of things to come.

How inspiring, though, can a Jewish commitment based entirely on preventing intermarriage be to a young Jewish student? In today's society parents adopt an 'anything goes' attitude to their children's abandonment of, or failure to adopt, tradition, but will suddenly put on the brakes when it appears that this lack of Jewish involvement will result in a non-Jewish daughter- or son-in-law.

This kind of negative, preventative Judaism is in itself designed to preserve rather than develop or enhance, and it is bound to fail because young ideological minds refuse to remain stagnant: they are going to move in some direction, either towards Judaism or away from it. This policy of containment is at best self-defeating, and at worst deadening and off-putting. Young people are not interested in hearing a message that consists of a list of cardinal offences which they must avoid. They want to hear a message of inspiration, motivating them towards practices that they should do!

Combating Anti-Semitism

Another point to consider is how much the focus on combating anti-Semitism serves as the impetus for our Judaism. Is Jewishness really a positive experience if it is primarily defined by having to look over one's shoulder for demons and goblins?

There can be no question that for a great many Jews it is the fight against anti-Semitism which gives rise to their Jewishness. I would even contend that half to three-quarters of world Jewish resources are poured into the area of combating anti-Semitism. Living here in Oxford, it has never ceased to amaze me how the fight against anti-Semitism, Fascism and racism fires the passions of Jewish students. For some it is their only means of identifying as Jews, and for most it is their primary way of identifying. At the L'Chaim Society we have speakers of varying degrees of fame: while the truly international Jewish speakers, such as Elie Wiesel, always attract a huge Jewish audience of hundreds or even thousands, lesser known speakers, even when well-advertised, will attract a group of fifty to sixty, and sometimes under ten. Yet when an anti-Fascism meeting or rally is announced by the Union of Jewish Students or a similar organization, even when the speaker is totally unknown, Jewish students we have never met suddenly pop out of the woodwork in droves.

This is perhaps the ultimate negative reason for remaining Jewish. In this scheme of things, one is Jewish because there are anti-Semites who want to harm or oppress Jews. The fight against that oppression is their *raison d'être*. It seems odd that the world Jewish community, and especially idealistic young students, should allow themselves to be primarily identified by what others find distasteful about them, rather than by some intrinsic form of internal identity. More importantly, it seems incredible that we should attribute our Jewishness to our opposition to those who hate us and would destroy us. This is exactly what anti-Semites desire. If they cannot rid themselves of the Jew, then at the very least they seek to control the Jew. What better way to control them than to actually define their very being!

Force of Admission Leads to Shame

In his monumental work *Holocaust*, Martin Gilbert, whose principal home is in London, but is an Oxford history don, describes the negative feelings associated with having Jewishness forced upon us by external anti-Semitic forces. Describing the effects of a one-day boycott of Jewish shops and goods staged by the Nazis in 1933, Gilbert writes:

> The impact of the one-day boycott was considerable. 'Many Jews on this Saturday were depressed,' wrote the editor of the German-language *Judische Rundschau*, Robert Weltsch, in his editorial on April 4. They had been 'forced to admit their Jewishness', not for 'pride in a magnificent history and in noblest human achievement', but by 'the affixing of a red placard or a yellow badge', and by the sticking of placards to their windows, and the daubing of their window-panes. During these boycott activities, the storm troops had painted the Star of David on the windows of Jewish-owned shops. 'They meant to dishonour us,' Weltsch noted, and

went on to declare: 'Jews, take it upon yourselves, that Star of David, and honour it anew.' (*Holocaust*, page 35).

Abraham Flees and Abraham Runs

It is imperative for us to identify positive reasons to affirm our Jewishness. If not, while we will never be lost as a people, we will lose thousands. But there are other very important reasons as well.

For a proper investigation of the difference between positive and negative reasons to remain Jewish, let us examine the famous *Akeida*, the binding of Isaac, when Abraham was prepared to sacrifice all to serve his Creator. A singular phrase is used when the command is given to Abraham. He is told, 'Go you to Mount Moriah.' The rabbis are intrigued by the use of the phrase, *Lech lecha*, for it appears only twice in the entire Bible, both in connection with Divine commandments given to Abraham, although the two words appear separately many times. The pairing of the two appears only twice; the first time, when Abraham is commanded, *Lech lecha* – 'go forth from your country' – when we are introduced to Abraham in the Bible, and the second time in the story of the *Akeida*.

Rabbi Levi ben Chidah observes, 'The phrase *Lech lecha* appears twice, but we do not know in which situation Abraham showed greater merit: when he left his father's house or when he went to Mount Moriah. However, since the text says "Go you to", specifying the destination, clearly, the merit was greater in the second instance.'

Rabbi Levi's initial doubt about which action was most meritorious arises from the fact that both cases involved a response to a Divine command; both cases called for enormous sacrifice. In the first instance, forsaking father, mother, family, lifelong friends and familiar surroundings, never to see them again, involved a wrench as severe as the threat of possibly losing a son. Yet it is the second instance which is considered greater, indeed greater than any test ever faced by Abraham. And not just because it involved sacrificing his son. The first call put him in flight from something. In the second calling he was given a clear perception of where he was going.

Escaping a Bad Situation into the Unknown

Abraham did not know where he was going. He was just told 'go, get out, leave your father's home. Your spiritual development is being stunted in these surroundings. You cannot expect to father a great and holy nation, dedicated to the principles of monotheism, if you are stranded here in the midst of these idolatrous people.' But he was not told where he was going. When Abraham fled from Mesopotamia, he was motivated by a fear of absorption and assimilation. He was afraid lest the idolatries and immoralities of his native land might overwhelm him, and if not him, his seed, wiping out the vision of God and morality that had come to him. So he started out for a new land, a new society, new surroundings where he could live out his dreams and beliefs without danger of suppression. In the words of Rabbi Philip Lipis who, in a sermon, eloquently describes Abraham's odyssey, 'In military parlance we would say he travelled under sealed orders; destination unknown. The text states plainly, "Go you to a land that I will show you." It does not specify where.'

The second Divine command clearly defined his destination. 'Go you to Mount Moriah.' The rabbis play on this word, *haMoriah*. Rabbi Chiya says it is a word which means 'the place from where *learning* went out to the world'. Rabbi Janai disagrees and says 'the place from where *reverence* went out to the world'. These sayings are a reference to the rabbinic tradition that the site of the *Akeida* was exactly the same site on which Solomon was later commanded to build the First Temple. In amalgamating the two opinions, we would say that Abraham was lured by the ideals that were fashioned on Mount Moriah, where the Holy Temple of Jerusalem was destined to stand, and where the Sanhedrin wove the fabric of Judaism from within the Temple courtyard.

What Rabbi Levi ben Chitah is effectively saying is that it is good for us to know what we fear, for we will protect ourselves against it. But it is infinitely better that we know what we love: for then we will not be refugees driven by our fears, but pilgrims drawn by our loves.

The Secret of Positive Jewishness is Love

For everything in life there must be a motivating energy. It can come in two forms: an attraction, or a repulsion. We are either drawn towards something because it is attractive and lovely, or we are repelled from something because of distaste or fear. I have seen this clearly in my five years at Oxford in the form of students becoming more Jewishly involved. There is always one of two reasons. They are either running from a bad situation, which can take various forms: a failed relationship; intense quarrels with parents and a rejection of their values; problems with academic work, and the like. In this case, they become involved with L'Chaim not out of a real attraction for what Judaism can offer. Rather, they are escaping unhappiness. They will almost go anywhere. It just happens to be that we are open, inviting and available. But then there are those whose lives are stable and fulfilling. Yet they see in Judaism an opportunity for greater meaning and enhancement of their lives. They are pulled, as if by a magnet, to embrace their heritage.

To be sure, fear is not inherently bad. It is fear of crossing the street that keeps us safe when traffic is heavy. Fear of sickness builds hospitals, clinics and the whole apparatus of a nation's health and welfare system. It is fear of old age that created 'old age pensions', social security, nursing homes and the science of geriatrics. Fear of war erected the machinery of detente and peace, however creaky it was during the Cold War and continues to be. And fear of the possible destruction of our beautiful planet by pollution has produced environmentalists and a new ecological awareness.

Fear Lacks Creativity and is Reactionary

Even at its best, though, fear cannot be affirmative, only defensive; neither innovative nor creative, but reactive. Fear and the emotions and commitment which it conjures up are inherently limited in their productive capacity. If we were filled with an enthusiastic love for safety, there would not be massacres on the highways of the world; a love for health, then we would not content ourselves with curative medicine, we would be concerned with preventative medicine. Were all people filled with a love for their fellows, a love for peace and a love for life, they would go far beyond the measures of precaution; they would display a desperate concern for the dignity of life and the worth of others.

Modesty: Internally or Externally Motivated

As an example, let us consider some rules which are very unpopular. The Jewish laws of modesty are grossly misunderstood in today's world. In all the time that I have been in Oxford I have heard many young women complain of the 'excesses and prudishness' of Halakha's (Jewish law's) emphasis on long skirts, buttoned-up blouses, and generally conservative dress. Many see it as a tailored prison. Invariably, the argument against these laws is the same. 'Just because the Torah thinks that men can't control their eyes, do we have to lock ourselves up in layer after layer?' This complaint misses the central premise behind these laws.

There are two possible reasons for locking up our houses at night and bolting our doors. One is to keep an intruder away and on the outside. The other is to protect the people and valuable contents of the house which are on the inside. The two seem similar, but there is a tremendous difference in emphasis. In the first instance it is fear which motivates the action. Since the house's inhabitants lock out the outside world, they become prisoners in their own house. They lock their home not because they choose to, and not because they wish to be alone, but because they are forced to. It is the rascals and scoundrels on the outside who serve as the motivation for closing the door.

In the latter scenario, it is the precious goods of the house, indeed the preciousness of the householders' lives, which motivate them; not to block what is outside, but to preserve what is inside. They are not prisoners in a house, but inhabitants of their own home. They close the door and simultaneously create their own world, an intimate environment. The outside world is not the reason they close the door, but rather to establish a safe, comfortable and private *inside* world. A world which is theirs to share alone.

The same applies to a man and a woman's body. If the motivating factor in modestly covering human flesh is to block out Peeping Toms and errant stares, then indeed the victim is a prisoner. However, if the reason to protect the privacy and intimacy of the body, to preserve a place of intimacy within ourselves so that later it can be used to great effect when we decide to open that world of intimacy to an invited partner, then we are not locked in by our clothing. On the contrary, our clothing then serves the same function as the door on the bedroom of a married couple. They close the door because they wish to be alone, to lock themselves into a position of secluded isolation, not because they fear wandering eyes. The emphasis is on them, not on the people outside. Likewise, the laws of modesty nurture our private selves, thus enabling us to experience private moments. If our bodies have no door, if our flesh is public property, then how special can a chosen moment of intimacy really be? One cannot choose to reveal oneself when intensity is desired if so much of oneself has already been casually given away.

Fear of Communism and a Love of Politics

Throughout the Cold War, the governments of the leading democracies in general, and the United States in particular, initiated far-reaching aid programmes to Third World countries in an effort to keep those developing nations under their sphere of influence. What began with good intentions went seriously awry. Since the end of the Second World War it was principally the fear of Communism, rather than the love of democracy, that dictated American and NATO foreign policy. This central fear produced a policy of worldwide containment of Communism. This was instituted through aid to Greece and Turkey, through the Marshall Plan, through the NATO and SEATO alliances, through the Latin American Alliance for Progress, through the Korean 'Police Action', the war in South-East Asia and Vietnam in particular, the initial blockage of admission into the UN of the People's Republic of China, and military and economic 'aid' programmes all over the world.

On the theory that 'the enemy of my enemy is my friend', an alliance was forged with any kind of government as long as anti-Communism was professed. This was done without taking a close look at the nature and quality of those governments or friendships. No demands for democratic reforms were made of those nations: as long as they resisted Soviet friendship, they were armed with western money and weapons.

The result was that the United States was led, in the name of democracy, to embrace every conceivable form of reactionary government, even though they made a shambles and a mockery of popular representation in their own country. Arms were supplied to governments and then used, not to halt the spread of Communism, but to repress nationalistic sentiments and crush the democratic impulses that were struggling to find their way into the light.

In the 1960s, the United States suffered terrible embarrassment when the rulers of Cambodia and Thailand, whom the United States had backed with shiploads of money, guns and military manpower, announced publicly that they were through with the charade of democracy, and would rule through personal dictatorship. In South Vietnam, where so many young Americans laid down their lives, and even more were maimed and crippled for life, incredible billions of national treasure were consumed for nothing. The result was that the United States was itself torn apart at home, all for the announced purposes of giving the inhabitants of those countries a free choice – to choose their own kind of government. But the farce of so-called democratic elections was later revealed for the whole world to witness and continues to be a stain upon American history.

Failures of the Cold War

Had the leading western governments been filled, not only with the fear of Communism, but also with the love of democracy, we would have taken all the necessary steps to protect ourselves against aggressive Communism, and we would have done more. America and the western alliance would have used its great power and influence to liberate the free spirit of those nations that possessed the revolutionary impulse which had already created democracy in the United States and other western powers, rather than obtaining solidarity only through opposition to others.

The Cold War years brought a strange kind of peace to the world, the most significant feature of which was the containment of rivalries within the two opposed factions of the West and the East. In the veiled hostilities emerging in the West, and the open factions that have arisen in the East, the artificiality of the old peace grounded on opposition to a common enemy is revealed. Real peace can only be achieved by genuinely united action and concerns. This is a lesson which Israel and its Arab neighbours must address in their current efforts to achieve a lasting peace.

Positive and Negative Reasons for the Creation of Israel

Here we return to the issue of the fear of anti-Semitism serving as the primary impulse for Jewish identification. Ironically, it cannot be denied that in many areas anti-Semitism has been good for the Jewish community. It has returned to us many gifted sons. In the late nineteenth century, a young and prominent physician in Odessa had gone throughout the Jewish communities preaching the doctrine of Russification. Leo Pinsker said, 'Assimilate yourselves into the ways of the Russians . . . Drop the customs and ways that keep you apart, and be like your neighbours in dress, in speech and in culture, and all will go well with you.' When the brutal May Laws of 1881 were introduced, the scales fell from his eyes. He recanted, and began to preach a radically different doctrine, the doctrine of auto-emancipation: 'Do not look for freedom at the hands of others. Seek your freedom through self-effort.' He became the forerunner of Herzl, the father of political Zionism.

What Impelled Herzl's Calling

Theodor Herzl was himself an assimilated Jew, a leader of Viennese culture who came alive Jewishly because of the Dreyfus case in 1894. He saw that it was more than one man being judged when Dreyfus was framed; that the entire Jewish people was on trial in France. On hearing the cries of the mob, '*Mort aux Juives*,' it was as though he had received a blinding flash of illumination. He re-examined the basic assumptions by which he had been living his life, and this led to his emergence as the leader of a revolution in Jewish life in the West: the spearhead of modern, political Zionism.

Since both Herzl and Pinsker were motivated more by the growing spectre of anti-Semitism than by love for historical Judaism, they were both ready to accept a territory, any territory, in any part of the world, that held out the hope of relief for multitudes of suffering Jews. At one point, Britain offered Herzl Uganda, and he was ready to accept. It was the Russian Jews, those very ones who suffered the most, who fought the proposal with all vigour. Led by Ussishkin, Bialik, Ahad Ha'am, Smolenskin and Lilienblum, in whom there burnt brightly the passion for Judaism, they refused to entertain any proposal other than the land of our fathers, which cradled our faith and our people.

The fact that today we have our own country in our ancient homeland, the land of Israel, which serves as a home of Jewish exiles from every corner of the globe and a democratic light unto its belligerent neighbours and the world at large, is because the lovers of Judaism prevailed over those frightened by anti-Semites.

If we could learn from this and begin to dedicate the majority of our resources and concerns toward Jewish education rather than reacting to anti-Semitism, we would guarantee a flourishing world Jewish community with no danger ever of extinction. While there can be no forgetting that we live just fifty years after half of the bright lights of our people were extinguished, there can also be no forgetting that the primary challenge to our survival today is not an intruder from without, but neglect from within. If the present trend of out-marriage and assimilation continues, and the latest statistics show that close to sixty per cent of Jews in the United States marry outside of the Jewish community, then we will have depopulated ourselves of millions well before any aggressor can reach us.

The world Jewish community in general, and the younger generation in particular, are ready and eager for a positive affirmation of Judaism. It must be our mission to provide it. By doing so we will prove ourselves worthy of the age-old messianic adage, that in this perfect age promised to us by our prophets of old, 'No Jew will be left behind.'

Chapter Sixty

AN ARGUMENT FOR JEWISH STUDENTS TO DATE AND MARRY JEWS

It seems that throughout this work I constantly find myself saying that my main objective as a campus rabbi is to keep Jewish kids Jewish, and even to motivate them to develop and enhance their Jewishness. As I have already pointed out, there are two ways of going about this. The first is almost purely a reaction to the secular world we live in: combating anti-Semitism, convincing young people not to marry out, and focusing on tragedy to engender a feeling of Jewish solidarity. The alternative is far more positive and life-affirming: cultivating within students a positive image of their Jewish self as their most basic identity, bringing in its wake a moral imperative to develop their full potential.

For this reason, I always try to remind myself that in essence I am not attempting to impart a sense of heritage or tradition to my listeners, but rather trying to provide a stimulus to facilitate self-discovery of their underlying Jewishness. In other words, a rabbi's purpose is not to try to make people 'more' Jewish. There is no need for this, inasmuch as every Jewish individual possesses an innate filial attachment to their roots. Rather, the rabbinic objective is to penetrate, unearth and expose the underlying attachment to things Jewish, which every descendant of Abraham, Isaac and Jacob possesses by virtue of birth.

Translating a Grandfather's Memoirs

For example, in the Michaelmas Term of 1991, a Jewish student who had no conscious interest in studying Judaism sought me out to help him translate a book written by his grandfather, an early Zionist pioneer. He made it clear to me that our weekly session together was for the sole purpose of translating the Hebrew text, and not for him to be preached at. Yet as time progressed he began attending our Friday-night meetings regularly, until our weekly reading session was transformed into an in-depth exchange on Judaism which was gradually becoming very real to him. That summer he travelled to Israel and attended Discovery, the well-known three-day outreach programme sponsored by *Aish HaTorah* in Jerusalem.

When he returned to Oxford, he surprised me by saying that he had decided to cease attending our Shabbat meals, and he informed me that he was terminating our study sessions. The reason he gave for this abrupt halt to what had previously been a steady climb in Jewish commitment was this: when we met weekly to read his grandfather's book, he was becoming more committed to his Jewishness, but without being consciously aware of that commitment. By virtue of his exposure to me and the material we were covering, it was something that transpired automatically. When he went to Discovery, which served as the quintessential intellectual investigation into the validity of Judaism and its claims, he had to make a conscious decision as to whether he agreed with what they taught, and whether he found their arguments convincing. In such an environment, he felt himself obligated to scrutinize every fact imparted, and then make a decision as to its veracity. In other words, they were trying to *make* him Jewish, to make him become something which he did not feel himself previously to be, and he staunchly opposed being 'taken for a ride' without giving firm, intellectual resistance. He said he personally found their arguments riddled with holes and intellectually flimsy (which is not to say that they were so in reality), and so he was compelled to reject them: in his opinion they lacked depth and profundity of thought. One of the things which he claimed bothered him most was the tendency, whenever he challenged them with difficult scientific questions, to point to their watches and claim that the time was running out and they did not want to go off on a tangent. Since he was a zoologist and staunchly challenged their dismissal of evolution, this happened quite frequently. The result was that he ceased to attend our society's events and vented his Jewish interest in Israeli political causes only, bereft of any deeper religious conviction.

The lesson, in my opinion, is to accept and understand the limits of intelligent exchange. If anything, one should engage a student in intelligent debate, not as a means to prove that Judaism is true, or to defend Judaism from unfair assault. This only serves to cast the student in the role of the adversary. Nobody likes to lose arguments, especially in Oxford. Rather, once a representative of traditional Judaism has established a rapport and imparted a sense of Jewishness to a student, to the point where the student is somewhat in touch with his or her Jewish identity, he or she can then use intelligent arguments to help the student overcome any inner resistance to the restrictions and commitments that Judaism imposes, which to the uninitiated, and even to the initiated, are not inconsiderable. The emphasis is therefore on intelligent connection and a shared interest, rather than attempting to prove that your intellectual opponent is wrong.

For every argument there is a counter-argument, and often disputes over the truth of Judaism are merely exercises in futility. There is, however, no counter-response to discovering that there is an essential dimension of one's identity that has been systematically ignored, and being told that something must be done about it.

The above serves as an entry into the most difficult and the most pressing of all issues which I deal with at Oxford. That, of course, is intermarriage.

To Date and Marry Jewish

It is increasingly difficult to address the subject of why my students should date Jews and why, even if they date non-Jews, they should only contemplate marriage with a Jewish partner. I discourage dating non-Jews as vociferously as I do marrying out because, taking a realistic view, it is impossible to go out with a non-Jew and discount the possibility of marriage. I have met many intermarried Jewish individuals who tell me they had never planned to marry outside of the Jewish community. They had merely innocently dated a non-Jew and things developed. The lesson: be honest with yourself about the volatility of your emotions. Dating a man or woman, even without the intention of marriage, can of course easily lead to that. I would even say that it is fairly indecent to take out a non-Jew for dates and not tell them that you have no interest in getting serious with them, and would never contemplate marriage, because of your religion. To do so is to be dishonest and misleading and will not cast the culprit in a great light with his peers, as has happened all too often here at Oxford. I have never encountered a non-Jew who didn't understand why I felt it was important for Jews to wed Jews. What I have found, however, is tremendous animosity to those Jewish students who will date a non-Jew and then, just as they are about to get serious, break it off because of their Jewish commitments. In every instance, the non-Jewish partner feels used and very cheap, and they are absolutely justified in their rage. This is no way for any decent person to behave.

Those students who arrive from committed Jewish backgrounds usually understand the need to marry a Jewish partner, but those who come from families who are assimilated need much convincing on the point. Compounding this problem is the fact that often a student is completely unwilling to discuss the matter because of the very hostile response of family and friends, and at times the lack of any reaction whatsoever when a non–Jewish partner is introduced.

A First Attempt at Counselling

I have often found myself wallowing in mental darkness on this, the most emotive and difficult of all modern Jewish subjects, admittedly doing more harm than good, in my attempts to encourage Jewish students to date and marry other Jewish students.

I shall always remember the first time I was called on to give counselling in a case of intermarriage. The young woman who came to me was a twenty-four-year-old mathematician from Brazil, studying at Oxford. Two weeks before, her non-Jewish French boyfriend had asked her to marry him, and she had gladly accepted. She told her parents, and they were heartbroken that she intended to marry a Gentile, but they were powerless to do anything because they were so far away. They demanded only that she should go to speak to a rabbi. She looked in the telephone book and I was the only Oxford entry, so there she was on my doorstep. I was twenty-two years old, and my approach to the problem was simple and straightforward. If Jews marry non-Jews there will no longer be any Jews, therefore it is wrong. I felt confident about my position and my ability to articulate it.

Is it a Crime to Fall in Love?

She arrived in my living room, sat down and described her predicament. She told me that she was a very proud Jew, and had been brought up rather observant. She had no intention of ever giving up her identity, but could not help being in love. She had met her boyfriend at the Sorbonne, and he made her happy. What were the possibilities?

I tried to look sympathetic, although it was hard for me to feel it at the time, and began to raise three fingers in quick succession. 'The first possibility,' I told her, 'is to break up.' She made it clear that this was not a possibility. 'Well,' I said, 'this brings us to the second option. He can convert, and in this too there are two possibilities. He can have a proper Orthodox conversion which would make everybody happy, but this is beset by two major pitfalls: one, he must be sincere in his desire to convert, motivated by a love for Judaism and a desire to share the fate of the Jewish people and not just a wish to marry a Jewish maiden; two, it takes a long time and involves major commitments of both education and action, on both your parts. It would involve nothing less than a complete reorientation of your lives to full Jewish observance.'

The other sub-option was to have a much faster, far less committed, Reform or Liberal conversion, but this was beset by an even greater pitfall. The authenticity of his conversion would be rejected by about seventy per cent of the world Jewish population, and would not achieve their purpose acceptably. She indicated that she wanted to hear the third possibility.

That of course was the most straightforward. She could marry without conversion, and perhaps live happily ever after, unencumbered by the snares of traditional Jewish ritual. Here I launched into the customary Jewish polemic: that this was the worst of all possible choices because of blah . . . blah . . . blah . . . A gush of the oft-repeated, forever regurgitated, and utterly weak and impotent Jewish opposition to intermarriage poured forth from my mouth. I told her the standard rhetoric about her having obligations, not only to herself but also to the entire Jewish people, how she would serve to sever the link in a chain going back thousands of years, how she would serve as a destroyer of her people instead of a builder, and if every Jew were to embrace her choice there would be none left . . . and so on.

She listened patiently, thanked me for my time, got up and left. *And she never came back again.* She did get married eight months later, with only her mother in attendance (her father refused), and I did occasionally bump into her on street corners and at two Oxford Union debates. She was barely friendly, though, and treated me more as an adversary than a compatriot.

Clearly, my approach had failed miserably. This led to a lot of soul-searching and I immediately drew two conclusions. The first was that I had spoken to her as someone who had done, or was about to do, something wrong: whereas in reality the only thing she had done was to fall in love. The second was that in reality there was a fourth possibility which superseded and transcended all the others. Much as I feared it, it had to be acknowledged. This was that, whatever she chose, she would always remain a *bat Yisroel*, a member of the Jewish people. We would always love and cherish her, regardless of what choices she made in her life. Of course, the flip side of the coin was that whatever choices she made, she would always have obligations to the Jewish community. Even if she married her non-Jewish boyfriend, she would still be expected to attend synagogue services from time to time, light Shabbat candles, and give her children a Jewish education. However, I did not say this to her and because of my neglect I for ever closed a door to her that I had no right to close. I am not the God of Israel but I live by His rules. And He stipulated that to be a Jew is an immutable state of existence, and that every Jewish individual is a member of a family unit with bonds that can never be broken.

As the years went by, the problem got worse and worse. More and more Jewish students were turning up at society functions and Shabbat dinner with non-Jewish partners. As I began to understand the nature of the problem, I began to develop a completely new method of dealing with the question of intermarriage, which I shall discuss below.

The Crime of Love

The first and most important premise to understand about those young people who date non-Jewish partners, and in regard to those who even go on to marry them, is that they have no desire to sever their links with the Jewish community. They are usually proud Israelites and, in their own way, committed. They do not understand, nor do they accept, that the step they are taking is in any way a rejection of the Jewish people or an act that leads to its destruction. They feel that the logic which claims that intermarriage is a cardinal vice within Judaism is flawed. Even when you point out the practical loss of Jews through intermarriage, and that if a man marries a non-Jewish woman his children are lost to his people for ever, they do not accept that the entire future of the Jewish people hinges on them alone.

These arguments require deep philosophical thinking in a matter which they feel is instinctive. 'I simply fell in love. What do you want from me?' Because they are accused, they become irritated and defensive, but I believe that in truth they are correct. What is their crime, and does a relationship naturally have deep philosophical underpinnings? Can we demand of a young person such deep feelings of commitment to the abstract concept of allegiance to their people, when a tangible, loving young companion with whom he or she has shared so much sits before them?

A Second Attempt

In my second year at Oxford, and a few months after the events of the previous narrative, I was introduced to a young Jewish Rhodes Scholar from Louisiana, called Jim. He came from a small town that had only a handful of Jewish families, and he knew all of them. To date, he stands as one of the finest young men I have ever come across at this university. He had everything: lightning-fast intelligence, tremendous personal charisma, a hilarious sense of humour, good looks, and a deep love and respect for all people. He came from a Reform Jewish background and his parents had taught him to be proud of his heritage and of Israel. He was a fourth-generation Southerner who called his grandparents 'Bubbee' and 'Zeide' with the strongest Southern twang, which made it sound very humorous. While he was not observant, he was the type that, wherever he travelled (and armed with funds from the Rhodes trust he did so quite a bit) he would always visit the local synagogue, not just as a site of antiquity, but to hear the Torah read and 'get an *aliyah*' (be invited to follow the reading in the scroll). The stories he related to us were quite moving and very funny. He turned up at a synagogue in Paris with long hair and beard, cut-off jeans shorts and T-shirt, asking if they would give him an *aliyah*. They slammed the door in his face and called the police. He was just seized by a desire to be surrounded by Jewish things and people, even though, on this occasion, the warden of the synagogue misjudged his sincerity. He had a soft spot in his heart for his Judaism.

To Run and to Hide

As time progressed, he became my closest friend in the university. When he saw me from afar he would run screaming like a madman, pick me up and twirl me in the air. Now, it must be said that some of the Jewish students, even many who are close to me, are somewhat apprehensive about acknowledging an association with me in public, because of the kind of light it casts them in. When they are with their non-Jewish friends they may suddenly see my beard, dark suit, and *tzitzit* as an embarrassment. But Jim was different.

In October 1989 we started the Oxford University L'Chaim Society and shortly after Jim was elected as one of our presidents. He served the society faithfully and through his considerable influence with Oxford students as one of the most outspoken and politically active Rhodes Scholars, he raised the prestige of our fledgling society to heights it otherwise could not have reached so quickly. Oxford is an ancient city with an old university. New things never quite flourish at this university, but L'Chaim did, and it was in no small measure due to Jim's devotion to the project. We studied, argued and played squash together virtually every day. I even put up a massive *mezuzah* on his door at Corpus Christi College, a photograph of the ceremony appearing in the largest student publication.

With everything I have said so far, one might think that although Jim may not have become observant, he would surely marry a nice Jewish girl and go on to be a staunch supporter of Jewish causes and communities. The latter was true enough but the former was not. Jim was a great lover of humanity and he could not accept that he should specifically search for a Jewish girl to marry. He felt deeply uncomfortable with the notion of immediately cutting out two billion women from being his prospective bride. He met a truly lovely young woman at the university, whose only shortcoming, as far as he was concerned, was that she was not Jewish. That was not enough to cause him to break it off. He made it clear to me that this was an issue he would not discuss. He loved his Judaism but he would not allow it to conflict with his sense of egalitarianism. The relationship developed and, in his third and final year at Oxford, they got engaged.

How to React to the News

Amazingly, he did not tell me. It was not until we were sitting together in my *Sukkah* two months later that he mentioned the engagement, as an aside. I was taken aback and torn as I had never been before. On the one hand, I loved him and wanted him to be happy, and frankly, she was a remarkable woman with proper values. On the other hand, he represented the cream of Jewish youth, and we were going to lose a part of him.

I congratulated him and felt myself partially turning off. In a matter of minutes our relationship, cultivated over three intense years, had changed.

I suddenly could not be natural with him. I knew he wanted me to be sincerely happy for him, but only half of me could. The friend within me wanted to hug him, but the rabbi within me wanted to plead with him not to go ahead with it. Yet I have always believed in synthesis. There were not two disparate beings inside me: the same person who loved Judaism enough to become a rabbi was the one who loved Jim's goodness and respected him enough to be his best friend. Frozen by confusion, I gave a lame excuse of some household chore that had to be done, and left the *Sukkah*.

I did not see him for three days. On the fifth night of Sukkot, while we were celebrating the *Simchas Beit Hasho'eivah*, one of the most festive of all Jewish days, he turned up, looking very upset, but he nevertheless danced and rejoiced with everyone else. When the band had finished and the people had left, he came back with me into the house. We had both had many Jewish toasts to the festival and we sat laughing and reminiscing about past stories and events. Then he got serious and I will always recall the scene. He sat on the counter of the kitchen with his feet dangling and began to cry. It was completely out of character for him to do so but that didn't stop the streaming tears and the woeful voice.

It was easy for me to judge him, he said, having been brought up in a place like Miami, surrounded by Jewish people and Jewish friends. In Louisiana, he told me, he knew only three Jewish girls. They were friends whom he would see all the time, at synagogue, at Jewish youth groups. That type of intimacy made it impossible to view any of them in a romantic light. Some type of female companionship was needed and he found it in the form of a non-Jewish woman. Once you begin dating, marriage is just one step away. 'What then,' he asked me, 'have I done wrong, and how can you judge me?' Worse, he could not believe that I was not happy for him. Were we not friends? He emphasized that he had made a decision, he loved his fiancée and he was not reneging on his commitment.

Bonds which Transcend Religious Convictions

I found it difficult to say anything, and we parted. The incident with the student from Brazil still rang in my mind. The next day I called him up, asked him to play squash, and picked him up in my car. As he entered, I told him that I had only one thing to tell him about the events of the previous night and it was this: 'You are a Jew and you shall always be a Jew. Neither all the baptismal water in the world nor a non-Jewish spouse can undo that essential fact of who and what you are. You must never forget that. As such, you have obligations to the Jewish God and the Jewish people. Marrying outside of the faith is not a licence to disengage oneself from Jewish life. I therefore expect you to continue coming to Friday-night dinner, studying and arguing Judaism with me, and to continue your immense contribution to our activities. As for us, we shall always remain friendly, like brothers, because the friendship we have transcends any decisions either of us make in life, bar hurting or being unkind to each other. And as far as your wife is concerned, she will be as welcome as you and any other student in our home and in our centre.' I advised him against converting her in a token way, just to please his conscience or his parents. She deserved better than that. If he would be a good enough example of Jewishness to her, then perhaps one day she would seriously consider exploring Judaism with a view to embracing it and joining his people. In fact I encourage this type of display. 'Bring her to the synagogue with you, impart to her Jewish wisdom and values, celebrate shabbos and teach her the serenity and beauty of a divine day of rest. By doing so you may kindle a real love of Judaism within her.'

The result of this approach was that he remains deeply committed to his Jewishness, and we remain the closest of friends.

Is Intermarriage a Rejection of Everything Jewish?

The attitude described above is anathema to most Orthodox, and even many non-Orthodox, Jews today. Modern Jewish thinking automatically interprets intermarriage as a rejection of everything which is Jewish. It sees marrying out as incompatible with a continued commitment to Jewishness and its specifics such as attending synagogue, keeping kosher, or observing Shabbat. To understand why this is so, and which view is more appropriate, we must first explore the issue in greater detail. We must offer compelling reasons to young people as to why they should marry a member of their people, and what to do if they choose to ignore our advice.

Different arguments have been proffered over the past few decades. Yet I have found that the majority serve to exacerbate the problems since they tend to be inherently guilt-oriented and leave the individual in question feeling that Judaism is naught but a negative encumbrance; I have been told as much by several students. For example, the argument that marrying a non-Jew leads directly to the destruction of the Jewish people casts the student in the role of a destroyer of Israel instead of being an integral part of a faith community. It offers no positive or personal reason to abstain from marrying outside of that community. Effectively, before young people have been made to feel the positive aspects of living with their kin, they are taught the negative aspects of breaking up a family.

Similarly, one of the commonly used preventative techniques is to take the person who wishes to marry out into a synagogue, give them a Torah scroll to hold, and then order them to drop it on the ground: the rationale that their inability to execute the order is indicative of a latent desire to preserve the Jewish people is often missed by the young person and it is interpreted as a sinister gimmick used by rabbis when they lack an intelligent response to a losing battle. With almost sixty per cent of all Jewish marriages today being out-marriages, we are clearly losing the battle.

The Reason We Marry

The argument which I have found to be most effective revolves around the intrinsic reason for marriage. After all, in today's liberal society, why marry at all? Living together seems to be an equally viable, if a less institutionalized, alternative. The reason, of course, is that when two people truly love each other they desire to solidify that love in the form of an unbreakable bond. Marriage serves as an unrivalled framework within which two people can eternalize their commitment to one another.

Stated in other words, the nature of human emotion is such that when one feels something very strongly, one wishes to do something about it. Real emotion makes us feel ourselves bursting at the seams. Emotion must find expression in action and deed. It is not sufficient for a father to sit at his daughter's wedding in rapturous delight. She will not believe him when he claims that he is very happy. When someone is ecstatic they stand up and run around the room. That is why joyous dancing is always associated with a wedding. Conversely, can you imagine someone who becomes furious about being wronged by a friend just sitting coolly, having no desire to get up and do something about it?

The nature of emotion is that it has to be expressed: when a couple are truly in love they want to get up and do something about it. So they seek to get married. They undertake tangible action which conforms with and reflects their feelings toward one another. Marriage is the most profound statement of that feeling.

Can a couple be said to be married if, at some subliminal, deep-rooted level, the two lovers are dissimilar? What if, on the deepest and most intimate plane, the couple lack common ground? Imagine a Jewish husband married to a non-Jewish wife who switches on the radio at breakfast to discover that an Israeli soldier has been killed in an ambush in Lebanon. He feels saddened by the news. It leaves an indelible impression upon him. His wife says, 'Honey, do you care for more eggs or coffee?', not because she seeks to be insensitive, but because it does not affect her in the same way that it does him. Nor can he expect her to feel the same way that he does. It is not a tragedy of her people. If at that level they cannot communicate or feel a similar sensitivity to the same subject, then marriage can never truly join them *completely*, for in a very significant aspect they are not the same. The same would not be true, for example, if an Englishman were to marry a Frenchwoman. True enough, they have dissimilar cultures and they must surmount the obstacles inherent in cultural differences. But being English is not the same, does not strike nearly as deep, as being Jewish. The proof is this: when Jewish individuals meet each other anywhere in the world, they immediately feel something special in common, far more than nationality. This is a fact known to Jews the world over and requires no elaboration. Two Americans who meet each other in Greece would not feel the same. They may speak of baseball, President Clinton, or other subjects which are not discussed by the natives. Yet they will not feel a sense of peoplehood, ancient comradery, a commonality of history and destiny, that two Jews would feel.

An Illiterate Farmer

There is a famous Chasidic tale of a peasant who is illiterate. He receives a letter from his father every month and he brings it to the local scholar who is kind enough to read it to him. This ritual goes on for years, the peasant anxiously bringing his latest letter to the scholar and the latter patiently reading it to the excited young man. One day, the scholar opens the latest instalment, stands up, and looks shaken. 'I don't know how to tell you this,' he turns to the youth, 'but your father has died.' Immediately upon hearing the terrible news, the peasant faints.

The question arises as to why the scholar did not faint. After all, it was he who read the letter personally, and it was he who conveyed its message. The answer of course is obvious. It was not his father who had died. Just as a wife could never expect her husband to feel the same way towards her family as she does, so a Jewish spouse could never expect their non-Jewish partner to feel towards the Jewish people and their fate in the same way they themselves do. This in itself demonstrates there is an essential gap that is not bridged even by an institution as intimate as marriage.

There are many illustrations of this truth but I seize upon one important contemporary incident. In the wake of the Six-Day War in 1967, when the global Jewish community experienced an unprecedented renewal in feelings of Jewish identity, primarily due to the miraculous Israeli victory, there was a simultaneous surge in the number of divorces of Jewish individuals who had non-Jewish partners. The reason was that as the imminent danger to Israel became clear, with Nasser blockading the Suez canal and ordering the United Nations to remove their peace-keeping forces, Jews the world over panicked and vented their concern and support for Israel as never before, but non–Jews wedded to Jewish spouses could not share the same concern or support. Sadly, this resulted in the collapse of many such unions.

Let me make it clear that I see this as a tragedy. Every divorce, regardless of the faith of its partners, is a tragedy. And I find reprehensible any efforts on the part of an observant Jew to break up the marriage of a Jewish and non-Jewish partner, preferring instead to pursue alternative paths of reconciliation, as I shall discuss later. Nevertheless, we must be realistic about certain differences which are exceedingly difficult to bridge. A Jewish person having a non-Jewish spouse faces one such chasm.

Contradictory Objectives

I personally know of an American Jewish doctor whose wife was not Jewish. He flew to Israel amidst his wife's fierce objections in the first days of the Six-Day War. He had wanted to offer his services in attending wounded Israeli soldiers. His wife simply could not understand how he could endanger himself, given his obligations to herself and their children. Of course, for his part he could not fathom how she did not laud his sacrifice. They found this an impassable obstacle and the result was a formal separation.

This is not to say that a non-Jewish spouse will never be sensitive to things Jewish, and there are indeed many instances in which the gap has been bridged. I personally know of many intermarried couples living in Oxford in which it is specifically the non-Jewish spouse who makes a tremendous effort to ensure that the family celebrates Passover, Chanuka and even Shabbat. But this only serves to enhance my point, which is that a sensitivity to things Jewish and an active participation in Jewish ritual is for them not automatic and does indeed require an effort. And who can fault them? After all, they are not Jewish and it would be completely unreasonable to expect them to feel a filial attachment to Judaism and the Jewish people. At the same time, the fact cannot be ignored: whereas concern for the welfare of the Jewish people, for example, will be intuitive and congenital for the Jewish partner, it will require an effort, usually solely for the sake of emphathizing with one's Jewish husband or wife, on the part of the non-Jewish spouse. It will not come naturally.

This is not to say that there are no exceptions to this rule. Indeed, many non-Jewish spouses are exceedingly concerned about the safety of the Jewish people. But in almost every case I am familiar with, if the spouse is of this type, having a strong interest in Jewish affairs and having reached the point where this feeling is automatic and requires no great effort, then they are also willing, or actively seeking, conversion to Judaism. I am not aware of any isolated incidents where a spouse shares the Jewish partner's love of the Jewish people but does not want to be Jewish him or herself.

The Most Basic Identity of a Jew

Of course, my entire argument above has no validity unless it can be clearly established that the underlying and most basic identity of even the most assimilated Jew is in fact their Jewishness. If this can be validated, then, logically, every person contemplating a marriage outside of the Jewish people will have to concede that at an essential, congenital level, in their heart of hearts, they and their proposed spouse lack complete compatibility. This does not in any way mean that they will necessarily divorce, nor need such a negative line of reasoning be adopted. Such arguments are offensive and anathema to Judaism. An intermarried couple can be very happily married and share identical concerns. What it does mean is that the Jewishness of the Jewish partner will always serve as a divide.

Even if they remain happily married for years to come – and I believe that once a couple go ahead and marry we must sincerely wish that the marriage succeeds, regardless of its contradiction to faith – it still will not achieve the highest, most desirable state. They will find it difficult to be synthesized completely as husband and wife. So, while this in no way guarantees a future break-up of a marriage, it does guarantee that they may never be completely joined. There will always be an essential level at which they cannot marry.

That this is true can be seen from how the great majority of Jewish people who marry out, actively seek, even compel, their intended spouses to convert to Judaism. Even if it is an obviously token conversion, they still wish them to 'become' Jewish. I would argue that this is not merely to appease their conscience, or their parents and families. Rather, they truly want their husbands and wives to be Jewish, as if they understand that that part of their partner is missing, and the marriage would be far more perfect if only they were Jewish. It is as if they feel there is a certain element of imperfection in the state of their marriage as it is.

In my time at Oxford I have counselled perhaps two hundred couples of different faiths who desired to marry. In each case, the Jewish partner professes their love for their non-Jewish partner. When I ask the Jew, 'Tell me honestly, if you could wave a magic wand, say "abracadabra", and make your partner Jewish, would you do it?' the answer has always been, 'Of course!'

Therefore, I do not apologize for attempting to prevent intermarriage, or the very least to encourage the non-Jewish partner to seriously study and explore the Jewish faith, with a view towards conversion.

The Credibility Gap

In general, success in preventing any intermarriage or persuading the couple not to marry until the Gentile partner has had an halackic conversion, which is at best very elusive, must be predicated upon a firm understanding of the root causes of the epidemic. Intermarriage is only the overt symptom of an underlying, ruinous chasm. The reason is simple and it is this: today's world Jewish community cannot find a positive reason to remain Jewish. We search in vain for a common cause, only to discover a litany of special interests and uninspired motives. Our young people sense this, and rebel against it.

Once a month, on a Monday evening, I deliver a class at a large Orthodox congregation in London. On the occasion of Chanuka, I asked the audience why they felt the Maccabees had sacrificed all to fight the Assyrian Greeks for the preservation of Judaism. If we could tap their convictions, we might become impassioned modern Maccabees ourselves.

Surprisingly enough, not one person was able to offer a coherent response. I have since tried this with various Jewish audiences with differing degrees of observance, but have yet to find one argument which all agree is convincing and inspiring enough to die or even to fight for.

Ancestral Motivations

To glance quickly over the responses which were proffered, the most popular reason to remain Jewish was that Judaism is something which has been practised by one's forebears. 'If my grandfather and his father did it, then I feel obligated to pass it on to my children.' Yet, in my experience, today's students find this argument utterly unconvincing. The logical response is, 'So what? Your forebears didn't attend university, were not secularly educated, and may not have kept anything if they were living in a more enlightened time, such as we live in today.' Practically speaking, the line of tradition has in many cases been almost severed. It is no longer true that tradition must be preserved because all our forebears kept it and the young feel little compulsion to perpetuate something already discarded by previous generations.

The students at Oxford often joke about this. Once, when we were entertaining a group of students at our home for dinner, one of them asked me how many hours one must wait to have milk after eating meat. I responded 'six'. Another student said that their custom, transmitted from their ancestors, was to wait only three hours. The student who originally proposed the question then said, 'Well, the custom that I have from my father and grandfather is to eat cheeseburgers at McDonald's and fried chicken at Colonel Sanders. Can I then continue with that?'

Judaism is Enjoyable

Another popular, similar response to the question of why we remain Jewish is the enjoyment such simple things as going to synagogue or lighting Chanuka candles can bring. I know, though, that Judaism can be just as cumbersome as it is enjoyable, and besides, there are plenty of other enjoyable things in life which do not demand the same degree of responsibility, sacrifice or commitment.

A Regimented Life

Some of the audiences I encounter argue that religion in general, and Judaism in particular, offers a highly regimented, family-oriented lifestyle, along with an absolute code of morality and ethics, all of which constitute welcome alternatives to the modern world's transient ethics, confusion and social chaos. But if truth be told, the army offers the very same. The security that Judaism offers is probably no more than a good job or a robust economy. Far be it from those who have striven to preserve Judaism over the course of three millennia to accept the argument that we have done so in order to protect our sense of security. Similarly, the argument that leading a Jewish life ameliorates any feelings of guilt and offers a wholesome, wonderful, spiritually satisfying feeling doesn't wash either. In fact, if we had lived just fifty years ago, under Hitler or Stalin, then our Judaism would have offered us anything but security. Yet even amidst adverse conditions, Jews have still clung steadfastly to their Jewishness. The answer must therefore lie elsewhere.

Israel as the raison d'être *of the Jew*

A surprisingly large number of people told me that the modern state of Israel is the most positive reason to remain Jewish, with many using the state to define their own Jewishness. Thus Israel, or devotion to Israel, inadvertently becomes one of the principal methods by which one's Jewishness is measured.

The problems with this simplistic definition are many. Foremost among them, especially in recent times, is the transient nature of support for Israel. When Israel is universally praised and inspires reverence, even wonder, such as in the case of the Entebbe rescue, then world Jewry raises the Israeli banner as its standard. Conversely, in the wake of international criticism and hostility, such as that which followed the war in Lebanon, Israel is ostracized even by once loyal Jewish supporters.

The other problem is that it transforms the means into the goal. Israel was a country which Jews, having preserved their identity and having remained committed to Jewish survival for two millennia, returned to build. It was not the state of Israel which built the Jewish nation but the Jewish nation which built the state of Israel. To say the opposite is to ignore the blatant fact that, contrary to all historical predictions, Jews have remained Jewish without a homeland for 2,000 years. And the most obvious objection to this reasoning is that Israel is not even half-a-century old, while the Jewish people are thirty-three centuries old. Surely, something must have sustained them in all that time.

The final and most convincing argument as to why the modern state of Israel should not serve as the primary reason for Jewishness is that it simply does not maintain that Jewishness. It has failed most noticeably among those who should have been most affected by it: the Israelis themselves. By the latest estimates, nearly one million Israelis have emigrated since the country's founding forty-five years ago. Zionism without God and Jewish nationalism without a soul, while perhaps able to provide brief moments of inspiration, have no lasting effect and offer no sense of permanence. The Jewish people are at heart a spiritual nation who require constant spiritual nourishment.

We must reach for something deeper, more religious, than mere territorial integrity to preserve our nationhood.

An Argument for an Inner Identity

In truth, the only plausible reason to remain and affirm Jewishness, and the one which many feel in their gut to be true, is, as already mentioned, that it is one's true, inner identity, and it transcends defined explanation.

Asking a Jewish individual to provide a positive reason to be Jewish is like asking a parent to give a reason why they love and care for their child. The question itself provides the answer, 'I love my daughter because she is my child.' There is no other reason. It is just so. And the parents feel it to be so.

This can also be compared to asking a human being why he concentrates specifically on developing his human side, as opposed to his animal dimension. For example, why does one go to college and study physics instead of learning how to sharpen a spear and hunt? The question, once again, is ludicrous. Because one is human, and possesses the higher faculties of intellect and understanding, one seeks to nurture and develop these talents, above and beyond any commonality with an animal.

Intrinsic Jewishness

The positive reason for promoting and protecting one's Jewishness is existential. It is the state of being itself which calls for that nurturing. We must not intermarry and we must remain committed to our Judaism simply because that is what we are. On many occasions in history we have even attempted to deny that Jewishness consciously. Alas, it was a wasted effort. One way or another we have been reminded of what we are and the fact that we are different. It follows, therefore, that something must be done to cultivate and nurture this Jewish dimension. It cannot be ignored.

In other words, to be Jewish is to be part of a people. What links the Jews of the world together is not just Torah, a common history, or common beliefs. Nor is it race or ethnicity. Rather, what we have in common is forefathers, the same ancestors; it is this that makes us all one people, including those righteous Gentiles who have joined with us. There can be no avoiding it.

Often in Oxford I encounter young people who are severely troubled by this idea. They feel trapped into something about which they have not been given a choice. A question put to me often is this: If God wants us to have freedom of choice, then why did he not give us the choice to be or not to be Jewish.

Plea for an Excommunication

This is exemplified by the following incident. One day I received a phone call from a seventeen-year-old young man who was attending one of the élite, private (in Britain they are, ironically, called 'public') schools in the area. He told me that he needed to meet and talk to a rabbi and that it was urgent. I was rather worried, so I told him to come over within the hour and he did so.

He walked in and the first thing he told me was that he wanted to be excommunicated. 'What?' I asked. 'Excommunicated! What on earth for? Do you even know what excommunication means?' Clearly he did not if he really desired to be legally ostracized from the Jewish community.

He was very persistent, though. A week earlier a Roman Catholic priest had visited his school and, in the process of discussing the differences between the world's leading religions, the priest had mentioned that, whereas to be Christian one must believe in Christ, to be Jewish one merely had to be born a Jew, and there was nothing one could do about it.

Now, the young man told me he was taken aback to discover that he was drafted into a religion he had not himself decided to join. He asked how it could be done against his will. At the very least we should be kind enough to excommunicate him.

After arguing with him I discovered he was absolutely adamant about this excommunication: he would not leave without it. Finally, I wrote the following on my computer: 'I, Shmuel Boteach, rabbi to the Jewish students of Oxford University, hereby declare Steve Whiting excommunicated from the Jewish people henceforth and for ever more.' I printed out the Excommunication Form, and once he had signed it, I said to him, 'That will be £400, please.' He loudly and forcefully expressed his horror to me: 'Four hundred pounds for an excommunication, are you crazy?' 'Of course I am not crazy,' I replied. 'How do you think we rabbis make a living?

Weddings cost £200; Bar Mitzvas £150; circumcisions £300, because they are so messy; and excommunication is £400 because it costs more to get out than to get in.'

He was taking me seriously and was clearly flabbergasted. So that's what Judaism and rabbis were about. He made it clear that this made him even more sure that he wanted no part of us and was only interested in getting out. There was a problem, though: he reminded me that he was a student, and he said he could not afford the £400. 'OK,' I told him, 'since you are a student, we'll make it half price.' But even that he could not afford. He then got angry, and told me that he simply felt it intolerable that 'we', the Jewish community, could tell him what and who he is. It was unfair and he just wanted out, he said.

A Jew For Ever Remains a Jew

I told him, you can run around convincing yourself that you are not Jewish, you can laser-print certificates to show others that you are excommunicated or you can have all the baptismal water in the world poured upon you, but that will never change the essential fact that you are Jewish. Nothing can change that fact.

If you have a Jewish mother, you are Jewish, because she is a daughter of Sarah, Rebecca, Rachel and Leah. What good is it to complain that you were not given a choice? You can run around claiming that your mother is not your mother, or that your grandmother is not your grandmother, but your claim is not true simply because you say it. If you insist on saying that although you were born male, you feel yourself to be female and you are upset that no one gave you the choice of which sex to be, will expressing your lack of choice do anything to change your gender?

It is absurd. Being Jewish is simply a fact of our existence. That is what we are. Instead of devising fruitless methods to rid ourselves of it or protesting about the lack of choice, we should do something positive about developing it by recognizing what we are in our very essence. We are Jews and we must develop a sense of pride, because there is no changing the fact of what we are. It follows, then, that when it comes to the single most important decision of our lives, the choice of who we marry and with whom we spend the rest of our lives, it should be someone with whom we have Jewishness in common.

This message is what must be conveyed to our young people, however difficult or elusive its realization may be. The fact that Jewish martyrs throughout the ages have included many who were ignorant of or uncommitted to their Jewishness, just goes to show that subliminally they were always connected to their Judaism, although they may not even have felt it consciously.

Rabbi Manis Friedman tells the story of having heard a Roman Catholic bishop being interviewed on Israeli radio. When he was asked to define a Jew, in contrast to a Christian, he replied, 'A Jew is someone who is religious without knowing it.' Indeed it is amazing that it should take a Catholic bishop to capture and express perfectly the essence of being Jewish. A Jew is someone who for ever remains attached to his roots, although this may manifest itself only sporadically.

The Uniqueness of the Jewish Martyr

Both Jews and non-Jews throughout history have suffered martyrdom for their ideals. Many are the accounts, for example, of Christian martyrs thrown to the lions to entertain the Roman masses. And while it may be true that Judaism has tragically had many more martyrs and sacrifices than any other people, this difference is of course only quantitative but not qualitative.

There is, however, a deeper difference. The important distinction between Jewish and non-Jewish martyrs is the *kind* of Jews who died. In almost every religion, political system or other ideological group, those who have felt compelled to sacrifice themselves have been those who were leaders, or at the very least those who adhered to their ideologies or faiths to the best of their ability. But who ever heard of a non-believing Christian dying for Christianity? And who ever believed a defrocked Communist would die for Communism? It has always been those with the strongest faith in their particular beliefs who died for, or were prepared to die for, their ideals.

Yet the Jewish record of martyrs is saturated with the blood of non-observant, Hellenized, Anglicized Jews who died rather than convert to another religion and lose the title 'Jew'. Throughout history, the Jewish masses have been ready and willing to forfeit their lives rather than give up their Judaism. Now why would those who had almost totally abandoned Jewish practice suddenly have been prepared to die in order that they might remain Jewish? The explanation could be that the Jew has a subliminal attachment to his or her God and people, and that this attachment completely transcends anything rational or comprehensible. This is what makes the Jew: not a rational, but an intrinsic relationship to God, predicated on the possession of a Godly soul within every Jewish individual, regardless of observance or lifestyle.

An important contemporary example is the furore that arose over the *Mi hu Yehudi* (Who is a Jew?) question, in the wake of the Israeli election of 1988. There can be no greater proof of the subliminal desire for each and every Jew to be counted among the Jewish people than this. Jews the world over, many or most of whom counted themselves among the Reform wing of

Judaism, with little or no observance, raised an international outcry because they (mistakenly) believed that the Orthodox did not consider them Jews, or that legislation would be introduced in the Knesset, through the coercion of the small religious parties, that would question their Jewishness. But why all the fuss? If someone does not feel they must lead the life of a Jew, why do they protest over someone removing their title? Yet not only did they care, but vast reserves of Jewish funds were spent in an orchestrated international media campaign to counter the claim, and Prime Minister Shamir was inundated with letters from Jews around the world fighting the 'Who is a Jew?' question. There can scarcely be a greater corroboration of the subconscious affiliation that every Jew has with his or her people than this.

The message therefore is that we must seek to educate ourselves to be Jews, and to marry Jews because that is what we are. It is something that cannot be changed. To an extent, questions of whether this is negative or positive, good or bad, are irrelevant. Jewishness is a fact. Of course, we believe it to be a privilege, but first and foremost it is something that must be acted upon.

Responding to Those Couples Who are Already Intermarried

So far, we have only dealt with the problem of preventing intermarriage. The question of how couples who have already intermarried should be treated has been bungled by the Jewish community from the start. For five decades now, the orchestrated response of the world Jewish community to those who intermarry has been to make them feel that they have crossed a point of no return. They have been ostracized, sometimes in the strongest and most uncompassionate way, by parents, siblings and friends.

The result of this most un-Jewish response is that those who do intermarry use their banishment as a licence to rid themselves of any sense of responsibility or filial attachment to the Jewish community. It is no coincidence that even those who were brought up in Orthodox Jewish homes and who attended traditional synagogue services generally sign up as members of Reform and Liberal congregations when marrying out. This is simply because they feel themselves to be anathema to Orthodoxy and are made to feel such. But is this really productive? Is this what we want?

No Jew ceases to be Jewish as a result of intermarrying, and even those who cannot be persuaded to break a relationship with a non-Jewish partner before they marry must be told, in the most forceful terms, that they are still Jewish, are loved for being Jewish and that nothing they do will ever change that. They are Jewish for all eternity, regardless of who their spouse is, and they have responsibilities to the Jewish community and to perform *mitzvot*. Marrying out is not a licence to cease all Jewish activity or affiliation and far be it from any Jewish communal leader to portray it as such.

Break-up of the Jewish Family

Even those who advocate hostility to those who marry out do not themselves argue that intermarriage is a cardinal offence, requiring excommunication. They are also aware of its negative consequences for those marrying out, that it will doubtless make them feel as though the Jewish people are no longer an extended family for them. Despite these strong reasons for exercising caution, they argue that the only way to prevent others from doing likewise is by placing the culprit in a state bordering on excommunication, to forewarn others from doing the same by witnessing the scorn shown by family and friends.

It is becoming increasingly clear that treating the Jew who marries out as a leper and outcast has proved a colossal failure. It has not stemmed the tide of intermarriage at all. The statistics prove that this method has had little or no impact. If anything it has caused us to lose twice as many Jews: not only are we now losing the offspring of those who intermarry (especially in the case of a man who marries out – his children are not automatically Jewish), but we are losing those who marry out themselves, completely, by pushing them from us with both hands.

Final proof of the folly of this method is that no one dares to advocate that the same be done to homosexuals or Jews who wish to remain unmarried, both of whom are guilty of virtually the same crime as the person who marries out. The lifestyles of all three lead to the decimation of the Jewish people through neglecting to produce Jewish offspring; yet it is only those who intermarry that are made to feel that they have ridden into Jewish oblivion. The *only* justification for treating the intermarried differently from the bachelor, spinster and homosexual, in the eyes of those who advocate this hardline approach, is the supposition that he or she sets a dangerous, and more tempting, precedent, which other Jewish youth must be deterred from following. Yet, as we have seen, to castigate and vilify the intermarried has proved to be no way of combatting the problem.

Building Broken Bridges

The time has come to expend every effort on welcoming back all those who have married out, to confirm and encourage their obligations to the Jewish community and to themselves. They are entitled to be greeted with open arms and encouraged to rediscover their Jewishness. They must not be treated as individuals who have consciously rebelled against their people or their religion. When dealing with someone who has married a partner outside the Jewish community, I always try to remember that they did so because they were in love, not because they consciously sought to reject their people. We must understand that when a man marries a non-Jewish woman, he is impelled by an attraction to that woman and not by a loathing or repulsion for Jewish women. He does not perceive his action as being a fundamental contradiction of his Judaism, since to him all he is doing is impulsively pursuing his feelings. He is in love and he wants to wake up to this same woman for the rest of his life. From my experiences, negative feelings and anger come almost as a complete shock to the Jewish man or woman bringing home someone non-Jewish they hope to marry. They do not perceive that their action of marrying outside the community has any greater ramifications than their immediate lives and cannot understand what all the fuss is about.

Of course this is not a licence for intermarriage. It is, however, a licence for all Jewish people who have non-Jewish partners to reaffirm their Judaism. They have done nothing to invalidate their identity because, indeed, their Jewishness is so much a part of themselves that there is no way in which it can be compromised.

As I see it, the essential lesson is to distinguish between attempting to prevent intermarriage – in which case we must be aggressive in promoting a case for marrying within the faith – and dealing with couples who are intermarried, in which case we must be aggressive about welcoming the Jewish partner back into the fold.

How to Treat a Non-Jewish Spouse

Inevitably the question arises as to what should happen to the non-Jewish spouse. If we begin to invite and welcome an intermarried Jewish man into synagogue, and into our homes for Shabbat and festivals, should we just ignore his wife, pretend that she does not exist, and focus only on him?

Of course not. When a Jew has a non-Jewish spouse, we must do our utmost to be as welcoming and considerate as possible to them both. Firstly, because this is just and decent, and secondly, in the hope that the latter will be inspired by Judaism and consider the possibility of a proper, halakhic conversion. In my view, this is the only reasonable course.

To support my reasoning, let us consider the options for a moment. As far as the Jewish community is concerned, there are three choices. The first option is outlined above: a loving acceptance of the individual as an immutably Jewish person. The second is to ignore the couple and treat them both as outcasts and traitors. That is ineffective, repugnant, un-Jewish, and contradicts Halakha, as we have already seen. The third possibility is to encourage the couple to separate or divorce. This can either be actively or even subtly pursued through inviting the Jewish partner to participate in Jewish life and leaving the non-Jewish spouse behind. This response is even more repugnant, and yet many observant Jews are under the impression that this is, or should be, the Orthodox Jewish line. Can Judaism really countenance this kind of response? Can we condone a policy that seeks to destroy marriage? Are we to believe that we should advocate that children should grow up without a father or mother and pursue a policy of being home-breakers? Anyone who has studied Judaism and has had an opportunity to grasp its essence will find a layer of humanity, goodness and truth which underlies everything which Judaism teaches and the way in which it seeks to shape the human race. Are we to believe that actively seeking to split up an intermarried couple is part, in the name of religion, of that essence?

Always Room for Contingencies

Our precious religion, each word of which we believe was transmitted to Moses at Sinai, is not just a collection of antiquated truths and dogmas. Judaism does not only live in books. It lives on through the generations, through the constant application of its ancient truths to modern times. Judaism deals with a reality and it is full of possibilities and contingencies. There is no such thing as an inability to extricate oneself from a situation even if Judaism warns against pursuing it from the start.

There is an old Chasidic aphorism: What is the difference between a *chacham*, a wise man, and a *pikke'ach*, a clever man? A wise man is someone who will not allow himself to get into a situation from which a clever man can extricate himself.

To be sure, Judaism insists passionately that a Jewish person must marry a Jew, for reasons that transcend a religious calling. But if someone has intermarried, can we come up with no better response than to wreck homes and deprive children of their right to live with both their parents? Can we blatantly disregard the deep feelings and love that these two individuals have for one another, especially in the light of the fact that they have committed themselves to one another in marriage?

In practice, my approach can be shown to be effective in helping Jews who have married out to remain Jewish. Invariably, on any given week in Oxford at our Friday-night table the ratio of single students to married couples is about five to one. Of the couples who attend, nearly half are intermarried. In most cases, the non-Jewish partner has a very warm and friendly disposition to Judaism. What I have noticed is that when this is the case – when, say, a Jewish husband sees his non-Jewish wife getting more involved with Shabbat, festivals, and studying the Torah – he is ecstatic and relieved. In every case I have seen, the Jewish spouse will encourage this. Moreover, there is the increasingly common situation in which the non-Jewish spouse serves as the primary impetus for the *Jewish* partner to start taking part again in Jewish life. What a turnaround!

Robert Maxwell, an Oxford Resident

Here in Oxford there was a well-known Jewish publisher by the name of Robert Maxwell. He had sprung from a Chasidic Jewish family in Europe, most of whom were murdered in the Holocaust. He escaped to Britain, where he became a war hero and then a wealthy businessman. He married a Protestant woman from France, and for reasons perhaps best known to himself cut himself off from the Jewish community in the UK for many years. It was his non-Jewish wife who compelled him to become involved in the community and to devote some of his considerable resources to the promotion of Jewish concerns. I became friendly with Mrs Maxwell – their principal residence was in Oxford – and she also involved her husband in our work and campaigns. Mr Maxwell became a supporter of our activities and sponsored two of our biggest events. Unfortunately, he was later discovered to have plundered money from his company's pension funds, and I, like many others, have not unravelled his psychology. However, he did offer us friendship which in no small measure was due to the influence of his wife. I know of many similar stories here in Oxford. I mention this case because it is the most famous.

I maintain that our position must be to act lovingly and accept the non-Jewish partner. We have a duty to encourage them through the most positive and life-affirming means, to examine their husband's or wife's religion seriously with a view to joining their people. This is not proselytizing, which Judaism does not condone. Rather, it is an honest recognition of the fact that one of our members has taken a spouse from outside the community, for better or worse, and we must now seek to involve them, in an authentic and halakhically acceptable way, in Jewish life and as equal subscribers to our faith. We must emphasize how this could only benefit the marriage and the children and, most importantly, that Judaism is something worthy of embrace. It was Judaism which revealed to the world its God, a God who joins together man and woman in wedlock, a God who commands a husband to treat his wife like a queen and never to commit adultery.

A Subconscious Embrace of Jewishness

To an extent, the most difficult part of the work is already done for us. If a non-Jewish individual married a Jewish partner, their Jewishness must have been somewhat attractive to them in the first place. For there is hardly a Jew in the world, even the most assimilated and secular, who has not been influenced, either consciously or unconsciously, by their Jewishness. Our

Judaism is an integral part of our development and whether the principal Jewish influence to which we have been subjected is religious, cultural, social or political, it is still Jewish and it is indivisible from who and what we are.

If we can understand what particular qualities attracted the non-Jewish partner to a Jewish spouse, we can build upon that. We can encourage them to learn more about the Jewishness of their husband or wife and to begin, ultimately, to embrace their God, people and history.

Some will think me unduly brave in publishing these views, for on the whole they are deep anathema to the organized Jewish community. They fear that if they do not uphold their tough policy on intermarriage, it will open the floodgates to those who are contemplating marrying out but refrain from doing so because they fear the wrath of the Jewish community.

I shall never forget the first time that I summoned up the courage to publicize these views. It was at a large, very Orthodox synagogue in Manchester, to which I had been invited as guest speaker at their annual *melaveh malkah*, attended by 350 people. I spoke about the need for tolerance in Jewish society today, basing my words on the story of Joseph who had forgiven his brothers for their treachery towards him. I then dropped what they perceived to be a bombshell. *We must stop treating our Jewish brothers and sisters who marry out as outcasts*. I proceeded to defend my position with many of the arguments offered above.

This was spoken to an audience of very observant people, many of whom were *baalei teshuvah*, returnees to Judaism, who themselves had brothers, sisters and cousins who had married out. I began speaking at 9.30 p.m. and the lecture was meant to last a maximum of an hour. At first the response of the audience was one of surprise, as if they did not comprehend what I was saying. After the initial shock their attitude slowly turned first to a show of discomfort and then to outright hostility. I was truly unprepared for their reaction. I was cut off in the middle of my summation by angry questioners and the ensuing attack continued until 2 a.m.

Twisted and Emotive Thinking Clouding the Issue

One by one, they stood and challenged what I took to be a basic premise of Judaism. Firstly, some claimed that those who married out have rejected their people and we should show them the contempt they have shown us. On this first point there was significant dissent, with many in the audience disagreeing that this was the sentiment being expressed. On their second point, however, there was universal agreement: if we invite intermarried couples into our homes, the message we shall be sending our children is that it is acceptable to intermarry. Some were a bit softer in their approach. 'My younger brother married a non-Jewish woman,' said one young man. 'Although I am prepared to meet him for dinner and social outings, because I do not hold him responsible for his actions – after all he did not receive a firm Jewish education – I will allow neither him nor his wife into our home. After all, what message will this give to the children?' Thirty different couples must have stood and made the same argument.

When I was allowed to get a word in edgewise, I said this: 'Only the most twisted and warped kind of thinking would argue that because a non-Jewish spouse eats dinner at your home, this serves as a licence for your own children to marry out. By this measure of thinking, no non-Jews, or even assimilated Jews for that matter, should be allowed into our homes at all, for fear that our children will see this as a licence to emulate their lifestyles. It is completely absurd to deduce one from the other.'

Teaching Children Love for Others

On the contrary, I told them, do you know what your children will deduce from the fact that you invite your intermarried brother and his wife to your Shabbat table? They will see that Judaism is something alive which can never die. They will witness how the Jewish nation in general, and your family in particular, are so unified that they embrace all their members, regardless of their choices in life. They will reaffirm their love for Judaism because they will see that it is a loving religion. And finally, they will renew their Judaism because they will see that being Jewish is not something one practises, but something one is. There is nothing that can change this, and their uncle sitting at the table alongside them is proof of this essential truth. Although he may not have chosen a Jewish wife, he still finds himself at a Shabbat or festival table, because he remains, and will always remain, Jewish.

Most importantly, your children will learn the message of Jewish love: that regardless of the choices one has made in life, he must be embraced and always encouraged along a true and proper path.

What I Have Seen in My Upbringing

In my own home I have never witnessed any response from friends or family, other than this. I have many intermarried couples and non-Jewish people sitting at my Shabbat table every week, and yet I have every confidence that my children will grow up committed Jews because they are witnessing a dynamic Judaism, a Judaism that does not shy away from the challenges of modern society but engages the modern world and demonstrates its ability to convey to it a message of inclusion, love and tolerance amidst a steadfast adherence to tradition.

The most important lesson to learn on the subject of intermarriage is this: in the Chasidic yeshivahs I attended, in many far-flung communities of the world, we were never once told not to intermarry. It simply was not an issue. Because of the lives we led, it was obvious that this was not even a remote possibility. Whatever problems we may have had with our Jewishness – and in yeshivah there can be many – this was not one of them.

If you bring up children to understand that they are Jews, teach them about the Jewish God and give them pride in their heritage, instructing them then to marry a Jewish boy or girl, so that they perpetuate the Jewish people, is completely redundant. They will see no other possibility. They will be happy with their choice of a daughter of Sarah, Rebecca, Leah and Rachel, or a son of Abraham, Isaac and Jacob.

Chapter Sixty-one

ARROGANCE AND INSECURITY

It is not surprising that arrogance abounds at Oxford. Not all the time, and not nearly among all the people. But there is enough of it, as is to be expected wherever one finds 'the brightest and most promising' young minds. Most of the time it is harmless. At other times, it is not. The most arrogant person I have ever met was a brilliant Oxford student. Not only was he clever, but he was fortunate in that he knew how to use his intelligence. He worked steadily throughout his years here so that he came away with a prize-winning first class degree only one point below that of the top mark in the university; he was also an excellent sportsman, played in his college music group and had time to socialize and make a wide circle of friends. Despite his success, and his understandable pride in his achievements, he was missing something. Because he felt he was entirely responsible for his achievements, if anything went slightly wrong his whole world collapsed.

One term he was blissfully happy. Coming from a rather ordinary northern background, he had always secretly looked up to the self-assured students from the prosperous south-east of England who had attended expensive public schools. Even while he and his friends mocked them, pointing out that they had been 'born with silver spoons in their mouths', and therefore their achievements meant less than his because they were expected to go to Oxford and be successful, he craved their acknowledgement. According to the statistics, he should have been working in a factory, drinking seven points of warm beer a night and running through a couple of one night stands a week. Instead, he was one of the most envied students of an Oxford college. However, he felt his happiness was completed when an attractive young woman fresh from one of Britain's great public schools fell in love with him. At last, he was recognized even by the social élite. This affair gave him more social cachet than any of his academic or sporting achievements had done; he was no longer a name, but an essential part of the smart set's socializing. However, their relationship lasted only a few weeks and he was devastated when he was rejected by her. He could not understand what had gone wrong: how could she *not* be in love with someone so wonderful?

The problem was that he had always suspected this happiness and recognition was too good to be true. You see, all his achievements, all his arrogance about his success, were attempts to fill a great pit in his heart that could never be filled. He did not believe that anyone could love him for himself, so he had to give them reasons for loving him: 'I'm so witty, so clever, so successful, so popular . . .' but he could never simply say, 'I am me.' Only once did he allow his guard down and permit someone else's standing and achievements to take the place of his own, but when she let him down he never allowed it to happen again. From then on, everything revolved around himself and his achievements even more than it had done before.

The Indignity of Anger

In the first of his fourteen-volume compilation of Jewish law, the first undertaken in history, Maimonides codified a series of laws which he called *Laws of Attitudes and Character Dispositions*. In it, he listed all of those character traits which everyone should try to embrace until they become part of one's character, as well as the negative character traits which should be repulsed by the individual.

The general principle which Maimonides laid down, the novelty of his approach, was that one should always try to remain somewhere in the middle, embracing 'the golden medium' between all character dispositions. Thus it is, of course, good to be charitable, but one should not be generous to the point where one's own family suffers as a result of one's philanthropic activities. Neither should one be cheap and insensitive to the needs of others; avoid being too much of a glutton, but also avoid fasting too much. Do not indulge too much in worldly pleasure, but never allow your body to suffer from material neglect.

Deadly Love in the Extreme

Maimonides believed that people were naturally extremists, and it was far easier to pursue an extreme path than a path of healthy moderation. That people are naturally extremists can be viewed across the panoply of human life and experience. In June 1993 there appeared a story in the *International Herald Tribune* of a little girl living in the south-eastern United States who, at seven years old, jumped in front of a train and killed herself. The reason: her mother was dying of cancer in the hospital and she wanted to be together with her in heaven. This kind of intuitive, extreme display of love on the part of an impulsive child is probably far more natural than displaying a healthier, more moderate love, in the same circumstances, such as sitting with one's mother during her hour of greatest need and offering all help, comfort and assistance within the bounds of human limitation.

I have mentioned a similar story of a man living in my native home town, Miami, who one day drove up to a hospital car park, put a gun to his head, and killed himself because his brother was dying there in need of a heart-transplant and he offered his own heart, which was compatible. We should not respect these seemingly wonderful displays of sacrifice too much; they are far easier to perform, taking the extreme way out, than, say, for the same brother to take care of his brother's widow and orphans, should his brother have succumbed to heart disease.

Extremism in Religion

Perhaps the greatest form of human extremism which I witness on a continual basis is with religion itself. All too often students will begin to frequent our activities and my classes and develop an inordinate interest in Judaism. But as virtually any rabbi will attest, they often become involved too quickly and adopt a very extreme position. In Oxford this can sometimes take the form of a student desiring to give up university and study permanently in a yeshivah. Or it can take the form of a student dropping his former, 'irreligious' circle of friends and adopting a completely new social life which revolves entirely around religion. Both of these reactions, which I have witnessed all too often, are early steps along very misguided paths. The real challenge of religion is moderation, or in this case, to remain completely human and to be committed to Godly endeavour: to have one's ear attuned to the calling of heaven, but with one's feet firmly planted on earth.

To Usurp the High Priesthood

We should not seek to emulate the path of Korach, for example, the first cousin of Moses who remains infamous in the Bible for challenging the leadership of Moses personally, and accusing him of nepotism for having afforded the High Priesthood to his brother Aaron. Senior biblical commentaries have always been perplexed at Korach's motives. By all accounts, including that of the Bible, he was a great and exalted man. How would he suddenly have become so petty? According to the Lubavitcher rebbe, Korach's motives were sincere. Why else would he complain against Moses and risk Divine retribution and even death, which he received, just to become High Priest? Did his desire for high office supersede his desire to live? What the rebbe explains, however, is that Korach fell into this trap of excessiveness. He allowed himself to believe that the only way of achieving proximity to God was to have the title and duties of High Priest, the man who goes into the holiest place on earth, in the Temple, and enjoys direct Divine communion. His mistake was to assume that he was not better off developing his own inner potential. He also erred in thinking that he must emulate the role of another human being in order to enjoy proximity to God.

A similar mistake is made by all those Gentiles who, impressed with Jewish spirituality and sense of community, feel that they must become Jewish in order to partake of the same. There is no end of this outlook in Oxford. Hardly a fortnight passes without a non-Jewish student, usually someone who has had considerable exposure to our activities and classes, asking to see me privately to discuss conversion to Judaism. My response to them is always the same. Don't be an extremist. Whatever life-affirming spiritual virtue Judaism possesses can be incorporated into one's life without becoming Jewish. The idea that one must become Jewish in order to enjoy a fulfilling spiritual life is not one with which Judaism can concur.

As Great as Zusia

Perhaps the story which best illustrates this sentiment is this: Rabbi Zusia of Anapoly, when on his death-bed, began to cry in front of his assembled gathering of students. He had always served God with the greatest of joy while alive, and so it was highly uncharacteristic of him to exhibit such melancholy even at the moment of his death. His students inquired about his tears. 'Surely, Rebbe, you served the Creator with every fibre of your being. Why, then, are you so sad?' 'Because,' he told them, 'when I come before the heavenly throne and the Almighty asks me, "Zusia! Why weren't you as great as Abraham?", I will have a response. "Because, Master of the Universe, you did not make me Abraham. I am Zusia, Your servant." And when the Almighty then turns to me again and says, "All right. Then why weren't you at least as great as King David?" "Because, Master of the Universe, you did not make me David. I am Zusia, Your servant." But when the Almighty turns to me and says, "Zusia, why weren't you Zusia? Why weren't you as great as Zusia could have been?" Then, what will I say?'

Traits which are Completely Harmful

Returning to the discussion on character dispositions, Maimonides also names those human characteristics which are regarded as harmful and unacceptable. Concerning these, his advice is completely different. Whereas before, Maimonides advocated what he called 'the golden medium', in the third law of the series he writes, 'and then there are those character dispositions which it is forbidden for man to embrace in a middle path, rather he must distance himself from them to the utmost extreme.'

The very first of these is arrogance and haughtiness: the *only* proper path is for a person to be humble, and to possess a contrite and lowly spirit. The Bible says concerning our master Moses that he was 'very humble', and it does not only say that he was humble. Our Sages have taught us that a person should be contrite of spirit: whoever is proud denies the existence of a Creator, as it is written: 'and your heart will be lifted and you will forget the Lord your God.'

This statement of Maimonides requires explanation. Is Maimonides advocating that we should never have any pride in our achievements or accomplishments, that we should only pursue a path of humility? Should we never defend ourselves against attack or public ridicule; should we never derive satisfaction from the sacrifices we make to practise goodness? Surely this is a very destructive view for a person to take of him or herself: consistent denigration of one's achievements can lead to a profound destruction of the will, leaving one lifeless and immobile.

Feeling Good about Goodness

Furthermore, one of the things I encourage most among the students in the university is to be genuinely proud of themselves whenever they sacrifice something, big or small, for the benefit of someone else, or for a higher cause.

One young woman, who was not particularly observant, had the last of her final exams on the Sabbath. After we discussed the matter, she decided to defer the exam until Sunday, even though it entailed significant sacrifice, such as being invigilated. Also, there are huge festivities awaiting a finalist outside the Examination Schools upon the completion of their exams. As she would be taking the exam on her own on Sunday, she would be giving up a pretty serious celebration, three years in the making. After all was over, she came for dinner, and told me she felt good about herself. It sounded as if that made her feel uncomfortable. 'And what is wrong with that?' I asked. Well, she said, one should do the right thing because it is right. One should not necessarily feel good about it.

But I disagreed completely. 'The entire reason that people choose to do bad and evil things is because they feel good. So, for example, a person steals a car because they want it and will enjoy it. Shouldn't doing the right thing also feel good? And how can goodness compete if it is not accompanied by the same degree of pleasure, albeit in a different way, as doing something evil?'

Thus I believe it essential that people derive personal satisfaction from their goodness. Is Maimonides contesting this?

Attributing Success to Divine Endowment

One of the profound explanations given to lend insight to Maimonides' pronouncement is that of the rebbe. He explains as follows: Humility does not mean that a person lies to himself and pretends that he has no superlative character traits. In the case of Moses for instance, surely, although the Bible does indeed say that he was the most humble man on earth, it was not because he walked around thinking, 'Yes, I'm the leader of the Jews, but I'm a nothing.' Nor did Moses walk around saying to himself, 'In terms of importance, I am exactly like the water carrier.' It goes without saying that Moses was very wise and was therefore fully cognizant of his superior position, and his unparalleled access to the Almighty, above and beyond the other members of the nation of Israel.

Rather, what true humility means is that a person fully recognizes and is completely honest about his unique traits, accomplishments and achievements. However, instead of crediting ourselves with those various achievements, we should understand that they are largely a gift, that they are manifestations of the providence of God who instilled within us this unique ability, whether it be intelligence, or emotion, or writing skills. We should attribute our ability to God's providence and God's kindness, fully understanding that the reason we have this greatness is because we were blessed and fortunate in that we were given special ability from the heavens. It follows that if one takes this advice to heart, humility, as well as supreme gratitude and thanks, are sure to follow in its wake.

Homage and Humility

But even this is insufficient. This approach could still lead a person to believe that although he or she attributes their virtue to God, they still recognize that they and no one else possess that gift. Recognizing that they possess great virtue over and above the people around them still gives them a feeling of arrogance; maybe God did give it to them, but they can still say, 'I have it and no one else does.' At the same time one pays homage to our Creator for this wonderful endowment of gifts, one can also thank the Almighty for having given us the gifts, to the exclusion of everybody else. The result is the same as above: arrogance.

Greater than Moses

Therefore there is a further step in acquiring humility. Simultaneously with recognizing their particular virtue as a gift, the person must think, 'Who is to say that if my gift had been given to someone else they would not have achieved far more with it?' This is how Moses felt. He fully understood that he was the prophet, the leader and the law giver of the Jews. Surely, not one of his brethren was equal to him and there has not been someone of his stature in all of Jewish history. Nevertheless, he also recognized that he was chosen by God for a specific mission and was given great spiritual character coupled with immense spiritual potential: had those same gifts been given to another individual, Moses reasoned, they might have made themselves into a man far greater than Moses.

This is a particularly salutary lesson for those who find themselves in one of the world's finest universities. Oxford students often confess that the automatic status accorded to them by those who are unconnected with the university can lead to a certain inflated sense of their worth, to the denigration and condescension of others. Paradoxically, this is despite their often profound sense of worthlessness when they compare themselves with their peers at the university.

Inverse Bragging and Snobbery

For example, nearly every member of the university has come across the phenomenon of 'inverse bragging'. Like its cousin, inverse snobbery, the game is to be proud of things which are traditionally despised, such as laziness, and to transform them into a virtue. Oxford undergraduates tend habitually to claim that their studiousness and dedication are far below the average. They remind their peers from other institutions that the terms here are officially only eight weeks long, making the total amount of teaching time in a year a mere twenty-four weeks. The students then speak of how many essays they should have completed, usually twelve or sixteen in a term, but remark that in fact they only managed half of this amount because they spent so much time training on the river for Eights Week, rehearsing for a play, or at the college JCR and pub. Finally, when they do achieve reasonably good results, they leave other people to draw the necessary conclusion: they are absolutely brilliant to do averagely well when all the odds were against them. What a ploy! You can't lose in such a system. This is their secret source of pride.

Potential from Inception

It is always tempting to believe that one is smarter, wiser, more charismatic, and more accomplished than similar people one's age, but one must also accept that, although all this may indeed be true, it is often not largely due to one's individual efforts undertaken in a vacuum. All human efforts stem from potential that is present from conception and birth. If the same potential had been given to another person it may well have yielded even greater results. The same is true of the economic or social situation which may significantly contribute to one's success and which may not be afforded others.

Anger and the Denial of Divinity

Maimonides states that 'He who is arrogant denies the existence of God.' The meaning behind this pronouncement is that the arrogant believe their achievements and accomplishments are their own. They cannot accept that they have anything to do with God, and in doing so they deny the omnipotence and existence of God. Arrogance is the belief that all of one's achievements and accomplishments are due to one's own efforts, and not through any God-given potential. It is absolutely consonant with a complete and utter denial of a Supreme Being who endows humanity with spiritual and physical potential, a recognition of which leads us at once to thank the Creator for His graciousness, and to form bonds with our fellow men who are meant to be the beneficiaries of all God's gifts.

Chapter Sixty-two

FREEDOM OF BODY AND MIND: LESSONS FROM PASSOVER

Many of those students living in Oxford who repose faith in God complain to me how they cannot help feeling that their beliefs are constantly challenged by the secular milieu in which they live. Apparently, the norm in western society in general, and its incubation centres, the universities, in particular, is now atheism or at most a gentle deism or agnosticism: those who genuinely believe in an all-powerful Being who takes an active governing role in the universe are definitely in the minority. In such an environment, it can sometimes appear to the religious student that he is engaged in a battle.

I say that this feeling, while of course common in society in general, is particularly prevalent in the intense atmosphere at Oxford University in particular because the students and dons present here are those who wish most to get on in the world, who will not be held back, and so of course they often feel that to be successful they should assume the character of the institution. It is quite difficult to be different at Oxford. I once asked a black Oxford student, of whom there are few to the point where the void is glaringly apparent, if he lamented the fact that there were so few black students. His reply: Of course I do. Because if there were more, I would feel so much more at home and comfortable.

Indeed Oxford does have a tendency to make those who are different feel slightly awkward. Of course, black students, with whom, interestingly, I feel an instant affinity and closeness in this city, do not possess the choice as to whether they will admit and affirm their ethnicity or not. But the Jewish students do, and many make a conscious effort to discard their ethnic and religious differences and submit to the various pressures that make people feel they must conform. At the time, such pressures seem impossible to resist. Later, however, they can betray themselves as largely self-imposed and trivial.

Bad Taste in China

A woman I know, who is now a tutorial fellow, came up to one of the ladies' colleges from a small provincial town in the 1960s, when the Oxford portrayed in *Brideshead Revisited* was still enough of a reality for the young students to look forward to three years of the very best that society living could offer. Within her first week she was on the telephone to her mother in floods of tears: all the other young ladies with whom she had been taking civilized afternoon teas possessed delicate tea sets of real bone china. She had never thought that her homely mugs (holding a third of a pint of tea each) would humiliate her, but they had. Her mother came down for the weekend and helped her to choose a suitable set of tea things so that she too could take part in entertaining friends and dons in her rooms. At the time, this seemed the most important thing in the world to her.

This story of relatively minor peer pressure has a more serious sequel. In 1969 the summer of love came around and with it the need to conform in other ways: the free love of the Sixties took Oxford by storm, and so the social whirl became as concerned with sexual abandonment as much as it had previously been obsessed with flirtation and marrying well. Unfortunately, the future tutor was not emotionally prepared for the new rules of the game: she dutifully played at picking up and dropping men as though they were items of clothing, but she knew her heart was not in it. In fact, her heart was attached to one of the men she had met at a party, been involved with and then parted from, pretending to be completely unaffected: she was in love with him, and yet to be madly in love, wanting a house and two children, was the most unfashionable thing in the world then. Finally, she decided to get what she wanted rather than what the rest of her peers expected from her, so she married him, and lived happily ever after.

Of course the students of today must face similar pressures from their peers, and at the time the choice seems to present enormous difficulties, but none of us has to throw off the influence of a group of people who are *legally* our masters, as the ancient Israelites did. We rarely have to battle against formalized oppression.

Slaughtering an Oppressor's God

The grand finale of God's efforts against Pharaoh and his people was the exodus of the children of Israel from Egypt. One of the final commandments given to the Jewish people was the enigmatic decree which came immediately prior to their departure from Egypt. Five days before they were to leave, they were to take a lamb, one of the deities of Egypt, and slaughter it, placing the blood of the offering on their doorposts. So great was the importance of this offering that it constituted the means by which the Jewish people commemorated Passover in Temple times, and remains the single most important obligation associated with Passover.

Among the various rationalizations presented as to the meaning of this offering, the most interesting involves a profound psychological insight.

There are two types of freedom: freedom of the body, and freedom of the mind (or soul). We are all familiar with the 'Jewish mother syndrome, which has become the butt of many jokes. When a mother is too overbearing with her children, she induces a state of dependency from which it is difficult for the child to escape. The result is a kind of bondage. The child cannot independently make decisions, feeling the need to consult or be accompanied by parents in every important sphere of life.

A Suffocating Dependency

The Jews had been slaves in Egypt for 210 years. This was enough to induce a suffocating state of dependency. The Jews relied on the Egyptians for their food, clothing and daily decisions. No aspect of their lives was so private that the Egyptians did not enjoy supreme authority as to how it should proceed. There remained the possibility that, although God was to free their Jewish bodies from enslavement, the Jews might always remain psychologically intimidated and dependent on the Egyptians, remaining for ever enslaved in spirit.

Slavery, by definition, requires a total subjugation and state of fear to be imposed upon the slave community by their masters. Just as reclaiming physical independence involves casting off the slave-master's physical oppression, so too achieving psychological independence involves garnering the courage to confront the whole system of slavery. The Jews needed to establish an identity independent of Egyptian culture and values in order to be truly free.

Burning Effigies of Hitler

For this reason, God commanded that before the Jews left Egypt they were to have one personal confrontation with their immediate masters, to cast off the yoke of slavery for ever. They were to perform the most courageous act imaginable: taking their masters' objects of worship, the very symbol of Egypt, and slaughtering them. To understand the gravity of the act, it is somewhat analogous to Jewish inmates of a Nazi concentration camp taking pictures of Hitler and publicly burning them. Through acquiring the courage to execute the act, the Jews became free for ever.

Disguised Blessing in an Embattled History

We are not often fortunate enough to witness God's hand in history, and often it is overlooked. In 1948, the Jewish people achieved a great milestone when they set up an independent state after 2,000 years of oppression. This came at a terrible price: thousands of young soldiers lost their lives in hellish battle. Amidst the tragedy, a hidden blessing lies beneath. Perhaps, had the state come about only through peaceful means and United Nations resolutions, had the Jews not been forced to stand up militarily to those who would destroy them, there might then have been an independent Jewish state in name only. The tough, independent nature of Israelis today is legendary, and largely due to the terrible hardships that they have endured.

Battle for the Jewish Soul

The battle for this freedom continues today. Our bodies may have been freed from Egypt, but we still fight for the freedom of the soul on every front. Immersed in western culture, among people who may still sneer when seeing a yarmulka, among even Jewish colleagues who are not sympathetic to those who will only have a drink in a kosher restaurant, we are effectively in a state of bondage. We rarely feel free to pursue the lifestyle which we truly desire, simply because we feel a sense of dependency on the environment which surrounds us and dread not fulfilling its expectations.

A very high proportion of students coming through the Oxford system tell me, upon graduating, that they cannot wear a yarmulka at their law or investment banking firms, or even put a *mezuzah* on their office doors, because 'it's just not done'. This attitude, however legitimate, serves to perpetuate a kind of captivity and reliance. It betrays a belief that it is temporal institutions which sustain us, and not the providence of a benevolent Creator.

Employers and the Nile River

Another Egyptian deity which God attacked was the Nile river. Many ancient peoples naturally looked and prayed to the Almighty for their sustenance, because they witnessed their dependency on rain falling from the heavens; but in rainless Egypt, they worshipped the Nile river which overflowed its banks and irrigated their fields. What the Egyptians failed to appreciate was that even this was an act of heaven caused by the Almighty. This simple oversight led to a base and corrupt society in which the worship of brick and mortar and the beautiful Egyptian architecture and pyramids supplanted a search for the benevolent Creator. We must not repeat their mistake. A pay cheque comes from an employer who may or may not appreciate Jewish observance, but this does not make them the employee's provider, nor the first institution to whom one is obliged. After all, corporations are not charities: they pay you for the work you do, and not because you depend upon them as a supplicant; the employer would not retain your services if you were not contributing at least as much to the firm as your pay. To extend the analogy to God is of course ridiculous: we cannot hope to provide the same service to Him that we do to an employer. But we must endeavour to offer something.

Business Presentations at Oxford

Several times a year in Oxford many respected multinational corporations and law firms make presentations to the students to persuade them to come and work for them. Some are more impressive than others. The truly impressive ones, such as those offered by Goldman Sachs, IBM, Linkletters (the large UK law firm) and Salomon Brothers, are by invitation only. Those students who are invited are ecstatic. They put on their finest suits, their most posh accent and most ingratiating persona. But what they also do is ask me whether or not they should mention they are Jewish. And the observant students ask me whether they should mention in the first interview that they will not work on Shabbat or Jewish festivals. God Almighty! *Should they mention that they are Jewish?* What is the value of thousands of years of religious tradition and hundreds of years of progressive liberal thought when the brightest students in the land have to question whether they should hide their identities when seeking employment?

Non-Jews Respect Jewish Affirmation

In virtually every instance with which I am acquainted, and there are many, non-Jewish employers and employees show a great deal of respect to a Jew who insists on retaining his or her identity within the world of the market place.

One of the purposes of religion is to free humans from societal bondage so that they can be free to serve their Creator. We cannot be free to be Jewish if we are totally dependent on a foreign culture or way of life, if we believe Judaism is something only to be practised in the privacy of the home, and insist on leading a compartmentalized lifestyle. When the Jews departed from Egypt, it was with heads held high, looking forward to a glorious future. We are that future and we must regain their sense of pride in a treasured heritage, and a dependency only on the 'outstretched arm' of the One who redeemed us from Egypt.

Chapter Sixty-three

AN INFINITE VOICE WITH NO ECHO

Like all idealists, students feel that the world is worth the huge effort required to change it. The number of student societies dedicated to social improvement and modification at Oxford is amazing, and they thrive because students are young and unstoppable in their enthusiasm to make the world a better place and not to repeat the mistakes of their forebears.

All these societies try to get as many freshers as possible to sign up with them at the beginning of their first term here in a huge fair that is held in the maze of the building called Examination Schools. Freshers emerge slightly dazed from their bombardment by enthusiastic tiddlywinkers (for some reason they always tell you that you could get a quarter blue by representing the university against Cambridge if you stick at it long enough), members of the Medieval Society and devotees of the Psychedelic Club. But in many ways the organizations that do the most important work are not the ones that tend to devour innocents at Freshers' Fair. But what this does go to show is that even students understand the importance of advertising and getting their messages across.

Making Messages Meaningful

Modern society increasingly attributes great importance to the power of words. Whether these words are the 'bits' of a computer, the formulae scientists use to understand complicated aspects of the physical world, or are written by politicians in treaties, we can no longer ignore the fact that our world is becoming regulated by words as much as it ever was by the power of force. In Oxford, philosophers have for centuries attempted to understand the meaning of the universe, but the current trend is to understand through analysing language itself: Wittgensteinian/linguistic philosophy has really taken hold here. Words seem to be the key to all knowledge and all power.

We seem to be forgetting something, though. What does it really mean when a government signs a treaty to protect free trade, for example? Does the paper itself guarantee the free movement of goods amongst countries, or is it the threat of sanctions and trade blocks that keeps the world market moving? The words are worthless unless those who agree to them feel they will be backed up by action. The same with the computer I use: the binary codes it uses to store information are incomprehensible to me, but this is not a problem because I want to use the computer to achieve my objectives. As such it is only a means to an end. The language of a computer programmer has no intrinsic value to me other than the fact that it can be utilised to realise my goals. The way my computer processes information is largely irrelevant unless it starts making mistakes in the things I want it to accomplish and needs to be rectified.

In fact, words and information are valuable when they are translated into something that is meaningful to human lives, not in themselves. The same is true of the ultimate word, the Word of God. This was so important that it has been made into a part of us, not just an optional layer that we can choose to have or not to have as the fancy takes us, and because it is important it demands action.

Therefore on an autumn night we celebrate Simchas Torah, the festival of rejoicing with the Torah. We do not just express our joy at the Word of God in words, we dance and act joyfully. The next morning we complete the reading of the last section of the Pentateuch with the sublime words, '. . . before all the eyes of Israel', and start reading it once again with the words, 'In the Beginning . . .'

No celebration can ever be complete, no festival can possibly be translated into its full potential for joy, unless one truly understands the reason for celebrating. What, after all, is the Torah, and what makes it unique? Only through an absolute comprehension of the essence of the Torah and what it is trying to do can I put on my dancing shoes, and find the energy to shake, rattle and roll for twenty-four hours non-stop as we do with students in Oxford.

An Infinite Voice

At the giving of the Torah at Sinai, the voice of God that was heard by the children of Israel is described as a '*kol gadol ve'lo yassaf* . . .'; it was 'a great voice that did not end', in other words, 'an infinite voice'. The *midrash* gives three explanations of what an 'infinite voice' is like. The first is that God's voice at Sinai split into the seventy languages of the world so that it was understood by all nations in all tongues. The second explanation is that the voice heard at Sinai served as the source for all prophecy throughout the ages. The most interesting of all the explanations of the 'infinite voice' is the third explanation, and it is also the one which I believe best conveys the essence of what the Torah is.

The *midrash* explains that when the Ten Commandments thundered forth from Sinai, there was no echo. The powerful voice that emanated from Sinai was absorbed by the mountains, the rivers, and most of all, by the people themselves. The voice did not rebound from any physical barrier. This is what made it an infinite voice. Normally, the greater and mightier the sound, the greater the echo, so when God spoke at Sinai with an infinite voice, one would expect that it should have rebounded in such a powerful and awesome way as to shake the entire earth.

On the contrary, the voice at Sinai was authenticated and proved beyond the shadow of a doubt to be God Himself talking because His words were absorbed by creation. The ten utterances did not merely rebound from the mountains and the people, but permeated their whole being. In other words, the greatness of the voice was that it left an imprint on its listeners, not that it dispersed. Those who heard God speaking at Sinai could not be passive. They also could not ignore or remain apathetic to His message. It disturbed them too deeply. They had to wake up and heed its call.

There are many people who love Shakespeare and other classics of English literature. Still, it is rare for someone to come out of a performance of a Shakespeare play to find that it has changed his or her life. One might be inspired by Shakespeare, or start thinking as a result of a play, but the words tend not to force us into human action. They do not make us march. The great power of the Torah is that it directs and affects our actions. It is absorbed in a very personal way, and does not merely rebound from our senses.

The Call to Action

After the death of our forefather Abraham, God appeared to his son Isaac and told him not to worry: 'I will always be with you and bless you.' The reason given was: '*Eikev asher shoma Avraham bekoli.*' While this is taken to mean, 'Abraham followed in my footsteps', the verse literally reads 'because his heel followed me'. The effect of God's words on Abraham was such that even the lowest, most mundane part of his body was permeated with holiness.

While the mind is the seat of the intellect, and the heart represents our emotions, the heel represents our actions. The sublimity of God's message to Abraham was that even his heel, his actions, were influenced by God's calling. The ultimate directive that should be adopted by a religious person is that one must 'know God in all of one's ways', '*bechol derochecha doeihu*', in everything one does, not just in the higher mental faculties, but primarily in the so-called mundanity of action.

Ascertaining the Authenticity of Scripture

In this city, there are scholars who sit with a finetooth comb dissecting every letter of the Torah to ascertain its historic validity. Many questions are being examined; for example, was it written by a single author or many? To me, the real test of the Torah's truth is its ability to be absorbed – even by a thirteen-year-old boy at his Bar Mitzva.

This is where the difference between the Torah and mere literature lies. Yes, Shakespeare can fire one's emotions, and Byron one's passions, and Blake one's imagination. The real question is whether their work changes what you do. Not what you feel, but what you do! Does it make you into a better person? Is the voice which you are hearing an infinite voice, or a man's voice? Does it change only the heart and the mind, or does it shape the heel, your very actions?

The Torah with which we dance on Simchas Torah is designed to transform us into good people. It is not there to make one feel good or look good, but to *be* good.

This is also the reason why there is a Jewish custom throughout the ages that when a rabbi dies he insists on being buried with his lectern and the table on which he studied the Torah. In many Jewish communities, the actual coffin was made out of the table and the lectern. Even these inanimate objects had absorbed his words of wisdom, and should come with the scholar to his eternal place of rest.

Aristotle the Philosopher and Aristotle the Man

The story is told that Aristotle was once seen by his disciples walking out of a house of ill-repute. They were flabbergasted. 'You! Aristotle! The great philosopher!' 'Calm!' he shouted to his students. 'When I teach you, only then am I Aristotle the philosopher. But now, I am Aristotle the *man*.' Judaism is different. When we observe a religious Jew not acting in accordance with religious teaching, cheating in business, lying or being mean, we call him or her a hypocrite, and say that their action has made a '*chilul hashem*', 'a desecration of God's name'. And it is. Not because the person claims to be religious and then acts in an irreligious fashion. Rather, the hypocrite's action demonstrates that although he or she has studied the Torah, it has not influenced their being. Actions that are irreligious belie and undermine the potency of the Torah. The hypocrite may even appear to be living a Jewish life, but it is not the kind of life which follows from an infinite voice if it does not lead to the right kind of actions. Refusing to act as well as understand treats the Torah as the equivalent of mere poetry or literature.

The challenge given to our generation and the many young people who study at this university is not whether the Torah is powerful enough to influence actions: of course it is, it even penetrated solid rock. The real question is whether we are willing to listen. Are we brave enough, distinct enough, to at least open our ears and allow Judaism to work its magic?

This is the message of the Torah reading which is read every year on the Sabbath immediately preceding Simchas Torah. All Moses asks of the people is to listen: 'Open your ears', '*Ha'azinu*'. Listen to the infinite voice. Notwithstanding how infinite it is, it is still a voice. It requires some kind of receiver, someone who listens as well as hears. Make that tiny little effort. You will see that it will impress you and lead you to live an extraordinary life.

To be Attentive and Listen

No one asks a student to jump into the sea of the Talmud and learn to swim just like that. Nobody asks a young person to climb mountains alone – Moses was much better at this than us anyway. What is required of us is to be attentive enough to listen. Oxford is a wonderful place for secular learning, let us make it a place for spiritual knowledge also. Judaism has an eternal message. The time has come for you to be the carrier. So absorb the message and become a participant.

'*Ha'azinu hashamayim va'adebeirah*.' 'Listen, O heavens and I will speak, the earth, to the utterances of my mouth.' Moses cried out, 'I will speak words that will shake the heavens and rattle the earth.' Will it penetrate your heart?

If it can leave no impact, it appears that the Torah is not an infinite voice that can permeate and affect all our actions. The test of the Torah's truth is its ability to be absorbed.

Search for the Perfect Groom

A wonderful story is told of one of the great Torah Sages of the previous generation. He wanted to marry off his only daughter, so he travelled to the great yeshivah of Valozhen in Lithuania, banged on a table, and said, 'I have a daughter of marriageable age. She is beautiful and wise and I will allow only the finest to marry her. I have a difficulty in the Talmud which I am sure none of you can help me with. If you can, you will have her hand in marriage.' He wrote the question on a piece of paper, stuck it to the noticeboard and said he would take answers every day of the week from 9 to 12. The first morning, three hundred students queued up to try to answer the question, but none of the answers were adequate. The next day there were a hundred, the next day only fifty, and finally there were three. All three gave the wrong answer, as all the others had before them.

The rabbi stood up, thanked everyone for trying, saddled his horses and was off. In the distance he saw a young boy, struggling with a large volume of the Talmud, chasing after him. Stopping the horse, he asked the boy why he was following him. 'Do you have an answer?' 'No,' said the young boy, 'but before you go, I'd like to know what the answer is.' 'Ah!' The rabbi jumped with joy. 'You're the one I was looking for. When I said the finest, I did not mean the brightest, but the one most interested in learning, in listening.'

After the serious times associated with Rosh Hashanah and Yom Kippur, times in which we are pressed and squeezed in serious judgement, Sukkot and Simchas Torah arrive, and we celebrate by dancing with the Torah. The question that is often asked is, 'Why dance with a closed Torah? On the contrary, open it up! Read it! Appreciate its message. Study it and be impressed by its wisdom.'

Dancing with a Closed Torah

The reason we dance with the Torah closed is to acknowledge its power even while it is not being read. It is the association with the Torah that has kept us Jewish through three millennia. Many Jews were not able to understand its verses or fathom its depths. Even they saw the Torah as their inspiration. They lived Torah lives and they rejoiced at the thought that a Torah existed, even if they could not understand it. Thus we dance with the Torah closed. We are not celebrating the fact that the Torah is so intelligent, or so inspiring. We are celebrating the fact that the Torah *is*. Its very existence makes us happy.

Have you ever seen relatives meeting at an airport? They hug and kiss before they even speak. The message given is, 'Before you even make me laugh, or tell me fascinating tales of your travels, I am plain thrilled just to see you. I am ecstatic at the mere thought that you are here. I love you.'

The same message is conveyed on Simchas Torah. We rejoice in the fact that we are lucky enough to possess a Torah, and hope that the joy we experience on that day will permeate the rest of our year.

A number of years ago the movement which calls itself 'Jews for Jesus' began a massive advertising campaign in the USA. It started with thousands of newspaper advertisements across the USA which proclaimed the enigmatic message 'I found it', without really clarifying what it was that they had found. It was only later that they made it clear that they had found Jesus. The Jews of the USA responded with a campaign of their own: tens of thousands of car bumper stickers which read, 'I never lost it. For three thousand three hundred years.'

On the day of Simchas Torah, as we dance and celebrate the fact that the Torah is, we do not lose sight of the essential message. Let us stand and proclaim every day: Five thousand seven hundred and fifty odd years after creation, I am willing to listen. I am prepared to be part of an extraordinary tradition. And I shall never lose it!

Chapter Sixty-four

THE RETURN OF THE ABRAHAM JEW

For an institution so renowned for its serious scholarship in many fields of knowledge, it might at first seem illogical that Oxford University is also famous for the capacity to have fun. Apparently, hard work needs hard play to set it off and make it all worthwhile, and the extravagant way in which Oxonians enjoy themselves has caught the imagination of the public at large, featuring in many people's idea of what the university is all about.

Play at Oxford tends to be either largely passive or manically active: punting lazily in summer sunshine on the Isis with a bottle of wine and a gramophone playing, or rounding off a tough academic year by staying up all night dancing at a Commemoration Ball.

Trashing after Finals

A less well-known celebration is the near-mandatory 'trashing' when Schools are over. The final examinations (Schools) at Oxford are extraordinarily demanding: the papers are rarely separated by more than a day, and on most days two three-hour exams must be endured. Even the rooms are daunting: they are like beautifully designed spaceship hangers, extraordinarily large L-shaped rooms with huge clocks ticking away the minutes of an exam for three hundred people. To round off and complete this intimidating experience, on which the whole of your academic career depends (there are few second-year exams to spread the burden of work, and certainly no continual assessment), you must submit to being humiliated by your friends and supporters. In 'sub-fusc' (exam attire of black suit, white shirt, white bow-tie, gown and mortar board), the lass or lad who has just finished the hardest round of exams in their life must stand still to be 'trashed'. Those who have loyally met the finalist on coming out of Schools every day cover him or her with a mix of wet and dry foodstuffs – flour, eggs, baked beans, you name it. These erstwhile attacks have become so troublesome for the traffic on High Street and have attracted so many hundreds of tourists that a few years ago the police felt they had to step in and ban the festivities at the risk of arrest, fine and, worst of all, being sent down from the university. Thus, in addition to the colourful pageantry which awaits the Oxford finalist at the conclusion of his or her exams, they can now also look forward to the stern looks of Oxford's uniformed police trying to maintain order with polite but firm nods, and 'Please keep on moving, just move right along.'

Transcending Limitations

No one is able to tell me the meaning of this ceremony. There is no logical reason for it, yet every year a large number of (supposedly) the most intelligent people in Britain allow this to happen to them. They might complain that they find it revolting, but they show only token resistance and certainly offer no logical arguments against it, apart from suggesting that their best suit or clothes might be ruined, in which case the 'trashers' sometimes let the victim change first. If I personally hear this from a student, I will endeavour to pour even more mush upon him or her, in an effort to help them learn to transcend their 'limitations.'

A few years ago, one of our financial supporters, who was in the cosmetics business, and who was due to make a payment to us but could not, instead donated three hundred cans of shaving cream, telling me to sell them. I don't have much use for shaving cream myself. I am quite bearded in the Chasidic tradition, and I have not had much success in selling them. But they do come in handy every June for greeting my students who are finishing exams. Rationality is entirely suspended and symbolically ignored when they enact this most preposterous ceremony in order to celebrate the end of the intellectual exhaustion of Schools.

Contradictory Logic

Yet these are so often the same people who find religion off-putting because it seems to them illogical. They will not participate fully because they cannot understand everything intellectually; their only understanding is intuitive or emotional, and that type of belief seems to make religion less true. Clearly, to believe we do not only have to understand, we also have to have the confidence, the love of the thing for itself, to overcome gaps in our knowledge . . . and to do something about our beliefs, even though they are not readily apprehensible.

Abraham, the first Jew, was the first to discover a Creator. For a moment, let us contrast God's revelation at Sinai when He gave the Torah and revealed Himself to all as the Master of the Universe, with Abraham's self-discovery of God in his youth. At Sinai, the world came to know that there was a God because the Almighty made Himself known. It would be difficult for any Jew standing at Sinai to deny that God was there amidst the spectacular spiritual firework display that ensued. There was thunder and lightning, a heavenly voice, and a host of assembled angels. Stated simply, at Sinai God revealed Himself to the Jewish people.

But God did not reveal Himself to Abraham. Rather, Abraham used his higher cognitive faculties to reject the prevailing idolatrous notions of the time, and to embrace and propagate the knowledge of an infinite, invisible Creator. Abraham was not forced to believe in a Creator, he *came to know* that there was a Creator. Stated simply, Abraham discovered that there was a God of his own accord, not through Divine intervention.

Surely, this was an unparalleled feat, deserving mention in the Torah. Yet the Torah makes no explicit mention of Abraham's greatness, or his discovery of God in his youth. We know of it only from rabbinical *Aggada* and *midrash*. The Torah's first mention of Abraham, in fact, is many years later when he is given his first Divine command: '*Lech lecha*' – 'Leave your father's household and go unto the land that I will show you.'

A Choice Independent of Merit

The Maharal (Rabbi Yehuda Loew) of Prague, immortalized for all generations to come as the creator of the Golem, wrote that the Torah does not divulge why Abraham merited God appearing to him, because that would imply that God's choice of him was dependent on his sublimity or virtue. If the Jews were not worthy of God at some later date, God might annul His choice of them. The Torah does not speak of Abraham's virtue, so that it is not implied that God's love for Abraham and his descendants is dependent on their righteousness. Rather, theirs is a parental love which bonds them for ever.

This insight can serve as an important lesson for our generation. Committed Jews today can be divided into two groups. The first is the traditional type, namely those who were educated in a Jewish way of life by their parents. We might describe this generation as that of *revelation*, not only because, in most cases, they trace their observance through an unbroken chain back to the revelation at Sinai, but also because their Judaism did not come about through a process of self-discovery. Rather, they practise what they were taught to practise by their parents.

Return of the Abraham-Jew

Amazingly, today's generation of Jews incorporates a second dimension in which Judaism has at last come full circle. We are witnessing a resurgence of the generation of Abraham. There is a significant number of committed Jews to whom no Judaism has ever been revealed. Rather, they have embraced its truth of their own accord, through trial and error and through experimentation. Their faith has mainly been achieved by logical thought, through a process of self-education. Like Abraham our forefather, many today are returning to the fold through a personal process of investigation.

Those who are part of this wonderful process of self-discovery carry with them the virtue of Abraham, but also one danger. By assuming a completely rational approach to their Judaism they run the risk of rejecting the less rational elements of the faith and dissociating themselves from aspects of Judaism that are socially unacceptable in a secular world.

Maintaining Support for Israel

The state of Israel has of late, since the election of the Labour government headed by Prime Minister Yitzhak Rabin, once again become fashionable. When it was being governed by a right-wing government that was deeply scorned by the West, many Jews eschewed any overt affiliation with the state. Now, the popularity of the Rabin government has brought these Jews back into the fold. Although no one is suggesting that Jews should stand blindly behind policies which they deem to be morally objectionable, at the same time the Jews should enjoy a deeper association with Israel than allow it to be dependent on the latest *New York Times* editorial. The Jewish attitude to an Israel that they feel has gone astray must be the same as parents who have a daughter who may be in need of moral and spiritual education. They still love the child, not for her righteousness, but because she is a part of them. The parents are willing to work with the child to better her ways.

The *Jerusalem Report* interviewed and reported on one international fashion designer and the negative comments on his Jewishness that he was said to have made to a prominent German journalist: 'Being Jewish makes me throw up . . .' His explanation of his nausea was matter of fact. 'Of course anything that makes life tough very often makes one upset . . . If I were bald in a young man's society of curly hair, it wouldn't make me cheerful. I think anything that makes life tough is not to be welcomed . . . If one lives a certain kind of life and wants to achieve certain things, it's annoying to have in one's way such extraneous matters as anti-Semitism.'

Clearly, if the designer's Judaism involved more benefits than sacrifices he might be more of a committed Jew.

Consistency is a Sign of Significance

The truly special things in life are those to which our commitment remains constant. Those to which our attitude fluctuates are often less significant. The same is true of a person's Judaism and attitude to the Jewish people. Questions of popularity and personal benefit should be of little consequence to the truly committed individual: one must strive to transcend a purely rational attachment to one's tradition and people to reach an appreciation that will never waver amidst social and personal upheaval.

It was this thought that the Maharal was trying to convey in his explanation of why the Torah omits any mention of Abraham's merit. God's love for Abraham struck deeper, was far more permanent, than Abraham's good behaviour on any given day. By this, God was teaching Abraham a lesson. His rational approach to Judaism was most commendable, but it was only the first step in a process that would culminate in revelation (at Sinai), a time when the Jews would witness God's appearance. God's presence would become something that they could never forget, could never deny, and to which they would always remain steadfastly loyal.

We must endeavour to take this timeless message to heart, today.

Chapter Sixty-five

WHEN RELIGION BECOMES A FOREIGN GOD

The summer term at Oxford is a time of dramatic contrasts, and not just because of the changeable British weather that brings chill winds one day and blazing sunshine the next. In the other two university terms, there seems little to distinguish between those in their first, second or final years. But in summer, finalists are slowly driving themselves over the edge by panicking about their forthcoming examinations, while those in their second year are indulging in a surfeit of laziness: punting, picnicking, playing croquet, watching Renaissance plays in the open air, chatting in fragrant college gardens . . . and having the occasional relaxed but very productive tutorial. One history don likes to refer to the garden where the students of his college relax as 'a sink of idleness', but they are never quite sure whether he genuinely disapproves, or if he is simply not being serious, in keeping with the spirit of the summer term.

For those with time to think, this term is the perfect opportunity to assess one's goals in life. The time spent trailing a hand in the water of the Isis or messing around on the thousand-year-old Port Meadow with a football is not time wasted, it is time spent finding out what things are worth striving for and being committed to. Suddenly things may come into focus, and the task is then to keep them in mind through the stress of finals, when nothing seems more important than getting through those horrific exams with a decent pass.

It is so easy to let the peripheral issues get out of hand, to attribute such importance to them that if the slightest thing goes wrong our whole world seems to disintegrate. University is a complete education, not just the passing of a few examinations; and likewise religion is a way of relating to God and those around us, not an end in itself.

I know a student who grew up in the Christian tradition; her father is an enthusiastic born-again Christian. Every time she goes home to visit her parents, he asks her if she would like to go to church on Sunday, and every time she answers 'no'. She knows that he would love her to go, but she cannot bring herself to attend a service in the church that first put her off religion when she was a little girl. When she visits her fiancé she is happy to go to church with his mother, who is a Catholic convert; when she visits her sister, she often goes to church with her; but she cannot participate in a normal service in the parish church of her home town that has so many negative memories. She is only just realizing that she cannot reject God just because she associates Him with the oppressively middle-class church that she grew up with, where politeness was apparently regarded as more important than goodness. She is only now learning to dissociate the goodness of God from the errors of the past.

The Torah too addresses this issue of the relationship between goals and the means of achieving them, and has a clear pronouncement on what we are to regard as really important. By investigating this theme we will also learn much about substituting a means for an end, and vice versa.

Binding of Isaac

One of the most courageous, yet enigmatic, stories of the Bible is that of the binding of Isaac ready for a sacrifice. God tested Abraham by asking him to bring his beloved son, the son whom God had promised would prosper into a great and mighty nation, up to the altar as a burnt-offering. Without hesitation, Abraham enthusiastically pursued God's wish.

Even today, the Akeida, as it is known, is read as part of the daily prayer liturgy, and is read from the Torah on the Jewish New Year, Rosh Hashanah, as well as on other auspicious Jewish occasions. It serves as the ultimate symbol of Jewish sacrifice and readiness to fulfil the will of the Creator. Although martyrdom is not uncommon to our nation, the submission Abraham was prepared to make was obviously a very special case. Many Jewish parents throughout history, notably Chanah and her seven sons associated with the story of Chanuka, have been called upon to make the ultimate sacrifice, but Abraham was willing to offer up his own son and to do it himself. He was prepared to sacrifice Isaac, not in opposition to the enemies of the one God, but as a sacrifice to Him.

It may seem strange, but I guarantee that the following is true. In all the time that I have been in Oxford this has been the most recurring question and challenge to Judaism that has been put to me: How could God desire a human sacrifice? Why did Abraham not object to God's calling on this occasion, especially on religious grounds? Where was God's compassion, and where was Abraham's humanity?

God as the Epicentre of Existence

The reason for Abraham's enthusiastic acquiescence as well as the subsequent praise he received from the Creator for his action is this. One of the most fundamental tenets of Judaism is the proscription against worshipping a foreign god. This does not only entail not bowing to a piece of marble.

Rather, an idol is anything which replaces the One God as the epicentre of one's existence. If a man lives only to make money, then mammon has become for him an alien god. Similarly a person who is arrogant, and lives only to fulfil his or her heart's desire, has supplanted God with the human self. There are those to whom religion too can become a foreign god.

The only purpose of a systematized religion, of any system of beliefs and practices believed to be of Divine origin, is to bring people closer to God. A religion without a God, or one that neglects or forgets about God, or His will, becomes a foreign god in itself.

The Talmud speaks of a man who watches a woman drowning in the river, yet refrains from saving her for reasons of modesty. The Talmud calls this man a fool, but the case is worse than that. He is an idolater. He has replaced God, who values human life above all else, with religious concerns of modesty. He has forgotten that the only reason to behave modestly is that it is God's will. The same God commanded that human life supersedes such concerns.

Similarly, a yeshivah student in Israel who, in a time of terrible danger, objects to fighting for the protection of his people because he must study the Torah, has a new god. The Torah, not the God of life who delivered it at Sinai, is the one to whom he now pays homage as he abandons his people.

Relating Only to Oneself

Imagine a husband who travels the world as a merchant, not to support his wife, but to earn the necessary money to buy her beautiful gifts and to give her an extravagant life. As she loves him, she is miserable because they are rarely together, yet he insists this is the way to make her happy. This husband is not in a relationship with his wife. He relates only to himself. He has forgotten that marriage, or any relationship, serves only as a vehicle to coming closer to another person. The relationship is a means, not an end. He must ask his wife what makes her happy, and not suppose that his conception of the way in which the relationship should operate is necessarily correct. Otherwise, he is not married to his wife, but to his own conception of marriage.

What is the real quality of the love a father has for his child if he cannot bring himself to punish her, even after she has put herself in danger by running into a busy road. Such a parent has supplanted his child's well-being, perhaps even the child herself, with his love for the child. The ultimate purpose of love, of any emotional effusion, is to bring people closer together. Yet this parent's refusal to act reveals that he has a greater desire to feel for his daughter than to act on the child's behalf.

Love is not an end, but a means. It is not enough to feel affection and love, one must do something about it.

Love for Children Takes Precedence over their Welfare

This is a very important lesson for today's parents who seem utterly helpless in guiding their children along a preferred path. Very often parents will come from London and tell me of their children studying in the university along with an unfortunate situation gripping their child's life, and how they feel helpless to persuade their child to choose an alternative path. 'Rabbi, will you please speak to our child?' they ask. And why can't you speak to him or her yourself? 'Well, Rabbi, we fear we may lose him if we push him.' Thus fear of alienating one's child has caused an untold number of contemporary parents to abrogate their natural responsibility of providing insight and guidance to their children to navigate the confounding pathways of life.

One set of parents came to see me to tell me that their seventeen-year-old daughter was dating a twenty-eight-year-old Hell's Angel, complete with leather jacket, motorcycle, tattoos, and a terrible propensity to smoke pot with their daughter in her upstairs room. He also insisted on touching very private areas of her body in their living room, where they would make out on the couch. I knew the girl and they asked if I could do something. They felt they couldn't because she threatened that she would not come home from Oxford to visit them any more. Of course, I offered to help. But I also told them that they should never put their love for their child, and their fear of losing her, before the welfare of the child herself.

Idolising Religion

The same applies to the religious individual. The Jewish man who throws a stone at another Jew driving on Shabbat, in the name of God, has made religion into an end, not a means of coming closer to God. The religion says that the Sabbath is holy. The stone-thrower feels the Jew in the car is desecrating its holiness. He feels he must therefore take action. He lifts his stone. He does not consider whether the Almighty, to whom religion is designed to draw him closer, is pleased with this action. Religion has now become his god – a foreign god.

When I was younger I was engaged in trying to bring a little more Jewishness to the streets of Jerusalem. My friends and I would stand in the thoroughfares of Ben Yehudah, one of the busiest shopping districts of the city, offering Shabbat candles to the women and asking men if they would like to don *tefillin* before Shabbat. We had always been careful not to coerce people, so one Friday evening when we were standing in the summer heat trying to catch the attention of passers-by, I was shocked by one woman's reaction to my offer of candles. She was absolutely livid; not just offended when I had asked her to take the candles, but deeply, almost uncontrollably, angry. She started screaming at me, 'You want me to accept those after what you've just done to me? I can't believe it!' she went on, using inflammatory language and being very abusive. I was flabbergasted. Obviously there was more to this than met the eye, so I asked her what the matter was. After a while she calmed down enough to tell me, and what she said grieved me to my heart.

She had been walking with her two young children in Jerusalem, seeing the sights and enjoying the blazing sunshine of the Jerusalem summer, and she had decided, like so many others before and since, to see Meah Shearim, the Hundred Gates, the district of the so-called ultra-Orthodox Jews. She had taken a bus to this area that is more than anything else reminiscent of an eighteenth-century *stetl*, and alighted to be confronted almost immediately by a highly indignant man. As it was so hot she was wearing a dress with no sleeves, and this contravened the strict dress code expected in the area: the man who came up to her was elderly, dressed all in black with hat and overcoat, and was talking to her in Yiddish. She had no idea what he was saying, but as he went on his voice was raised higher and higher, until at last he was shouting at her as loudly as he could.

Finally, he spat in her face, and at this point her two little ones, who had become increasingly fretful during his tirade against their mother, escaped her hand-hold and darted into the crowd. She turned her back on him and set off, shaken by his abuse (of which she had not understood one word, although she gathered he was upset by her dress), but more concerned to find her children.

She told me that she had found them only after hours of searching, and her search had brought her near to the street where we were then, five blocks away from the scene of her ordeal. When she found them, she had vowed to take them from the *cheder* where they had been studying each Sunday, because she wanted nothing more to do with a faith that was so intolerant. She explained that as soon as she had seen my Chasidic clothes she had associated me with the man who had abused her and made her children run away for fear.

I told her that I dissociated myself entirely from this man's un-Godly behaviour, and by the end of our conversation she was willing to accept that his abuse would not be approved by our Bible, by our rabbis or by the majority of Orthodox Jews. It was a hard struggle to convince her, though, and one that would have been unnecessary if the man had respected his God before his religion in the first place. He was wearing the garb of Judaism, but his deeds were representative of a faith in his own interpretation of his religion, and not an indication of his respect for God.

Aversion to Creating False Gods

Abraham knew this only too well. He understood the danger of replacing God with religion. At the time of the Akeida, Abraham, the first Jew, was old. The only living person who could have continued the religion that he had discovered, the monotheistic belief that he laboured so hard to establish and disseminate, was his son, Isaac. Yet the Almighty asked him to kill Isaac, to destroy the heir of all his belief and religion. With the slaughter of Isaac, all the religious ideals which gave meaning to Abraham's life, including the belief in a benevolent Creator, who keeps his promises, would have been shattered. Judaism would have been lost to the world. How then could he contemplate obeying God's command?

Abraham understood that a religion without a God, or a religion which neglects the very desire that God expressly requests, however irrational it may appear, has become an idol. Abraham made a living out of abolishing idols. He was careful not to make monotheism into the latest pretender.

Moses Requests to Enter the Land of Israel

Moses was the supreme leader of the Jews throughout their sojourn in the wilderness. He had an extraordinary connection with God, so much so that his brother and sister were rebuked for criticizing his judgement. God made it clear to Miriam and Aaron that Moses had His protection: 'And he said, Hear now my words: If there be a prophet among you, I the Lord will make myself known unto him in a vision, and will speak unto him in a dream. My servant Moses is not so, who is faithful in all my house. With him will I speak mouth to mouth, even apparently, and not in dark speeches, and the similitude of the Lord shall he behold; wherefore then were ye not afraid to speak against my servant Moses?' (Numbers 12:6–8).

Yet despite his special privileges, his first and only request to God was blankly refused. Throughout the Bible, Moses supplicates God to be allowed to enter the Promised Land. The *midrash* expands this request and insists that even if the price he had to pay was the loss of all his limbs or if his first breath there was to be the last of his mortal life, he simply wanted to breathe the holy air of God's promised destination of the Jews.

The biblical commentaries all attempt to explain why Moses, having led God's people through the wilderness for forty years, was not permitted to enter the land of Israel. The reason God explicitly states is that Moses was punished for hitting a rock to obtain water for the people in the desert of Zin when he had been commanded to speak to it.

God had commanded Moses to make a spectacular demonstration of His power by telling inanimate stone to give water for the people: 'Take the rod, and gather thou the assembly together, thou with Aaron thy brother, and speak ye unto the rock before their eyes; and it shall give forth his water, and thou shalt bring forth to them water out of the rock: so thou shalt give the congregation and their beasts drink' (Numbers 20:8).

Moses was supposed to show that the power of God is so great that even if His servants merely command an object that lacks any consciousness, it will obey. Instead, he used physical force on the rock to make it give water: 'And Moses lifted up his hand, and with his rod he smote the rock twice: and the water came out abundantly, and the congregation drank, and their beasts also. And the Lord spake unto Moses and Aaron, Because ye believed Me not, to sanctify Me in the eyes of the children of Israel, therefore ye shall not bring this congregation into the land which I have given them' (Numbers 20:11–12).

But the source of his error runs deeper than mere disobedience. Essentially, Moses failed to make a *Kiddish Hashem*, a sanctification of God's name. Moses' error has nothing essential to do with the fact that he hit the rock; it centres on his omission of the greatest imperative a Jew has, namely to make God known to His world, to serve as a light unto the nations.

Light Creates and Brings into Existence

Examining this light metaphor, it will be appreciated that without the benefit of light, things just as well may not exist. If one, for example, tours the Louvre but it is pitch dark, will it really matter whether or not there is a *Mona Lisa* hanging on the wall to be admired? As far as the observer is concerned, it simply does not exist. Stated in other words, light does not merely illuminate, it actually brings things forth into existence. Whereas four out of five of the human senses operate directly between the sense and the object, and thus one can smell a flower, feel a table, or taste a dish, or hear an orchestra, when it comes to seeing our eyes are useless without the benefit of light. It is not enough to have eyes and to have a painting in front of you. One must have light. And it is only once one has light that reality is translated from the potential into the actual and, presto, the world comes into existence in its boundless beauty and colour.

As this applies to the Creator, God may indeed exist, but of what use is this existence if no one is even aware of it. If the Almighty is shrouded in darkness, if no earthly beings know of His existence, then He can be denied. If scientists postulate theories which, at the very least, remove the necessity of a Creator, if not deny His existence outright, then does it really make a difference if God does indeed exist? If people refuse to see it, how can it shape or effect their lives?

A Nation of Light

Hence the need for light, or a nation of light. The mission of the

Jewish people was to bring the knowledge of God, and the accompanying moral and Divine imperatives, to the far corners of the globe. They were designed to be the catalyst through which the inhabitants of the earth came to know that there was a Creator and that He makes demands of men for moral and ethical excellence.

The Jews do this primarily through the act of *Kiddish Hashem*, sanctifying the name of God in all their actions. People observe the Jewish spiritual life and listen to their spiritual ideals and take the message of Godliness to heart.

Thus if a Jew instead embarks upon a path which does not bring light but darkness, which does not enhance the Glory of God on earth, but detracts from it, it is not that they are punished for a misdeed. Rather, they negate the very reason for their existence.

This was the story of Moses. How was he punished so severely for hitting a rock instead of speaking to it? Because by speaking to it he was afforded an amazing opportunity to sanctify God's name. As Rashi points out, had Moses spoken to the rock and it had obeyed his commandment, the Jews would have taken to heart the message of how even an inanimate object strives to serve the will of its Creator: how much more so they, human beings with a conscience, must make an effort. But this opportunity was lost and for a brief moment Moses, who has done more than anyone to bring the knowledge of God to earth, and to unite God with his people and his world, failed to add more light. The result was that the leadership now had to pass on to other hands.

Dark Religion

The lesson from this as it applies to our previous discussion is that Judaism and all other forms of religion must first and foremost be a conduit to light. The moment it itself becomes a false god, the moment it brings not brightness and illumination but darkness and despair, it has negated its very purpose, as have its adherents.

When pious Jews put the consideration of Jewish law before human dignity and respect for our fellow man, then indeed Halakha has become a foreign god, enforced by its idolatrous worshippers who value the tenets of the law over and above the people to whom the Torah is designed to bring them closer.

Every Jew, and every religious individual, must always strive to ensure that they are emissaries of light to whom people on the outside point and say, 'This person is a bearer of a glorious tradition. Perhaps that accounts for why their deeds are so loving and special.'

Chapter Sixty-six

INTRINSIC WORTH: ARE STUDENTS RIGHT THAT THEIR PARENTS RUIN THEIR LIVES?

Those who have been fortunate enough to go on to higher education often say that their college days were the happiest of their lives; a large part of the positive experience is the opportunity for witty and stimulating discussion with very fine minds on a wide variety of topics. Students are renowned for their love of disputation, and very often their whole purpose is simply to argue, not to come to any solution or reconciliation. On one day a bright young undergraduate may argue passionately one way, on another they might be arguing the opposite. It is possible for them to see the contradiction in this because the important perspective for them is the context in which the discussion took place; often the meaning of their argument is to refute what the other person has argued for, not the position itself.

This came out strikingly in one candidate's final examinations for law, which would decide the rest of his career. He is a very ambitious man, and his dream is to teach law in Oxford University; this would almost certainly depend upon gaining first class honours in his final examinations. But even his great hopes for the future could not rid him of the habit of living his life by reacting to what others say and do. When a paper asked questions in the typical Oxford format, using 'he' throughout to refer to men and women, he took the time to balance his answers carefully with 'he' and 'she' so that he included everyone and was, so to speak, 'politically correct'. But when he came across one paper which he knew had been set by a feminist and which used 'she' throughout, he responded by changing his style: he used 'he' in all he wrote. It was not that he objected to the examiner's ideology, but that he could not help reacting against her words. Even if his chosen style might irritate his examiners, he felt compelled to write in the opposite way to that of the question paper.

This habit of reacting to what others think, say or do can extend to one's very definition of oneself. Many a student at Oxford has a profound problem with their identity. Sometimes they have no real idea of who or what they are, and constantly define themselves by other people's standards and systems. Ask what an Oxonian's life means and you will receive a vague definition based on achievements to date, home background, career hopes . . . but nothing that intrinsically defines them and only them in the concrete here and now. This identity crisis is evidently one that has to be confronted practically, and not merely discussed; we human beings have a deep need to know who we are, in terms that would not change even if the rest of the world were to disappear or alter its opinion of us. We need positive ways to define our identity and meaning.

Thus one of my most important functions is to try to impart to the students a feeling of essential worth and identity, completely divorced from any academic, sporting or financial achievements, something that in the modern world, which rates men and women according to their achievements, is certainly not an easy task.

Two Fires

The Jews were commanded by God to build and consecrate a tabernacle, a tent where God would meet with His people, in the wilderness. Moses himself enacted all the rituals which were associated with the tabernacle for seven days, but on the eighth day he ordained his brother Aaron, and Aaron's sons Nadav and Avihu, as priests. From then on they would take over all the practices inside the tabernacle. 'It came to pass on the eighth day that Moses called Aaron and his sons, and the elders of Israel; and he said unto Aaron, Take thee a young calf for a sin offering, and a ram for a burnt offering, without blemish, and bring them before the Lord' (Leviticus 9:1–2).

There had never been a bigger celebration. God was finally going to have a physical home on earth where people could see His fire descending from heaven consuming their offerings daily. Through this they would know that God was in their midst and His presence dwelt among them. First Moses brought all the offerings. In verse twenty-four it reads, 'And there came a fire out from before the Lord, and consumed upon the altar the burnt offering and the fat'. When all the people saw this they rejoiced and fell on their faces because they saw that God had accepted their offer. It was a wonderful feeling for the Jewish people to witness God's love for them and His selection of them as His people.

Tragedy in the Face of Celebration

But then something went tragically wrong. The two sons of Aaron were so joyous about what was happening that they acted spontaneously, outside the instructions that had been given to them. The younger priests each took his censer, put fire in it, and then added incense on the fire, and brought it before the Lord. God had already brought them a fire which had descended from the heavens, indicating God's acceptance of the Israelite's offering. But now they brought their own, a fire which He had not commanded them. Flames went forth to consume them and they died before the Lord, in this greatest moment of national celebration.

Aaron witnessed his two sons dying in front of all the people, and Moses said to his brother, 'This is it that the Lord spake, saying, I will be sanctified in them that come nigh Me and before all the people I will be glorified.' This means that God loved Aaron's children very much, and that is why He had to use them as an example to all people that a foreign fire cannot be brought before the Lord. God has to use His own fire to consume the altars; He specifically chose to use the people close to Him as an example, even though they suffered for it. Aaron kept silent, he did not complain, and he was rewarded for his silence later.

All the commentaries attempt to explain why these two young men were punished so severely. After all, it doesn't seem very fair: they had consecrated the sanctuary, brought the sacrifices of the Jewish people, God's fire consumed the offerings, and then they also brought their own fire to show that they loved God. They loved the service of the altar, and they died. One of the most widely accepted interpretations of the Talmud is this: they were drunk, completely intoxicated. This interpretation can be corroborated by the fact that merely six verses later God spoke to Moses and Aaron, saying, 'Do not drink wine nor strong drink, thou, nor thy sons with thee when ye go into the tabernacle of the congregation, lest ye die: it shall be a statute for ever throughout your generations: and that ye may put difference between holy and unholy, and between unclean and clean.' Immediately after they died, God said to the survivors, Aaron and his remaining sons, that they should never consume strong drink again; therefore everyone assumes that the two who died were drunk. Still, being drunk doesn't seem reason enough to be punished with death.

Artificial Joy

A profound explanation, which also serves an important lesson for life, is offered by Rabbi Yosef Zevin: there are certain occasions in life which are so special, so unique, that we should naturally feel their enormity and gravity. We should not need artificial inducements to be happy. This is what happened here. The Jews finally had God in their midst; He had built a home with them: but this was not enough for Aaron's sons. They still felt the need to drink to be happy. It was almost as if they discounted the whole gravity of the celebration; they couldn't get excited enough without the extra, and artificial, stimulus of wine.

Drinking on the Wedding Day

Suppose the groom thinks his own wedding is complete only if he wears the best clothes, or he will be truly happy only if he gets first-rate presents;

his new wife will feel very insulted that he needs such artificial incentives to make him happy on the most special day of his life. Something is drastically wrong; it means that he is not wholeheartedly looking forward to marrying his fiancée. The same applies if a groom feels the need to get very drunk at his wedding in order to celebrate more. Surely his bride would not take this as a compliment. Likewise, if your parents needed to get overly drunk at your wedding in order to dance and be happy, you would assume that they did not feel the joy of the occasion properly.

This was the transgression of Aaron's sons: they needed to drink in order to celebrate. Even though they were priests, it was as if the revelation of God's presence meant nothing to them.

My Son the Doctor

Many people say that the greatest crisis in western society today is the breakdown of the family, and many people point to the rising number of divorces. The problem is not just that of couples separating, though. Even if sons and daughters are lucky enough to have both parents still living together, they often feel at a distance from their parents because they have grown up thinking that their parents do not want them for themselves, but for what they can become. Such scenarios lead students to question their intrinsic self-worth and define themselves by their achievements alone.

I can't begin to tell you how many of the young people who come to this university feel angry, or even hate their parents. Many blame their parents outright for destroying their lives. And what is their primary complaint? Parents no longer want children, they want *successful* children. Before they say 'I love you' to their children, they tell them that they have to seek achievement to win their approval. Although parents may love their sons and daughters anyway, they rarely tell their children that they make them feel good just for being, that the very fact that the child *is* brings happiness to his or her parents.

Many of today's young generation have grown up thinking that unless they become successful they will never be special to their parents. So a son or daughter isn't enough any more, but a child who studies at Oxford or Cambridge is truly desirable. All the friends I grew up with in Miami were pushed by their parents to be outstanding people in their school, and then to go on to be doctors, lawyers, or similar professionals. The ones who don't come up with the goods feel that something was missing in them, and it makes them feel like failures. Surely, there is a very fine line which separates parents necessarily motivating their children to success, which is an important parental responsibility, and making a child feel that success is the most important aspect of life, and the primary reason for a parent's love.

There is a Jewish joke which describes the card sent out by Jewish parents announcing the birth of a son: 'Mr and Mrs Harvey Jacobs are proud to announce the birth of Dr Jeremy Jacobs.'

Have you ever sat next to a man at a bus stop and talked about families? If he pulls out pictures of his son, he seldom merely tells you, 'This is my son. And he is such a good person.' Instead, he says, 'This is my son the doctor.' As if the essential relationship which the phrase 'father and son' describes has been replaced by 'father and doctor'. He is saying, 'I love him because of what he is.'

Children begin to feel that their mothers and fathers seek approval for them from the outside world rather than seeing their worth as defined by the intrinsic parent–child relationship. They stop feeling loved, and they acknowledge frustration with their parents.

Of course it is the greatest blessing for a mother and father to look at their child and see a part of each of them there, blended together; it is the truest form of unity they will ever know, and it can be seen in the most living, loving form. So often the fact that parents can have children is seen as not enough. We are going to make our children feel that our love is contingent upon this or that goal being achieved; and when that has been attained, we will give them another one.

Intrinsic Blessings

Stated in other words, one of the greatest human tragedies is a failure to acknowledge those things which are intrinsic blessings. As it applies in the story of the death of Aaron's children, it wasn't enough that God resided among the Jewish people for Aaron's sons; they needed another inducement to be happy.

There is a real crisis in this university; hardly any of the very successful and ambitious young people here seem to come from families who give them the stability they need. It is not that their parents don't care, but rather that they care in only one direction. Even if their parents do feel the intrinsic worth of their sons and daughters, the pity is that they do not express it enough to make it a reality to them. The result is a whole generation of students with deep insecurities, especially in the better universities, who float from one male–female relationship to another, in search of someone or something with whom they will eventually find stability and security.

Once I knew a student here who did not do very well. He was sent down because he did terribly in his exams, but his father called me (his son was in college, so he could not be telephoned directly) and said, 'Please tell my son that we love him. It is fine, no big deal. Of course he has other things to do, he is going to be something great anyway.' This fortunate young man had parents who were thoughtful enough to break the mould.

I meet very few truly stable students in this city, and among the ones I do meet, one in particular stood out amongst the thousands in the years I have been here. He has no problems at all, he never needs me; in fact, I complain to him. He is one of the students to whom I can pour my heart out when things are difficult and my efforts meet with frustration. I know his parents very well; I met them in New York, and they are the exact opposite of the typical pattern I discussed above. Before he came to Oxford his parents said to him, 'We couldn't give a damn if you are a garbage collector, because the greatest thing about you is that you are our son. Becoming President of the USA won't make that better, and becoming a garbage collector won't make that worse. Of course, because we love you, we would like to see you succeed and be happy. But it is because we love you that we push for your success, and not the other way around. We will not love you more because of your success.' The fact that they are parents and child is an existential statement about their relationship that cannot be altered or modified, deducted from or added to.

Support for Israel in Oxford

Of course the same problem can occur with our relationship to our homeland. When Yitzhak Shamir became Prime Minister of Israel in 1983, and as he pursued and encouraged his policy of settling Judea and Samaria amidst western pressure to the contrary, we witnessed an almost total disintegration of respect and support for the Israeli cause among the Jewish students and academics of Oxford. It is fair to say that most Jews at the university expressed real embarrassment for the actions of, and tried to distance themselves as much as possible from an association with, the Jewish state. Israel has always had its enemies and detractors at Oxford, and at other leading universities and bastions of liberalism. It is part and parcel of championing the underdogs, whom the world now perceives the Palestinians to be. The Oxford Middle East Society has sponsored many large and respected speaker meetings, the greatest of which was a lecture by former US President Jimmy Carter, whose outcome was to disparage Israel. Clearly, there are also many countries who are not favourably predisposed to the existence of Israel. Even the United Nations enacted resolutions against Israel, the most infamous of which was in 1975 when it passed its 'Zionism equals racism' resolution.

The Withering Away of Jewish Support

But amidst this intractable opposition, Israel could always count on one thing: support from the world Jewish community. Israel was a real part of us, we would do anything to sustain its security and existence. But when a strongly right-wing government was elected into office and Israel became unfashionable in western eyes, even that was lost. Once upon a time, Israel was the darling of the nations: she won spectacular victories around the world against people whom everyone saw were evil, she combated terrorism, brought Ethiopian Jews hope and salvation, saved Russian Jews, and took in Jewish refugees from Arab countries. We all applauded these actions, and we supported her.

The moment it got ugly, when Israel had to suppress an insurrection and Jews watched on television as children who were only throwing stones were shot with rubber bullets, then the Jews suddenly looked askance. There was widespread Jewish condemnation of Israel. Now I have no problem with Jews criticizing Israel *per se* because there are two types of criticism. Good criticism is like parents rebuking their child because they love him and want him to be better; bad criticism is more like a parent saying, 'She is not really my child, she is an embarrassment.' I think the criticism of Israel took the second form; Jews were saying, 'Don't equate these things or people with us, that is not like us, these are Israelis.' They distanced themselves from something that was an essential part of them. Israel, after all, is the Jewish national homeland.

Israel's War Hero in Oxford

One of the things which hurt me most during this period was the reception accorded many of the L'Chaim Society's distinguished Israeli speakers, especially the military men and heroes, and the utter hostility displayed toward them by many of our students and supporters. For example, we hosted the Israeli war hero Avigdor Kahalani in November 1991. His feats in the Yom Kippur War, how he and his battalion saved the north of Israel against an invasion of thousands of Syrian tanks, are immortalized in the book, *The Heights of Courage*. He lost his brother in that war, who was only married one week, as well as most of his original comrades-in-arms with whom he began the war. To discover the magnitude of sacrifice displayed by him *and* his soldiers, you must travel to the Golan Heights where you will see 'the Vale of Tears', the site where one of the greatest tank battles in history took place, and see the wreckage of many of the remaining tanks.

Yet when he arrived in Oxford he was greeted loathsomely. Too many students had already begun to perceive the Israeli army as the enemy to accord him sufficient respect or acknowledge the services he provided to his country and people when they were attacked on the holiest day of the Jewish calendar. He spoke very eloquently and with great compassion and humanity, about the history of that war. But the fact that he had been advertised as an Israeli general already served to discolour the students' opinion of him before even opening his mouth.

Israel an Intrinsic Blessing

Two millennia of exile and the gravest suffering of any nation in history wasn't enough for us to attach ourselves to Israel, to love her and recognize that she is a blessing in herself. Over fifty years ago, Jews sought refugee status in countries; huge cruise boats with one or two thousand Jews had to return to Germany after months at sea because no country would accept them. Their journey ended in the crematoria of Auschwitz. Having our own country means this could never happen again. But now, people treat Israel as a blessing only if she is perfect. The Jews forgot what their lives were like before Israel, when there was no one to stand up for them anywhere, when there was no place to run and no place to hide from hatred and persecution. They had been totally alone; people were dying and being killed because there was no army to defend them. Again, like Aaron's sons, cloud-dwelling isn't enough, we have to drink as well.

Entitled to Happiness?

People forget what life was like before. This is the mistake people make in all kinds of relationships, including marriage. When people complain about their parents, I tell them, 'Look, you're twenty-four years old, that relationship with your parents is not going to change. Your parents do love you, even if you feel they made mistakes and continue to make mistakes. But what you must do now in any event is to recognise the limitations of that relationship. It will not significantly change from the way it is now. Stop complaining, and get yourself a husband or wife, someone who loves you in a completely different way.' The ones who do, feel happy, and completely different, of course. Their problems with their parents fade into insignificance. Then one thing goes wrong and they are unhappy. They forget what they were like before, and I remind them, 'You were complaining about something completely different a few years ago! Can you not now at least learn to appreciate your spouse or partner?'

In modern life we forget to recognize that marriage itself, having a husband or wife, is a special experience. We tell ourselves that we need something above that fact in itself; she has to be not just my wife but the most perfect wife; he has to be not just my husband but the best. And if any one of those things you think you are entitled to is missing, the marriage itself begins to be affected. The moment you find out he or she has a temper and you have one argument, things begin to suffer.

We have made happiness the ultimate god. Parents say, 'I'm being a good parent as long as my children are happy.' My response to that is that a lot of kids are happy taking LSD, so what is wrong with that?' 'Oh no, no no . . .' they reply; they know it would be wrong to encourage vulnerable children to take such substances, but parents don't seem to realize that other things are destructive in their own way, too.

Elusive Quality of Happiness

When children are spoiled and get whatever they want, they learn to be dependent, instead of learning the value of an equal relationship. Parents see them smile and that is good enough for them, and later their children take a selfish and destructive attitude into marriage. They think the purpose of marriage is to be happy. The moment they are not happy they think, 'Why did I marry this person? Did I make a mistake?' They run to all their friends, lamenting decisions, and speaking badly about their spouse behind their back.

I do not think that in the modern era people are worse husbands and wives than they once were. So why are there so many incidents of divorce? Because the reasons people have for going into marriage are completely different. Once upon a time people married because that was what life was all about; there was no explanation, life was about getting married, it was something you did and you were happy about it. Nowadays one marries because one wants to be happy and only for that reason. It is lovely and romantic while you are young and running around with each other, but the moment you get married there are bills to pay and a lot of tension. You wake up with the same person every day, and you complain and wonder why you got married.

Once you have this attitude, you don't work on solving problems any more, you just work on complaining about your spouse. People waste so much time complaining about their spouses that they don't have time to take care of their problems. And if they would instead sink the same amount of energy into their marriage and spouse, they might put completely new life into their relationship.

If people look forward to marriage because up to now they have made each other happy, they love each other and feel they have to look after each other, that's great. But I guarantee there will be moments when they do not feel happy because they are married. There will be major arguments, because everybody has them. What is going to keep them together at that time? Just that piece of paper with the writing on it, up on the shelf? In today's society, the chances are that nearly one out of two couples is not going to be together after about five or six years. We have to adopt a new attitude, and I think the first step is to begin to look at our partners as a part of ourselves, because we need more to keep us together than the assumption that marriage is only about happiness.

Wholeness

Sometimes we are very unhappy with our personalities or bodies, but do we even consider that we should abandon them? No. I may know how unhappy I am with myself, but I am still me. I am me because that is the way it is, not because I'm happy or unhappy. If you look at marriage as a stage of completion, of making you whole, it is the same. I want people to be able to say, 'My husband or wife is now me, a part of me. Marriage is something that I have to deal with. I don't need it to be the most wonderful marriage in the world in order to want it to work. All I have to do is recognize the fact that marriage is an intrinsic blessing, that I am extremely fortunate not to have to be alone and to have someone alongside me who completes and loves me, makes me whole.' Through their recognition alone, it will become the happiest and most satisfying marriage ever.

When you marry you are giving each other more than happiness can ever give you, you are giving each other wholeness, the knowledge that you never have to be alone; just as the Jewish people were completed by Israel. Without a land to call their home, they were pushed from place to place, and they were nothing. Everyone saw them as scavengers stealing other people's wealth, moving into other people's countries and controlling banking, publishing and the media. People thought, 'They don't have their own country, so they come into mine and they dominate it. They are un-whole, they are taking what is mine. Let them become whole through somebody else, let them satisfy and work their appetite in some other country, let them not steal from me and my children.' When the Jews finally got a state of their own no one could say that again. People who live in Israel are never going to say, 'The Jews are stealing the media, the Jews are controlling the government', because it is a Jewish state. Marriage gives you that wholesomeness, which is much more than empty happiness could ever give you. And if we were only to recognise this, we would never be sad or unhappy ever again.

A Sense of Belonging

The Jews may have had happiness and success in the USA and other places, but they would not have had the same feeling that righteousness and dignity can give. Israel affords the Jewish people a sense of belonging, because that is what your home gives you. When you come home, you're hugged; you created that house together, and it is yours. If work is unsatisfying, it is no big deal because that is only something you do, it is not something you are; when you come home, you are you. A place to call 'home' lends one human dignity. At home you can be whatever you wish to be. Your spouse gives you that ability to express yourself, to be yourself – that is much more important than what is commonly called happiness.

Although you may be happy in your job, it is never yours and you never feel completely at ease or comfortable. You are still not free to behave the way you want to. Even arguing at home is better than being happy at the office, because it is yours, it is you. Jews squabbling in Israel are better than Jews marvelling in the USA, because they are still bickering about what is historically theirs.

What this all means is that we must learn to recognize those rare things in life which are so special and constitute such an amazing blessing that irrespective of the direction they take, they must be appreciated for what they are. We cannot allow ourselves to make the same mistake of Aaron's sons and look for an artificial or external reason to be happy for the most special occasions. Not everything in life is only good or evil relative to something else. There are those things which are intrinsically a blessing.

Your Problem is Our Problem

One of my favourite stories about marriage is the one told by Rabbi Aryeh Levine, who was known as the *tzadik* of Jerusalem. At one time he was a rabbi to a hospital; he saw one of his congregants at the hospital at 4 a.m. The man was perfectly fine, so Rabbi Levine asked him, 'Why are you here? You look fine.' The man pointed to his wife who had just appeared and was limping, and said, 'Our foot hurts.' It wasn't that his wife had a problem, that her foot hurt. Rather, her foot hurting was *their* problem. This man recognized his wife as part of himself and thus felt her pain as much as she did, or at the very least endeavoured to do so.

What happens if a couple marries and one of the partners proves infertile: is it her problem, his problem, or their problem? Surely, in areas such as these everyone would recognize this as being a joint problem irrespective of which partner is actually infertile. But isn't it amazing, it is only when it comes to couple's fertility and other such issues which are by definition a mutual problem that couples look at it as their problem. They know it is something, we have to have a child together, so it is now our problem. But in every other area we speak of 'his' problem or 'her' problem.

Supposing a husband gets really angry. Is it that *he* has this problem? No; if you were living by yourself in an apartment it would be no big deal if you ever got angry; you could always scream at the walls. The angry husband or irate wife's problem is a shared problem *because* they are married and share a life together. Thus the husband and the wife have a problem.

Once you look at it that way, then instead of thinking, 'Should I have married him/her or not?' you think, 'What must I do, because this is part of me, this is our problem.' How then can we alleviate this problem? Every time an unmarried person has a problem, they don't immediately think of jumping off a bridge; we all know we must deal with our personal problems, so why not in a marriage?

Being Mature and Ready for Marriage

I am not implying that there are no legitimate reasons for divorce. But this does not mean it should be the *norm*. If it is true that one in two married couples in the USA divorce nowadays, *and they have legitimate cause*, then marriage as institution is a failure and we should just stop it altogether. This is a very important perspective to take.

I recently met a couple who were engaged, and then it was discovered that she had a cyst on one of her ovaries. She had to fly to the USA for treatment, and then, God forbid, they thought she had cancer. Immediately her fiancé came to me saying, 'This is destroying my life, it's terrible', and I agreed with him that it was a very sad situation. But then he started saying, 'No, no, you don't understand. What I mean is, it's terrible making a decision whether I should still go ahead with the marriage. I mean, she's not well.' And I looked at him and said, 'You shouldn't go ahead with the marriage.' He looked very surprised, so I explained, 'You are not ready for marriage. The moment you start saying "she has this problem, should I marry her?" – you are not ready to be married.'

It was so easy to say, 'She has a problem.' Because the Torah is a living document, something can be extracted from it all the time. It teaches that marriage is a blessing in itself, it doesn't need anything added to it to make it more of a blessing; not even health. Of course it is great to be happy in your marriage, but happy marriages never come automatically, they have to be worked at.

In the past, people always put a tremendous amount of effort into getting married, and they still do to an extent. Every man knows that a woman needs to be wooed, and every woman knows that a man has to be impressed. You are on your best behaviour all the time. Even when you are engaged, you buy your fiancée little presents and flowers. For some reason people think that the moment they get married, that is it; you don't have to do anything any more. The truth, however,is that we have to make an effort throughout our married lives.

Becoming One

However, no amount of effort put into a marriage will ever be successful unless we see marriage as the creation of a unit, instead of two people who share a house or whatever.

I am speaking from the vantage point of someone who came from a divorced family. One of the things that I witnessed throughout my parents' hurtful marriage was that they always spoke about each other's problems, and they never really solidified, they never became a unit. They were always to some extent not married. Real marriage means coming together as a new entity. That is why we use it as a synonym for words like bond, unite and join; it really should mean those things to us.

Not until there is absolute trust will you feel that deep sense of wholesomeness which comes with marriage, and which most people today end up not feeling at all. Let me give you an example. One of the things I witness most is that people often remain as attached to their parents after marriage as they were before marriage. If the couple fight over where they will live, the parents will get involved. Whenever there is a problem, each partner will run to his or her parents. How could any marriage be a success if you don't attach yourself to your husband or wife as firmly as you attach yourself to your parents and much more? This is an increasing refrain. Not only because so many people are willing to go back to their parents, but because parents don't know anything about how to go about helping their children who are in marriage. They sometimes end up making a bad situation worse because they are not impartial and are the worst people to be brought into an argument.

You are meant to develop a whole new family. If you trust each other absolutely, you will have no need to depend on the old relationships. By remaining stubbornly attached to your parents you are hedging your bets; if things don't go so well, then I've still got my parents. In the Jewish scheme of things, when you get married, that is it. Even your immediate family, your brothers and sisters, become secondary family because a completely new unit has been created.

Cut Flower Ethics

All of these lessons that we draw from Judaism cannot exist in a vacuum. There is a book called *Cut Flower Ethics* in which the author points out that we habitually say things like, 'Yes, I think religion has a lot to teach us, but I'm not prepared to be religious. I'll extract the best things from religion, the ethics, the values, but I won't be religious.' It is like saying, 'Flowers are beautiful but I can't bring the whole garden into my house, and I refuse to go out to live in the garden, so I'll just buy some cut flowers and put them in a vase.' Of course they die after a while. Values and ethics can only really be preserved in a much larger framework.

For example, many people say to themselves, 'I'm very impressed with the idea of marriage so I'm going to extract it from religion. I'll seek to make it work and make it a holy institution.' Then they find it much more difficult than they supposed. The reason is that they have forgotten that marriage is an important institution *within the framework of religion*. Outside of religion, living together is what should be done; there is no intrinsic reason in the world why people should marry, merely legal and practical considerations that result from our society's longstanding preference for marriage. If these disappeared, as they are slowly doing, marriage aside from conviction would be an empty form. Why compromise so much of your independence? This extra level of commitment comes only from the fact that God said that people should live together in a holy way in which they respect each other and live by certain laws. From this framework marriage assumes a new degree of importance. Not just as a statement of love, but a statement of wholesomeness. Such worth cannot exist otherwise. The idea is absurd. Marriage is sacred and holy, and what is holiness outside the framework of religion?

Curbing Marital Infidelity

For example, although marital infidelity may not be as big an issue for newly weds, it becomes one for every couple who are married for many years and whose sexual passion may not be the way it once was. One of the most effective ways to stop infidelity is to remember what marriage means. You are not just committed to someone, so it's not a case of saying, 'If they don't know they are not going to be hurt.' Infidelity pours heaps of unholiness onto something which is deeply holy, destroying its sanctity. When marriage is no longer sacred, you can say, 'I know I made a mistake but it was no big deal.' You fundamentally damage a holy entity.

Think how we see children. Parents can look at children as biological organisms that they have brought together and created, but if that is all a child is to you, you divorce your son or daughter from all the connotations of innocence that Judaism associates with them. You won't mind sitting them in front of a television and allowing them to absorb a large dose of sex and violence. But if you begin with the attitude that you have to guard that child's innocence and sanctity, then you'll never let them watch such rubbish. It is usually religious parents who guard what their children watch because their children are seen as innocent beings, and if they get corrupted they are going to blame themselves. If you look at marriage in the same way you won't let these things happen. It is an innocent, loving and sacred institution, and if you allow things to penetrate it, it is going to be dissolved. The marriage will still be there but it will lose that innocence.

Intrinsic worth is a concept that is fast disappearing from this planet, and in its place have been substituted names and ideologies. Rather, what we need is to resensitize ourselves, not only to the pursuit of happiness, whose logical outcome is to reject and be unhappy with all those things which do not bring happiness in their wake, but to life's greatest blessings which complete us and make us impregnable to the outside world: among which are marriage and the beauty of having children.

Chapter Sixty-seven

DEFENDING ISRAEL AT OXFORD

Having made the case of why it is important for a Jew to have an intrinsic relationship with Israel and the Jewish homeland, irrespective of international sentiment or condemnation of the Jewish state at any given time, I now offer a short history of the battle for Israel's reputation that has raged in Oxford since my arrival some five years ago.

A Propaganda War

In February 1990 Abu Sharif, the Chief Adviser to the PLO leader Yasser Arafat, lectured in Oxford. His words were well received by the two thousand or so students who attended, and there was also a great deal of media interest in his appearance. Abu Sharif was such a success that they invited him back to debate a dovish Israeli Knesset member a few weeks later. We felt that the aftermath of these events marked one of the lowest points of morale for Jewish students in Oxford because of the propaganda associated with Mr Sharif's appearances. Indeed it seemed quite odd that Mr Sharif, who was himself once a self-proclaimed terrorist, could be accepted with such glee in a liberal bastion such as Oxford, but there was more to come.

The Middle East Society also brought Noam Chomsky from MIT, and he too gave a speech that was highly critical of Israel. But the highlight of the Middle East Society's propaganda campaign against Israel was the visit to the Oxford Union of former US President Jimmy Carter, whose lecture, on the state of the Middle East, was highly critical of Israel.

Hanan Ashrawi at Oxford

A few years later, the Oxford Middle East Society hosted their 'Middle East to the Year 2000' conference, which featured leading pro-Arab politicians as well as prominent Arab speakers. This was a full-day conference which took place at the Oxford Town Hall, directly across the street from the L'Chaim Society Centre. Some of the major speakers who were present included Senator George McGovern, the pro-Arab 1972 Presidential candidate, David Gore Booth, formerly head of the Foreign Ministry in Great Britain's Middle East desk, and many others. By far the most famous speaker was Hannan Ashrawi, the spokeswoman for the Palestinian delegation to the Peace Conference in Washington.

When she spoke the crowd, about five hundred strong, was made up of a very large pro-Arab faction, a few dovish Jewish students who supported her position (that of the conference as a whole), and myself. I had been invited by the leaders of the Middle East Society; although we are rivals in speakers, we do co-operate and I have become quite friendly with a number of their presidents. After all, although we approach the Middle East and its complications from completely different angles, our events are very similar, and are of mutual interest to each other's members. We invite the student leaders of the Middle East Society specially to our events, and they invite me to theirs. Mrs Ashrawi began an hour's tirade against Israel, saying how intransigent the Israeli position was on the subject of the Middle East Peace Conference, and also claiming that Israel had unleashed death squads against the Palestinians. She claimed they were indiscriminately killing Palestinians in the Territories.

Condemning or Condoning Violence

I was deeply upset by her comments and her ridiculous statements about Israel systematically attempting to kill off the Palestinian people. Three days before her lecture a young Israeli girl of seven had been stabbed to death in Bat Yam, a small suburb of Tel Aviv, in Israel. When Mrs Ashrawi had finished her diatribe, after speaking for a venomous hour against Israel, I walked up to the microphone, and I said, 'I've heard what you said about Israel setting up these death squads. Three days ago a seven-year-old Israeli girl was waiting at a bus stop . . .' As I was asking my question, the entire crowd started to boo. I was completely overwhelmed. When their abuse petered out, I completed my question: '. . . and she was stabbed to death by Palestinians. If you accuse the Israelis of indiscriminately killing non-combatants, and are opposed to the murder of innocents, then can you at least condemn her death?' She just looked me in the eye and said, 'This is the cost of occupation; when you oppress a people there is no telling how extreme they will become, and although I don't condone her murder I can't condemn it either. I understand the frustrations of the people who committed it.' When she said that, there was tremendous applause throughout the audience and I began to leave the microphone. As I walked away there was also a thunderous 'boo' from what seemed to be all the participants. I must admit, it required a fair amount of courage and belief in the justice of the Jewish cause to withstand this abuse.

Israel's Greatest Spokesman

We resolved that we had to start a campaign to counter the effect that this kind of incident had on our morale, and so we brought Mr Benjamin Netanyahu, currently head of the opposition Likud Party, for a lecture. His timely visit impressed us very much and inspired us with confidence at such a difficult time.

The main event was his eloquent speech at the Oxford Union, which did a tremendous amount to counter claims of the Palestinians and, more importantly, to boost the morale of the students. As he arrived, there was a demonstration against him; about 160 Palestinian students standing outside had been bussed down from London. They were chanting over and over again. 'Netanyahu, you should know, we support the PLO.' He invited them in, and some of them agreed to hear what he had to say. At the end of his speech, many of the left-wing Jewish students who had been at the demonstration, alongside the Palestinian students, gave him a standing ovation. He defended Israel eloquently.

Home Comforts

He also impressed us with his demeanour. For example, we had a dinner with the American Jewish Rhodes Scholars at my house. Mr Netanyahu was there for a whole day, giving lecture after lecture, so he asked to have a room where he could rest. We hired a very fancy hotel room for him, but when he heard of the booking, he insisted that he didn't want to waste our money just for two hours, and asked to be taken to our house. We took him to our house, but we didn't have a bed ready for him, and to my wife's horror he lay down on a bed without a sheet. She felt so embarrassed. When I told him how embarrassed we felt because there was no sheet on his bed, he said, 'The army was much worse.' He used to sleep on the ground.

Difficult Times

Then on 29 November 1992, the Oxford University L'Chaim Society intended to host former Israeli Prime Minister Yitzhak Shamir, who had just been defeated in the election against Yitzhak Rabin. Everything was arranged, and on the Thursday morning before the lecture Mr Shamir's office called to say he was very ill and would be unable to attend. Aside from our concern for him, we panicked terribly because we had planned a very big event to welcome him, and we had already sold two thousand student tickets for his lecture at the Oxford Union. We thought this to be a terrible débâcle. In addition, there was a glamorous dinner planned in his honour at the magnificent Oxford Town Hall where many of our supporters and distinguished academics from the university were set to congregate immediately before the Union lecture.

By a stroke of fortune, thank God, it happened to be that Benjamin

Netanyahu, at the time the front runner to succeed Mr Shamir as the leader of the Likud Party, was in Great Britain, raising funds for his campaign. Although Mr Shamir was seriously ill, he telephoned from his sick-bed to ask Mr Netanyahu to step in for him, and so he agreed to come to Oxford a second time.

Democracy in Conflict

The second lecture which he delivered at Oxford was one of the finest political speeches we had ever heard. He argued that it would not be right for the world community to press Israel into peace with the Arabs because their countries are not democracies. He said, 'Democracies have a certain way of alleviating their disputes.' And he gave the example of Mexico and Canada's disputes with the United States. In democracies, they work things out with diplomacy, but totalitarian dictatorships settle disputes with war and aggression. He maintained that this was the essential cause for the Arab–Israeli conflict. Other regions have also had some severe disputes, although perhaps not as intense. Nevertheless, democratic countries have peacefully overcome many difficult scenarios. But the problem in the case of the Jewish–Arab conflict is, in that the Arabs possess no current democratically elected governments, they choose to settle disputes with war. The reason Mr Netanyahu gave for this is that in totalitarian dictatorships it is not the people who elect to go out to war but the dictator. Now, whereas the people would rather solve territorial disputes through diplomacy rather than war since it is they and their children who will die, the dictator who is sending other people's children into battle possesses no similar sensitivity. Therefore, he argued, the only method by which to ensure a lasting peace in the Middle East is by democratizing Israel's Arab neighbours.

Presenting Bibi to the Oxford Union

My introduction for Mr Netanyahu at the Oxford Union included the following remarks: 'First of all, I would like to welcome the Lord Mayor, who has graced us with her company this evening. I will make my remarks very brief as I know many people have been waiting here for us. Very quickly, there is a famous story that Richard Nixon was so impressed with Moshe Dayan, the great general of Israel, that he approached Golda Meir and said to her, "We will give you three of our best generals for Moshe Dayan", and quick as a flash Golda Meir replied, "OK, we want General Dynamics, General Electric and General Telephone!"

'If there is one politician in Israel today about whom that story could be told, it is certainly Benjamin Netanyahu. He has achieved worldwide recognition not just as Israel's ablest spokesman but as one of the finest and most skilled diplomats in the world. He has appeared so many times on ABC's *Nightline* and BBC's *Newsnight* that people have often mistaken him for Ted Koppel. This is the second time Mr Netanyahu is to address the Oxford Union. We are very grateful to him for coming back after three years.

'A few months after Mr Netanyahu last spoke in Oxford, he got married, and I would like to welcome his wife who is here with us tonight. I brought him a present in the Foreign Ministry in Israel (I hope he remembers this story). I brought him a silver wine cup in a little box, to say the blessings on Friday night. The security man outside his office asked me what it was, and I said it was just a cup. The guy didn't even open it up to see what it was! I brought it into Mr Netanyahu's office, and he later asked me, "Was that cleared, I see that it isn't opened yet?" And I said, "Don't worry, I can't blow you up because I need you to speak in Oxford at a later date." Well, that later date is now here.

'Mr Netanyahu is the son of a world-renowned Jewish scholar, Professor Netanyahu, and also brother to someone who will go down in history as one of the greatest Jewish martyrs of all time, Yoni Netanyahu, the famous leader of the Entebbe rescue operation for Israel in Uganda, and the only Israeli casualty. Mr Netanyahu is a graduate from MIT, and from 1967 to 1972 he served as the commander of one of the élite Israeli commando units; he then served as the Minister, or Second in Charge of the Israeli Embassy in Washington. He rose to world prominence as the Israeli Ambassador to the United Nations, in the years 1984 to 1988. The Jewish people will for ever be indebted to one of its most illustrious sons, Mr Netanyahu, for in those four years, like the blazing sun at high noon, he emerged on the international stage as a towering spokesman for Israel and the Jewish people, combining great eloquence and a strong sense of conviction and responsibility and love of his people.

'Finally may I say that it is appropriate for Mr Netanyahu to stand in place of Mr Shamir this evening, for after the events of just two weeks ago, when Mr Netanyahu won an important election in the Likud Party, he is seen as being the successor to Mr Shamir as the leader of that party. And given that the next Israeli election will involve a direct election for the Prime Minister for the first time in Israeli history, and that Mr Netanyahu is certainly one of Israel's most eloquent and most loved politicians, there is a strong possibility that tonight we are listening to Israel's next Prime Minister.

'This is my last remark. I must thank the four organizations without whom this evening would not have been possible. The first is Faith Shoes, our major sponsor for this evening and for the entire term; secondly another of our sponsors, Vogue Computers and Curtis Maclean; thirdly the Young Presidents' Association, David Pollack, who is the President, and Maurice Ostro who has done a tremendous amount to help us, and of course Charles Coleman who arranged all of our transportation and the beautiful cars which brought Mr Netanyahu and his party; and I really want to thank all the students of the L'Chaim Society for their continued hard work which enables us to host the leading politicians and thinkers of the world.'

SECTION SEVEN

A CERTAIN TYPE OF JUDAISM: LUBAVITCH, MESSIANISM AND ORTHODOXY

Chapter Sixty-eight

JEWISH MESSIANISM AND THE ADVANCE OF CIVILIZATION

In February 1993, my second book, *The Wolf Shall Lie with the Lamb: the Messiah in Hasidic Thought*, was published by the American publisher Jason Aronson. I delivered a broad overview of the subject on the occasion of its official launch, which took place both in Oxford and in London. At the launch I debated secular versus Jewish messianism with Danah Zohar, the world-famous author of *The Quantum Self*. I wanted the audience to consider whether a perfect world can be achieved by human efforts alone or whether, as I believe, God's assistance is necessary before all wrongs can be eradicated.

The Quantum Self and Society

Danah's book has so far sold over one hundred thousand copies around the world. It is a brilliant synthesis of quantum physics and human consciousness. In the book, she constructed an entire world-view based on what she refers to as 'the new physics', arguing that the insights of modern physics can illuminate our understanding of everyday life. Drawing on the strange and fascinating workings of the subatomic realm, she constructed a new model of human consciousness, and addressed such questions as whether modern physics can explain how our consciousness can continue beyond death, and whether there is a subatomic wellspring from which our creativity, our empathy with others, and our feelings of unity with the inanimate world originate.

Her book was such a success that it is being developed into a trilogy. The week that my book was published, she completed the second volume, *The Quantum Society*. In this new work, Danah argued for a new societal perspective which can be culled from the new physics. Because the overtones of the book are blatantly secular, and yet messianic, I asked her to debate with me the subject of Jewish messianism versus the alternative visions of secular messianisms which have been promoted, with increasing frequency, over the past two centuries.

Danah and her husband Ian Marshall, a well-known psychotherapist, are regulars at the classes on Chasidism and Jewish mysticism which we provide here in Oxford, and which are delivered primarily by myself and Dr Tali Loewenthal, author of *Communicating the Infinite*, published by Chicago University Press. As a result of these classes, Danah admits to having many of her ideas deeply influenced by Chabad Chasidic thought, although she has always complained to me that the one great setback within Chasidism is its parochialism. She claims her approach is far more universal. To her, Judaism suffers from its distinctiveness, and could offer the world more if it were to promote a universal religion, embracing all peoples and all cultures.

For my part, I do not think her allegations are accurate. I see inherent universalism within Jewish messianism, and I felt the launch of my book was an ideal opportunity to debate the subject of whether or not humanity can usher in a utopian age without Divine assistance. Danah was adamant that messianism cannot be representative of just one group or even just one messianic figure, but should be more collective so that humankind as a whole represents the messianic redeemer. This is largely what her book *The Quantum Society* is all about. I told Danah at our debate that I guess we will have to wait for the publication of her book to see which sells better, and with these figures in hand determine who is right. In the meantime, my case went something like this:

Deep Flaws Within Creation

There is a tale of a man who brings some material to a tailor and asks him to make a pair of trousers. When he comes back a week later, they are not ready. Two weeks later, they are still not ready. Finally, after six weeks, the trousers are ready. The man tries them on. They fit perfectly. None the less, when it is time to pay, he can't resist a jibe at the tailor. 'You know,' he says, 'it took God only six days to make the world. And it took you six weeks to make just one pair of trousers.' 'Ah!' the tailor says. 'But look at this pair of trousers, and look at the world.'

This joke ostensibly describes a fact which is almost universally acknowledged to be true: the world is deeply flawed. Even the greatest optimist cannot help but notice the prevalence of injustice, disease, suffering and deep unhappiness in the world which we inhabit.

The disparity between God's perfection and the imperfection of the world He created inspires much of the humour about God. Indeed, while the Bible itself may contain little humour, it does have plenty of complaints. 'Awake, why sleepest thou, O Lord?' the Psalmist cries out (Psalm 44:23), in protest at God's seeming indifference to the Jews' suffering and oppression. The Talmud records the bitter reaction to God's silence during the Roman destruction of Jerusalem. 'Who is like You among the dumb?' (Gittin 56b). The question, 'God, why do You permit the righteous to suffer and the wicked to prosper?' seems to lie at the root of almost all the biblical and rabbinic complaints. The complaining spirit that runs through many anti-God jokes and witticisms is, in part, rooted in the Bible and other Jewish holy writings.

No Jewish text has ever answered the question of suffering satisfactorily, although the prophets repeatedly insist that because God is good, justice will one day triumph. Contemporary Jews, most of whom lack the prophets' religious faith, do not usually find this response consoling.

Why Do We Not Despair?

If indeed we long ago accepted the inherent design flaws within creation, how can we still simultaneously hope for the future? Human beings seem to be obsessed with perfecting the world, as if we somehow know, contrary to all the evidence, that it is indeed possible. Why have we not reconciled ourselves to the fact that there will always be war, famine, tyrannical regimes and mass murder?

Here at Oxford I have found that young and idealistic students are usually completely unwilling to accept the injustices of society. The students not only preach utopia, but devote a significant proportion of their time and energy to organizations and efforts which actively seek to rid the world of cruelty. Some students volunteer for the National Society for the Prevention of Cruelty to Children, Rhodes Scholars against Apartheid, or Oxfam, not to mention all the Jewish charitable and relief organizations, such as the Oxford Campaign for Soviet Jewry. But what is it that tells them that they are not just wasting their time? If you are here at Oxford to earn a degree, what impels you, what serves as the motivation to divert large amounts of time from study and the pursuit of academic excellence, to a goal which seems at the best of times to be elusive?

Inspiration Behind the United Nations

The victorious allied nations who emerged from the Second World War formed the United Nations. What led them to believe that they could indeed found an international regulating body which could intervene in territorial conflicts and avert destructive war? What served as the inspiration behind the idea of a community of nations? Is it mere coincidence that on the Wall of Peace standing in the Plaza of Nations at UN Headquarters in New York, there is a single line from Isaiah etched in stone, which reads: 'Swords shall be beaten into plowshares . . . Nation shall not lift up sword against nation, neither shall they learn war any more' (Isaiah 2:4).

Although we are impelled to strive for higher and higher states of perfection that even allow us to dream of a global outbreak of peace, this occurs while we inhabit a tiny bubble of hope surrounded by wholesale slaughter. It has become increasingly illogical for anyone to still believe in the redemptive power of the human race. Amidst global outrage, what motivates humankind to dare to wish for better, with the immense weight of history posed against it?

No greater evils have ever stalked the earth or killed more people than in this century. If it were possible to calculate the number of innocent victims killed in the twentieth century in war, state terror, hunger, pestilence and starvation, the figure could go into the hundreds of millions. Communism in the Soviet Union, China and Cambodia was responsible for the murder, both active and passive, of at least seventy million people, while Nazism claimed at least twelve million innocent lives. The two world wars claimed a further fourteen million in lives of combatants and civilian deaths, and there were many smaller but very bloody skirmishes. To be sure, in generations gone by there have been many wars, and the case can be made that people did not possess modern methods of mass slaughter or weapons of mass destruction, hence the number of casualties was smaller. Even so, it is the programmes of genocide and mass murder initiated in this century which have no equal in the annals of human history.

Even against the backdrop of the terrifying crimes perpetrated in the lifetime of many of the readers of this book, we still hope for an era of peace and brotherhood between all persons. To take this idea further and project it onto a more universal plane, what gives the people of the world the hope, the certainty, that we can eventually conquer AIDS, cancer, and other debilitating or lethal diseases? What makes us think that we can somehow rid our streets of drugs and crime? Certainly, no one has succeeded before. Yet we still speak in political, social and academic circles alike as though it were not just a remote possibility but something at hands' grasp, always inducing us to make more of an effort. But whence springs this glimmer of hope which refuses to fade?

It springs from Moshiach, the Messiah, which has been the fountain of human hope for over three millennia.

The Power to be Positive

There is an awareness in the hearts of the Jews that Israel is a promised land. The promise, a destiny to be fulfilled, is the cause of our present exertions; it is not the result of a conglomeration of past events. The drive on the part of the Jewish people to perfect the world, whether consciously or subconsciously, is fuelled by anticipation, by something beautiful and miraculous which defies precise formulation, which calls out to us and beckons from a not-so-distant horizon.

Even secular Zionists, who formally decried all religious terminology and motivations, often spoke with messianic overtones. They believed that although Jews were scattered throughout the world, and although Jews were largely lacking political rights and entirely lacking in nationalist claims, they could somehow refocus the Jewish agenda on re-establishing a Jewish commonwealth. Something gave these Jews the belief that they could somehow reconstitute themselves as an independent entity.

They were secular, and yet they lived by messianic expectation: they believed that the Jews could be revived. No student of history would expect that we could be a strong, independent and revitalized people after what has happened to us. It was the ancient prophecies of people like Isaiah, standing in public squares foretelling of a time when 'the knowledge of the Lord would cover the earth' that made the Jews once again believe that they could change the world. It was these promises of the future, forever ranging in the ears of the Jews, that taught them they could still hope for the society they would bequeath to their children.

With all of history posed against us, and with the knowledge that all those who embarked on similar quests for perfection before us have failed, we still dare to keep up the struggle. Why? Because the Jews are the bearers of a dream which we must translate into reality through the Messiah.

Peace – the Central Tenet of Messianism

The title of my book of Jewish messianism is *The Wolf Shall Lie with the Lamb*. It is taken from a verse in Isaiah which foretells the wonders that will be seen in the age of the Messiah: 'the wolf shall lie with the lamb, the leopard shall lie down with the kid, the calf and the young lion and the fatling together, and a little child shall lead them.' Essentially, this is meant to convey the central theme behind Jewish messianism and the messianic epoch: peace, harmony and wholesomeness, as is stated by Rabbi Yossi HaGellili in the Talmud, 'The Messiah's first message will be Peace!' (Aboda Zara, 3b).

Sometimes people ask whether the Messiah might already have come without the Jews being fully aware of it. There is only one answer to this, and it is provided by the great Sage, Saadia Gaon. He said simply, 'The Messiah cannot yet have come, since we see the nations actually warring and fighting as violently as possible' (Emunot VeDeot, 933, 8.8).

We should face the uncomfortable fact that to date messianism has been responsible for anything but peace. On its theme has been built a religion which for centuries persecuted and oppressed the Jews because they rejected its claimed Messiah, and the many other claimants to the messianic throne who have brought the Jews naught but death, destruction and disillusionment.

Despite Judaism's fervent anticipation of the arrival of the messianic age, history has taught Jews to be sceptical about predictions that it is imminent: they have had too many bad experiences with putative Messiahs. In the first century, Rabban Yochanan ben Zakkai taught: 'If you should happen to be holding a sapling in your hand when they tell you that the Messiah has arrived, first plant the sapling, then go to greet the Messiah.' Less than a century later, after Rabbi Akiva urged Jews to follow the would-be Messiah Simeon Bar-Kokhba, Rabbi Yochanan ben Torta prophesied to him: 'Grass will grow out of your cheekbones, and the Messiah still will not have arrived.' In the twelfth century, Moses Maimonides counselled Yemen's Jews not to waste their time in mystical speculations concerning the date of the Messiah's arrival.

There is reason to believe that many Jews in Yemen chose not to follow Maimonides' good advice. According to one medieval folktale, two men arrived in a Yemenite town and told the inhabitants that the Messiah was arriving that night to transport them all to Israel. The people were instructed to remain on their roofs the entire night, but the Messiah did not come. In the morning, when they came down from the roofs, the strangers were gone – as well as the townspeople's possessions.

The bitterness engendered by false Messiahs has not gone unnoticed in Jewish humour: the following joke is typical. A man comes home from synagogue and tells his wife: 'They say the Messiah is coming any day, and will take us all to Israel.' She becomes hysterical. 'Oh no! That's terrible. It took years till we could finally move into this neighbourhood, and buy the house we wanted. Now we've spent a fortune fixing it up. I don't want the Messiah to take us away.' 'OK, OK, don't worry,' the husband says. 'We survived Pharaoh, we survived Haman. With God's help, we'll survive the Messiah too!'

The conflict between Judaism's optimistic assertions that the Messiah is coming and that the world will be made perfect (*tikkun olam*), and the Jewish people's experience of oppression, engendered just the sort of sceptical atmosphere in which humour flourishes. If things are really *this* bad, more than a few Jews thought, are they really going to get *that* good? The prophets unequivocally answer, 'Yes!' According to Isaiah, a wonderful future is coming. Jews will be restored to their own, independent homeland, and there will be world peace. He even prophesied changes in the innate character of animals: of course, the wolf shall lie with the lamb, 'And the calf and the lion shall lie down together, and none shall be afraid' (11:6).

The Lion and Calf Who Dwell Together

Another joke puts it in this way: A man visits a zoo and is taken to the lion's cage. He witnesses there the literal fulfilment of Isaiah's prophecy

– a lion and a calf in a cage together. Amazed, he calls over an attendant. 'How long have you had a lion and a calf living together?' he asks. The zookeeper tells him that it has already been done for well over a year. The man is amazed. 'Why, it is a miracle!' 'Not really,' the zookeeper replies, 'we have to put in a new calf every day.'

The next anecdote is an old Chasidic tale that demonstrates how easy it is to hijack an important idea or concept and substitute a cheap alternative that it is not even vaguely similar to the original.

Once upon a time, a man called Saul the Dreamer heard about a faraway country where onions were unknown. 'No onions!' mused the Dreamer. 'Now what kind of pleasure can they derive from their food without onions? I'll go there and introduce this delicious vegetable!'

He took a wagon-load of onions and started out, and when he arrived he said to the emperor of the far-off country: 'Your highness, I bring you a new vegetable that possesses the unique quality of improving all savoury food. I urge you to try it.' The king loved the taste of the new vegetable so much that he kept the whole wagon-load and gave Saul the onions' weight in gold.

When Saul returned home he told his tale of a land where gold was cheaper than onions. The entrepreneur Kolboynik thought to himself: 'Garlic is not only more expensive than onions, but infinitely more fragrant. Surely, if Saul was given gold for onions, I'll get diamonds for garlic!' So Kolboynik set out for that country with five bags of garlic.

The garlic was relished even more than the onions. As Kolboynik had guessed, the emperor said that gold was inadequate remuneration for such delectable food. Therefore, he decided to reward Kolboynik with the most precious commodity in all their kingdom: Kolboynik returned home with his reward – five sacks of onions!

Ever since the prophets of the Jewish people foretold of an era which would see the perfection of civilization and humanity itself, the concept of messianism has been fraught with controversy, not least because there have been many imitations and pretenders.

The Mechanics of the Messianic Age

The perfection spoken of in the messianic idea is twofold, and could be summed up as follows. First, there is the concept of all people striving to do their best, based on the principles of justice laid forth in the Torah, to bring about a better world. Then, when the Almighty sees how much the earth's inhabitants desire a perfection of the world, He will provide the finishing touches in the form of a glorious messianic redeemer who will harness the world's resources and ideals, weave them all together, and usher in a complete utopia, an age in which Godliness, goodness and peace will pervade the earth and no one will know hunger, disease or death.

At the root of this concept is the idea that humanity is a junior partner in creation. Since everything is created by the perfect God, it must necessarily be perfect. The world we inhabit is so deeply flawed because God wanted us to be His partner in the perfection of Creation. We have a choice: to improve the world and the lot of our fellows, or tear the world asunder. God wants us to better the world. Through the steady perfection of society and civilization, through the performance of more and more acts of kindness and *mitzvot*, the world achieves perfection. The actualization of that process in its entirety will be the messianic era.

When the world reaches a critical mass of goodness, God promises that He will provide the finishing touches. He will do those things that we are incapable of fully accomplishing on our own, such as the eradication of illness and all forms of hatred. The result will be a better world – people who treat each other better, and a manifestation of the underlying Godliness of creation. A world in which all people can maximize their potential without intimidation and without contention. A world in which no tears of sorrow or tragedy will again be shed. A world in which the dreaded diseases of the past will be nothing more than a memory. A world in which no parent will ever be bereaved of a child, or a wife of her husband.

Intellectual Attraction of Messianism

The greatest obstacle to Jewish messianism was and is that, despite centuries of promises, nothing has yet materialized. One Jewish fable speaks of a small Russian *shtetl*, where the community council decided to pay a poor Jew a rouble a week to sit at the town's entrance and be the first to greet the Messiah when he arrives. The poor man's brother came to see him from his own village, and was puzzled why his brother had been willing to take such a low-paying job. 'It's true,' the poor man responded, 'the pay is low. But it's a steady job.'

Despite this obstacle, messianism has been immensely appealing to people in many different societies and civilizations precisely because it points towards a better world than we have today. There are few people so enamoured of the world as it is now that they would not be attracted by promises of an ideal society.

In the last few centuries, messianism has had an increasingly wide appeal for liberal, secular thinkers, especially Jewish thinkers, because it speaks of the perfection of our world, and particularly humanity itself, as a distinct possibility. It is truly remarkable that even amongst the secular Jewish intellectuals who dismiss Judaism virtually in its entirety, it is still Jewish messianism that always captures their imaginations. They see these promises of a perfected world as ample reason never to despair of hope in humanity and the world, even amidst palpable darkness.

It was for this reason that Deutsch proclaimed, 'It is the comforting and uplifting faith in the Messiah which has sustained the Jews through the fateful times of oppression' (address, 2 July 1839). Klausner added that 'the messianic idea is the most glistening jewel in the glorious crown of Judaism!' He even attributed the very advance of civilization almost single-handedly to messianism, exclaiming that 'the Jewish messianic Faith is the seed of progress which has been planted by Judaism throughout the whole world'.

Another leading member of the enlightenment echoed Deutsch's thoughts: 'From this belief in the Messiah who is to come, from the certainty which they have of conquering with him, from the power of esteeming all present things of small importance in view of such a future, springs the indestructible nature of the Jews' (Rosenkranz, *Philosophy of Education*, 1848, page 249). 'The existence of Judaism depends upon clinging to the messianic hope' (Skreinka, *Entwickelungsgeschichte der Judischen Dogmen*, 1861, page 75).

In the world of yesterday, Zweig gave eloquent voice to the understanding that it was specifically the call to messianism which had always caused the Jews to listen: 'Whenever anyone, prophet or deceiver – throughout the two thousand years of exile plucked this string, the entire soul of the people was brought into vibration.'

On the other hand, there was also a profound sense of unease felt within the heart of the intelligentsia about the very concept of a coming Messiah. This unease was largely a result of messianism's heavy reliance on Godly intervention. The very *raison d'être* of the secular intellectual is the idea that humankind, by using their own innate intellect and pushing the expanses of reason beyond their limit, can solve all of their own ills. The very bedrock of western secular academia is its presupposition that humans are the masters of their own destiny. Every moment spent supplicating even a benevolent Creator is a moment wasted from advancing the cause of the human race through humanity's own efforts.

Modifications in the Messianic Ideal

The Jewish enlightenment especially sought to release the Jews from the strict shackles of dependency on a concept of the Divine, and many of the Jewish intellectuals of the era became prophets of the power and worth of humanity. Interestingly, these intellectuals used the tragic story of Jewish history to their advantage, just as the messianists did, but with a completely different emphasis. Instead of a story of triumph over persecution, Jewish history was portrayed as a disaster alleviated only by human triumphs:

'The omnipotent Creator that we so often speak of was nowhere to be found in the Jews' greatest hour of need.' Holdheim announced that 'Israel required no Messiah in the generally accepted sense of the word because it itself suffered and agonized for its faith . . . died for its faith and was resurrected time and again' (Philipson, *Centenary Papers*, page 94).

Of course, the greatest Jewish 'death and resurrection' is still a recent event, and is still hotly debated in both academic and social circles. An event that came long after disillusionment with the promises of the messianic age had set in: the slaughter of the Second World War. In the twelfth and most famous of his Thirteen Articles of Faith, Maimonides wrote: 'I believe in the coming of the Messiah, and though he tarry, I will wait for him on any day on which he comes.' During the Holocaust, countless Jews sang these words on their way to the gas chambers.

Given the preceding two centuries of 'enlightenment', it was to be expected that secular Jews would react scornfully towards such literal messianism: many contended that these same Jews whose last breaths of life invoked the age-old promise of messianic redemption received anything but that redemption. They say that God, if He exists at all, cannot be relied on to save the world and the human race.

Born from this apparent dichotomy, on the one hand the great appeal of the messianic idea in general, on the other hand the distrust of any reliance on a creator, was the largely inevitable movement of secular messianism. The overall plan to better the lot of society and all people was preserved, but the mechanisms were modified. In some cases, the adjustments were slight, but in others the alterations to the original concept of messianism were so profound that, as in the case of Christian messianism which preceded these newer secular alternatives, the original bore little resemblance to the newly organized product.

The 'March of Progress' and Secular Messianism

Furthermore, the Jewish enlightenment noted that it was precisely the Christian nations of the earth who had undergone a spiritual reformation from strict Catholic observances that were contributing the most to the fields of literature, the arts and sciences. It was assumed that the Jews should consider pursuing the same course of action. Having contributed the concept of a Messiah to western thinking, because it lies at the heart of Christianity, the Jews had finally seen it transformed from a religious to a secular ideal. Then, a proportion of Jews were willing to take the altered concept back again and assimilate it into their own understanding of the world, even though it was precisely because the messianic prophecies of world peace and redemption were not fulfilled in Jesus's time that Jews reject Christianity's messianic claims.

The Jewish intellectuals were willing to take on a new kind of messianism because the age-old promises of redemption had failed to materialize: they could not believe there was any divine hand in the salvation of mankind and were massively disillusioned. The Jewish novelist Franz Kafka bitterly summed this up: 'The Messiah will come only when he is no longer necessary; he will come only on the day after his arrival' (*Parables*, translated Greenberg, page 65).

In many cases, humanity as a whole was substituted for the messianic figure. The German Jewish intellectual Guttmann stated that 'Judaism does not hold that the Messiah redeems mankind from sin, but declares that when mankind shall have set itself free from the sway of sin through its own powers of amendment, and shall have matured to true moral perfection, then, for it, the Messiah will have come' (*Idee der Versöhnung*, 1909, page 15).

Similarly, Schulman wrote in 1924 that 'Israel must always await the Messiah. It must never acknowledge any person or event as the complete fruition of its hopes. Indeed, the essence of Jewish messianism is the hope in an infinite ideal' (*Menorah Journal*, 1924, x.318).

Even Abraham Joshua Heschel, who was himself a Jew of profoundly held belief, could not help but partly succumb to the great temptation of substituting the efforts of mortal humans and humanity as a collectable entity for the Messiah: 'An architect of hidden worlds, every pious Jew is, partly, the Messiah' (*The Earth is the Lord's*, 1950, page 71).

The Secular Replaces the Religious Tradition

In a deeply secular age, these predictions seemed to make sense. God and religion had largely been consigned, if not to the dust heap of history, then at the very least to the backwater of life. Judaism became important only as means of preserving an ancient tradition, but not as an affirmation of a way of life or a path to the salvation of the human race. It was now the collective belief in the ability of humankind which transplanted a need for a redemptive creator.

The achievements and accomplishments of science bolstered this view. It appeared as though we had pushed back the frontiers of our world and there was no stopping us. Atheism was in fashion and scientific evidence appeared to back it. In fact, it was religion that now looked indefensible.

It was also the age of the superstate and the great leaders in whom everyone had supreme confidence, a fact which automatically lent itself to radical secular messianism. Why await the Messiah when the world's great leaders are already here? Immediately prior to the Second World War there were Churchill, Roosevelt, Stalin and Hitler, and although the latter two exemplified the epitome of cruelty and wickedness, they were nevertheless powerful leaders who engendered uncritical trust on the part of most of their respective citizens. Nothing was outside their ability to conquer.

Then the war came, and suddenly the concept of the secular utopia was in tatters. Whereas many survivors of the Second World War atrocities contend that the Holocaust ended our belief in God, the real story is that it ended our belief in humanity. How could anyone continue to believe in humanity or human institutions when one of the most culturally advanced nations of all time slaughtered twelve million people in the most gruesome and barbaric way imaginable? In fact, many scholars contend that it was precisely *because* Germany was so advanced that it spawned the atrocities of that war. They made culture and race their God to the exclusion of law and morality.

Fortunately, people finally recognized that the utopian overtones of Nazi Germany and Communist Russia were false. Both foretold of the perfection of humankind, Hitler through establishing the Aryan race, Stalin through the effective rule of the proletariat, but both equally were ideologies that advocated the advent of a secular utopia. What they delivered of course was not a utopia but Auschwitz and the Gulag Archipelago.

The Legacy of the False Messiahs

As a result, we who live in the present age have developed a deep fear of utopian ideas in general, and messianic claims in particular. This fear is compounded by the fact that a great many throughout history, as well as in the present day, have claimed that they were the Messiah. Instead of bringing redemption to their flocks, their leadership has almost always resulted in unbridled cruelty and suffering to the masses who followed them.

At the time of writing this, there was a fanatical and apparently insane leader of a messianic sect in Waco, Texas. He and his followers murdered four federal agents, yet he claimed that he was the Messiah, the bringer of peace.

Despairing of Redemption

The Jews have had their hopes dashed by false messianic expectations as well. The most famous of all the impostors is Shabbatai Zvi, but there are many others. One was a great Jewish Sage, Moses of Crete. He claimed that he was the Messiah and told the Jews of the island that he was there to deliver them from the hands of their tyrannical oppressors. As they marched behind him in their proposed exodus, they came to a great sea-cliff that left them nowhere to go. Moses of Crete then instructed them to hurl themselves over the cliff into the water, and he would cause a great miracle to happen in the form of the splitting of the sea, as his namesake had done for the Jewish people upon their exodus from Egypt. Needless to say, no miracle transpired and many hundreds died.

The Talmud has always warned that 'the redeemer will come when men despair of the redemption' (Sanhedrin, 97a). We certainly find ourselves in an age that has despaired of the coming redemption. So impossible in our minds is the concept of a righteous redeemer coming along to radically change the world for the better that today, in the wake of the worldwide Lubavitch campaign to raise the awareness of Jewish messianism and the Moshiach, most Jews the world over have responded with a cynical curiosity at best, and outright scorn and derision at worst.

Allowing ourselves to fall into a pit of despair or disillusionment because of past events is something one must be very cautious of when dealing with Jewish history. Here we may return to the question of how, amidst everything described above in terms of the human suffering and disillusionment that the human race has witnessed for thousands of years, we can still hope for the future and even dream of a glorious age when peace will spread throughout the earth.

Covenantal History

The great Jewish thinker, Rabbi Joseph Soloveitchik, who sadly passed away in 1993, explained: 'The Patriarchic Covenant introduced a new concept into history. While universal (non-Jewish) history is governed by causality, by what preceded, covenantal (Jewish) history is shaped by destiny, by a goal set in the future' (*Man of Faith in the Modern World*, page 70). He argued that in universal history every event is brought about by a preceding cause. Such history develops almost mechanically; origins determine events; the present is precipitated by the past. Most historians are guided by this principle, namely that causality dictates unfolding events.

Jewish history is different; therefore when secular scholars try to interpret Jewish history in this manner, they inevitably arrive at bizarre conclusions and distortions. Covenantal Jewish history is propelled by purpose and Divine covenants pertaining to the role of the Jewish people. The destiny of the Jewish people emanates from a Divine promise foretold about the future, rather than by events from the past impelling them to act in a given way. Jewish history is pulled, as if by a magnet, towards a glorious destiny; it is not pushed by antecedent causes.

The word 'destiny' is of course etymologically related to the word 'destination'. What determines Jewish historical experience is not one's point of departure, but one's destination. The destination of the Jewish people, as foretold by our prophets, is a state of perfection and redemption, not just of the Jew, and not even just of all humans, but of the entire universe. Rabbi Yehuda Loew of Prague, famous as the Maharal who built the Golem, writes, 'The essential function of the Messiah will consist of uniting and perfecting all, so that this will be truly one world.' The words of the prophet Zechariah still ring in our ears: 'And the Lord shall be king over all the earth: in that day shall there be one Lord, and His Name One' (Zechariah 14:9). This is the messianic dream of Judaism and the spiritual goal of Jewish history.

It is this covenantal understanding, and only this, which can account for the Jewish obsession with perfecting the world accompanied by the certainty that it can be achieved. If Jews took any notice of the history that has gone before, we would have given up the dream long ago. The glorious destiny that is foretold is an obsession that has nagged us throughout history as well as being the source of our infectious hope and enthusiasm for the future. How else can we explain why it is specifically the people who have suffered the most who are also the most hopeful and dedicate so much of their imagination and creative talents towards making a better world, or at the very least dreaming a vision of its possibility?

A Refusal to be Crushed

There is a passionate, almost irrational, determination to lift up the Jewish people by every means possible, be it creating our own homeland in this century after nearly two millennia of exile, or rescuing Soviet, Syrian and Ethiopian Jews from their oppression, or even something as everyday as building Jewish day schools throughout the world and promoting Jewish education amidst mass assimilation.

These actions bear witness to an innate belief in a glorious destiny and a supra-rational determination to force the arrival of the Messiah. There is no political, sociological or nationalistic explanation which can otherwise account for the intensity and solidarity of the Jewish people in relation to these goals, despite their having been raised in distant lands and immersed in disparate cultures. Other nations have suffered lesser catastrophes and have succumbed to the imperatives of historical decline. Where are the ancient Egyptians and the ancient Greeks, the ancient Romans and the Roman Empire today?

Judaism, with its vision of a perfect society, has influenced, no, brought into being, many movements and 'isms' which can be referred to as secular messianic utopias. Judaism has influenced and had its impact even on those Jewish visionaries who have not led Jewish lives.

It is more than sheer coincidence that so many of the world's political ideologies have come about through Jews. On the contrary, the desire of secular Jews to perfect the world through every means is a direct outgrowth of their exposure to the teachings of the Jewish prophets, and the promises those prophets gave of a glorious culmination to the march of civilization.

Robert Maxwell addressing the L'Chaim dinner in honour of Elie Weisel. Mr Maxwell, who later fell out of favour with the British public, was an Oxford resident and lost many of his relatives in the Holocaust.

Dr Jonathan Glover, university lecturer in Philosophy, makes a case of why we don't need God to be good in a debate against Dennis Prager that was quoted in articles around the world.

Dennis Prager, leading Jewish thinker, ethical monotheist and American radio personality, debating with university Philosophy tutor Dr Jonathan Glover on whether we need God to be good.

Dr Jonathan Cohen, university lecturer and world authority on philosophy, talking with Sir Claus and Lady Moser of Wadham College at a L'Chaim dinner.

Rabbi Adin Steinsaltz, translator of the Talmud (second from right), lunching with Nobel laureate Dr Baruch Blumberg of Balliol College, Oxford, Professor Saul Kripke and Sir Zelman Cowen at the Master's Lodgings.

Actor Leonard Nimoy, famous for his portrayal of Mr Spock in *Star Trek*, at the L'Chaim European premiere of his Holocaust testimonial film, *Never Forget*. Over 1,500 enthusiastic students crammed into the debating chamber of the Oxford Union for his lecture.

Leonard Nimoy receiving a menorah and a L'Chaim Society sweatshirt at the conclusion of his lecture.

Mel Mermelstein, Auschwitz survivor, warns students of the dangers of modern day Holocaust denial. Mr Mermelstein was the subject of the film *Never Forget* and was portrayed by Leonard Nimoy.

Mel Mermelstein signing copies of his book *By Bread Alone,* telling of his teenage years in Auschwitz. More than 600 non-Jewish students bought copies of the book.

Rabbi Boteach and Cory Booker at the Purim celebrations at the L'Chaim Society.

Oxford students enjoy a whisky tasting evening sponsored by United Distillers with Master Blender Ian Grieves at the L'Chaim Centre.

Richard Dawkins, author of *The Selfish Gene,* argues against religion with a panel of religious scientists that included fertility specialist, Professor Robert Winston.

Rabbi Boteach with Mr Gorbachev and some Oxford students. To Mr Gorbachev's left is Toba Friedman, L'Chaim Society President and the first female from a yeshiva background to win a Marshall scholarship.

Yoram Sheftel was the Defence Attorney for Ivan Demjanjuk, who was acquitted by the Israeli Supreme Court of being 'Ivan the Terrible', chief operator of the gas chambers at the concentration camp, Treblinka. This fascinating case captured the world's attention. To the left of Mr Sheftel is the original photospread shown to Treblinka survivors in order to identify 'Ivan the Terrible'.

Mr and Mrs Edmond Safra present Mr Gorbachev with a century-old Russian menorah which he said he would place in his museum of Perestroika in Moscow.

Even those Jews who have abandoned Judaism are still driven by its vision, but they reject a Divinely ordained messianic epoch for the concept of a secular utopia. The early fathers of Communism spoke almost straight out of the Bible, of a time when all of the earth's inhabitants would have according to their needs, when no one would go hungry, when there would be peace and harmony between all nations. The only real difference between what Communism promised and the facts of the Jewish messianic ideal was that the former hailed a Bolshevik Messiah who was to save the people, a Marx or a Lenin; what was promised was still a utopia. Even secular Jews such as Karl Marx have had this drive to improve mankind's lot, which is a direct outgrowth of their exposure to Jewish messianism.

Indomitable Spirit

Three thousand years of promises of hope hardened the Jew, who emerged from the Holocaust, not depressed and distraught from the blows of the past, but energized with superhuman zealousness by a dream about the future which the flames of the crematoria could not extinguish.

With regard to the state of Israel, for example, there is an awareness in the hearts of the Jews that Israel is a promised land. The promise, a destiny to be fulfilled, is the cause of our present exertions; is not the result of a conglomeration of past events. The drive on the part of the Jewish people to perfect the world, whether consciously or subconsciously, is fuelled by anticipation, by something beautiful and miraculous which defies precise formulation, which calls out to us and beckons from a not-so-distant horizon. Even secular Zionists, who formally decried all religious terminology and motivations, often spoke with messianic overtones.

Therefore the Jew never despairs. A Jew feels deep in his or her bones that destiny, not causality, is the mechanism behind the Jewish people and constitutes the dynamics of covenantal history. The future is responsible for the past.

Why We Need a Messiah

All this leads us to address the most important of all questions related to messianism, touched upon above, and that question relates to its modern-day relevance. If this Messiah is the one who will bring about a positive transformation of the world, why should we work for the betterment of our world today? Or, looked at from another perspective, why wait for something spiritual and elusive which we can carry out today via sociological, academic, or political means? The belief in the Messiah seems at odds with the belief that *humankind* is capable of making a better world.

Ironically, the concept of the Messiah superficially appears to me most un-Jewish. If someone who was vaguely acquainted with Judaism was asked what to her was the very essence of Judaism, there are many things she might answer. She might answer that Judaism believes in charity, or that Judaism believes in the family, or that Judaism is communally based. All of these answers scratch the surface of what Judaism really is. They are mere components, and not the essence. Nor do they truly sum up Judaism because they do not readily distinguish between Judaism and the other religions of the world. In the end she would have to answer that Judaism puts its emphasis on action. It believes in doing, accomplishing. It believes in conquering and mastering. It believes in perfecting, talking, arguing, whatever is needed to make a better world, that is where Judaism lies.

Judaism is concerned with perfecting the world through positive steps on the part of humanity, so the question becomes how Judaism can relegate the ultimate perfection of the world to a Messiah. Here stands Judaism, the most goal- and action-oriented religion ever to appear, and its ultimate message to us is this: 'By the way, we want you to work as hard as you can, but ultimately there are things which you cannot do. You will have to wait for a messianic epoch, for some legendary figure who will come on to the world stage, and he is the one that will ultimately perfect the world.'

How can we reconcile leaving the perfection of world society to a Messiah with the Jewish religion's demands that we better our world? Surely we are capable of adding the final touches ourselves, without any messianic redeemer?

Is Mankind Not Capable of Perfection?

Clearly, this is exactly what secular Jewish intellectuals like Marx thought. Their motto, in essence, was, 'Why wait for the Messiah? Let's do it today! By joining together we are wholly capable of creating a utopia ourselves.' Why was Marx wrong? Why was the vision of John F. Kennedy inadequate when he started the peace corps in the Sixties promising to cure the world's ills by focusing the attention and the effort of the younger generation on a solution?

The same question can be asked in relation to secular Zionism. It was the secular Zionists, many of whom were brought up in strictly Orthodox, even Chasidic, Eastern European homes, who rejected the Jewish concept of waiting around for a Messiah, and seized the initiative to go up and re-create a Jewish homeland. They didn't just talk about it, they achieved their objective and created a remarkably successful and impressive country in the process, which in turn has become the pride of the world Jewish population. The state of Israel has become the object of adoration which Jews have lacked since the destruction of the second Temple. There is hardly a Jew alive who does not swell with pride at the achievements of the Jewish state and pray for its security and survival.

So who is right and who is wrong? Is Judaism the one religion that always told people to go out, conquer, and change, also saying we must now wait?

The Root of All Evil

The answer comes from seeing how evil and goodness fit into the deepest structure of the world: what makes our universe what it is, and what would have to be changed to achieve the wonderful perfection that all messianists, secular and religious alike, look forward to.

First of all we must face the unpleasant truth: we live in an imperfect world. No one can say the world is perfect, no one truly thinks they themselves are perfect. But what is the world's primary imperfection? What is it about our world, and ourselves for that matter, that makes us so willing immediately to pronounce it imperfect?

According to Chasidic thought it is this: the first human, Adam, was born into a perfect world. God is perfect and what He creates must necessarily be perfect. Adam and Eve were put into the Garden of Eden, which we are told was also perfect. However, the Torah itself attests to the fact that there was evil in the Garden of Eden: there was a tree from which Adam and Eve were not permitted to eat. It was not good for them. In fact, it would harm them. God warned our first parents that if they did indeed eat from the Tree of Knowledge of Good and Evil, they would die. Surely this is proof that not everything in the Garden of Eden was good. Some things were so bad that they could kill. So how was the Garden perfect?

Distinct Entities of Good and Evil

The perfection of the Garden of Eden was not that it contained no evil, but rather that the good and evil were completely distinct entities. Good was good and Bad was bad. God was able to 'point His finger' and indicate conclusively, 'This is a bad tree. But this one, over here, is a good tree. This tree has good fruit, this one has bad, diseased fruit.' In the Garden of Eden, Adam and Eve were clearly aware of what to pursue and what to stay away from. Who the good people were, and who the bad people were. What this meant in practice was that in the Garden of Eden, if one chose to pursue good actions, there would be no worry about evil consequences. When one took medicines which were supposed to cure, there were no harmful side-effects. That was what the Garden was all about.

In other words, the evil forces that operate today within creation existed even in the Garden of Eden prior to Adam and Eve's first sin. Yet the difference between then and today was that evil was easily recognizable, and so it could easily be avoided. All our first parents had to do to avoid the evil was to obey God's commandment and refrain from consuming it.

However, Adam and Eve did not listen: they mixed the two fruits, the two trees. They decided to commit the ultimate sin, for which we all suffer to this day. They interwove good with evil. They took all the blessings that God gave them as human beings – intelligence, insight, a spouse, a residence in the beautiful Garden, sustenance – and abused them. Adam and Eve used God's goodness to defy God's will and commit evil and, for the first time in history, there was an admixture of good with evil. This was the beginning of the confusion between good and evil which reigns till this day.

So great was Adam and Eve's confusion of good and evil that God gave the human race the Torah, His infinite wisdom, whose very purpose is to undo their evil. The purpose of the Torah is to teach us once again to be discerning and to extract good from evil. That is what the Torah is. The essence of the Torah is that it is a way of identifying what is good and what is evil. The Torah says, 'There are seven days in a week. Working on six of them is good for you, but working on the seventh is a mistake.' 'There are all kinds of animals in the world, but the kosher ones are good for you to eat, the others are not.' 'There are all kinds of peoples on this earth, this you may marry, this you may not.' 'There are different ways of doing business, you may behave this way, but you may not do deals in this manner.' The Torah is the means by which to discern and teach what is harmful and what is beneficial. The Torah is the guide for our struggle to undo the sin of Adam and Eve.

Evil and Sadness from Goodness and Joy

Even with the guide of the Torah, though, life is sad. We are all too aware of the confusion between good and evil. Life is hard because everything is chaotic, and there is no lucidity. We enter life being taught that there can never be a beautiful moment that will not be accompanied by hardship, and there can never be a tragedy from which something good will not be derived. This is 'the curse of Adam'. Had our first parents heeded God's prohibition, we would know what is good, and what is bad, and there would be no confusion and no pain caused by the inability to decide or the frustration of not knowing the outcome of our choices. As a result of the first sin there is no black and white, only shades of grey.

We go through life making decisions, making choices, feeling confident that what we have done is the right thing, only to discover later that what we thought was good was disastrous, and vice versa. None of us is ever really sure if the path and the courses we embark upon will yield the desired result. If we try to help our neighbours they may be insulted by our assumption that they cannot cope on their own, or they may be glad for our concern. If we invest in a business, we may become rich, or we may lose everything, even our homes. Life is fraught with uncertainty.

Every newly-wed is told, 'Don't worry if you fight, expect to fight!' That is the imperfection of this world. Even amidst the most beautiful occasions we know we should expect some harmful consequences. Even while couples are preoccupied with preparing for their wedding, many are simultaneously drawing up pre-nuptial agreements in case the marriage breaks up. There is nothing in life that is only a blessing. When you have a child there will be times when you will be swearing, 'Why would I ever want another one?' Similarly, the fact that we can learn even from our grossest errors, the fact that we cannot just dismiss them as unfortunate and forget them, is our pain and our curse. Even in tragedy there can be happiness, even when the worst possible things transpire, there will always be some light at the end of the tunnel. It is sad that in something so ugly there can be something so beautiful.

All this is said about life in general. However, on a more personal level, within ourselves, we know that through some of our ugliest human facets we are able to achieve the most beautiful and warm human accomplishments. I was once invited to speak at a Chanuka party in East Berlin, and my visit was the first time I had set foot in a Communist country. Anyone who is accustomed to the beauties and comforts of western living would have been shocked. The cars were about as big as bumper cars. The people looked impoverished and depressed. It was very unimpressive. Why? Because when you take away capitalist competition, contention, ambition, and even jealousy, when one removes all those things which we in the West habitually say are ugly and condemn and deplore, what you are left with is an ineffective group of human beings. In other words, some of our ugliest human character traits have brought about a very impressive and technologically advanced western civilization.

A Role for Jealousy

Interestingly, Jewish law has a brief comment on this. In talmudic law, if one *cheder* teacher is already in a city, it is permitted for a new one to move into his territory to teach children the Torah, even if this will encroach upon the business activity of the first. The reason the Talmud gives is simple. The Jewish people need the best possible Torah teachers, and 'jealousy amongst scholars increases wisdom'.

Here at last we have the reason why, ultimately, we need a Messiah. We will never be able to perfect the world on our own. The moment we say,

'We declare war on jealousy, contention, ambition, discord, arrogance, strife, intuition, in short – let's rid ourselves of all those causes which make us hate each other and act indecently towards one another', at that moment we will simultaneously be killing part of ourselves. We will be annihilating a part of ourselves which makes us tick, which makes us human, which makes us successful. If we were to succeed at ridding ourselves of all conceit, desire, vanity, arrogance, aspiration, pretension, and supplant them with contentment, satisfaction, lethargy and indolence, what we would be left with would be a very 'nice' but a very inadequate human being. That is the curse of Adam. And that is why we need a messianic redeemer.

This is also why Judaism contends that, strive as you may, you only serve as a catalyst to usher in the messianic era. Ultimately you are not going to solve the problem because the problem is not out there in the world so that you can find it and kill it. The problem is within us. The problem is not just that the world has some evil bits – famine, hunger, disease, murder, and insensitivity – and we must simply cure them and create a utopia. The problem is that the only way to rid the world of these ills is by calling upon some of our own inner ills, perpetuating the problems arising from evil still further.

It is specifically the scientist who competes to win the Nobel Prize for Medicine or some similar international recognition who eventually finds a cure for a terrible disease. And it is the competitive, ambitious young entrepreneur who sometimes must behave quite ruthlessly in business, who succeeds financially and is able to donate the money that will alleviate someone else's hunger. And it is the politician who wishes to be remembered as a great and humane statesman who sends his army into battle to combat the dark forces of the world, as in the case of George Bush and the Gulf War of 1991.

If we kill that part of ourselves that aspires to these heights, the world will disintegrate. Parts of the machinery that makes us what we are, that makes us successful, is not the greatest or most pleasant things which exist within us. That is why we need the Messiah.

Good and Evil Finally Separated

Hence we find that Rabbi Chaim Vital, speaking in the name of the great kabbalist Rabbi Isaac Luria, known as the Ari, stated that 'When good and evil are finally separated, the Messiah will come.' Similarly, Chama of Tzepori proclaims in the Midrash that 'the Holy one will repair the damage [of Adam's sin]. He will heal the wound of the world' (Genesis Rabba).

We need, ultimately, God Himself to come, after we've made a gallant effort to show Him we really want to be better, to help bring about a transformation in the human condition itself, whereby we can actually be successful and compete alongside other human beings without wanting to outdo them. This is one area in which no human has yet had true success.

Being a good person does not entail being weak, or having no great achievements. Rather, it means that while you may be fantastic and successful, the world is large enough to contain a great many successful people, and a great many egos. Being ambitious is seen in Judaism as desirable, so long as it does not intrude upon someone else's ambition. The problem is that self-development usually entails outdoing one's fellow and agonizing when the achievements of other people surpass our own victories.

As a comment on this, here is a story of the Tzemach Tzedek, Rabbi Menachem Mednel of Lubavitch. A young student from the yeshivah came to him and said, 'My life is miserable. I am leaving the yeshivah.' He was a new student, not from a Lubavitch family, and he was sure the rebbe would encourage him to stay. 'I can't take it any longer,' he complained, 'everyone steps on me. Everyone abuses me.' The Tzemach Tzedek said to him, 'Before you leave the yeshivah, I want to ask you one question. Who asked you to spread yourself out over the entire yeshivah so that at every place someone steps, they step on you?'

This is the secret to getting along with other human beings. It is the ability not to 'spread yourself' everywhere. One must be 'large enough' to transcend one's natural fear of other people's success to leave room for the expansion of those others. Ultimately, it is specifically through that kind of attitude and approach that people have climbed the highest heights.

Retaining Wholesomeness and Competition

We need God to give just that little ingredient which will bring about a human transformation so that we can take all of ourselves into a better time: so that we don't have to leave part of ourselves behind. None of us wants to do that. None of us hates ourselves so much that we believe we really have to kill off part of ourselves in order to be better and more caring human beings.

This is why, for instance, people do not like festival days like Rosh Hashanah and Yom Kippur, although we always look forward to Purim and Chanuka. Rosh Hashanah and Yom Kippur are those days we would rather avoid, because one hears those terrible words, *teshuva*, repent, return. One reason people distrust this concept of *teshuva* so much is because they feel it is saying to them, 'Leave part of yourself behind. There is a part of you inside which is undesirable. Get rid of it!' No one likes to be told that there is a little beast inside him or her that must be squashed and sacrificed on the altar of God in order to get closer to Him.

The messianic era is one which will involve transformation, not eradication. It is not about exterminating the undesirable elements in the world, nor about leading a crusade and saying, 'Capitalism is bad, we will adopt a different way.' Rather, it is about bringing all of ourselves into a better time. It is about recognizing that it is the human totality which can bring about a better world, and that we simply need to redirect some of our human drives so that they can be utilized for goodness as well.

The same applies to Israel. Just the existence of Israel is of course an extraordinary achievement. It is incredible that finally we have a place that can be defended by Jews, but it is not yet a part of the longed-for messianic era. Brave young men and women must serve in the army from eighteen to twenty-one years-old, and mothers have to cry over their young who die in battle. We are looking for a better, more prosperous world, where we will be intrinsically Jewish but we will not have to fight for it. Where people can be good without having to defend goodness. Where decency, honesty and morality will ultimately triumph and not only prevail over the forces that oppose it, but win over those forces and bring them into the sphere of Godliness and goodness. We await a time described by Maimonides, the leading medieval Jewish thinker, 'When the Messiah comes, war will end, God's blessing will be on all men, and none will risk his life for money' (Commentary to Mishnah: Sanhedrin, 1168, 10.1).

We hope and pray for the imminent arrival of the Messiah. May it happen now!

Chapter Sixty-nine

SHOULD OXFORD HAVE PUBLIC DISPLAYS OF JUDAISM?: THE LUBAVITCH LOUDSPEAKER

Although it is probably true that our presence in Oxford has always been a source of controversy, this is especially so among certain quarters of the Jewish community. This is primarily because of the high-profile nature of our activities. Britain in general has a low-key approach to life, and the English habit of understatement is of course legendary (I use English advisedly, as Scottish, Welsh and particularly Irish are very different in style). While Americans pepper all their conversation with loaded adjectives like 'very', 'the greatest' and 'unbelievable', one will generally only elicit from the English the word 'quite'.

The most pertinent indicator of this is in the field of politics. A British candidate for Parliament who used a US-style election campaign with big bands and thousands of balloons would be laughed off his or her soap-box, and for two reasons. Firstly, the idea that one can buy oneself into office with a slick advertising campaign is anathema to the British style of democracy. Everyone, rich or poor, should be able to be elected on merit alone. That is why all major parties have free time on television for Party Political broadcasts, and why Members of Parliament receive a wage, so that political power is not only available to the wealthy. Secondly, Britain as a nation is wary of those who 'blow their own trumpet'. Saying, 'I'm the best' automatically invites disbelief, so politicians have either to bad-mouth the other parties, as was noticeable in the 1992 General Election, or stick to talking about policies and facts. Something special does not need to be *made* special. On the contrary, the more dressed up an idea or subject has to be before we appreciate it, the more this betrays its lack of any intrinsically unique characteristic.

Even the Americans understand this, but only with the really special things. For example, the stationery from the President just says, in small blue letters, 'The White House'. There are no emphatic italics to make it read *The* White House, or multi-coloured logos that re-emphasize this is a letter from one of the most powerful men on the planet.

Recognizing Intrinsic Beauty

In truth, this is also an important Chasidic principle. The Jewish Chasidic custom is not to put a *mezuzah* in an ornate or embroidered case, simply because a *mezuzah* is a beautiful object in itself. The same is true of a *Sukkah*. Whereas many people install the most beautiful decorations in a *Sukkah*, often to the point where the *Sukkah* itself is no longer visible, the Chasidic custom is to leave it bare. A *Sukkah* has intrinsic beauty and does not need artificial decorations.

Unfortunately, this difference between the Americans and the British has had negative repercussions for their relationship in Oxford. Firstly, there is an incredibly high number (there goes my American superlative again) of Yanks at Oxford. In the graduate community they can make up as much as fifty per cent of any given year. Of course, most American students come here for a uniquely Oxford experience, and the best way of doing that would be to get to know a lot of British students, but this simply does not happen. The American and British students often remain two distinct and separate communities, and all too rarely is an American successful in crossing this figurative border to be fully accepted into the company of an all-British crowd.

A Clash of Cultures

The American visiting students always complain about this to me. They feel that their British hosts are not very welcoming toward them and that they are treated not so much with contempt as with a general indifference. They think that the British students are not very friendly, but this is not true at all: it is just that the British are naturally more reserved. This is largely because they see the Americans as being brash, rather arrogant and pushy. The British students also tend to treat them as invaders. There are, after all, so many of them. Of course, the Americans are not so much brash as very outgoing, and at ease with expressing their opinions. So there are misconceptions on both sides which serve to perpetuate this 'gulf' that separates them.

Of course, this also spills over into the British seeing a loud American rabbi, like myself, who is intent on staging high-profile activities and who brings very high-power speakers, as yet another brash American invader. This is compounded by the fact that there is a natural ambivalence among the established Jewish faculty members towards noticeable religious displays: they fear such behaviour on the part of a minority religion and community might invoke the hostility of the 'real' Oxonians. As I have said, I have heard umpteen times that my activities can engender anti-Semitism, albeit from a small group of Jewish dons, and usually those who are more advanced in age.

Fear in Sydney

This reaction is not confined to Britain. I shall always remember the time I organized a large Sukkot celebration in the Waverley Oval in Sydney, Australia. Sydney Jewry had never before put on a large Jewish outdoor display that had been advertised throughout the city, and here we were staging an event, attended by most of the city's leading politicians, including the mayor, that would attract thousands of people, complete with a loud band, scores of clowns and jugglers, and a lot of fanfair. While most of the city's Jewish population loved the idea, there were also many older residents, particularly Holocaust survivors, who objected most vociferously on the grounds that the event would generate anti-Semitism. We were basically being told that we were living in someone else's land, and we should behave ourselves and keep our heads down.

I responded by telling them the well-known story of two Russian Jews who were sentenced by Stalin to execution by firing squad. The soldiers were putting the blindfold around the eyes of the first when he brushed them off and told them that he would like to look at them as he died. The second Jew turned to him and said, 'Stop arguing, you'll get us into trouble.'

The point is that when people label Lubavitch activities as 'wrong' because they draw attention to the Jewish minority, they misinterpret the purpose of these actions. Their assessment misses the vital issue. My particular kind of high-profile Judaism is not the result of being American, being brash or whatever. It is however due to my being Lubavitch. The attitude of Lubavitch, with its *mitzvah*-mobiles, high-flying *tefillin* campaigns, and broadcasts of the rebbe's talks on worldwide satellite cable television, to name but a few examples, has always been that there is no place that Judaism does not belong, and therefore there is no reason to hide it in a box.

Because this concept is strange to many people, it requires further elucidation.

Doubts about Lubavitch

In late 1992 I was asked to go to Cambridge to address the Jewish student and academic community there on the subject of Lubavitch itself. The community wanted to know more about the aims and objectives of the movement, and they were particularly interested in the importance to Lubavitch of the concept of the Messiah. The question of the Messiah had arisen at this time due to extensive publicity about messianic fervour in the Lubavitch of New York and in Israel. Some of this media coverage had been unfavourable, and had conspicuously failed to understand the historic dimension of messianism in Judaism in general and its proper place in the intellectual basis of the movement in Chabad philosophy. I thought it proper to give the understanding of the Messiah in Lubavitch and recent events in their correct context so that everybody could gain a balanced reading.

I published this account a little later for the students in Oxford, as the students here had similar questions. The circulation of the lecture here also made the students aware of the fascinating and complex history of Lubavitch. Many did not know that the movement is over 250 years old (which for the sake of comparison makes it almost the same age as the Oxford Methodist movement) and that everything Lubavitch does is directed by Chabad philosophy (a profound religious philosophy of real intellectual depth and rigour) which is ultimately derived from the teachings of the great Jewish mystic and teacher the Baal Shem Tov (1698–1760) of Russia.

Practically, I wished the students to be aware of what my objectives, as a Lubavitch rabbi and emissary, actually are in Oxford – and more particularly what they are not. It will be seen in the following that Chabad emphasizes inner change and transformation towards Godliness. The challenge of Lubavitch in Oxford is not to usurp or replace existing Jewish structure in the university, or to make everybody Lubavitch. Its purpose is to enhance and extend the Jewish life and Godliness that is already here, and to do it in a way that is both spiritually and rationally satisfying.

The Baal Shem Tov and the Origins of Chabad Chasidism

The Chasidic movement was started by Rabbi Israel Baal Shem, known as the Baal Shem Tov, at the beginning of the seventeenth century in Russia. The Baal Shem Tov was a renowned mystic who aimed to teach people to discover the Godliness of creation. He showed people how to discover the intrinsic holiness which exists within the world, even though the Godliness in creation is superficially obscured in material existence. This was to serve as the central doctrine of all Chasidic thought and development in subsequent generations. Chasidism is typified as a branch within Judaism that emphasizes the transcendental in human and earthly existence: human character must be fully developed in order to serve God because it is inherently Godly. The Baal Shem Tov's principal disciple was Rabbi DovBer of Mezritch, and in turn his principle disciple was Rabbi Schneur Zalman of Liadi. Rabbi Schneur Zalman, born in 1745, was the founder of the Chabad Chasidic movement, and he achieved this largely by his remarkable distillation of Chasidic thought in his monumental work *Tanya*, published in 1768.

The Principles of Tanya – *the Foundations of the Chabad-Lubavitch Movement*

Rabbi Schneur Zalman expounded two vital doctrines which have shaped and inspired the Lubavitch way of life, and accounts for its role in disseminating Judaism throughout the world Jewish community.

On the first page of *Tanya*, Rabbi Schneur Zalman, known as the Alter Rebbe (Elder Rebbe), introduced one of the most radical ideas in the history of Jewish religion, if not all religion. First, though, he said that to the untrained mind, righteousness seems to be a state whereby one constantly eradicates the evil from within one's soul. Man can transform himself by dispelling and annihilating the natural predisposition to be materialistically inclined, with lusts, jealousy, insubordination and irrationality. Eventually one reaches the stage where one learns to embrace Godliness, Divinity, prayer, faith, acts of charity, kindness, and all other things which we associate with religious commitment. That is what we usually accept as righteousness. It is the *avoda*, the Divine service of the talmudic and righteous individual, whose principal interest in life is the eradication of all evil from within his or her being, even to the final extent that he or she no longer feels any desire or sense of pleasure in transgressing the will of God. For such an individual, materialism has no comfort or pleasure. This concept had long been accepted by many creeds and religions. However, Rabbi Schneur Zalman went on to describe an alternative superior way of serving God that is completely different to the first. This does not focus on the negative aspect of humanity and of creation by seeking to eradicate the evil within on the path to Divine service and realization. Instead, the emphasis is reversed: one realizes God by affirming that which is already Godly and positive in the creation. Here humankind serves God by striving each day to choose that which is right, so as to release and manifest the existing Godliness inherent in creation. This concept is radical and unique because it does not deny the intrinsic Godliness of human and material nature, but it enhances and affirms the importance of the intrinsic transcendental Godly reality in the world.

Enter the Intermediary

In detail, Rabbi Schneur Zalman had introduced the vital concept of a *beinuni*, an intermediate person who serves God not through purging the evil of the human soul, but through fighting every day to choose what is right. This concept emphasized that serving God is an intrinsically human activity: God does not desire that we be righteous, or that we stop the natural human inclination towards earthiness. Rather, God wants us to be confronted with a series of choices on a daily basis to condition us to fight the natural evil inclination, and finally we will choose goodness instead. In this manner, God becomes an active part of our lives, who is chosen on a daily basis rather than being chosen by the Jew long ago at the beginning of one's life.

Rabbi Schneur Zalman went as far as saying that this way of serving God is greater than the perfection of the *tzadik*: the *beinuni* has to deny evil on a daily basis without the courage and Divine assistance that the *tzadik* is given. The *beinuni* seeks to enhance the glory of God and to affirm and release the transcendental in the material through his very mundane and daily activities.

An Unconscious Commitment

The second important doctrine that the Alter Rebbe introduced in *Tanya* was that every Jew has a natural and constitutional relationship with God. The Jew is naturally bound to the being of God at all levels of his or her existence. Crucially, Jewish spirituality and identity is founded not just in the conscious or even the subconscious, but in the unconscious itself. The Jewish relationship to God is not primarily the result of consciousness and action, but is an utterly basic and spontaneous condition and movement of being. This doctrine can be readily and pleasingly summarized by reference to the understanding of the Jewish religious identity and essence given by a Roman Catholic priest during the Israeli war against the PLO in Lebanon. While being interviewed by Israeli Radio (where the interviewer was trying to understand what it was like to be a Roman Catholic priest and to live in a country where he was a religious minority) he was asked what he understood was the essence of being Jewish. The priest responded, 'To me a Jew is someone who is religious without knowing it.' And there he stopped. In this simple statement there is no greater summary of the central idea the Alter Rebbe is communicating in the *Tanya*. While many people believe that religion is the conscious activity and participative movement of the individual towards God, the Alter Rebbe introduced the concept of an inherent substructure and foundation for our spiritual life, a part within us which naturally assumes to draw us closer to God. It is a part of us that never needed to be acquired or cultivated, for it is a part of us that makes us Jewish, just as we are human.

A Philosophy for Personal and Historical Transformation

The philosophy of Chabad and the *Tanya* has not merely been one of learned theological importance; this dual philosophical system is intended to have practical effects that change the world and its people. It has in fact inspired and directed the entire development and growth of the Chabad-Lubavitch movement since the eighteenth century. Moreover, it accounts for the dynamic growth and dissemination of Lubavitch worldwide since the Second World War.

Much of the character and dynamism of Chabad-Lubavitch since the war is undoubtedly the result of the current rebbe, Rabbi Menachem Schneerson. Born in the Russian town of Nikolaev in 1902, he moved to Berlin shortly before he married, in 1929, Chaya Mushka, the daughter of the then Lubavitcher rebbe, Rabbi Joseph Isaac Schneersohn. Although he is a renowned Jewish sage and scholar, his intellectual roots are not confined to the rich soil of Judaism: he studied philosophy and mathematics at the University of Berlin and engineering at the Sorbonne, and he is fluent in ten languages.

When the previous rebbe died, Rabbi Menachem Schneerson was asked to succeed to his father-in-law's place, but he was reluctant to do so for some time. Eventually, though, he agreed and since 1950 he has been the high-profile leader of the international movement of Lubavitch, reaching out to forgotten or forgetful Jews the world over and showing us all that traditional Judaism can be exciting and creative. His administrative centre is not in Israel but in the rundown and racially divided neighbourhood of Crown Heights in New York City, and that is where one may find him every Sunday, handing out dollar bills to the thousands who seek his presence.

Perhaps the most revealing incident I know of him dates from the time when he was far too young to be thinking of the great future that lay ahead: as a nine-year-old he saved the life of another boy, who had fallen into the Black Sea from the deck of a moored boat. Even then he thought of others before himself. His own life was less important than the life of this other child.

Today and throughout his years of leadership one of his prime objectives has been to send emissaries all over the world to inspire Jews in their religious life and observance. The rebbe has not only sent such *shluchim* to areas where there are thriving Jewish communities; he has often sent them to remote places where Jews are impoverished, or completely lacking in Jewish education or awareness. That such importance has been attached to this work comes from the belief of Chabad philosophy that every Jewish soul is unique and important because of its intrinsic connectedness to God, and the need for individuals to realize their spiritual essence and existence. We shall return to this point later.

Sacrifice and Leadership in the Gulag Archipelago

Between the Alter Rebbe and the present rebbe there were five other leaders of Lubavitch, most of whom were father and son. Immediately preceding the current rebbe as leader of Lubavitch was his father-in-law Rabbi Joseph Isaac Schneerson. Rabbi Joseph Isaac was the first of the Lubavitch leaders to send many emissaries to outlying provinces and neglected Jewish communities. His emissaries often experienced great hardship, and many were killed, because of the importance they attached to the individual Jew and his or her connection to God. I personally am not from a Lubavitch family, but many of my friends in the yeshivah I attended were named after Lubavitch grandfathers who were executed by the Bolshevik authorities for disseminating Judaism, opening up *cheders* and *mikvahs* in places as distant from the city of Lubavitch as Georgia and Ukraine. It is no exaggeration to say that Lubavitch single-handedly saved the Judaism of the Jews of Georgia and many other remote Russian areas. When any of the previous rebbe's Chassidim were caught by the Bolsheviks, they were put in front of firing squads. Often, when the rebbe sent his emissaries to open a *cheder*, they knew full well that they would never come back and would never see their children again. Thus Lubavitch had to go underground with all of their activities, and this elaborate underground Jewish educational network remained in place and operated with great efficiency throughout the Cold War.

An Enemy Who Looks up in Awe

To give the reader just some idea of the extent of Lubavitch work to save Jews and Judaism through the torturous years of the Cold War, I quote a brief excerpt from an article by Rabbi Marc Gellman, leader of Conservative Judaism in New York City, who wrote the following in an article which is actually highly critical of Lubavitch: 'In Vienna a high [American] official told me that when the CIA want to get a message quickly into the Soviet Union they call the rebbe! He has had people working in Russia since the Revolution and his lines of communication are always open and secure. The rebbe is not the head of a cult. He does not brainwash or coerce his followers. He is, rather, the powerful and charismatic leader of Jews who want to do *mitzvot* for the Jewish people and for the leader they will follow until their death or his. I am the enemy of the rebbe, but I am in awe of him. No simple-minded analysis can capture what he has begun to do for or to the Jewish world' (*The Jewish World*, 2 December 1988).

This level of sacrifice demonstrates the radical and humanitarian nature and effects of the application of the philosophy of *Tanya*. It also vividly illustrates the reality of the notion that the religious life of the *Beinuni* is one of a struggle, to choose good and to resist evil, in the face of human fallibility and sometimes great odds.

In the final analysis, the rebbe and his followers undertook their fateful task in Russia because Judaism is ultimately rooted in an unconscious reality. The rebbe and his followers could not countenance deserting millions of Jews trapped inside the newly formed Soviet Union upon the rise of Bolshevism and Stalinism.

Defying the Opponents of Judaism at All Costs

It is well worth recounting the work of the previous rebbe in this context. After the rise of the atheistic Communist state, Stalin sought to crush religious observance and religious doctrines with a mighty hand. One of the tools he used was the NKVD, the secret police, the precursor of the more well-known KGB. They launched a systematic campaign against all forms of Jewish religious observance, closing and outlawing all yeshivahs and Jewish day schools, and seeking to make all of Russia atheist. The great spiritual leaders of the era believed it was imperative to encourage their followers to leave the Soviet Union in order to escape this unprecedented wave of governmental atheistic coercion. Indeed, virtually all the great rabbis of the time departed, taking all their followers with them. But Rabbi Joseph Isaac refused to leave. His attitude was that if they were to leave there would be many Jews who would not or could not follow, and the result would be mass Jewish religious ignorance, with its consequent assimilation and the loss of millions of Jews. Not only did he send the first of the Lubavitch emissaries to all the corners of Russia, he also sent out emissaries to places like Georgia and Mukhar, knowing full well that most would never return as they would be assassinated by the NKVD for their religious activism. Lubavitch lost thousands through political assassination by the Soviet secret police.

Justifying the Loss of Life

The previous rebbe was asked how he could allow this. It was suggested that it contradicted all of Jewish law, as Jewish law mandates that Jews *must* transgress any of the laws of Judaism when confronted with a capital penalty for performing them, in all except three cases: idolatry, sexual immorality and murder. Jewish law does not in the least countenance Jewish education as a cause for martyrdom. They asked how he could take it upon himself to ask his followers to die in their thousands? His response was that regardless of the law there are those things which are so important they transcend the law. If Lubavitch and all of its followers and emissaries were to leave Russia with the rebbe, there would be a near-collapse of Jewish life which would result in the loss of millions of Jews, something which Judaism in Russia would never recover from. It is for this reason that there are few Lubavitch families of two generations ago who did not lose at least one member to the Russian police. I personally know of two friends from yeshivah whose grandfather and great-grandfather, respectively, were assassinated by the secret police.

It was largely through the efforts of Rabbi Joseph Isaac that any semblance of Jewish learning and consciousness remained in Russia until the present day, when the Gorbachev revolution freely permitted religion again. Thus the Lubavitch organization in the Soviet Union was the most extensive and reliable network existing in the Union that was not a client of the state. This was the remnant of the extensive network of contacts that had been laid down in the days of Rabbi Joseph Isaac.

The Suffering of Rabbi Joseph Isaac

Finally it must be emphasized that the rebbe himself suffered persecution for his work. When the Russian authorities caught up with Rabbi Joseph Isaac they imprisoned him and sentenced him to death for insurrection against the state. But the sentence was later commuted to exile in the Urals through the personal intervention of President Herbert Hoover of the USA. After many years of exile, the rebbe was finally expelled from the country, and later he lived in Warsaw for ten years. He lived through the bombardment of Warsaw by the Nazis and barely escaped with his life.

He finally arrived in the USA in 1940 on the last ocean liner to cross the Atlantic Ocean prior to the German U-boat blockade. Upon his arrival he was greeted by hundreds of followers in New York, but he refused to leave the ship until they guaranteed him a central yeshivah the very next morning where rabbis could be ordained, and Jewish pupils taught again. Their response to him was that '*America iz anderish*', in English, America is different, this is a different country and the same rules of public Jewish affiliation and education did not apply as they did in the Shtetls of Russia and Poland. It was a secular acculturated country which deeply believed in a division between church and state. Jews felt that people would not respect the antiquated practices of Judaism in such a modern and progressive society. His response was that America is *nisht anderish*, that America is not different. He said that according to the teaching of the Baal Shem Tov and Chassidus there is no place which is devoid of God, even America. He added that although the home and religious life of the Jews for many centuries had now been destroyed, what was left had to be preserved. Their new home in the USA was no less holy, nor did it have less capacity to be Jewish than the previous one.

Rabbi Joseph Isaac was accompanied by his eldest son-in-law and his daughter. His second son-in-law, whom he had sent to study at Leningrad University, the University of Berlin and the Sorbonne, barely escaped with his life but finally managed to make the crossing from Portugal in 1941, and arrived to be with his father-in-law. A third son-in-law and daughter with ten children were not as fortunate and died at the Treblinka death camp.

The previous rebbe continued his programme of sending emissaries to different corners of the world such as Australia, Italy, and the West Coast of the USA. But Lubavitch was still a very small movement with only a few hundred followers. Rabbi Joseph Isaac was confined to a wheelchair for most of his years in the USA because of the damage done by the extreme torture he had suffered under the Bolshevik authorities and in Bolshevik prisons. Still, he would not allow his disability to curtail any of the vast Jewish educational and social welfare activity he initiated in his ten years in the United States

The Present Rebbe, and the Worldwide Dissemination of Chabad

Rabbi Joseph Isaac died in 1949, and the question as to his succession became pressing. His younger son-in-law Rabbi Menachem Mendel Schneerson was the obvious choice, as he was a direct descendant of Rabbi Schneur Zalman of Liadi (the original founder of Lubavitch). He was already a noted Torah scholar, and he had the unique (and extremely rare for a Chasid) qualification of having been educated in the leading secular universities of Leningrad, Berlin, and the Sorbonne in Paris. Initially, he refused to accept the leadership of the Lubavitch, and so for a year the movement was leaderless. Finally, after much pressure and persuasion, Rabbi Schneerson agreed to assume leadership.

A Vision of Expansion

In one of his first public addresses he presented his vision of Lubavitch having a global operation, opening centres in all continents to disseminate the ancient wisdom and knowledge of Judaism throughout every nation. While at yeshivah I recall being taught by one of the original Chasidim of the previous rebbe who attended that public lecture over forty years ago. He retold how the people listened with disbelief to the rebbe's words; here was a small and impoverished group of bearded and black-clad and black-hatted men, whose ranks had been decimated by Stalin and Hitler and yet whose leader dared to talk about opening centres for Judaism worldwide! Now more than forty years on the astonishment has ceased, for the rebbe has fulfilled his vision and even surpassed it.

Lubavitch Comes of Age

Today Lubavitch is the largest Jewish social welfare organization in the world. There are over 1,548 centres, and they employ about 150,000 full-time workers. The Tomchei Temimim central yeshivah, which was begun the day after the previous rebbe arrived in New York, has ordained more than 24,000 rabbis who serve in communities around the globe. Today there are few Jews in any part of the planet who have not experienced the impact of the Lubavitch message and benefitted from Lubavitch activities and programmes. The movement has a presence in over thirty countries, and has helped tens of thousands of Jews discover their Jewish heritage and the contemporary relevance of the ancient verities of Judaism in their lives. The rebbe uses revolutionary means to disseminate age-old truth. He fully utilizes every form of modern telecommunications, including satellite networks. Of course, this contradicts some preconceptions about Lubavitch. The use of high technology by Lubavitch shows that the movement does not shun modernity but fully embraces it. This is because innovations which may increase the effect of good actions over what was possible in former times are to be regarded as a desirable means and opportunities for goodness which must be harnessed, even if they have been born out of burgeoning secular culture that may be contrary to religious life.

It is important to realize that the success of Lubavitch in its worldwide mission is not solely the result of effective use of publicity and media. Success rests very much on the application of the insights of Chabad philosophy to Lubavitch work and the modern situation. Essentially, the movement has succeeded because Chabad and the rebbe seek to find and to draw out the Godly which is in every situation, because of their fundamental belief that nothing in creation is intrinsically un-Godly. Therefore, there is no need to shun any part of the world and contemporary society, provided it can be brought to serve God or to manifest Godliness. What this means in the practical dealings of Lubavitch is that they do not have to usurp the existing pattern wherever they work. Instead, the spirit of Chabad is to transform and elevate a situation from within, working from the bottom upwards. Thus Chabad encourages change and Godliness by the redirection to Godly ends of existing actions and situations that may not at present be recognized as good, special or holy.

The importance of the role of the rebbe in the work of Lubavitch must be stressed. The success of the rebbe is not just due to his skill as leader and organizer. On the contrary, the rebbe is important and influential because of his place in the religious life and philosophy of Chabad and Lubavitch. The rebbe is regarded as a *tzadik*, a holy person, who has attained an unusual degree of personal sanctification. Because of his tireless efforts, love and dedication to the will of the Almighty and humanity, the *tzadik* enjoys a special attachment to God. The *tzadik*'s personal fulfilment of *mitzvot* has reached a pitch where his person and actions reveal the Godly in a dynamic and unique way. This means the rebbe is a point where the individual can become aware of the Godly in a more complete and concrete way than is normally possible. Therefore, the rebbe is the focus for the religious efforts of Lubavitch, and an important exponent of and manifestation for the Chabad philosophy and ethos. The rebbe and his predecessors are intrinsic to any understanding of Lubavitch and indeed to the purpose of my personal work as emissary in Oxford.

Making Peace with Oxford

My work in Oxford has been deeply inspired by the rebbe and the principles of Chabad. The principle of change and transformation from within means that one does not have directly to challenge the whole ethos of the university, which is in many ways very secular and liberal, by knocking it down in order to bring in Godliness. Instead, I have emphasized to the students that being Jewish and Godly does not mean a complete denial of what they already feel to be important, and that it does not necessitate a repudiation of the cherished principles on which the university prides itself. On the contrary, I have urged that one should continue to do what one is doing at present, but direct it towards Godly ends.

We have at the university many highly ambitious students. I tell them that there is nothing wrong in their ambition, if it is directed towards the ends of goodness and holiness. Thus to one of the medical students I said that there is nothing wrong in being ambitious to become a famous doctor: if one wants to direct that ambition to the good of others and not just of oneself. If this particular medical student's ambition inspires him to develop a new drug or treatment to the benefit of others, then he has transformed the human character trait of ambition into one that truly serves the Divine. In short, the success of Chabad lies in the way it refuses to deny or usurp any aspect of the world or a person's life it merely endeavours to direct what already is to an affirmation of Godliness and goodness, transforming it from within by a qualitative transformation not a substantive transformation. People are born special and goodly. What Lubavitch seeks is to reveal it.

Dealing with the Secular Modern World

The strategy of Chabad successfully addresses the challenge of modernity. Since the eighteenth century, many of the strategies and endeavours adopted within Judaism to preserve and advance itself in the face of new ideas and social conditions have proved inadequate. This is because they set off from the starting position of denying certain aspects of existence as relevant to the realization of Godliness, and in so doing they denied an aspect of the underlying Godliness inherent in all things. They failed properly and completely to synthesize all aspects of the Divine and the material. This problem has compromised both conservative and liberal approaches to this issue. The Orthodox elements have tended to emphasize withdrawal from the modern world into a protected core-region of Jewish life, the liberal have emphasized the compromise of distinctively Jewish practices in order to assimilate Jews into the surrounding culture of modernity. In the first instance, the assumption is that the modern world is not capable of being made Godly; in the second instance there is a failure to assimilate the existing religious tradition to Godliness: it is regarded as a hindrance to modern spirituality. The result has arguably been further to erode and lose the essence of Jewish life that these innovations sought to enhance and preserve. These problems and general types of response can be exemplified by examples taken from France and Germany in the period of the Enlightenment.

The French Revolution and the Granting of Rights

In the wake of the French Revolution, male Jews were granted new rights, including those of voting and property ownership, and also the opportunity to enter university and receive a secular education. But while revolutionary French society had taken the radical step of allowing male Jews equality with all Frenchmen as individual citizens, it was reluctant to acknowledge the individual Jew also to be part of the nation of Israel. The new French regime felt uneasy with the collective religious identity of Jews thus it was obvious that if French Jews accepted their individual liberty as citizens in the French Republic emancipation would tend to undermine their traditional religious identity as Jews.

As a result, there was a great wave of fear in the Jewish community, since the question was raised as to how Judaism could be preserved and protected in the midst of this new revolution. The Orthodox response was divided: one important response was that of the Chasam Sofer, Rabbi Moshe Shreiber, who advocated that '*chadash osur min HaTorah*'; that anything new was proscribed by Torah law, so modern secular society was to be rejected. He believed that Judaism would be preserved through its external institutions acting upon the internal conscience, though he also understood that many Jews would be lost as a result of the revolution to assimilation, or at least become accultured to secular French society. His strategy to save Judaism in Hungary and the remainder of Europe was to preserve a core of Judaism in a smaller number of trained Jews.

Cult of the Élite

Therefore, the Chasam Sofer instituted the concept of a yeshivah, the first of which he founded in Pressburg, an organized higher educational institution where students could study the Torah in much the same way one studied at university. Whereas before there were study halls throughout the world where people congregated around a talmudic master or a mystical teacher and studied the Torah, he now emulated the secular universities in his creation of the yeshivah. So now in order to enter yeshivah one had to pass examinations. Furthermore, subsequent sets of examinations were used to ascertain a student's development and standards, exactly like a secular university. Overall, his response to modernity was to compete with it by assimilating it within a confined Jewish enclosure. This all rested on a belief that Judaism would be preserved and sustained through insularity and isolation. It was also, to an extent, an acceptance of defeat. What Rabbi Shreiber was doing was creating a spiritual élite who could successfully withstand the pressures of acculturation and survive to bequeath our precious tradition to the new generation. But inherent in this approach is a *de facto* acceptance of the loss of millions of Jews. Better to preserve something, he reasoned, than to risk losing all.

Stranded on an Island

There is a story which parallels and illustrates the attitude of Rabbi Moshe Shreiber to modernity and change. It is said that once when he was told that the Jews had been granted rights in Hungary and could now own property and vote, while all the Jews rejoiced, he began to cry. When asked why he was crying, he offered a parable in explanation. There was once a king who had a favourite son, but the son acted deplorably and so he was exiled by his father to a solitary life of great hardship on a small desert island. One day, the son looked up and saw a fleet of ships arriving with a great number of servants, and slaves, with gold and silver. When they had disembarked they started to build, telling the prince that they were sent by his father to build him a beautiful castle on the island. At this the son began to cry. When they asked why he was crying, he said, 'This means that my father intends for me to stay on this island and that I will be here a very long time.'

The Chasam Sofer did not see modernity as a challenge to be synthesized and transformed into something Godly and desirable; he saw it only as a terrible affirmation of the continued existence of the Jewish people in *Galut*, the Divinely imposed state of exile from the Land of Israel, their spiritual inheritance.

Elsewhere in Europe, the emancipation of Jews and the emergence of a modern liberal society encouraged differing responses by Jewish leaders in an effort to preserve Judaism and to adapt it so as to be suitable for modern conditions. These responses were both liberal and conservative. Arguably these other efforts had the same implications as in France in that they ultimately involved the assumption that God could only be relevant to and sought in part of Jewish existence, and that it was not necessary to find and incorporate God into all aspects of life, meaning again that Jewish life was depleted rather than preserved and extended.

Compartmentalizing Jewish Identity

In Germany, where Jews received extensive and early freedoms, Moses Mendelssohn, the first Jewish philosopher of the emancipation, argued that laws of the state and demands of religion were two entirely separate spheres. Mendelssohn saw no necessary or absolute connection between what he was as a Jew at home and how he conducted himself outside; his Jewish life could be an essentially private affair.

Mendelssohn himself was a halakhic Jew. His views did not prevent him being a practising Orthodox Jew, but their ultimate result was the decline of orthodoxy and the rise of the secular Jew. Many of his own children converted, describing Judaism as not a religion but their misfortune. They saw Christian baptism as the means to full entry into modern society and culture. Mendelssohn's innovations showed how a loss of part of Jewish life, and the particular assumption that God did not have to be included in one's civic life, and that one's identity as a Jew could be sufficient on an individual rather than a collective basis, led to a loss of Jewish identity.

Later on, the process started by Mendelssohn was extended by Geiger. Geiger did not think Mendelssohn's reforms had gone far enough. He said that Jewish integration into society was hampered even by religious practice in the privacy of the home, a point which the Germans themselves had argued. They said, 'They cannot eat with us, they cannot fight on Shabbat'; indeed, they said, 'The entire purpose of these laws is separation'. What was worse, the Germans said that Germany was only a temporary home for the Jews, whereas Palestine was the true permanent home of the Jews. In order to assuage these criticisms, German Jews opened the first Reformed Temple in 1817. They called it a temple to show that even in Hamburg there could be a Jewish temple. Here prayers were in German, and references to Zion omitted.

There was, predictably, also a conservative reaction to these moves. This was Zechariah Frankel's conservative 'positive historical' movement. However, the overall trend was strongly in favour of those such as Geiger and Samuel Holdheim who thought that the laws separating Jews were irrelevant at best, and at worst impeded the progress of civilization.

Dispersing the Community

The response of Chabad philosophy and the present rebbe is entirely antipathetic to this approach. The rebbe sees modernity not as a challenge or a hindrance, but an *opportunity*. The rebbe has notably denied and actively negated Chasam Sofer's principle of preserving an insulated core or heartland of Judaism as a bastion against modernity. The rebbe advocates the dispersal of the Chabad Jewish community by sending his followers abroad to teach and educate the entire nation of Israel so that no Jew will ever be lost.

Throughout history, Judaism was largely sustained by the nurture, kinship and enveloping contact of the community, a group of people held together by common interests and observances. The rebbe took the radical step of taking newly ordained young rabbis, and sending them out with their wives to the far corners of the earth, into cities and places where they would be virtually the only observant Jews. They were instructed to convey and impart their Jewish values by their welcome and positive example, without condescension, to the communities to which they were sent. This was motivated by the rebbe's belief that religious identity and spirituality must be something internal, and intrinsic to one's being and character, and not external. He utterly rejected the Chasam Sofer's assumption that it is sufficient to save a core élite who will retain the rituals of Judaism, albeit in smaller numbers. The rebbe's guiding principle throughout his more than forty years of leadership of Lubavitch has been that 'no Jew will be left behind'.

Attachment to One's Source

It must be emphasized again that the motivating force in the rebbe's action has been the principles of Chabad, the insistence that we can approach and find God in our everyday circumstances and in the material world, without a denial of either, so long as we elevate and sanctify the mundane so that it may manifest Godliness, and become a fitting home for God. By doing so we may cut through the dichotomy that seems to exist between the heavenly infinite and the earthly finite. In Chabad, the latter really reflects and originates from the former; it is not in actuality foreign or divorced from its source, and it is capable of being transmuted by human action clearly to show its real essence and origins. This insight avoids the mistaken view that when a human aspires to realize Godliness it is absolutely necessary to deny his or her physical reality and the world.

Engaging Earthly Existence

A common result of this misguided thinking has been the supposition that we should eat less and fast more, be celibate, abstain from earthly activity, meditate and withdraw on a mental plane from the world as well. But Judaism in general, and the rebbe in particular, have emphasized and re-emphasized that the true purpose of creation is for humanity to create a home on earth for God through everyday actions which, in accordance with God's law, sublimate and sanctify our physical existence. This accounts for much of the distinctive nature of Jewish religious life and ritual.

Instead of a general abstention from the gross physical world in order to transcend our physical condition and realize God, we find, for example, that Jewish celebrations always involve eating food. Of course, eating food is one of our most basic physical acts, and one which symbolizes perhaps better than any other our physical nature, condition and limitation. It is one that seems to deny our innate transcendental nature and connectedness with God, for what transcendental being needs to eat? Judaism subverts such an observation, as food becomes an important means of spirituality: we make blessings before eating food, place the eating of food in a spiritual context, and use food as an expression of spiritual ideas. There is a similar approach found in Judaism's attitude to and regulation of sexual relations. Sexual relations within the laws of Judaism are sanctified and holy, instead of an expression of various other thoughts, desires and motivations, some of which may purely concern physical self-gratification.

If we mistakenly emphasize the transcendence of heaven over earth and the spiritual over the physical, we may begin to think the attempt to perfect our world is not worthwhile. Acts of charity and kindness would, perhaps, be done with the intention of gaining a place in heaven, whereas they should be done with the intention of making a better world. Judaism has always had an obsession to '*lesaken ha'olam bemalchus Sh-dai*': 'to perfect the world within a heavenly kingdom.'

To Teach and to Learn

It is this philosophy which has dictated the rebbe's actions as the leader of Lubavitch for more than forty years. This is why the rebbe has sent young emissaries throughout the world; the world is Godly and it is our duty to precipitate the immanent and latent holiness in existence. What is more, the emissaries have been sent out not just because they have something to impart to their communities, but because they have something to learn from those communities as well, because of the underlying holiness spread throughout existence. This fact demands a certain humility in the emissary, as even the most assimilated Jew has an unconscious connection with God and Judaism. So one is not trying to intrude 'alien' Jewish values upon the individual, since one is at the deepest level only effecting the conscious recognition of an existing and latent but potent spiritual existence and relation to God in the Jew.

In this respect, the rebbe can be seen as one of the great visionaries of this century, someone who has literally transformed the Jewish landscape in the short space of under half a century. The rebbe can be single-handedly credited with the revival of Jewish education and learning, in commitment to Jewish works, and the raising of Jewish consciousness. Although there are many others involved in the field of promoting Jewish education and other Jewish works who are not Lubavitch, they have nevertheless all been directly or indirectly inspired by the rebbe's commitment to transforming the world and making it possible for Jews to be openly Jewish in the street, having a sense of Jewish pride and dignity, and not having to feel that Judaism is something to be hidden from the outside world to be reserved for the private domain.

The Importance of the Messiah to Lubavitch

If one understands and accepts the philosophical perspectives of Chabad offered in this book, then it is clear that a messianic era is logically and spiritually necessitated. This will be the culmination of thousands of years of spiritual effort to bring Godliness to the earth; it will finally lead to that hour when Godliness will become clearly visible on the earth. The world will live and be directed by a Godliness that will no longer be confused by anything else. At this moment, the world will be qualitatively transformed, even though there will still be the same material existence. This all follows from the dual premises that God did create the world, and God's principle intention in creating the spiritual and physical universes was the physical world. This physical world is as Godly as the heavenly; he created both in the same Divine act, for in the first verse of Genesis it states, 'God created the heaven and the earth.' The final goal of both human and Divine creativity is in the climax of the messianic era.

Extending the Perimeter of Holiness

It is interesting to note that this perspective has led to Lubavitch being criticized for not being Zionist. In reality this attack is unfounded, as the deep commitment Lubavitch has towards Israel can easily be recognized and witnessed. Lubavitch Chasidim serve in the Israeli army and contribute to every facet of Israeli life, aside from the fact that the Lubavitch religious commitment to Israel is unquestionable, with over 180 Chabad Centres throughout the country. However, this criticism does arise from the correct perception that Lubavitch avoids over-emphasizing work in Israel, although the profound theological reasons for Lubavitch spreading its resources more evenly around the world remain largely unrecognized by the critics. Basically, Lubavitch does not believe in concentrating all of the world's spirituality and all the Jewish people into one location. The Talmud promised that in the messianic era the land of Israel would spread throughout its borders, and that is part of that underlying philosophy that the objective of the Jew is to take the perimeter of holiness, and the synagogue, and to expand it so as to encompass the entire world. This is so we can show there are no real shrines or definitive holy places in a world of holiness, but rather that the entire world is Godly and holy. Disseminating holiness throughout the world is our mission.

While formal messianism may not be a popular conception in a modern and secular society, it is a matter of fact that messianic desire is a powerful and perhaps universal motivation among peoples. If anybody seriously wishes to make the world a better place, to change it permanently for the better, this person arguably implicitly desires a change in the world order that is similar, perhaps tantamount to, a messianic redemption. If we believe for example in the statement '*Shalom Achshav*', let there be peace now in the Middle East, and if we indeed take President Kennedy's Peace Corp seriously, and if we would like to rid the world of illness and destruction and contention and hatred, and all of those things which would bring humanity to war and jealousy, then we cannot deny that we really want a messianic redemption and a messianic world, in that we want a world permanently free of the historical travails of humankind.

Working Towards a Better World

The modern era has reached the stage where a universal and permanent peace among nations is desired, and it is seen as a sufficiently realistic option that we have organizations such as the United Nations to work for this; we also seek to eradicate disease from the world with such organizations as the World Health Organization. These facts indicate a change in the consciousness of humanity and the growth of a vision that was not general in our ancient or even modern history. In an earlier age, men became kings and emperors because of their ability to wage war against other countries; men revelled in their ability to subdue their neighbour, and the greatest accolade to be attributed to men was their skill in combat. The idea of universal peace and freedom from the travails of human struggle was only propagated by a few Godly individuals, such as in Israel where there was a group of elderly white-bearded men, the prophets of Israel. These men stormed through the Judean countryside, or stood in public squares, and foretold of an era of peace; an era in which men would collectively beat their swords into ploughshares and where one nation would never wage war against another; a world in which every person would also seek an inner peace and harmony which would permit others to achieve and even exceed them without arousing jealousy. A world in which we would all understand how special a human being is and we would never feel that one person's accomplishments in any way compromise our own position; a world in which we feel joy, and not jealousy, when we hear that someone we went to school with now chairs an important corporation. A world in which we would be able to feel the joy of humanity as one.

The rebbe has tried to bring us closer to that world through his efforts. He has dedicated an entire movement to the purpose of outreach and inspired young men and women to dedicate their lives to others, Jew and non-Jew alike. Lubavitch sponsors thousands of activities for all kinds of people in both religious and social welfare. The movement's time, money and energy is equally distributed between raising Jewish educational standards and meeting social welfare needs, such as offering counselling advice to those who find themselves in difficult situations, drug rehabilitation programmes, food programmes and services, and material benefits as well as a host of other things. In some respects it is germane that the Lubavitch movement is judged more on these works and the genuine contributions that have been made in the field of alleviating human suffering and ignorance, than by an untoward and narrow concentration on the movement's push towards the millennium and its messianic ideals. But this being said, one of the central challenges of Lubavitch is precisely that there is a culmination of history in the Jewish Messiah, and that the deepest purpose of humanity, and the fulfilment of our purpose, is in working for this.

Transforming Human Character

The major complaint that people raise against the messianic era is that they feel we should depend on our own efforts to bring about perfection of the world, rather than relying on Divine intervention and miraculous means. It is felt that relying on God is too easy and enables us to avoid the issue of personal responsibility in change. The problem with this is that some negative traits of human character really are incorrigible, that is, we are incapable of making the fundamental changes to human character that would be necessary for us to perfect the world. In Chabad, the final resolution of the struggle in the human psyche that differentiates the *beinuni* from the *tzadik* is effected by God. This is not to say that we are not capable of effecting good; as we saw earlier, the essence of the *beinuni* is a struggle, but one where all qualities of character and action are channelled to good ends. Therefore human effort is capable in a qualified sense of perfecting the world, but the final touches must be supplied by God.

As an example, a scientist may compete for the Nobel Prize purely for the purposes of self-aggrandisement, but this purely selfish motive may nevertheless be the cause of the discovery of a cure that may be of great benefit to all humanity. In this case, there is a clear example of a human being effecting great good and change in the world. While one may not like this scientist's egoism, the priority is not for us to criticize their integrity, but for us to encourage them to continue to make their vital discoveries. Finally, though, for true perfection and transformation to occur in the world, change will have to be made at the personal level in the scientist, and this change will always have to be Divinely effected.

Women in Lubavitch

The role of women in Lubavitch is of some significance in the achievements of the rebbe. The rebbe made a significant innovation in that he was the first to institute true fulltime higher academies of learning for Jewish women, as opposed to the women's teaching seminaries and yeshivot that had existed before. For example my wife studied at the Ohel Chana Women's Institute in Melbourne. There she studied as many hours as any yeshivah student, from nine in the morning to nine-thirty at night, and sometimes later as well. Perhaps even more significant is the fact that the rebbe insisted that the women's seminaries study Chasidut and Jewish mysticism, which was the first time in history that these subjects were made available to women within a traditional Jewish framework.

The rebbe was also the first to ensure that whatever was done for the male *shluchim*, male emissaries, around the world, would be done for the women. For example, when the International Conference for *shluchim* began in earnest eight years ago, with 1,500–2,000 people attending every year, the rebbe insisted that the same be done for the women. Thus they have their own *shluchot* conference annually.

The rebbe also insisted that women be brought to the fore of Lubavitch life. There are now many famous Lubavitch female lecturers who do the international circuit every year, such as Rebbetzin Masha Lipsker of South Africa. The rebbe himself delivers many public lectures solely to women several times a year. When this happens there is the unique spectacle of one of the world's great Chasidic rabbis surrounded by thousands of women with no other men at all present. On these occasions he addresses women on precious subjects of interest specifically to female audiences, as well as mainstream Jewish subjects of learning and the like.

The rebbe's attention to the needs of women can be seen in small things; when the rebbe makes his weekly distribution of dollar bills and gives blessings to the ten thousand or so people who come to his court, he always insists that it is the women who come first. Historically this is highly unusual for a Chasidic rabbi. The rebbe really has done more than any other Jewish religious leader to promote the absolute centrality and equality of women, not just in Jewish communal life, but as an intrinsic part of global Jewish revival.

Chapter Seventy

THERE ARE NO HYPOCRITES IN RELIGIOUS FAITH

Lizette Nieves is one of Oxford's special students. In 1992 she and a Jewish colleague, Toba Friedman, respectively won a Rhodes and a Marshall scholarship, the first time these awards have ever been won by students from Brooklyn College. (Toba's achievement is unique because she is the first girl from a strict yeshivah background to win the Marshall scholarship, and we in Oxford are very proud of her.) I was introduced to Lizette through Toba when they both arrived in Oxford last October. Brooklyn College obviously made a big celebration of their victory, but it is not the Rhodes award which makes Lizette special, but rather the reason for her having won it in the first place. To be sure, winning the Rhodes is recognition of academic excellence, but Lizette was also given the award in recognition of her tireless work in social programmes which benefit people of all races and ages. While still at Brooklyn College, she was involved in many local and national social welfare organizations, and by no means was her involvement just on a token basis.

Now Blackbird Leys, located just five miles from Oxford, is one of the most troubled neighbourhoods in Britain. It is a council housing estate known for riots, crime, violence, and a low standard of living. If ever two areas were incongruous, it is Oxford and Blackbird Leys. On arriving in Oxford, Lizette, together with a few other black students, initiated a campaign to help train and educate many of the Blackbird Leys youth. While most of Oxford's residents did nothing but lament how Oxford's proximity to Blackbird Leys dragged the entire city down, and led to incessant theft and nightly violence in the city centre which I witness from my perched office above Carfax, these students went and committed their limited time and energy to making the area better and lending hope and care to its inhabitants.

Lizette's background would not instantly guarantee a career of academic achievement. She was born into a working-class Latino family in the Bronx, New York. Obviously, her rising above these barriers to become an Oxford Rhodes Scholar made her a star. Yet she never rested on her laurels and always dedicated herself to helping those in need. And this is precisely my point. There are many other students as dedicated to others as Lizette, and I only use her as an example. There is, for example, Lisa Kaul, a Rhodes Scholar from India whose greatest dream is to use her knowledge and erudition and, upon returning to India, help contribute a greater degree of stability to her beleaguered nation. She does not merely talk about kindness, but embodies it in her every dealing with other people. There is Ross Kriel, a South African student, who was overwhelmed by the injustice of apartheid and promised to return to his native country so that he can dedicate his life to guaranteeing equality for all inhabitants of that country. There is Cory Booker, another black Rhodes Scholar, who has participated in many programmes to benefit black children in the American inner cities, and continues to struggle to uphold minority rights within the university.

Devotion from Ethnic Minorities

The point which I would like to make is this: the majority of students who do devote so much of their time to social and charitable work while at Oxford are from ethnic minorities. There is good reason for this. They look around at their family and friends, they instantly understand how fortunate they are to be in the position in which they find themselves, and feel they must give something back.

It was once like this with the Jewish students as well, but is becoming increasingly less so. The simple truth is that with the continuing success and progress of the worldwide Jewish community in many different areas, the results have been that there is no longer the same sense of urgency to contribute to and advance the society and situation of the Jews.

When I first arrived in Oxford five years ago, there were many students who were involved in the Campaign for Soviet Jewry. Any of these meetings, even the most trivial, could attract upwards of one hundred students. There was a sense that although these were privileged Jewish students studying in one of the world's finest universities, their Jewish compatriots in Russia were suffering the torment of being prisoners and not being able to live with their brethren in Israel. Marches and rallies were organized, telephone campaigns tied up the switchboard of the Soviet embassy incessantly, and there were letter-writing campaigns to Members of Parliament. The students did everything within their ability to make a difference.

How Judaism Has Become a Lost Cause

The same was true of the campaign for Syrian Jews, which also drew many student volunteers, although not on the same scale as its Soviet Jewish counterpart. But when Soviet Jews began emigrating en masse to Israel, and after President Assad of Syria announced the lifting of travel restrictions on Syrian Jews, brought about through American pressure, there was little left to campaign for. And I have definitely noticed the difference. There are just not as many Jewish students involved in student initiatives as before. And this affects not only the dearth of current student programming, but even the number of students who will attend a Friday-night meal or synagogue. The effects are very far-reaching. The cause is simple. Even those students who once only affiliated through negative impetus, such as campaigning against Fascism or for Soviet Jewish freedom, either intentionally or unintentionally found themselves in the company of other Jewish kids, motivated by a Jewish cause, and thus they did the same things as the rest of the group. Even if they had no desire to attend a Friday-night dinner, they found themselves being pulled there by virtue of the fact that many of their fellow activists were attending as well. But when in the minds of the students there are no legitimate causes left, then Judaism itself becomes a lost cause.

On the other hand, the black, Indian, South African, Israeli and Arab students can point to injustices or lack of opportunity within their own communities and dedicate their time and energy, since they feel themselves fortunate, to correcting those wrongs. Many of them will even express to me a sense of guilt. Why should they be so lucky when so many others are so miserable? Why should they pore over the love poems of Shakespeare, Byron and Yeats, when only poverty, misery and suffering is in store for many of their people? Usually guilt is bad, but in this case it is constructive. Because these students translate these negative feelings of guilt into positive aspirations and actions to change the lot of their fellow man.

Simon Wiesenthal and the Right to Remain Alive

One of the finest examples of transmuting feelings of responsibility or guilt into positive motivation and dedication to others was provided by the legendary Nazi hunter, Simon Wiesenthal, upon his visit to Oxford. First, some background information about his visit.

In November 1990 the L'Chaim Society staged one of its biggest and most significant events in its history. Simon Wiesenthal visited Oxford from Vienna under our auspices and took part in five engagements. This was Mr Wiesenthal's first appearance at Oxford, something we were quite proud of. In fact, when I first collected Mr Wiesenthal from the airport he remarked to me that this was his first time speaking for a Chabad organisation and then he began to extol the virtues of Chabad. He mentioned to me that he had spoken in some of the world's biggest universities and some of the world's smallest universities, including some which had a Jewish student population of under thirty. Yet he said that wherever he went there was always the Chabad rabbi or representative with his table full of Jewish books attempting to encourage Jewish observance and Jewish identity among the Jewish community. He maintained that he was continually amazed at the far corners of the world that Chabad never failed to reach. He also expressed a great interest in and knowledge about the Lubavitcher rebbe and we spent most of the hours on the trip home from the airport discussing the kind of person the rebbe is and his accomplishments.

Upon his arrival at the Chabad House in Oxford, in the days preceding the L'Chaim Centre, Mr Wiesenthal held a press conference which was attended by five of England's national newspapers, three television stations, and four radio stations. It was amazing that all the press correspondents were able to fit into Chabad House's small meeting room. Our press releases said that Mr Wiesenthal's press conference would be encouraging the next Prime Minister of the UK – Mrs Thatcher had just resigned and John Major had not yet been appointed – to keep Mrs Thatcher's pledge of bringing Nazi war criminals to justice. The press conference went on for approximately forty-five minutes, segments of which were played on all local television and radio stations, and two national papers also wrote lengthy articles.

Mr Wiesenthal's second engagement was a luncheon at Chabad House held in his honour, attended by fifty students whose names were chosen from many more by lot. Mr Wiesenthal answered questions and spoke of his experiences in tracing Nazi criminals. Mr Wiesenthal's third engagement was a tea at Exeter College which was attended by university scholars, professors, academics and heads of college. The tea was also attended by the Lord Mayor of Oxford, who at that time was a woman, as was her successor.

After the tea we held a dinner in Mr Wiesenthal's honour at the Oxford town hall for university academics and distinguished supporters and guests. The dinner was extremely lavish and was attended by many Oxford dignitaries, including Colin Blakemore, Professor of Physiology at Oxford, and Dr L. Jonathan Cohen, both of whom publicly greeted Mr Wiesenthal on behalf of the university.

After the dinner came the main session and the main purpose of Mr Wiesenthal's visit to Oxford, a major address to the Oxford student and academic communities entitled 'Justice Not Vengeance'. Even we were surprised by the incredibly large turn-out to Mr Wiesenthal's lecture, which totalled over eleven hundred students and academics. The lecture was held in the main lecture theatre of Oxford town hall which is one of Oxford's largest speaker venues. I introduced Mr Wiesenthal and he then proceeded to deliver a lecture which related personal stories recounted to him by survivors who asked him to find the barbarians who wiped out their families. There was complete silence the full length of his ninety-minute talk and the audience was visibly moved by his words. There was thunderous applause and a standing ovation at the conclusion of his lecture and many who attended told me it was one of the most memorable occasions of their lives. I thanked Mr Wiesenthal at the conclusion of his lecture and brought the evening to a close. The next morning I drove Mr Wiesenthal to the airport where he extended a very warm invitation for me to come and visit him in Vienna and gave me a tight embrace. I was extremely moved by his warmth. He treated us, his hosts, at all times with respect, courtesy appreciation and love.

A Responsibility to Those Who Perished

But returning now to the original point, during his visit Mr Wiesenthal was asked by one of the students why he had dedicated his life to chasing Nazis. Wasn't that being vindictive? He paused a moment for reflection and then he answered. When the war was over, he glanced across the landscape of European Jewry. All he found was death and desolation. Then he searched for the survivors of his own family and discovered that nearly all had perished. 'So I asked myself, "What right do I have to be alive?" And I concluded that I had no right at all. When so many millions were dead, I had no reasons above theirs to live. I was not better than any of them. So I decided to give them my life. I dedicated my life to them. I dedicated my life to bringing their murderers to justice.'

That was then. But what have the Jewish students to campaign for in today's times? Increasingly little.

In purely lifestyle terms, the world Jewish community has perhaps never been better off. To be sure, there are still many outbursts of anti-Semitism or pockets of rabid Jew-hatred throughout the world. But none of these seem nearly as menacing as they once were. Aside from the terrible violence that continues in the Middle East with Israelis of all ages and persuasions dying from knifings and attacks on an all too regular basis, the major Jewish communities in the diaspora are flourishing. Which all leads to one significant question. How much of a reason, then, do Jewish students still have for being Jewish? And the answer. Not much. Which is why we are witnessing increasingly few who are willing to act in a leadership capacity or assume the role of the activist.

Judaism Suffers without Hatred

Why is this happening? The reason is simple. Because for far too long Jews have defined their identity in relation to the actions of the Gentiles around them, and without any reason from within. And this is the price we are paying for that neglect.

Similarly, I can testify that this significant decrease in the number of students working on behalf of Jewish concerns in Oxford has not affected the more observant Jewish students, however small their numbers may be. Whereas the students who fight anti-Semitism treat their Jewishness as a calling, and they are thus always available to help in moments of crisis, the observant students treat their Judaism as a way of life. Therefore, the suffering or success of the world's Jewish populace has absolutely no effect on their commitment to their Jewishness or to people, which always operates at or near full throttle. Their identities spring from within and are independent of any ephemeral social winds.

But a further problem which this topsy-turvy Jewish commitment creates is a perception of disingenuousness or hypocrisy. Those students who are not always involved in promoting Jewish interests at the university, and do so only sporadically, begin to disengage themselves from helping out when sometimes they are needed most. They rationalize their lack of interest by maintaining that it is hypocritical to be involved only part of the time. I have witnessed hundreds of Jewish students who, upon arriving in Oxford, are very interested, then slowly opt out because if they get involved, they wish to do so all the way. They do not wish to feel torn asunder by questions of commitment or lack of it. The easiest solution, therefore, is, instead of attempting a difficult balance, to fall to one side or the other.

This sentiment is very destructive and must be countered. Accusations of personal hypocrisy, inconsistency or disingenuousness waged against oneself in matters of religion not only pose the perfect excuse to relieve oneself of heavenly responsibility, but betray a shallow and un-Jewish understanding of the whole religious undertaking, the authentic Jewish view of which we shall now explore.

Being the only rabbi resident in Oxford I am the obvious target for questions about what we should be doing to please God, a question which comes from Jew and non-Jew alike. Most people assume that those who really follow God's wishes have somehow been enabled to achieve and maintain saintliness, once and for all, but I disagree. When I am talking with students and others, I contend that in today's society we have a misguided understanding of what it means to be religious. As a logical result of this, I also argue that this misunderstanding creates wrong responses to the conflict between good and evil in our hearts. First, a lesson from the Torah about miracles.

Two Kinds of Miracles

Although the Torah recounts many stories of miraculous events, they may still be subdivided into just two classes. First, there are those miracles which actually transform material existence as we know it. Then there are those miracles which merely suspend physical existence for a time. In the first type, the laws of nature are not only suspended, but nature has actually been transformed by God. With the second type of miracle, nature has not in any way been changed, except for the time in which the miracle acts upon the world. The difference between these two classes of miracles is whether another miracle or Divine intervention is necessary for life to return to its original state.

To illustrate this contrast, take for example one of the signs which God gave to Moses to authenticate his message to the Jewish people when he took on the Divine mission to free the Jews from Egyptian slavery. 'That they may believe that there has appeared unto you the Lord . . . put now your hand into your bosom. And he put his hand into his bosom, and when he took it out, behold his hand was leprous, as white as snow. And He said, Put back your hand into your bosom, and he put back his hand into his bosom; and he took it out of his bosom; and when he took it out of his bosom, behold it was turned again as his flesh was before.'

In this instance it can be clearly seen that what transpired was the first type of miraculous event, a transformation of the material world. Moses' hand had changed. The miracle had made it leprous and it would have remained so without a second miracle to restore it to its original healthy state. In other words, the miracle would have physically changed the permanent nature of the hand, had not God decreed otherwise through a second direct act of miraculous intervention.

Water Which Became Blood

Contrast this with a different type of miracle, the kind of miracle which strikes every person's imagination deeply. When God transformed the Nile to blood, the entire time that the water remained as blood was miraculous; a complete contradiction of natural law. But the water remained as blood only as long as Divine intervention was acting upon it. The miracle did not change its physical make-up. Only on a transitory and superficial level did the water become blood. Intrinsically, it remained water, therefore as soon as God's intervening powers receded from the Nile it immediately reverted to water. The proof for this is provided from the fact that, whereas there was need for Aaron to strike the Nile river in the first instance to transform it to blood, there was no need for any other intercession on the part of Aaron for the blood to revert to water.

Splitting of the Sea

In the Book of Exodus we read of another 'transitory' miracle, also one of the most famous stories in the Bible: the parting of the Red Sea. The Torah states clearly that this was a temporary change in nature: 'And Moses stretched out his hand over the sea; and the Lord caused the sea to go back by a strong wind all the night, and He made the sea dry land, and the waters were divided.' As long as the gale-force wind which split the sea acted upon the water, it remained divided, but when the wind subsided, the walls of water through which the Jews escaped crashed down in fury and drowned the Egyptians. The water was not physically transmuted. It did not become a wall. Rather, it was held as a wall.

Having established that there are two methods by which to change material existence, one permanent and the other transitory, let us apply this lesson to religion and the art of becoming a religious person. There are two possibilities involved in becoming a religious individual: the first is where religion changes us and we become different people, as in our first kind of miracle; the other is where religion still poses a constant struggle to conform to its norms.

Sweet or Spicy?

Two hundred years ago, the great Sage Rabbi Shneur Zalman of Liadi established the Chabad Chasidic movement and disseminated its teachings largely through the publication of a single volume of Jewish mystical thought. To this day, the *Tanya* serves as one of the most profound statements of Jewish religious teaching.

The novel ideas which Rabbi Shneur Zalman introduced served to make religion a much more intuitive, natural and human endeavour. In the *Tanya*, he described a basic human desire to merge with the Infinite. Each soul 'naturally yearns to separate itself and depart from the body, in order to Unify with its origin and Source . . . the fountainhead of all life.' Nevertheless, Rabbi Shneur Zalman viewed the process of spiritual growth as lifelong, requiring tireless self-discipline and the appropriate use of both intellect and emotion. The system was called ChaBaD, an acronymic abbreviation of the Hebrew terms for the higher faculties: wisdom (*chochma*), understanding (*binah*), and knowledge (*da'at*). For this reason the movement's followers have for two centuries been known as Chabad Chasidim, as well as Lubavitchers after the town in Russia (which translates as 'Town of Love') that eventually became their communal base. In the 1960s, the Lubavitcher rebbe chose the name Chabad House for the Lubavitch campus centres that he was promoting, of which one exists here in Oxford.

On the very first page of the *Tanya*, Rabbi Shneur Zalman introduced one of his most controversial and radical concepts, yet one which, in my opinion, remade Judaism accessible to Jews of all levels of observance; namely, that of the *beinuni*. A *beinuni* is an intermediate individual, someone who can neither be classified as purely righteous, as the *tzadik*, but who is not evil either.

Rabbi Shneur Zalman explained that every individual is a hybrid of both good and evil. In the language of Jewish mysticism, every individual possesses not just a good and evil inclination, but a Godly soul and an animal soul. It is the Godly soul which harbours an attraction for and animates all of one's holy and goodly deeds, and it is the animal soul which pulls humankind down into an obsession with material, mundane, and sometimes even profane wants.

One of the immediate benefits of this system of thought elaborated upon by Rabbi Shneur Zalman is that it negates any accusations which can be lodged against the individual for duplicity or, more importantly, for being hypocritical. Given that all good comes from one side of a person's being, and evil and insensitivity comes from another, one should never shy away from doing a good deed just because one may not do so tomorrow, or because one's friends may accuse one of hypocrisy.

The first section of the *Tanya* deals almost exclusively with trying to explain what this intermediate religious individual is, and how such a person differs from the *tzadik*. Rabbi Shneur Zalman devoted so much thought to this theme because, as can readily be appreciated, the great majority of the human population falls into this category.

He explained that often we can understand God by applying some simple human truths. People love eating, especially tasty foods. There are two categories of tasty foods that we find most attractive; one sweet, the other tangy and spicy. While indeed sweet foods are desirable to the palate, they do not elicit the same kind of mouth-watering response that sharp, spicy foods do. Few people can have failed to notice the rapid spread and immense popularity of the primarily sharp and spicy foods from the Orient and the Middle East.

This principle which refers to our palate may be utilized to understand the kind of spiritual worship which the Almighty demands of human beings. The one is the sweet religious devotion of the *tzadik*. Sweet because it is removed from all sin and embraces only untainted holy acts and motivation and has totally subdued any evil forces. Then there is the spicy service of the *beinuni*, which entails not only good deeds but the constant struggle between good and evil, and the necessity to choose between the two.

The Tzadik's *Struggle has Ceased*

Although the above represents two ways of serving God, it is the latter that God prefers. The *tzadik* is someone who long ago in the past fought such a vicious battle against his or her evil tendencies that they were either completely annihilated, or turned to good; at the very least they are rendered completely impotent. The *tzadik* can rest assured that throughout his mortal days he will never fall into the mire of evil deeds, speech, or even thoughts. He has cast out evil. This seems very impressive, but there are two important shortcomings. Firstly, the *tzadik* does not need to battle or struggle. Having put down evil once and for all, long ago, his or her day-to-day religious activity does not entail the constant fight for supremacy of good over evil. The *tzadik* is not forced to make any decisions, since he or she is impelled only by good. To an extent, the religious worship of such a saint begins to resemble that of an automaton – a robot. A good robot, but a robot none the less. The *tzadik* has no choices to make, and there is only one possibility which is always set before him. He does not even notice the evil possibilities in this world because he has no feeling or attraction for them whatsoever.

The shortcoming in this is that the Almighty wishes our religious worship to entail, indeed reflect, the constant subjugation of all the evil in the world to the cause of goodness and Godliness. Stated in other words, what God truly desires, as described by Rabbi Shneur Zalman in his quotations from the Zohar, is not just for humanity to choose good, but also to reject evil.

The Triumph of the Struggle

The life of the *beinuni*, however, reflects this constant struggle between light and darkness. Every day of his or her religious existence must be a struggle to do, and choose, that which is virtuous. Every day, indeed every moment, sees a fresh battle raging within his or her being to decide whether or not to walk in the path of God or to capitulate to the forces of darkness. Who is there among us who is not drafted every moment of our lives into this incessant battle for the triumph of good over evil? Every time the *beinuni* sits in the company of friends who are gossiping and rumour-mongering, the desire to participate and add to the conversation is a challenge to their relationship with God. Every time the *beinuni* goes to work, he or she is confronted with the choice of being a conspicuous Jew or to lie low and 'not make waves'. When one is informed by a colleague of how they achieved a first class degree or earned a rise in pay, one is confronted with the choice of being jealous and spiteful, or rejoicing in their good news.

In short, every step in life sees new choices that must be made, and a battle for the very soul of the *beinuni*. Who among us can honestly say that leading a religious and ethical life, a life of exemplary morality, is or was ever easy? We are all at some time torn asunder by opposing internal forces. Not one of us can guarantee that just because we made the correct decision and chose goodness on this occasion, we will be sure to do so the next time. Each day sees another engagement between what we know to be correct, and what we feel would be more personally advantageous. The pursuit of goodness in life consists of an eternal struggle.

Battle for the Citadel

In the *Tanya* the Alter Rebbe described the situation thus: 'It is written . . . "One nation shall prevail over the other nation" (Genesis 25:23). The body is called a "small city" (Ecclesiastes 9:14). Just as two kings wage war over a town, which each wishes to capture and rule, that is to say, to dominate its inhabitants according to his will, so that they obey him in all that he decrees for them, so do the two souls – the Divine soul and the vitalizing animal soul that comes from the *kelipa* – wage war against each other over the body and all its limbs. It is the desire and will of the Divine soul that she alone rule over the person and direct him, and that all his limbs should obey her and surrender themselves completely to her and become a vehicle for her, as well as a robe [instrument] for her . . . that she should pervade the organs of the body, and the entire body should be permeated with them alone, to the exclusion of any alien influence, God forbid . . . However, the desire of the animal soul which is derived from the *kelipa* is the very opposite – and it is for the good of the man, that he may prevail over her and vanquish her' (Chapter 9). In a further discussion on the subject he adds, 'Therewith will be understood the commentary of our Sages that "Intermediate" people are judged by both [the good and evil natures], for it is written, "He stands at the right hand of the poor man to save him from them that judge his soul" (Talmud Berachot 61b). Note that they did not say "ruled" by both, God forbid, because where the evil nature gains any control and dominion over the "small city", even though but temporarily, one is at such times deemed "wicked". The evil nature [in the *beinuni*], however, is no more than, for example, a magistrate or judge who gives his opinion on a point of law, yet it is not necessarily a final decision to be implemented in deed, for there is another magistrate or judge who is contesting this opinion. It is, therefore, necessary to arbitrate between the two, and the final verdict rests with the arbitrator.'

This arbitrator is every one of us who must choose the right path and make decisions which will have a bearing on what we do and what we become. Thus, precisely because we are not 'righteous' and have not allowed for the complete dominion of the Godly soul over the animal soul, we are cast in the unique position of choosing good over evil on a daily basis. This is the true meaning of a 'religious' individual both today and throughout time.

Significance of the Struggle

In other words, what God desires is not righteousness, but *struggle.* He derives pleasure from our daily choice to do good, amidst a powerful inclination to do otherwise. The religious individual is not one who does not feel lust, or covet, or is jealous, or hostile. Rather, the religious individual feels all these emotions and yet tries his utmost to overcome them and do that which is just and righteous.

This is why, for all intents and purposes, Judaism will never truly become easy, and this is a matter of which I must remind the students of constantly, as they become more involved. No matter how many times one puts on *tefillin* in the morning, it will always be a struggle between sleeping in another few minutes and then having to rush through morning prayers, and the other choice of reciting the whole of the morning prayers with patience and concentration. No matter how many times one gives alms to the poor, whether they be on the streets of Oxford, London or New York, it will be just as difficult the next time around. And it is proper that it be so.

The Path is the Reward

God does not desire that we choose to become charitable so much as that we practise charity as a continuing process. Every Oxford graduate must learn to give ten per cent of their earnings to charity. Students struggle for years with only pennies in their pockets and suddenly, upon receiving their first pay cheque, they are expected to give a large portion of their net earnings to charity. You can be assured that it will hurt, but when it does the student should not feel guilty for lacking an intuitive charitable nature. If it did not hurt, if it did not come with great resistance, then the action, on the part of the giver, would not be worth as much. It is important not only that a poor person benefits from the donation, but that the one who gives has chosen, of his or her free accord, to subjugate an ungenerous or selfish nature. This is what religion is all about.

When God visited the world with His greatest and most memorable miracle, when the waves of the Red Sea were dramatically cloven, He did it in such a way that the world was left as it is. He did not change the intrinsic nature of His creation, in order to convey a moral point. The purpose of a Godly act, such as miraculous intervention in the course of events, is not to prevent us from being who we are. We are human, and there is a certain Divine beauty to that. To be human is to flow with the energy and vitality of life itself. We need not eliminate any part of ourselves in order to draw closer to God. On the contrary, we must arrive whole and complete. Every fibre of our being – intellect, emotion and intuition – is special and worthy enough, and holy enough, to be used in the service of the Creator. But we must use all these faculties to promote goodness in accordance with the Divine plan.

The world is not so evil or un-Godly that there is a need radically to transform its nature. What the parting of the Red Sea and other spectacular miracles demonstrate, however, is that in order for a just and happy ending we must exert constant vigilance and effort, just as strong winds acted upon the water through the night. That is what enabled the Jews, representing the innocent and the oppressed, to triumph over their base persecutors.

Human beings are not intended to be constantly annihilating their evil inclinations. Instead, we are to make an effort to utilize every part of ourselves so that it can be guaranteed that our every action, deed, and even thought, will bring the world and ourselves closer to a higher state of perfection. While perfection might not yet be achieved, for we live in an imperfect world, yet it must always remain our goal.

Of course it is proper to question why this struggle, as opposed to the eradication of evil from our hearts once and for all, is considered to be true righteousness. Why is the one who constantly wages a war against evil superior to someone who delivers evil a decisive blow? For all intents and purposes, it would indeed appear that the latter is greater than the former.

Contrast Between Love and Justice

To better understand the transcendence of the *beinuni* over the *tzadik*, and the constant struggle over a state of righteousness, we return to the analogy of the splitting of the Red Sea. There were two possible reasons why the Almighty took the Jews out of Egypt. The first was in order to correct an injustice. A nation had been unjustly and brutally enslaved by a murderous and destructive oppressor, so God freed the Jews and punished the Egyptians. According to this scheme of things, God plays a role analogous to a political liberator who possesses the power at once to free the Jews and destroy the Egyptians. However, a political liberator should be emotionally detached from the victim acting; they should act because of conviction and the pursuit of justice, and not due to any connection or feeling for the victim. Justifiably or not, this is the common perception of many supra-national organizations today: we in the West assume that the United Nations stands in and tries to redeem an enslaved or deprived minority because it loves justice. They do it for the sake of a sacred principle, and not for the sake of a person.

The other possibility, however, is that God came down to Egypt not in pursuit of justice, but to save His children. He came not to correct a wrong, but to show love to His people. He acted not to uphold a principle, however meritorious, but to save a nation that is the apple of His eye.

If God had transformed the water of the Red Sea into stone so that it stood like a wall, He would have been showing Himself to be just another liberator of any oppressed people. He would only do the kind of things that were necessary to save the Jews and vanquish the Egyptians. All that was necessary was for the sea to split; minimal effort on the part of an infinitely powerful Redeemer.

However, we know that He did not choose this path. He caused a wind to blow the entire night, in other words God actively intervened on behalf of the Jewish people throughout the long battle, even when His manifest intervention could have been far more limited. He was thereby demonstrating His love for the Jewish people. He was showing that He took an active interest in their welfare. He intervened not just once, and not just in a way that would have achieved His purpose, but constantly, in a manner which proved that He loved and cared for the children of Israel. He thereby demonstrated that the path, namely intervening and caring for his people, was far more important than the stated goal, saving them from their Egyptian oppressors.

And if He did not care, if He had abandoned the Jews after they were freed instead of nurturing them for forty years in the desert, they would have been a free people, but they would have been lost. Instead, he took them by the hand and stayed with them throughout their sojourns in the Wilderness, and escorted them to their land.

Correcting Injustice in Africa

As a secular and contemporary contrast, let us note the way in which the European colonial powers withdrew from Africa. These countries had colonized Africa over hundreds of years and in many cases had plundered its wealth and oppressed its people. But suddenly in the era after the Second World War they decided that they had to rectify their misdeeds. Therefore, in the Fifties and Sixties they granted their former colonies independence on a massive scale. The problem was that the colonial powers like Britain, France, Holland and Belgium, and also the United Nations which pushed the policy from behind under United Nations Secretary General Dag Hammarskjöld, were not motivated by concern and love for their fellows. Rather, they wanted to be seen to correct a historical wrong. They wanted to give back as quickly as possible the freedom that had been denied the African continent throughout the plundering which took place amidst colonial rule.

The former colonial powers simply granted the African states their freedom; they removed colonial rule, but without any investigation of the new African governments' capacity to rule fairly. There was very little nurturing of their former charges through the difficult transition from colony to sovereign state. Western Europe was out to correct a specific wrong, and it did, but in the process it left a mess so great that even now it cannot be cleaned up. In the first decades of free African states, thirty-odd civil wars were fought, which by 1978 had produced about six and a half million refugees.

The varied but on the whole sombre pattern of the African continent a generation after independence is reflected in the following summary of events in the 1970s. In 1979, there was an attempted coup in Sudan, while in Morocco there was a war in the western Sahara against Polisario guerrillas costing about £750,000 a day. In Ethiopia, 20,000 Cubans plus many more Ethiopian troops were fighting wars on three fronts against Eritrea and Somalia, a war in which there were more than one million refugees. In Djibouti there was an uprising in the Adar region. From Tanzania, 40,000 troops invaded Uganda when the mass-butcher Idi Amin (who had received a standing ovation from the United Nations in 1975 when he called for the 'extermination' of Israel), supported by 2,500 troops from Libya was ousted. In Ghana there was a coup by Flight Lieutenant Jerry Rawlings: three former heads of state and many other politicians were executed by a firing squad, there were public floggings and canings of 'corrupt' citizens, a police strike, and finally the whole country was officially declared bankrupt. There were Liberian food riots that killed a 'mere' seventy people. There was yet another coup in Mauritania: Ould Salack, who had ousted Ould Daddack in 1978, was ousted in turn by Ould Hardallah. Equatorial Guinea saw the overthrow of the dictator Macias, and the Central African Republic overthrew Bokassa. In Cape Verde over ninety per cent of the food consumed was imported from abroad at great cost. In Mozambique, the death penalty was extended as a punishment for the crimes of sabotage, terrorism and mercenary activities, and there were many political executions. President Machel attacked men with long hair and women with tight clothes, and the Catholic and Anglican churches were closed. In Zimbabwe, official white rule finally ended after a decade of civil war leaving 20,000 dead. In Namibia and Lesotho there was constant guerrilla warfare.

Had any of the colonial powers not acted merely on principle, but rather out of deep concern for human life, they would never have abandoned these fledgling countries to oblivion, even in the name of freedom and liberty, until they had seen them through the most difficult stages and made sure they had gained the capacity to stand on their own feet.

Goal Orientation and Means Orientation

This is the reason that the *beinuni* is superior to the *tzadik*. He or she demonstrates a love for goodness which has to be actively chosen every day. The *beinuni* demonstrate through their ongoing struggle between good and evil, and their passion for achieving goodness, a presence on the side of Godliness that shows they do not love merely a principle, but that they love God.

The *beinuni* shows that he or she loves God and casts his or her lot with Him, not just once, and not just when it is expedient or convenient, but all the time, and with ever growing intensity and fervour.

The lesson that must be drawn from this insight is that we must learn to respect the path over and above the reward. It is the means which are significant, not (just) the end. A human being is commanded by God to pursue goodness, without any recourse to thoughts of success of his efforts. What this means is that if someone sees, God forbid, a passer-by hit by a car in the street, and it appears as though any efforts to save the victim will eventually prove futile, one must nevertheless do one's utmost to save the life. Why? Because God never commanded us to ensure that every life be saved. Rather, He commanded us to endeavour to save life. Even the probability of our exertions meeting with failure can in no way justify the cessation of effort and caring.

A Wife's Anguish . . .

This, unfortunately, is not the way in which most people view the situation. Our society today is one which is almost entirely goal-motivated and achievement oriented. Those projects which seem forlorn are cast aside, and students are interested primarily in what they can accomplish rather than what they can undertake. The result, to our great misfortune, has been that whole sectors of human life and the perfection of society have been abandoned. I was speaking to a man who always got angry at his wife, shouting at her violently. They were married five years and his wife decided that she could take no more. They had already been to various marriage counsellors about the problem but nothing helped. Finally, he told her, 'This is the way I am. Either take me how I am or leave me.' Needless to say, she opted for the latter. But before she did so, she asked him to come and see me. He admitted to me that his inability to control his anger was the main cause of their marital strife. 'So why don't you try and change?' I asked him. 'Because I have tried and nothing has happened. This is the way I am. People never change, and that's just the way it is. Either she accepts me for what I am or we're through.'

. . . And a Husband's Caring

I had had enough. 'Who the hell said that you should only work on yourself and try and change if it will succeed?' I asked him 'You have an obligation to try and change yourself, to stop shouting and to treat your wife with respect regardless of whether or not you will eventually change. Just keep on trying and don't worry about the progress you're making.' When he finally heeded my advice, and I was very angry myself at his behaviour, their marriage began to heal. The reason was obvious. His wife hated being shouted at. But what she hated even more was the fact that he didn't care how she felt. She was even willing to forgive occasional bouts of anger. What she justifiably could not forgive was her husband saying to her, 'This is the way I am and I won't even make an effort to change.' When he resumed making an effort, she regained her love for him. But why? He was still shouting. The answer: because at least he cared. And the proof was that he was making an effort.

This is what God desires. Not necessarily that we succeed in upholding goodness, improving the world, and the lot of our fellow man. Rather, what He requires is that we at least care enough to do something about it, whether or not we will succeed. We still must always try; and we must therefore remember that it is the journey which is the reward.

Rabbi Yochanan on his Death-bed

The Talmud relates that the celebrated Sage Rabbi Yochanan ben Zakkai cried on his death-bed and exclaimed, 'I do not know where they [the angelic being who would escort him after his demise] are taking me.' His students were aghast. Surely a man as saintly as Rabbi Yochanan knew that he could only be going to heaven. The Gehenna was out of the question for such a saint. So what did he mean?

The rebbe, Rabbi Menachem Schneerson, once explained that Rabbi Yochanan really did not know of his own righteousness. You see, throughout his life he never focused on becoming saintly or holy, he only concentrated on his ongoing efforts to do the right things in accordance with Godliness and goodness. He never thought of the consequences of his action. Thoughts of whether or not he was simultaneously becoming holy or righteous never crossed his mind. Only now, in the twilight of his life, when he was disabled from doing any more, was he able to question whether or not he had become good, and by extension, whether or not he would be rewarded with entry into heaven.

And the lesson of this *tzadik*'s life, that it is the ongoing acts of goodness which are important and not achieving one's objectives, is what should sustain us through all of the hardships which life throws our way but which can never stop us in our mission as angels of mercy.

Chapter Seventy-One

THE REDEEMER AND THE COMFORTER: BATTLE BETWEEN SUCCESS AND GOODNESS

The most successful way in which a rabbi to a university can affect his surroundings is when his home and family become that of the students. The degree of trust and friendship that comes when students feel that their rabbi and his family are their extended family is second to none. Every educational institution is to an extent a lonely place, and Oxford more than most. The intense academic routine and fierce competition among students leads them to spend much of their time on their own studying or contemplating. For the majority of the British undergraduates it is the first time away from home, and for the many overseas students it is the first time that they are so far away from their families. Thus a warm, friendly, family environment is something welcomed by all students and accounts for why we have so many students who volunteer to baby-sit our children and become so attached to us, for which we are eternally thankful.

But being a Chasidic family we usually have something else to offer: the many celebrations for children born. For young students who have no desire to get married soon, it is quite incredible just how excited they become when we have a baby born. The hospital where my wife stays after the birth of a child has a constant stream of students coming to see the new arrival. We were used to this enthusiasm, but it does not compare with the parties for the new baby. There is dancing and singing for hours and hours.

So at the birth of our newest child and our first son, there was renewed joy. My wife and I had had three daughters and many of the students were here to witness all three. Thus when it became known that we were now expecting our fourth child, there was great anticipation for its birth and speculation as to the gender of the baby. Everyone told me that we would have another girl. Therefore, when the baby was born and the news was known that he was a boy, the students were surprised and ecstatic. On the Friday after the birth we staged the traditional *Shalom Zachor* for the birth of a baby boy and about two hundred students helped me dance on tables, finish about fifty bottles of whisky, and sing through the night. The *bris* itself was no less enthusiastic (except for the actual surgical technique which caught many of the students by surprise), and was held on Lag B'Omer, one of the most joyous days of the Jewish calendar; we had dancing and singing throughout the day. It was truly spectacular, and what was most impressive was how happy the students were for us. This was the ultimate token of their appreciation and respect, the fact that they could be so happy for my wife and me on the day of our celebration.

The students' sentiments, and this idea of the students being our extended family, is sometimes captured more beautifully in the words of the students than my own. The following letter was written by an Oxford Rhodes scholar from Yale who, though not observant, would come to our house regularly to argue various social issues. Since he was also a correspondent for a leading Jewish newspaper, he was interested in hearing the Jewish perspective on various contemporary issues.

Dear Debbie and Shmuley,
The bustle and excitement that accompany an important occasion frequently get in the way of expressing the sentiments and reflections prompted by the occasion itself. I am afraid that such has been the case for me on your recent important occasion, although Noach, in his toast, gave an eloquent statement of exactly what I had wished to say. Your hospitality – in the broadest sense – of opening your house, and even much of what would have been your own time, to students and others at Oxford – is legendary around here, and has made many people happy. So we are all glad to be around to witness some personal good news for you which, true to form, became an occasion (or rather several) for everyone to celebrate. Again – Mazel Tov. I hope that what you sacrifice in time and privacy is compensated for in some measure by having so many people share your celebration. Different people certainly benefit from your presence in different ways – but we're all glad you're here, and appreciative of your work.

Such a letter both warms my heart and lends me the fortitude to rise to the challenges of my job, as well as affords renewed enthusiasm for my work. I also wished to convey to the students not just the joy, but the introspection and commitment engendered by the birth of a child. So, the following were the remarks I made to the students about the aspirations and goals I have for my child, as well as the advice I give him for, above all, setting goodness as his ultimate goal in life, and achieving it.

Wishes a Parent Has for His Child

With the birth of another child, I have paused to reflect on the new life and potential that his birth means. Like any parent I wish my child to have the best that life may offer and to develop his full potential. I would most deeply desire that he will be both good and successful in life. I hope he will be a Godly and moral individual, and a help and blessing to all those around him. Also I hope that he may achieve any personal ambitions he will set for himself in the future, and have material sufficiency to provide for himself and his dependants, as well as to help others.

But these are mostly platitudes, and as I dwelled on this I have been disturbed because I fear that ultimately success and goodness are in conflict and may be mutually exclusive goals in life. This has always troubled me as a rabbi, and in my personal life and desires. As a rabbi and as an individual I have been motivated perhaps as much as anything else by the quest for this elusive quality. Throughout my life I have seen a world and relationships troubled and enervated by a lack of righteousness. I have seen unhappiness and failure caused by its absence, and I know people and situations that could have been so transformed by even a small infusion of it. A few kind thoughts, feelings and actions have the power to transmute even the darkest situations. The principal cause of my becoming Lubavitch was that I saw the Lubavitcher rebbe as a great and inspirational source of goodness and Godliness, whose teachings and life actually brought light and life to those he came into contact with. I wanted to be part of this too, so that I could in whatever possible way help the world to become a better place.

However, the conflict comes because I do not just desire to pursue altruistic aims in life; I have my own selfish ambitions, and I wish to have personal success and recognition in my life. One of my strongest desires is to have success as a writer, and to make a name for myself in the field of Jewish universal thought and publishing. This desire is to some degree an expression of personal vanity, as we all wish to be esteemed, exceptional, and to be remembered. It is certainly selfish because writing is a time-consuming business which excludes others. Time spent writing is time that one cannot be pursuing altruistic aims. Practically it is time in which I cannot lend an ear to the problems of my students, teach ideas that can enhance and change peoples lives, or offer my services as a rabbi.

I fear that these two legitimate desires towards goodness and personal success may ultimately exclude one another. At best their pursuit can lead to an unholy compromise between the life and actions directed to self and others. Have I then wished the impossible for my son; will he in the future have to choose which way he is to go in life, or to decide how much time he can spare at most for the needs of others when he has attended to his own ambitions?

A Solution Among Students

When I first came to Oxford as a rabbi to the students I hoped that I might find a resolution of my problem. I had hoped that by spending time with them I would be with idealistic young people who would in some way be able to transcend this dichotomy, who would be open to the vision of a world that can be changed for the better, and where people can live good and successful lives. I had also thought that the great universities such as Oxford would have the highest conception of academic life, where knowledge is pursued not merely as an end in itself, or as a foundation for a well-paid career, but rather as a means of bringing benefit to all of society from knowledge, so that students could fulfil themselves in and through the needs of others.

At yeshivah we were inculcated with this great idea. Education was presented as not only the acquisition of knowledge, but the learning and practice of how to be good, so that we could acquire a dexterity in devotion and service to others. In yeshivah we were taught that the entire purpose of knowledge, indeed the entire reason for our presence in this highly insular environment, was to train and inspire us to action for the benefit of others. Our teachers sought to instil deep within us the belief that life is not just about accumulating knowledge. The object of the knowledge we gained in yeshivah was to understand wherein lay goodness, so that our actions could fly straight to the mark as we came to practise what we had learnt.

The curriculum of the yeshivah closely reflected this philosophy. It demanded that we devote a quarter of our time to the needs of other people. We spent two hours each day teaching in high schools and colleges, as well as teaching in the community. The whole of Friday would be devoted to going out and meeting people, or visiting the elderly. In short, our education involved acts of kindness and charity; the primary purpose of our presence at yeshivah was to learn how to lead righteous and kind lives. I cannot claim to have achieved or become everything that was asked of me, or that goodness became an innate part of every yeshivah graduate. But by the time I and my fellow students had left yeshivah we all knew what was required of us, and how we could work in modest and great ways to help others. Through what we had learned and practised we all had a great sense of mission to the Jewish people and to all of humanity; a vision of not just teaching religion, but of teaching and enabling goodness.

An Ethos of Selfishness

Unfortunately, when I arrived at Oxford I soon realized that I had gained false expectations as to the nature of education here. I discovered that the students were generally pleasant; they were intelligent, considerate and caring. But I saw also that the students were selfish as well. When I say selfish I do not mean that they were unpleasant or uncouth, rather I soon found that many of the students were just too busy to have much room in their lives for anything other than their study and development. The university makes great demands on the students, and the students themselves are usually keen to acquit themselves as well as possible and to fulfil their curricular and extra-curricular ambitions. Thus they put their career, exams, essays and university work before absolutely everything else.

From certain Jewish perspectives this is correct, as it can be argued that students are here for their studies and self-development which in the long term will be of real benefit to wider society, even if it necessitates a degree of self-absorption now. On this basis, students are not here for social activism or for the needs of other people, because they are here for an education. To do anything else would be misguided and counter-productive as students will make better citizens and philanthropists later if they focus on their education and self-development now.

While this argument has a certain persuasiveness, I am not convinced of its ultimate validity. For as our rabbis said to us at yeshivah, if one can find reason to be selfish while a student, a stage of life when we are free of many of the pressing responsibilities of more mature years, then how will we find time and reason later to be of service to others? I would emphasize that much of the fault for this lies with the modern university institution and ethos itself.

How Oxford Has Changed

Many modern universities, particularly the more élite ones, actually encourage students to be selfish, and propagate a false and inflated self-importance in their students. The Oxford University regime has no communal work at all as part of the curriculum, and the burden of work they lay on students leaves them no time to dedicate themselves to others without great self-sacrifice. I cannot really fault the university authorities for feeling that their principal duty is to impart knowledge, and to distribute degrees but it is incomplete nonetheless.

In this respect Oxford has much declined from its former moral stature in the high Victorian era. In the late nineteenth century, many heads of college wanted to produce students of all-round excellence: students who were of polished intellect and culture, and most importantly embodied high moral and religious values, who saw it as their duty to serve another. There were also attempts by university leaders and students to serve local communities. The famous artist John Ruskin even instituted a programme of road repair work by students in isolated Oxford villages, so that they would know the 'pleasures of useful muscular work'. Villagers in North Hinksey were able to see Oxford students, including Oscar Wilde, toiling with pick, shovel and barrow to improve the material condition of their lives.

It seems that modern universities have gone astray from a nobler view of education because they no longer believe that personal development is as important as knowledge. More fundamentally, the problem that the universities fail to address today is that the western world suffers not from lack of knowledge but from a lack of goodness. Righteousness is no longer perceived as a supreme value. In saying this it is important to bear in mind that education is ultimately about what we believe people should ideally be, and any educational organization is deficient if it fails to have a holistic conception of its purpose.

What is worse is that it is clear that students often subconsciously imbibe the values or lack of values around them in the universities. I can clearly see that goodness is no longer a supreme value when students complain that they have no time to help co-ordinate or publicize Jewish activities, even for meals that they will participate in, and yet still find the time to go to movies and many other social events. This shows when I ask such a student, who complains that he or she has no time to devote to Jewish events on campus, why they have so much time for their social life. The usual response is, 'I work so hard that I owe it to myself.' This statement is breathtaking in its implicit assumption that leisure is not merely about enjoyment, but constitutes a duty that one has to oneself. Socializing and leisure are supreme values, and people feel deprived if they only work with 'no play'. In this situation we succumb to the assumption that the obligations which we have to ourselves are more important than the obligations to others. It is primarily the presence of people like myself outside of the university establishment that reminds students they have no less an obligation to their communities and to the world at large.

I remain convinced that we shall never bring forth a better world until being an upright person is seen to be as important as success. As a society we have become too much obsessed with doing well, with the result that we are encouraging a suffocating selfishness among our children, where they are taught firstly to conquer, and then only to share.

Abstention from Evil as the Equivalence of Good

An associated problem is that many people confuse absence of evil with the presence of virtue. In my work as a rabbi I often ask people if they think it is important to be good, and whether they consider themselves to be so. The common response to this question is indignation, and the declaration that not only do they believe it, but that they practise it. They say they do not lie, steal, cheat, murder, philander, or even speak badly about people behind their backs. To this I am forced to respond that they have only told me that they are not evil. Unfortunately, refraining from evil has become synonymous with goodness itself, and people fail to realize that abstaining from the bad only confers moral neutrality on them at best.

There is also a species of this problem recognizable in some people's view of the nature of religion. I have not infrequently come across people who think that being a good Jew consists of being honest in business and to one's spouse, and not being a demanding parent. They signally fail to appreciate that religion is very much about doing positive and specific exemplary acts, and not just avoiding evil.

Goodness as Selflessness

What goodness really means is selflessness. To act for the benefit of others, to participate in another's sorrow or joy, without immediate regard to the inconveniences posed for ourselves or how we will benefit or lose from it. It means shifting decisively from placing ourselves at the centre of our world, to placing God and, by extension, others at the centre of our priorities. It also entails restructuring our time so that we have a primary regard for the time of others rather than our own time which is rooted in our own desires and ego perceptions. More than anything else, goodness entails sacrifice, as there will often be a cost for helping others. Selflessness may place us at a personal disadvantage and loss. This naturally cuts right across the grain of the success mentality in which our personal gain is paramount, and a key measure of our worth.

With the birth of my son all of these issues have been sharply highlighted, especially as I realize that it raises an issue of some importance to us all. If there is ultimately to be a conflict between righteousness and success, then as a rabbi it would be my duty to affirm goodness and Godliness. But I fear that goodness without legitimate self-interest may ultimately be invalid, because there would be the real danger that the needs of others would be so placed above the needs of the ethical individual that the latter would become supremely passive and open to exploitation by others. This would be contrary to the very spirit of Judaism, which propagates dynamic ethics and the legitimate rights and needs of the individual. In short, without the legitimate self-interest of the individual a dangerous species of quietism could emerge, which could not be regarded as a good at all.

Enter the Comforter

I believe the name 'Menachem' that has been given to my son today provides an understanding of the conflict between success and goodness, and one important way (among others) to resolve it. The name Menachem means 'comforter', and in Jewish tradition it is also the name of the Messiah. 'His name is Menachem, the son of Chizkiya, for it is written, Because Menachem [the comforter], that would relieve my soul, is far' (Lam 1:16); (Sanh. 98b). Similarly, describing the day in which the Messiah is born, Midrash Rabba says in five places, 'That day Menachem was born, and thus it was a happy occasion' (Numbers 13:5). The way in which the Messiah will give to the world in the future as the comforter provides us with an important model as to how we can be individually successful and use that success to bring great good to others. It must be remembered above all that the Messiah will be a man of unsurpassed brilliance and accomplishment, and this ascendancy will be used as the very catalyst to usher in the redeemed messianic world.

You may ask what is there in a name, and why I am emphasizing the name of the Messiah so much. In Judaism a Hebrew name is of great importance. An individual's name is no mere label on which to attach their identity; a name is a mystical entity which contains the essence of an individual's nature, and helps explain the inner working of their destiny. There is a spiritual connection between the name of an individual and his or her soul. Similarly, the Arizal writes that the nature and behaviour of a person, whether good or bad, can be found by analysing their name. Even the numerical value of the name's letter is an indication of the individual's character and personality. Jewish tradition even maintains that a father and mother are imbued with a spirit of prophecy upon choosing the name which their child will carry.

A name can also be a prayer that the individual may live up to the potential expressed in their particular name. For to give a name to something is to define its nature and essence. Adam revealed his great wisdom when he named all species of creation. With his Godly intellect, every name he chose, together with the combination of its letters, defined the nature and characteristic of that creature.

To return to the name of Menachem, it is now clear that his name is intended to impart his essence, and his essence is about the way he gives to the world as the comforter. The way in which the comforter gives is one particular way of giving, among other ways. So to help us understand how the Messiah will give, it is constructive to contrast this with the way of giving of the other great leader and provider of the Jewish people, Moses.

The Redeemer vs The Comforter

The name of Moses means to draw, to cull, or to extract. Moses the leader drew forth of his self, and his unparalleled stature, to give to the Jewish people who had nothing. He was a redeemer who saw total impoverishment and need, and gave freely of himself to those who had nothing. He was the redeemer who brought the Torah down from Sinai. He drew the Torah down and it was done exclusively through him. So began a process of dependency that existed between Moses and the Jewish people for the entire forty years that they traversed the desert. In effect a leader in the form of the drawer is the kind of person who makes the people feel dependent because no one can match his stature. Only one Jew could bring down the Torah and only one Jew could redeem the Jews from Egypt, and that was Moses. A materially and spiritually impoverished nation could not redeem itself. His leadership was in effect leadership by the élite. He was acknowledged by all as the greatest of the Jews. But his greatness made everyone around him feel dependent. The Jews needed Moses in the wilderness. Everything from their food to their clothes rained down miraculously because of the merit of the great law-giver. The Jews needed to do nothing. They were passive. God provided everything through Moses, from the land of Egypt to the land of Israel.

In contemporary terms Moses resembles a philanthropist who comes to the destitute and downtrodden not with hope for what they can achieve, but with promises of what *he* can give. Moses is like a government which comes to the Third World with foreign aid. At its best the act is selfless and humanitarian, but it is also by definition a condescending action from greater to less, from the haves to the have nots.

To Counteract the Philanthropist

The name Menachem indicates an entirely different kind of giving. It is a type of giving that seeks to nurture and draw forth what is already potential in the person in need. It is not a giving of material, because the comforter offers encouragement that empowers the individual. The comforter is someone who offers nothing but belief in themselves. He gives nothing new and he is not a philanthropist. He offers to focus on what the individual he is comforting already possesses, to bring it into life and to help bring that person from darkness to light.

In contemporary terms we can imagine a man who after years of toil loses his business and goes bankrupt. He sits at home and sulks. A comforter comes along and, unlike Moses, he does not offer any money. Nor does he offer a good, high-paying job. Rather, he makes the businessman focus on what he already has. He says to him, 'You may have lost a lot, but just think of what you still have. You have your health, you have a loving wife, you have children, and most of all, you have the potential to rebuild yourself. If you made it to the top once, you can do it again.' The comforter doesn't offer a handout because the person doesn't need it. He has everything he needs to get back on his own two feet. All he needs is a restored belief in himself.

Once when I was in France on holiday with my family, I chanced upon the French Handicapped Skiing Championships. There was a young girl competing in a ski wheelchair with numbers on her front and back. Her number was about to be called and she was practising with her mother on a small slope. She kept falling over and could not get up. On the third attempt to rise, she burst into tears and called for her mother to lift her up. Her mother refused. 'But I can't move my feet,' she shrieked, sobbing. 'But you can move your arms', was her mother's reply. 'I'm not here to give you pity. So pick yourself up', and she did.

This is the role of the comforter. To remind us of our own innate potential, and to be a catalyst for us to become and achieve that which we should be. To remind us that even in the face of the greatest adversity, that indomitable human spirit cannot be crushed. The comforter neither focuses on what we do not have, nor promises to make up our faults. Rather, the comforter is the facilitator. He is there to remind us that we possess everything that he possesses, and that we are thereby not dependent on him. He reminds us of our potential. Whereas the redeemer focuses on the actual, the comforter focuses on the potential. When the redeemer sees the downtrodden, he bends down to lend a hand, and stoops to help. The comforter cannot accept that anyone should remain downtrodden and knows that everyone has the potential to stand erect. Thus he will not bend to help, but he will raise the other person up. Whereas Moses saw a slave nation which was in need of his salvation, the Messiah sees an able people who already possess the ability to change the world. The Messiah will not act magisterially and do it for them. Rather, he will serve as the catalyst to stimulate action and transformation. He will seek to bring us self-belief to make a coherent whole that will create the critical mass necessary to usher in the redemption.

Black Experience in America

Of course both modes of giving are valid and complementary, and each has their own appropriate time and place. A historical example from America, which shows this, concerns the history of black people, from slavery to freedom, and their relationship to American leaders. Abraham Lincoln was a redeemer to the black slaves of America who gave to them like Moses.

Lincoln's message to American black slaves was, 'Stand by, and I will free you.' The white north had the ability and the military might to translate a proclamation of emancipation from paper into reality. It was an emancipation that the slaves could not gain for themselves, and so they had to wait upon Lincoln for their freedom in the same way that the people of Israel had to wait upon Moses for their freedom.

Lincoln brought them freedom and the promise of a better life. For a time this has worked, but now we are watching it fail. There are now thousands of disaffected and angry black youths who are saying that they are tired of whites thinking that they can do everything for them. They acknowledge that much of their redemption was brought about through whites, but they are not happy about it. Many feel degraded and are tired of being told that they cannot lift themselves up on their own. Man feels a basic need for redemption, though he desires it more than anything else by his own devices. What this means is that the same will within us that wishes to be redeemed also wishes to retain human dignity and self-reliance. There is a part of us that will always resist being the passive recipient of help from a benefactor.

Taking Responsibility for Our Actions

The Mosaic redeemer has an ultimately limited role. After he has lifted needy peoples from a helpless and passive state, these peoples come to need and desire a messianic redeemer who will enable them to fulfil their own destiny through the catalyst of his person and their own ability and work. In the case of Israel, Moses lifted them from the very depths of despair and helplessness; he nursed them to maturity and independence. But once Israel was in full growth and established in the land with a temple, and had weathered the storms and travail of its history, the people of Israel needed a role in which they were in a partnership with God and depended on Him, and yet were maturely responsible for their own destiny.

It was as if Israel was in its dependent childhood under Moses, and had gained its adult stature and responsibility once in the land. The essential relationship of God to Israel in the land was that of Comforter, for once in the land God sought to encourage and to guide Israel to fulfil its potential and destiny which had been sealed with Moses at Sinai. God said to the people that the success or failure of the Temple and the Jewish kingdom depended on them. He said that if they led exemplary spiritual lives all would be well; if not, disaster would ensue. He made it clear that all rested in their hands, and that they had been given all the ability and potential necessary to do it.

As yet the Jewish nation is still awaiting the fulfilment of its spiritual destiny, and the Temple is not restored. The Jewish people are still scattered throughout the world, and is still suffering from the unspeakable disaster of the Holocaust. The reality that the Messiah Menachem is still to come reminds us all that we still have the ability to rise out of the ashes again and again if necessary, and that when the time comes we will arise and bring in the hoped-for spiritual destiny promised by the prophets. The Messiah is not just a symbol of the ability of Jews to attain their full growth and redemption whatever the circumstances, but he also represents the actuality in all human existence for us all to find our fullness, destiny and redemption.

Standing with Others at the Mountain's Summit

As you can see from this there is great significance in the name Menachem, the new name of my son. It is certainly a name to aspire to, it is also a name which indicates a vital way in which we can give to others and society, without needing to resort to unhealthy and un-Jewish self-abnegation. Moreover it shows how individual success can be a great asset and a help to all around us if it is used and directed in a Godly way. The key understanding is that self-development and becoming somebody in the world can be part and parcel of a life directed to others, if that success is built from the beginning to include the needs and aspirations of others. A success that seeks to leave the rest of humanity in a poorer state is no achievement at all. It is an abject human failure and tragedy, as it leaves the individual marooned on the island of their own egotism, cut off from the place of relationship, love and fulfilment.

I hope that my son will fulfil his name, and will be the enabler of others. I hope that he will ensure his success in life is never to the exclusion of others. Rather I hope that when he reaches the heights and stands on the mountain tops of achievement he will reckon success by how many others stand beside him in that high place because he helped to enable them. I hope that if by misfortune none stand beside him, he will have thought himself to have failed, and will return again to the plains to gather around him those with whom he will return again to the summits of success.

Messiah as Facilitator

Finally it is important to mention why my wife and I were moved to name our son Menachem, and not any other name. Though Menachem is named after the third Lubavitcher rebbe, the Tzemach Tzedek, in accordance with the Jewish Chasidic custom of not naming a child after someone living, our main intention in calling him Menachem was also to give honour to the present Lubavitch Rebbe, Rabbi Menachem Schneerson, who has led the worldwide Lubavitch movement for more than forty years, and who has been my constant inspiration and leader since an early age.

If there is any living person who is the embodiment of the inner significance and meaning of the name Menachem the comforter, it is the rebbe. His life, achievements, leadership and astounding self-giving have uniquely advanced and facilitated Jewish life since the war. The rebbe is certainly one of the most notable Jewish leaders this century, and has done as much as any individual, and perhaps far more, to revive and rebuild Jewish life from the smouldering wreckage of the Holocaust. He sought to remobilize the whole of world Jewry after the war, the broken and dispirited survivors of the Holocaust, and those who had watched helplessly and demoralized from the sidelines.

The Jewish people had just been through the trauma of the Holocaust. In the wake of every previous calamity, the Jews always seemed able to find comfort in their God and in their religion. But here for the first time there was nothing to console, nothing to comfort. Not only was Judaism not comforting its children, but there was a mass exodus away from Judaism. Suddenly the God of Israel seemed unable to console. As mentioned above, the ability to comfort arises when one is able to focus on something fortunate which has survived and still remains. One finds solace for what is lost in what remains.

For example, if, God forbid, a man loses a son, the rabbi comes to the place of mourning, sits next to him, and tells him how fortunate he is to have another son. He must focus on the other son and find comfort in him.

But of Jewish life in Europe, nothing remained. NOTHING. The Germans wiped out all of the communities. The only thing that was left were millions of fugitives, uprooted from their ancestral homelands, with no homes, no clothes, and riddled with hunger and disease. Whence were they to derive comfort? And who was there to console? Where was there any *Menachem*?

From Despair to Hope and Joy

The rebbe emerged from obscurity and reminded all that the light of the Jewish soul was inextinguishable, like the fire of the Torah. He sought to bring light back to the Jewish nation and to remind them of their unique heritage and historic mission and that they were not forsaken. Most of all, he taught that we are an eternal people whose destiny is impervious to the designs of wicked tyrants. At first with a small rag-tag band of Chasidim who were mocked and scorned by many, he started to revitalize Judaism as he sent his emissaries throughout the world. He organized a global campaign using every form of technology to transmit the message of Godliness and goodness to the most remote places. The Jewish world responded to his call and embraced him warmly as their rebbe.

More than anything else, he transcended the role of a Moses and became a supreme comforter of the Jewish people. More than anything else, the rebbe encouraged and inspired. From the first his message was about the ability of the individual to bring change and to transform. He showed that every human being is uniquely able to help to bring about redemption. Following the tradition of Maimonides, he emphasized the significance of the role of the individual in changing the world, even if they had mistakenly thought before that their contribution was minute and insignificant. The rebbe in all these ways has been a supreme comforter of Israel. Without his encouragement that I could succeed as an emissary in Oxford, I would never have imagined that, at a young age, I could come to one of the most famous universities in the world, make a positive difference to people's lives, and in my own unique way bring a contribution to the advance of goodness in Oxford.

Finally I pray that my child Menachem will grow up to follow in the rebbe's footsteps, to work for the good of others, and do all that he can to help bring the Messiah and usher in a time when everyone's life will be joyous and the world will be filled with plenty.

Chapter Seventy-two

WHY I REVERE ORTHODOXY AND TRADITIONAL JUDAISM

One of the leading benefits associated with my position is the opportunity to become familiar with so many of the world's foremost Jewish thinkers and personalities. Many of them are guests we ourselves bring over from the United States, Israel and other countries. Others are academics who come to do a Sabbatical or other form of study or research in Oxford.

Dennis Prager and Ultimate Issues

Of the many leading Jewish thinkers whom we have hosted and have had the opportunity to befriend, Dennis Prager ranks high among them. Most people do not immediately associate the name of Dennis Prager with the likes of Elie Wiesel, Adin Steinsaltz, or Manis Friedman, but the truth is that in the United States there are few Jews at all who are as much respected or exert the same level of influence on religious and political issues.

Through his quarterly publication of *Ultimate Issues*, which has over 10,000 subscribers, and his nightly radio talk show in Los Angeles on KABC Radio, which is easily the most popular in its time slot on the West Coast of the United States, to his best-selling books on Judaism, such as *The Nine Questions People Ask Most About Judaism* and *Why the Jews: the Reason for Anti-Semitism*, each of which has been translated into dozens of languages, Dennis Prager has fathered a return to ultra-rational Judaism. His basic approach to Judaism can be summed up in his words, 'Any teaching which says that we cannot understand aspects of Judaism is the most dangerous and the most objectionable I have ever heard.' He believes profoundly that Judaism can be explained in a rational guise, which will make it appealing. The flip-side of this approach, however, is that he is prepared to reject those laws of Judaism which are entirely supra-rational, much to the dismay of many of his Orthodox readers and enthusiasts.

Return to Jewish Rationalism

For my part, I am a considerable fan of his work and have thus invited him to speak here at Oxford twice, and can honestly say that the rational arguments he makes about the importance and pre-eminence of Judaism as a way of life are second to none. The first time he came here, he spoke on his own at a special Friday-night meal which we made at the Randolph Hotel in Oxford. He was an instant hit and there were three other lectures which he delivered to packed audiences.

However, this initial euphoria led to a certain degree of disappointment. There are always a certain number of students who are in the process of becoming more observant here at Oxford, and these young people could not accept that someone who would speak so eloquently about Judaism would not observe it completely, but would 'pick and choose'. For his part, Dennis feels that he is being honest about his convictions. He was brought up Orthodox but abandoned it, arguing that he would refuse to remain Jewish if Jewishness were just a way of preserving an ethnicity. He needed reasons for his Jewishness. He is absolutely committed to those aspects of Judaism which he finds a rational imperative to observe, but feels that he would be intellectually dishonest if he were to observe those things which he cannot accept. For my part, I must attest to the total sincerity and strength of conviction which Dennis brings to his Judaism. He has served to impress me and influence and inspire my work in Oxford to a very considerable degree.

Professor Kripke at Oxford

But not all people are convinced. The students who were 'returnees' to Judaism contrasted this attitude with that of Professor Saul Kripke of Princeton, author of the acclaimed *Naming and Necessity*, and considered one of the three leading philosophers alive. He is the man *Time* magazine said had one of the ten highest IQs in the world, who, when he ate with us over Sukkot with his wife, the philosopher Martha Gilbert, astonished the students by checking to make sure that he was eating within the Sukkah under the *schach*, the palm tree covering, which is demanded by the Halakha. Professor Kripke's sabbatical year at Wolfson College served as a real boon for the observant students because it is not every day that one of the most acclaimed secular philosophers alive demonstrates a continued and passionate commitment to Jewish observance and tradition.

The students' argument was that, if Kripke, who is no less a rationalist than Prager, can try to keep even those *mitzvot* which defy comprehension, then Prager must accept that he cannot possibly fit all of God's will into his human and limited mind. Indeed, it would appear a convincing argument to say that part of being a rationalist is to accept the limits of intellect.

Be that as it may, I continue to admire and respect Dennis Prager because there are only a handful of Jewish thinkers in the world who can make the case for Judaism, and the dependency of morality on a belief in God, as well as he can. I would go so far as to say that with regards to the latter he is simply the best I have heard. And he lives by what he preaches. He does not just talk about goodness, but practises it. We were stunned by the number of invitations he and his wife, Fran, issued to students visiting Los Angeles to come to visit them at their home, and his general good humour and charm enthralled all his listeners. Dennis has also been incredibly kind to me, amongst other things having written a 'blurb' for my second book, *The Wolf Shall Lie with the Lamb*, which began with the words, 'Shmuel Boteach is one of the leading Chasidic thinkers today . . .' If only Dennis could have seen the faces of the students who read that commendation.

An Ethical Monotheist

In the capacity which I described above, Dennis Prager is probably the world's foremost ethical monotheist, by which I mean someone who argues that ethics and religious belief are interrelated and interdependent. Thus, when it came to our staging a major debate on the issue of 'Can We Be Good without God', discussing whether religion is necessary for morality, which was to feature one of Oxford's leading philosophers, Dr Jonathan Glover from New College, we chose Dennis Prager of all the possible candidates we could have brought from anywhere in the world. And he did not disappoint us. This debate was one of the most exciting we ever staged and was, in the words of one Oxford graduate student, 'the most powerful exchange on the necessity of religion in the Nineties that I have ever witnessed in this city'.

The debate had all the essential ingredients for success. Strong rational arguments on both sides, addressing each other's points seriously, and with a great touch of humour. As it was, the debate, originally scheduled to last ninety minutes, went on for three hours, and could have lasted longer. We cut it in the spirit of our philosophy towards all of our events (something which I would encourage all impresarios to follow): that it is better to give the audience less than more of what they want, in order that they thirst for more. The internal discussion which the debate provoked amongst the students in the subsequent days was considerable. Which goes to show that while I cannot agree with many of the positions which Dennis has taken on Jewish religious questions, in arguments for the necessity of God in modern life he is unequalled at what he does and should be applauded accordingly.

An Authentic Jewish Denomination

There was one article written by Dennis with which I disagreed considerably, and I wrote him a letter for publication in his quarterly *Ultimate Issues*, which is where the article, entitled 'Which Denomination is Authentic Judaism', had appeared. In it he argued that all three major Jewish denominations, Orthodox, Conservative and Reform, together constitute authentic Judaism, and not just one in isolation. So it is wrong to argue that Orthodox Judaism is any more authentic than any of its offshoots.

Reform and Liberal Judaism at Oxford

This question of authenticity is one which arises all the time in Oxford. Reform and Conservative Jewish students at campuses are different from their older communal counterparts in that many of them are genuinely passionate about their Reform or Conservative Jewish convictions. They do not embrace Reform or Conservative because they are not yet ready to be Orthodox. Most suburban Jews do not actively choose to be Reform or Conservative, but rather their level of observance, or lack thereof, naturally gravitates them towards less demanding modes of Judaism: Oxford Jews tend not to choose these forms of their religion for any reasons of expediency. On the contrary, the Jewish students at Oxford who run to participate in groups such as 'The Progressive Jewish Society' do so, not only because in most cases they were brought up in a progressive Jewish tradition, but because they genuinely believe that Reform Judaism offers the best hope for the continuity of the Jewish people, and that it is the most inclusive denomination as well as offering equal religious opportunity to women. Whenever we do a Point-Counter-Point, a mini-debate between myself and a student, or other forum on the question of authenticity among the Jewish denominations, the numbers attending are always high and the discussion intense and argumentative.

Office of the Chief Rabbi

This is augmented by the fact that the Liberal, Reform, Progressive and Masorti denominations of Judaism (of which Rabbi Louis Jacobs is founder) do not have real representation outside the Jewish community, which is dominated by the existence of an official Chief Rabbinate in the UK, which is Orthodox, presently occupied by the extremely able, learned and dynamic Dr Jonathan Sacks. Because the non-Jewish world, including Britain's celebrated institutions of the monarchy and government, recognize and look to the Office of the Chief Rabbinate for guidance and information on all matters Jewish, a *de facto* legitimacy problem is automatically created for the non-Orthodox denominations, which leads to no end of anger and frustration.

Fortunately, Oxford is far too small for any unnecessary bickering to thrive amongst the various Jewish groups, and the various denominations live in harmony. Our society has hosted quite a few visiting Reform and Liberal Jewish rabbis at our services and events, including the head chaplain to the Jewish forces of the American military in the United Kingdom, a personal friend who is a Reform rabbi and who attended our Passover *seder* with a group of American Jewish airmen.

My Only Student to Follow in My Footsteps

In the university's Summer Term of 1990, the L'Chaim Society had a president by the name of Deborah Myers-Weinstein, an American student from Texas. Through L'Chaim and other sources, Deborah became more and more interested in Judaism, until one day she informed me that she wanted to be a rabbi. There was no room within Orthodoxy for such a role, so she decided to enrol in the Leo Beck Rabbinical Training Course. She is currently in her second year and in another two she will be a Reform ordained rabbi. Her ambitions for the rabbinate were sincere, and thus her decision was one which I applauded, albeit in a somewhat different permutation. She felt that she wanted to contribute something significant to the Jewish community, and I tried to persuade her that there are several significant routes for a woman to make such a contribution, which were still within the framework of halakhic Judaism, and outside the framework of being a rabbi. What of course weakened my argument was the very fact that I myself was a rabbi, and chose to make my contribution in this way. Notwithstanding her decision, our relationship was unaffected, and she still seeks my traditional Jewish perspective in many areas of her own Jewish study. Nevertheless, the prospect of a movement the likes of Lubavitch serving as such an inspiration to a Jewish woman that she decides to become a rabbi is interesting indeed, and this may have been a first.

I stand by the conviction that I have maintained throughout my life: Judaism is an immutable truth conveyed by God to Moses and the Jewish people at Sinai. Any attempt to tamper with these age-old Divinely revealed truths is dangerous as it serves to defeat the entire objective of a way of life that transcends humankind's ability to invent it. It was for this reason that I wrote Dennis my letter which addresses his issue of authentic Jewish denominations, and the main text of the letter follows.

Dear Dennis,

Inasmuch as there is no need for me to elaborate upon the great respect which I accord you and how much I enjoy reading your deeply thought-provoking and inspiring essays, I will get straight to the point. While I value the courage and motives behind your essay, 'Which Denomination is Authentic Judaism?', I take issue with its most central premise.

Had you titled the essay, 'Which Denominations Play a Vital Role for the Jewish People?', or 'Which Denominations Faithfully Serve the Jewish People?', I would not have disagreed so strongly. Because in truth your essay does not deal with authenticity at all, but rather with which denominations are making necessary contributions to Jewish life. Indeed you do not define 'authentic' or delineate guidelines on what constitutes authenticity. Rather, the entire article is devoted to displaying the utilitarian and pragmatic necessity of the three denominations and how, if Judaism consisted of only one denomination, there would always be a significant segment of the Jewish people who would be left alienated. I quote: 'Orthodox Jews could appreciate how, thanks to Reform, untold numbers of Jews remain counted among the Jewish people.' The essay may indeed demonstrate how a multiplicity of denominations caters to the needs of the Jewish people better than one, but this hardly makes the denominations that do so *authentic*.

A simple example will suffice. One of your most brilliant essays was last year's *Ultimate Issue* dedicated to the subject of homosexuality. In it you delivered an eloquent defence of the Jewish predisposition to heterosexuality and the nuclear family. Yet there are Jewish Gay and Lesbian Counselling Services, nay even Temples, strewn throughout the world which provide comfort and advice to Jewish homosexuals, thus creating a niche within the Jewish community so that they can fit in. Although I remain committed to the values of traditional Judaism, I still recognize that these groups provide a caring and sensitive service to a problem that Orthodox Judaism has largely ignored. But does this make their position on homosexuality Jewishly legitimate? Would you argue that the fact that they have helped untold numbers of young Jewish souls 'remain counted among the Jewish people' serves to legitimize their championing of homosexuality as a 'normative' expression of authentic Judaism?

Exclusion of Reconstructionism

The tone for the entire article is set immediately by your exclusion, in the very first paragraph, of Reconstructionist Judaism from the running. The reason: 'Reconstructionism denies Judaism's supernatural God and the chosenness of the Jews . . . Until the movement officially affirms Judaism's supernatural and personal God, one cannot honestly include the Reconstructionist movement as a normative Jewish vehicle to God and ethical monotheism.'

The contradiction that this immediately poses is obvious. By what criteria, Dennis, are you willing to accept one denomination as an authentic or, in your words, 'normative' denomination in Judaism? Clearly you have chosen Judaism's supernatural God and the chosenness of the Jews as your yardstick, and in this respect you are creating a personal catalogue of the essential articles of Judaism. Now, I will not be so dogmatic as to argue that one must accept the Maimonidean or indeed any other creed of the

Cardinal Articles of Jewish Faith, but I do maintain that one must have some method by which one adopts and establishes such Articles.

For instance, who is to say that Reformed Judaism's abandonment of the belief in a messianic age and a messianic redeemer does not constitute an abdication of *normative* Judaism? Or for that matter, without appearing to be offensive, who is to say that the Jews for Jesus's synthesis of the Christian redeemer with the Jewish religion serves as a renunciation of normative Judaism? They certainly contend that it is not. So what makes them wrong? Is it merely the fact that they are apparently not making a beneficial contribution to Jewish life that negates their claims to authenticity?

Omitting Mention of Israel

Less than one hundred years ago, many Reformed congregations were still omitting any mention of the return to the land of Israel from their prayer books, that is, until the creation of a state in Palestine became fashionable once again with the establishment of the modern state of Israel. Yet there are few Jews today who would accept any denomination of Judaism as being authentic if it repudiated a kinship, indeed, any affiliation, with the state of Israel.

Equally, who is to say that Conservative Judaism's abandonment of strict halakhic criteria for conversion, as in the requirement that the candidate undertakes an acceptance 'of the yoke of heaven and all the *mitzvot* of the Torah', and converts for no ulterior motive, is not a detachment from Judaism. On the contrary, surely the candidate who converts for reasons of marriage to a Jew alone, without any love or commitment to Judaism itself, has also rejected, or has at the very least not embraced, a desire to be affiliated with a belief in Judaism's supernatural God or its conception of Jewish chosenness, which you define as the criteria for Jewish denominational authenticity.

It appears to me that the essay is built on the arbitrary footing of having chosen a concept which you feel to be the most significant within Judaism, and then offering legitimacy to any of the Jewish denominations that accept that criterion. To this, I believe that Mordechai Kaplan, founder of Reconstructionist Judaism, would respond, 'Dennis Prager, what makes your criteria better than mine? Why do you immediately disqualify reconstructionism based on your personal vision of Judaism. I had a different vision and why is it not equally as valid as your own?'

Defining an Authentic Jew

The same criticism can be lodged once again towards the end of the article where you define 'an authentic Jew'. An authentic Jew, in your definition, is someone committed to God, the Torah, and Israel, and a Jew who is preoccupied with morality, holiness, and regularly studies Judaism.

Yet by what criteria do you arrive at this definition? Surely it is from your extensive exposure to Judaism and an attempt to extract the essence of what you have culled. But, by your own admission, since Judaism involves 'hundreds of obligations upon the Jew', which among those myriad responsibilities captures the essence? Should we allow Judaism to degenerate to a state whereby anyone who has an opinion to express is given the same microphone as the Talmud or ancient Halakha? Without being flippant or sounding offensive, which is certainly not my intention, given that your own personal criteria serve as the basis for these thoughts, albeit based on your extensive exposure to Judaism, it may be more proper to refer to this as 'Prager Judaism'.

It is particularly this last point of the 'authentic Jew' where I disagree most. Since your definition of an authentic Jew is someone who engages in the above, it appears as though you are defining one's Jewishness not as a state of being, but rather as a state of 'action', or a state of becoming.

To Be a Jew

Judaism has always defined Jewishness as a state of being. And all the holy, baptismal water in the world poured on the Jew, or all the atheism in the world embraced by a Jew, could never undo, or in any way compromise, one's Jewishness. For tradition maintains that Judaism is not something one practises, but rather it is something which one *is*. And there is an inherent beauty to this. It is an articulation of the belief that the Jewish people are a family. They are related by something innate which strikes much deeper than belief, doctrines, or creeds. Yet in your definition one is an inauthentic Jew if one does not embody the aforementioned criteria or submit to some level of Jewish observance.

Dennis, rather than speak in relation to the above individual's authenticity, would it not be more accurate to speak about their 'commitment' or 'observance'?

Unity of Halakic Judaism

I must also question your comments designed to prove that Orthodox Judaism is divided into disparate and sometimes opposing groups. Clearly the one unifying factor in all Orthodox groups is their commitment to both the written and oral elements of the Torah both of which together comprise the Halakha. Thus, when behaviour between these different groups varies greatly, what must be examined is which view best conforms with the Halakha, in the face of such radically different attitudes towards the same subject.

So, in your example of the Satmar Chasidim, the question must be asked whether the Halakha can stomach such a hostile response to Jewish people and a Jewish entity that the Satmar Chasidim have shown towards Israel and the secular Zionists who built it.

The same applies, dare I say it, to Chabad and their attitude toward their rebbe. It too can be investigated within Halakha to discover whether following a charismatic '*tzadik*' as 'authentic' falling within the parameters of halakhic Judaism or not.

The point is that the differences in *emphasis* that lie between the different Orthodox Jewish groups does not in any way constitute the kind of gulf that separates Orthodox Judaism from Reform or Conservative. Surely, whether or not an Orthodox Jew attends a movie, to cite your example, is immaterial in the face of whether or not a Reform rabbi administers at an interfaith marriage in a church, to cite yet another of the examples you employ in your article.

The reason why I affirm and revere Orthodox Judaism, and view it as the only authentic expression of Judaism, has to do with what Judaism purports to be: a Divinely revealed truth given to our ancestors at Sinai over three millennia ago. Now, it is perfectly logical to say that if God gave the laws, then Man cannot tamper with them, save in those areas where He gave Man jurisdiction to do so.

Although, as you rightfully point out, this can present numerous problems with modernity, if we abandon it or significantly modify it to conform with modernity, then we must be honest enough to give our creation a new name. I have no problem with the existence of Reform or Conservative Judaism. On the contrary, their existence is but an expression of the most important of all Jewish tenets: freedom of will and freedom of choice. I am perfectly willing to admit, as is so forcefully argued in your essay, that both movements have served a purpose within the Jewish community. The real issue would be, at what cost this is achieved. In any event, what I do have a problem with is their claims to authenticity.

Chanuka in East Berlin

Two years ago I was the guest speaker at a Chanuka party of the East Berlin Jewish Cultural Federation. Suffice it to say that Chanuka was not celebrated in the same way it would have been done in an Orthodox synagogue, but the people who run the organization told me clearly that they do not purport to be, nor do they advertise themselves as, a Jewish religious institution. They are a cultural organization. And they are absolutely right. I would expect the same kind of honesty from those movements within Judaism which have lost their line of continuity within the Halakha.

In response to the central argument in your thesis, namely that Judaism needs plurality in order to survive, I would counter that instead of a lessening of standards, or the modification of ancient tradition to prevent the large numbers of Jews who are not prepared to be Orthodox from leaving Judaism, what we should encourage is Jewish people who adhere to as many *mitzvot* as they possibly can, but wholesome *mitzvot*.

Shabbat on Wednesday

For instance, a former Oxford student had just obtained an excellent job. He came to tell me that he was forced to work on Shabbat. I did not advocate that he observe Shabbat on Wednesday, his only day off. The reason was that Wednesday isn't Shabbat. The sanctity of the day is not present, and even if one eats cholent it will taste more like cement than the delicious concoction of meat, barley and potatoes it really is. In essence, by keeping Shabbat on a Wednesday, one is keeping nothing. What I encouraged this student to do was keep three hours of Shabbat on Friday night, but keep them properly. No smoking or turning on/off lights, and to minimize his non-halakhic activity even at work. Thus, if there was a revolving and an automatic door at his investment banking firm, he should use the revolving door.

To this end, I highly respect the opinion you offered to me, Dennis, at our last encounter in Los Angeles, that you encourage people to keep Shabbat in their cars while driving to shule. You were revolutionary in advocating that just because people feel that they have to drive to shule on shabbos does not grant them license to turn on the radio or smoke a cigarette while in the car. This is right on, and I would hope to see you advocate similar unconventional thoughts that lead people to embrace Jewish observance at whatever level they are prepared for. But what is essential is that whatever they try and keep, it be something wholesome and real. Not the 'I keep Shabbat on Wednesday' scenario. Not the 'I married out of my faith, but at least a rabbi officiated.' And not the 'I don't keep kosher, but I keep kosher style' type of attitude. When one keeps kosher-style cooking one is keeping nothing. It is exactly like observing Shabbat on a Wednesday.

The problem is that most people today see Jewish observance as an all-or-nothing scenario.

As far as your question concerning the type of person I would prefer my children to marry, my answer is any Jew who is an extremely decent human being, is open to the truth, and harbours a love for their people and for humanity at large and is willing to translate that love into action. I would hope that my children would marry someone who had a love and knowledge of Judaism, which is my passion and the passion which I am attempting to inculcate in my children. In addition, marrying someone with whom you share the same values can only serve to enhance the prospects for compatibility and happiness.

I shall continue to look forward to each and every edition of *Ultimate Issues*, which sadly only arrive every three months. Although I live in a city which offers much in the form of intellectual stimulation, I nevertheless always look forward to your every lecture and printed essay. Even those with whom I disagree serve as one of my principal forms of intellectual challenge.

Yours sincerely,
Shmuley

Chapter Seventy-three

IS THE VENERATION OF THE REBBE FOREIGN TO JUDAISM?

In most universities throughout the world, wherever there is a sizeable Jewish population Lubavitch also has a presence. This is either in the form of a Chabad House, a student or Hillel rabbi, or a student organization. In terms of population alone, Oxford would probably not have had a legitimate reason for its Chabad House. There are probably about one thousand Jewish students here, and there are plenty of other universities with far larger Jewish populations which are still without a Chabad House. But Oxford University's influence by far outweighs its numbers, and this was one of the considerations for establishing a formal Lubavitch presence here.

Of course, there are many different types of students within the university, but some of them still come from the most powerful and élite families in the world. The year I arrived, just some of the students who were studying here included: the Crown Prince of Japan; the daughter of King Hussein of Jordan, whom we would constantly see walking with her bodyguards, especially in the Oxford Union; the son of the Prime Minister of Belgium; children of Foreign Ministers, United States Senators, British Lords and Cabinet Ministers, and other assorted members of the upper political crust. There are also many students who come from phenomenally wealthy families, and here I am not ashamed to say that the Jewish representation is extremely high. Many of the wealthiest Jewish family names are represented in Oxford.

Over the past few decades, though, Oxford has noticeably opened up: it is no longer exclusively a haven for the wealthy and powerful. There are many students who come from ordinary, and even extremely poor, families. Indeed, the majority of students here never seem to have enough money for anything, and constantly bicker and complain about any of the very nominal charges which we associate with our activities.

Students Surviving on their Own

The general lack of funds is at root due to the fact that, by and large, British students are not supported by wealthy parents: instead, they receive a means-tested grant which is supposed to cover 'maintenance'. Although of course this enables even the poorest of bright students to come to Oxford, it does mean that if they have no family or their family is unable to give them any extra money to live on, they have to subsist on the small government grant that is available. At one time the student grant was a reasonable amount of money to live on, but successive years have seen it dwindle in real terms so that now it barely covers rent for a year in Oxford. Unfortunately, though, because the grant system has been in place so long it has been assumed that it enables all students to have a basic standard of living, and so no effective measures to ensure that poor students do not suffer hardship during their education have been introduced. So those who cannot apply to their parents to help them out of the inevitable student debt are in a very difficult situation: they are reluctant to take a year out of study to earn money because it is likely to be looked on very poorly by university authorities.

This is a problem across Britain, but it is especially bad in the south-east, where rent and other costs are nearly as expensive as London and yet students do not get the extra allowance that their counterparts in the capital have. The students here are particularly galled by the situation because it was once proposed, when the country spent more of its GDP on higher education, to extend the 'London weighting' to Oxford, but the students of the 1960s themselves voted against the proposal.

It is quite interesting that many of those who complain throughout the year that they have no funds, and are given concessions on all of our activities as a result, suddenly come up with £130 or more to pay for a Commemoration Ball ticket. These events are all-night extravaganzas, full of the beautiful people of Oxford (as well as a few more ordinary mortals!) enjoying themselves in some of the most lovely surroundings in Britain. Now, the Oxford Union, our sometime partner and Oxford's largest society, currently charges £94.72 for lifetime membership, which is a hefty sum for most students. We, therefore, have gone in a different direction and decided to charge only £10 for annual membership, but then we charge for most events. Even so, the £10 entitles the student to our weekly mailings, and a discount at our three weekly events, as well as special pricing at our kosher restaurant when it is functioning.

Diversity of Religious Backgrounds

As well as the very different economic backgrounds from which the students come, they also embrace a wide variety of religious traditions. Within the Jewish community there is a wide range of observance, from the most atheistic to the strictly observant. Firstly, there are and have always been very few Orthodox students at Oxford: by and large, those who are good enough to be accepted by Oxbridge choose to go to Cambridge. This is a self-perpetuating situation: since Cambridge has the reputation of having more observant students and better facilities to accommodate them, those who are thinking of applying feel they will be more comfortable there and so they choose Cambridge over Oxford, therefore the facilities and Jewish environment are strengthened, and so on. At the last count, there were approximately fifty students wearing yarmulkas in Cambridge, as opposed to three at Oxford, and Cambridge has about 150 yeshivah-educated students, whereas Oxford has about seven.

Students Blessing Tutors

As an example, in Cambridge, since the students own their synagogue, and it states as much in their covenant, they can pursue whatever policies they feel just. The Cambridge students can ensure that their shule remains strictly halakhic, whereas the Oxford students share the synagogue with the community and can at times argue over many of the rituals which have either been modified or abandoned. There has always been a dispute about the validity of the Oxford *mechitza*, and until today this remains a source of some contention. Also, the Oxford synagogue does not permit the *birchat kohanim*, the priestly blessing, which is dear to many students. No one can quite remember why they removed it from the Jewish festival services, but various explanations which have come my way include the fact that the academics find the belief that only a certain type of person can bless another 'barbaric'. A simpler explanation, but which I must admit was told to me tongue-in-cheek, is that the professors and tutors dislike the idea of having their students, many of whom are *kohanim*, bless them. After all, Oxford is nothing without its hierarchy, and who ever heard of professors who need their students' blessing? In any event, this policy has led to more than one instance of the students walking out and setting up their own services for the festivals.

Because it appears to be so difficult for Oxford to attract Jewish students who wish to retain their observance, the Lubavitch Foundation UK decided to focus its limited resources on this university and city rather than Cambridge. However, if the truth be told, the much lower number of Orthodox students does not at all bother me. The Cambridge Jewish Society experiences somewhat of a polarization between the more and less observant students. Since the Orthodox students constitute such a large and powerful block in the community, they go about many of their activities with indifference toward the less observant, albeit inadvertently. Many of the less observant students from Cambridge with whom I come into contact complain of a certain 'cliqueishness' amongst the Orthodox students. They all seem to know each other, and this makes it difficult to integrate into their group.

The irony is that in Oxford there is a greater sense of cohesion amongst all kinds of Jewish students precisely because there is no single group big enough in numbers to dominate the scene. I feel very comfortable with this unity, and I'm proud to foster it as our community grows.

Although students in Oxford come from fairly diverse economic, social and religious backgrounds, it is striking that in certain areas, regardless of their roots, they all converge and the same things bother them about Judaism – regardless of how much a particular student may or may not know about a given subject.

Common Social Attitudes

The Jewish issues which seem to perturb all students from all backgrounds here in Oxford, many of which are dealt with in this book, include the social barriers that certain Jewish practices constitute, such as *kashrus*. On this particular subject what seems to bother them most is the issue of food which is forbidden for Jewish consumption just because it was prepared by non-Jews. Virtually all of the academic social functions in Oxford revolve around sherry and port, and not taking part seems a high price to pay for observing a rule that does not seem fair, or even seems racist, anyway. Other issues include a real distaste for right-wing Israeli politics; concern for some of the Talmudic pronouncements about non-Jews and their dislike of the Jewish people; a rejection of the traditional Jewish opposition to homosexuality; and real anger for the fact that the world Jewish community seems to be somewhat apathetic to the suffering of other ethnic minorities, or the starving people of Somalia and Ethiopia.

But even these important issues do not seem to engender the same universal hostility or sense of unease as the Lubavitch movement's veneration of their rebbe, Rabbi Menachem M. Schneerson. Such veneration seems to conjure up in their minds idolatrous or cultic overtones. Nearly every student or academic from every background, even those who publicly applaud the achievements of Lubavitch, and defend it aggressively in private, feel deeply uncomfortable at the esteem in which the rebbe is held.

As an example of this, let me cite the views of a leading expert on sixteenth- and seventeenth-century Spanish history and the author of *Power and Penury*, Dr David Goodman. He told me that, as an Englishman and a historian, he has always been wary of the German national character, not only because it perpetrated the Holocaust, but because of the underlying weakness which led to that atrocity. 'The Germans,' he said, 'have this fundamental need for strong, charismatic political leadership, be it in the form of Bismarck, Hindenberg, or Hitler.' He contended that this need which they have to subjugate themselves to their heroes is what made them ripe to pursue a programme of genocide on the scale of the Holocaust. For this reason he told me that, while he respects Lubavitch, he cannot respect *this* aspect of Lubavitch. I have been told as much by many other academics.

It was with this in mind that I devoted one of our weekly Point-Counter-Point discussions to this problem. As I have said elsewhere, these events pit a student volunteer, or, as in this case, an entire student audience, against me in debate.

To demonstrate the 'give and take' on these occasions, I have transcribed the debate from an actual recording, complete with my and the students' arguments. To make it easier to read, throughout the letters SB indicate my replies or points; other speakers' names have been changed:

Point-Counter-Point, 26 February 1992

DAN: Shmuley, do you believe that the rebbe is Moshiach?
SB: Hold your horses. We'll get to that.
DAN: I see this is going to be another lot of cosmeticized Lubavitch Judaism . . .
SB: What do you mean? I'll deal with all of your questions, but you can't just start with that. OK . . . Should people first voice their views on the subject and then I comment, or should I start it off? You want to say anything on it? I think people have preconceived notions on the subject that should be expressed. Go ahead, seriously. Come up to the podium.
LISA: Do I think the Lubavitcher rebbe is the Messiah? OK, well I'm going to cheat a bit and look at Shmuley's notes. The first thing in Shmuley's speech here is 'Surrender', and if venerating the Lubavitch rebbe means surrendering anything of yourself to him then I'm not very happy with that at all. I think he is a great man, and if veneration just means deep respect, that is fine. But if it is more than that, if it means dedicating your whole life to every word he says, worshipping the ground he walks on, and going to collect a dollar from him and never losing sight of that dollar ever again, then I really don't like that at all. He is a great man but that is *all* he is, he is only a man.

He may have inspired many people to do wonderful things, and I don't doubt that he himself has done superb things as well, but I really don't believe that there is anything miraculous in being so great and in being so good. It's really the limit of what a man can do, and therefore I think he should be acknowledged as a man. Not as anything more than that.

I mean, for example, I have a little anecdote. Funnily enough, the only anecdotes I hear about the rebbe end up quite happily. Somebody goes to him and says, 'I have a problem, what should I do about it?' or something like that, and . . . (this isn't a speech by the way, I'm just blurting out my thoughts completely incoherently) this is an anecdote about a girl in New York whose father needed a heart operation. Every time that the doctors said, 'OK, now it is time for the heart operation', and just before the father went under for the heart operation, he would go to the rebbe or he would have somebody ask the rebbe, who would say, 'No, not now, it's not the right time.' And he would go back, and go back, until one day the rebbe said, 'Yes. This time you can go and have the operation.' And he went and had the operation, and everything was superb. And now his daughter is just in euphoria, so is the whole family, and they are all Lubavitch, and everything is fine and great. *And I just don't understand it.*

SB: Is the daughter the one who told you the story?

LISA: Yeah, she's a girl I met in New York. It is just stories like that that make me think if there is a great man that you respect, then that's fine. But if there is a great man that you count on for questions of life and death, that is potentially very dangerous. Because he is such a superb person then in this certain case, in Rebbe Schneerson's case, it is not dangerous at all. He would never abuse his power, he would never distort anything he says for an evil end. Just to venerate that kind of *position* is potentially dangerous, and that is why I think that having a whole group of people who just go by this man's word is not such a great thing.

I think the concept of leadership, and the concept of having a *tzadik*, is nothing foreign to Judaism. I'm not trashing Lubavitch at all, in fact what I'm saying is that this man is a great man, and seems very dedicated to the Jewish people after forty years of leading people. It's just that I can't see why he should control people's lives if he's just a man.

SB: How do you know he is a *great* man?

LISA: Well, from what I hear . . .

SB: Aren't you following the party line with this?

To Hear and to Believe

LISA: Yeah, absolutely. He is a great man from what I've heard: I hear stories all the time, especially since I've come here, about how superb he is. But having those pictures of a man in every room that you have a *mezuzah* in is slightly exaggerating. I don't know what it is like in your house, but in houses of friends of mine who are Lubavitch it's slightly, I think, over the top. I really didn't want to make a speech.

What I wanted to say was that what is foreign to Judaism is not the fact of having a leader, having a great man that you respect, and that you listen to, but it is having a great man that you would follow to the end of the earth. Believing he would be the Messiah if it was the right time is potentially dangerous. Therefore I think the kind of worship the Lubavitch give to this man is foreign to Judaism.

I want to explain that my problem is not with the man himself, because he says that he doesn't want this kind of adoration. It is the veneration that emanates from the congregation that I'm opposed to, not the man, not what he stands for, not what he says, but how people have distorted everything he stands for and completely worshipped him and . . . is that enough? Can you trash me now?

Wait, there's another thing that really bothers me actually, and this just shows how not only some Lubavitcher completely twist everything, but they are really reducing him to some kind of idol figure, which I know is not what he'd want. I was in a plane and sitting next to a Lubavitch boy, and I started talking to him. He wasn't happy about this at all, and he really didn't want to talk to me. I think to shut me up he just gave me a little sticker he had of the rebbe, but obviously it furthered more questions. I said, 'What's this sticker?' – he had a whole load of them. He said, 'Oh, I've been sending them around Israel', and I'm thinking to myself, 'Is this a great man that you respect, or is this a man that you want to commercialize? That you just want to reduce to a souvenir-type idol that Madonna is?' I mean, he is a lot more than that, he is a great man. I don't know. Just don't worship him, respect him. OK?

SB: Ian, do you want to add something?

IAN: Yeah, it's true to say that in Judaism we do have the idea of such a thing as a *tzadik*. Each generation has to look up to someone to lead them. You had Shneur Zalman [the first Rebbe of Chabad] for his generation, Yiftakch for his generation, everyone in their own generations; you've got to look up to them and what they say in terms of Halakha, and what the Halakha is. I can't really argue with that.

To be honest, I'm not really sure of what exactly happens in Lubavitch, but the way I see things, I've got my own struggle through life to get on with, and it's my problem how I do that. I've got to somehow try and get through life and end up as close as I can to God. But is there such a thing as a rebbe somewhere who can sort of artificially lift me up higher than I can really get myself? Is it that he can do certain things and therefore I am, since I follow him, somehow lifted by that? I mean, I'm not quite sure if that's what venerating the rebbe means, but if it is so, and I'm not sure that it is, I don't want to follow that.

Personal Responsibility and Initiative

I've got to try and get as far as I can on my own two feet, following the example of people who are better than me, such as great rabbis or leaders. But how much I achieve is really down to me and what I do, and it's not really down to anyone else.

I don't think that just by auto-doing everything the rebbe says I'll be doing right. If I don't actually get down to the books and the sources and study Torah, say the dovening three times a day, and eat kosher food, I've not really got anywhere. I really think that it's what I personally do that counts, not what someone else does. I think Judaism is really down to struggle; what every Jew in their own hearts, own lives, goes through, and it is up to them to do that themselves.

SB: Is that it now? Can't you trash us a bit more? I thought you guys were going to really give me a hard time. This is too easy. What I'm looking for is some real fire or something. OK. How about Jonathan? David?

DAVID: OK, I'll give a different opinion from Shmuley because I'm pretty new in the whole game. But as for what Ian said, it reminds me of a story well known among Chasidim: it's the difference between Lubavitch and other Chasidim. So the story is, a Lubavitcher said, 'The fire is lit up in me when I'm close to my rebbe', and someone else turned his words back on him and said, 'Well, if you depend upon your rebbe for a fire to be lit up in you then you're really a dependent being and you're useless.' The point is, you shouldn't be dependent on the rebbe figure for your spiritual livelihood. He should actually foster independence, and he should encourage a healthy attitude of self-development.

When I saw Chabad House in different parts of the world or Lubavitch headquarters in Brooklyn which were so shabby, or whatever, I was appalled. Basically you've just got to look at it to see that I was being snobby. I thought high spiritual concepts shouldn't come into such low mundane things. I thought, 'It's like marketing spirituality.' And that is what disconcerts a lot of people about Lubavitch. Far from Lubavitch being the old sort of hoary town in Lithuania full of *shtetl* and lots of people going, 'Oooh!', now it's a sort of marketed Judaism: that turns people off.

And yet it's done because you have got to break the back of snobbery. You have to, because spirituality must infiltrate into the lowest run of life. So that you can have such things as Lubavitch sweatshirts, and Lubavitch this, that and the other.

The Necessity of Leadership

SB: Anyone else? I'll make a few points, then, and you can come back in when you want to, OK?

I want to get some perspective on the concept of leadership because I think that is the main issue here. I think that Lisa's speech especially helped focus our attention on why people feel so uncomfortable with the veneration of the rebbe. It is a question of leadership. But what is leadership? Is it a necessary evil that we expect gradually to be done away with as we perfect the world? Under what circumstances is leadership necessary? What kind of statement am I making about myself when I adopt a leader? Am I making a statement of weakness, admitting a deficiency within my own character because I must adopt someone else's charisma? Perhaps it's a statement of weakness that I am willing to be overwhelmed by a strong leader. Understandably, we need to look at these ideas.

Lisa said that the first thing written in my speech is surrender, and that's right because I think, again, that this is a central issue – surrender. I'll begin by looking at human relationships because I would like to try to explain tonight that the rebbe enterprise is one of the strongest and most elemental human relationships on which things can be built. You can progress once that relationship has been strongly established – by surrender.

In every human relationship the first thing that has to be overcome is the fear of surrender. What is this fear?

As you get older, you become aware of a sense of loneliness, a sense of longing, and nothing can compensate for your feeling of emptiness. So you seek a relationship, and immediately there are problems. It is very difficult for us to set up the perfect balance of surrender. To what extent do we surrender ourselves? Let's face it, every relationship involves two essential ingredients. Those ingredients are surrender and responsibility. And the thing is, good relationships involve both of these things, not one or the other. You have to behave as a responsible adult, but at the same time you have to make room within your life so that another person can approach.

You ask yourself, if I surrender myself completely, am I making myself too vulnerable? We fear vulnerability and that is why we fear surrender. Nobody wants to make themselves into some sort of carpet for another person to walk on. When you are completely passive within a relationship you feel that you have no place, you feel that you have no output; it is as if the person with whom you share the relationship does not need you because they completely ignore and neglect you. So we fear complete surrender.

Focused Surrender

We understand that a proper relationship is what we call a focused surrender. You focus on a certain part of yourself which you know can benefit from another person's love, and you open yourself up. You make a big gaping hole, but it is a particular shape of hole into which something else can fit. It is fair that we are not expected to tear ourselves completely open to have a relationship. We also understand what is expected of us in return and try hard not to be too aggressive. Every relationship is about maintaining that equilibrium; am I being taken advantage of, or am I being too pushy?

When it comes to friendships and male–female relationships, the main problem is to get the balance right, and we can accept that. We don't fear having a boyfriend or girlfriend and getting married because we know we will still recognize ourselves in the new relationship.

With the higher relationship between God and Man, absolute, unconditional and indiscriminate surrender is demanded. This we feel uncomfortable with. You take your complete self, give it to another and say, 'You can have it all.' Although you can of course choose to obey God only partially, ultimately you still know that what God requires is complete surrender. We feel very disquieted with that, to the point where, and I have seen this happen, people are willing to give up a very strong marriage, a very beautiful relationship with another human being, if one of the spouses becomes more religious, leaving the other behind. They will even divorce over it. The surrender demanded by a spouse is not nearly as much as the surrender demanded by a God, and a rift can develop.

Even this surrender we can rationalize, though. That kind of forfeiture is understandable because it is God demanding the sacrifice. If it can be proven, or if I can be led to believe, that this being brought me into existence, then He can rightfully claim that He wants to know how I tie my shoes, He wants to know who I love, He wants to know how I make money, how I treat other people, and that makes sense. We can rationalize that a creator has a right to that kind of demand.

But can we ever rationalize giving up our independence to another human being – is that not worship, is that not replacing the focal point of our lives, which should be God, with another human being? Throughout my years in Lubavitch, I have witnessed the most aggressive attitudes from people who oppose the veneration of the rebbe. I think they are hostile because surrender is the most difficult facet of a relationship for a human to come to terms with, even with a beloved spouse or God. How much more so to surrender unconditionally to another human being. People ask questions like, 'You mean, you ask him when you're going to have an operation?' 'You mean, you ask for his blessing for the person for whom you want to marry?' 'You mean, you ask him what city you should live in, and where you should go on *schlichus*?' How can anyone offer such indiscriminate surrender, and how can another human being *demand* it?

Fear of Invasion

This is the focal point of the problem. In every relationship we have to overcome this deep-rooted fear of invasion: we have our own lives, and we want to share someone else's life but we don't want to be completely taken over by the other person. Once you understand the problem then you can begin to come to a solution as to why it is necessary and why it could make sense.

Before I go on, is there anyone who says this is not the problem? Is there some other facet of submitting to the rebbe that you feel uncomfortable with?

(At this point, a student reminds me that the problem is not necessarily simply with what the rebbe might be said to claim for himself; there is the extra dimension of what people claim for him possibly getting out of hand.)

SB: It is a bit like what Lisa said: in order to justify our own surrender we begin to assign powers to him which are superhuman. It makes us feel better about our submission. Is that what you are saying?

I'll answer that, but before I go on I want to say something. A personal statement. I must say that in all my years, the thing that I despise the most as a Lubavitcher dealing with a non-Lubavitch world is that people devalue and degrade us as human beings because they see our surrender to the rebbe as complete and indiscriminate. As if we had no choice, as if the rebbe makes all of our decisions for us. When people are conversing with a Lubavitcher they think that every single response is a pre-rehearsed response; we feel what the rebbe tells us to feel, we go where the rebbe tells us to go, and they assume that they are not conversing with a human being, but an agent.

Robotic Response

I know what that feels like, because I'm guilty of it as well when I speak to a couple of Mormons I know and who are close friends. I'm angry with myself when I treat them as people who have been conned into a belief, not as people who have adopted a belief. I've been sitting with them over the past two weeks for quite a few hours. I sit there thinking, 'What day was it when they learned that response?' Because I think I'm not speaking to people, I can't respect their responses. I want to hear human initiative from them. So I can understand how some people see me as a Lubavitcher, but I'm angry with them and myself, too.

In fact, it is very refreshing sometimes to see the human side and to know that you are wrong. We were having a very serious conversation, these two Mormon missionaries and I, for both of whom I have developed a very strong respect, and one said to me, 'Oh, by the way, you do read and understand Hebrew?' I said I did. 'Well, do me a favour: my girlfriend wrote me a letter and she wrote something on the envelope in Hebrew and I'd like to bring it around. Can you translate it for me?' I said, 'Sure.' So his friend says to him. 'That's as long as it's not too dirty!' I mean, they tell jokes like that, and they are suddenly human!

We are all guilty of the same thing. When we believe that someone has surrendered unconditionally to a doctrine, we believe that they become that doctrine, that they forfeit their very humanity because they are a living, breathing idea. I think this is an important subject because I want to explore whether there can be room for maintenance of self even when we have completely forfeited our will to another person. So let us begin.

There are certain parts of the Five Books of Moses which can move you to the core of your being: the building of the Golden Calf, and Moses' defence of the Jewish people, is for me one of the exciting aspects of the Torah, but there is another one, too. When I was about fourteen years old, a boy in yeshivah, I first came across this fascinating passage in Parshas Pinchas (Chapter 27).

Moses' Last Request

I was following in the English as the Torah was being read in the yeshivah. We all know that Moses was most beloved of God: God loved him like a son and spoke to him face to face. Yet amazingly, Moses only wanted one thing from God for his whole life, serving the Jewish people faithfully. He had wanted to be allowed into the land of Israel, but because he had failed to consecrate God's name in the face of the Jewish people he was not allowed to do so. Moses didn't listen to God; he sinned and God said, 'Because of this you will not go into the land of Israel.' Because God refused to let Moses enter the Promised Land, we have one of the most beautiful and fascinating passages in the entire Torah. First of all, parenthetically, although the Torah says very often, 'God spoke to Moses, saying . . .' this is the only verse in the Torah where it says the opposite, 'Moses made a demand of God.' Just as God has the right to make demands of human beings, Moses spoke to God saying, 'this has to be.' This was his only request before he died . . . listen to the words, because they are very beautiful: 'Before I die, I ask only one thing. That the Lord the God of spirits, of all flesh, appoint someone over the congregation, over the Jewish people, who shall go out before them, and who shall come in before them, and who shall lead them out and who will bring them in. And let not Your people be like a flock of sheep which has no shepherd.' When Moses died he envisaged other leaders following his example as leader; he knew that the idea of a leader was not once only.

I remember a question I had at fourteen years old. If Moses was left with just one request before he died, why not ask, 'God, let me live for ever, let there be no death.' Or let him ask, 'God, let them always be kind to one another, let them develop a good heart.' Or, 'God, let them always be wealthy and never know suffering or hunger.' He feels that leadership is more important than all of that. Why?

Moses is saying that leadership is not a necessary evil, it is not just about congregating individuals. Twelve sheep may make a flock, but they are not a viable group unless they have a leader. One request before he dies, and all he asks for is that the Jewish people will always be complete, that they should have a leader. Right afterwards, the Torah declares that God said, 'Take Joshua and put your hands over his head and transfer your authority over to him, he will lead the Jewish people into Israel.'

Living by What One Learns

At this point I really want to stress what I believe to be the focal point of leadership. The most difficult thing that I faced in yeshivah was this: we were enmeshed in a world which valued money, and sex, and greed, and competition, and we were sitting and studying from books that painted a completely different reality. It was a world that said, 'Reject all of these things, there is something higher, there is something better, there is something spiritual.' And for the life of me, in all my years at yeshivah, I thought that we were torn animals. I began to hate myself to an extent. How the hell can we spend twelve hours a day reading from a book which says, 'This is not what the world is supposed to be, you can build a better world. You do not have to be a part of the rat race, you do not have to devote your life to the pursuit of money and power and wealth and greed and everything else. You can be something higher.' Close the book at the end of the day, walk out into the world and nothing was like that. It was the greatest irony that nothing we studied ever worked. I felt deeply depressed because I thought the world just wasn't what the Torah said it was. The Torah was wrong. It really disturbed me.

It came to a head when I was about seventeen. By this time I was in the yeshivah in Jerusalem, and we were studying thirteen to sixteen hours a day, devoting our lives to study: we were doing whatever we could, and it made no visible impact on the world. Every time we went out it was still there. I'll never forget the next phase in my life: I then went to New York for Tishrei, the Jewish month of all the festivals – Rosh Hashanah, Yom Kippur, Sukkot – and I was around the rebbe hundreds of times. Watching him for thirty days' time, it suddenly dawned upon me what being a true leader really meant. In the rebbe, for the first time, I saw that everything these books had said that the human race could attain, could be done. They said we can climb a spiritual mountain, and develop great spiritual excellence, be a great person, despite the kind of world we live in and the challenges it poses. I saw someone living it as a reality and it gave me strength.

I understood why the Jewish people need a leader. Not because we have to congregate individuals but because the world needs at least one person who does not live in just one of the two different realities of the spiritual and the mundane. You need one person who doesn't just study books but lives them. You need a Torah not just of parchment and ink but a Torah of flesh and blood. That is what the rebbe became to me. At seventeen I had that realization and it inspired me. From that time I knew that, regardless of how contradictory the world and the books of the Torah were, there was a man who was a living, walking, breathing Torah. The funny thing is that I did not see him as less of a human or more of a man because he was a living idea: it never crossed my mind to think that.

A Leader Provides a Challenge

No matter what excuse I found for myself not to climb that mountain, 'because it was impossible', I knew that he had already made it and he challenged me to do the same. I know that if he didn't exist, this would only remain a dead book that was written three and a half thousand years ago. Leadership means creating an alternative reality which is normally only spoken about here in this world. Don't preach it, live it. If you can do that, then you will gather people around you, a tremendous amount of people who will see with their own eyes and will follow.

Ariel Sharon established a very important rule in the Israeli army. It is only one word, but it epitomizes all the successes of the Israeli army – it is *acharai*, follow me. In most armies, the officers are the most vulnerable section of the force: they've been in training the longest, they've learned strategy, and so you cannot risk losing them. They stay behind the lines, in safely fortified positions, and say, 'Charge!' Then along comes a new army, and it says, 'No, no, no. We don't care. We don't care how much you study. You have to say *acharai*, follow me.' Why does that inspire a soldier?

I'll tell you why it is successful. An officer might tell the men and women of the army, 'You know what, human life is very important, all of you are sitting here in terrible fear wondering if you will live after this battle or not. And what you are thinking about is only your lives. Let me tell you something; your lives are *not* of paramount importance. There is something more important. The life of the people. The life of the country, your wives, your husbands and children behind you, the Zionist dream: that is more important.' But all of those are just damn words.

You don't feel them when you think you are about to die, all you feel is 'Will I live or will I die?' Before you walk into a battle, you're torn between two different realities: the reality of ideology and the reality of me. It doesn't work, all you feel is fear. But the officer who says '*acharai*' doesn't talk about another reality, the officer lives it. 'Follow me! I will show you that all of these things we talk about, the Zionist dream, protecting the country and the life of the people, are of greater importance than yourself. I will show you a new reality. Follow me!' When you see that, you are inspired, you think to yourself, 'That's right. How can it not be right? There it is, staring me right in the face', and you follow your commanding officer. The concept of a leader is the person who lives what they preach. If you can see it, then you can never deny it.

Leadership is not merely a necessary evil, it is a great good. Even in a modern capitalist society in which you are expected to do everything on your own, people need to know that there are higher things than themselves, and to see those things embodied in a human being. Even they need to follow.

By the way, this is what Moses was asking for. He was saying: 'God, until now, I was the intermediary between you, they saw me ascend a mountain and get a Torah, and because of that they knew that everything that I taught them actually existed. But when I die, how will they know?' And God said, 'There will be another walking Torah, his name will be a Joshua, but he will be there.'

Causes of a Deteriorating Society

Today I went from bookstore to bookstore, looking for a book called *The Day America Told the Truth*, a ten-year study of American lifestyles and social patterns. It is a fascinating sociology book done in the form of a running poll. Thousands and thousands of Americans were polled through the 1980s, and the book analyses the results. In the very first chapter, the authors looked at people's perception of American society. Everyone they spoke to agreed that American society is deteriorating. When they were asked why, they all replied, 'Lack of leadership.' People from the Deep South, from the North, drinkers, farmers, politicians, car-washers: they all said there was no one to look up to. In this day and age we lack the charismatic leaders who existed even in the Second World War era. There are no de Gaulles, no Churchills, no Roosevelts, the world is falling apart because there is no one to challenge us to climb. It is not that American society is weaker, it is because the leadership is weaker. The society is directly dependent on the quality of its leader.

This is why Lubavitch, in forty-two years, has been working strenuously to spread Judaism to the far corners of the earth. Amidst the greatest trials, struggles and tribulations we have never faltered because our leader has not weakened. If anyone should throw his hands up and say, 'I'm tired', what do you think Sholom Ber and I are going to do? Charge on!

That is just an overall perspective of what I see as the purpose of leadership. Before I go on, I want to try to show that this is not foreign to Jewish Scripture itself, but if you have any, I want to hear some comments.

The Man or the Office?

CHARLES: Is the rebbe given so much respect just because he is the leader of Lubavitch? What if he didn't live up to his position, would you still have to venerate him?

SB: I'm not saying it is by virtue of his office, but by virtue of his character. Let me tell you what I mean. There was something earlier about the rebbe being a great human being, and that is what I first saw in the rebbe. The first time I saw the rebbe was also when I first came to Lubavitch. I was twelve years old and I went to New York for Simchas Torah. A special group from Miami takes youngsters to New York. It wasn't totally religious, you have a lot of fun: we got to go to see the Empire State Building, and everything else, and of course you see the rebbe.

Virtually the only thing I remember from that trip is this. I have a clear picture in my mind, and you should see what it looks like! What I remember the most is that the rebbe had holes in his shoes. That's what I remember! I couldn't believe that a man who was the subject of such extraordinary adoration – every time he would walk into a room people would part to let him walk through – didn't mind that his shoes needed to be mended. For the first time in my life I saw someone who could have been on the highest ego trip, and yet he was so simple. It killed me. It made me feel humble, and it impressed me. I said, 'What a marvellous human being', and my respect for the rebbe developed from that.

A year later, when I was thirteen years old, I was able to get a private audience with the rebbe for my Bar Mitzva, which was very difficult at the time. He answered my questions, and while I was in that office he treated me as if I was the only person alive, even though he was seeing hundreds of people that night. Although I was a nothing in the cog of Lubavitch, a little thirteen-year-old punk, I remember the way he was half coming over his desk to answer my questions, showing his warmth and how much he cared. I thought of him as Lisa has said, a wonderful human being.

Let's remember, though, that a superb human being challenges you but does *not* merge the two realities, the reality of what God says the world should be, and what the world is. The rebbe is an extraordinary human being, but I also saw that he transcended that. He is not Divine, but he is someone who retains all of his human attributes when he incorporates spiritual faculties. He synthesizes as one what God has to offer, and the best of what humanity has to offer. I saw that it was the Torah that made him a great human being. I saw that he was a great person by virtue of his study and becoming a living embodiment of that ideology of which I was trying to be a part. He emerged not just a great humanitarian, but someone who can do what Moses did, merge heaven and earth.

Reconciling Internal Human Opposites

That is what each and every one of us has to do, that is what is so difficult. Even if you are not a religious person you still struggle with the same things: we all know what is good and we all know what is bad, our intellect says one thing and our emotion says another. We are often faced with two choices: one is to say 'To hell with it, I'll be just a hybrid of two different impulses,' the other is to say, 'I'll compartmentalize myself. Sometimes I'll do this, sometimes that; sometimes I'll try to be good, other times I'll let myself be evil.' The problem is that if you say that the part of me which is emotional and impulsive is not important you're ignoring a very beautiful part of yourself. That is what the academics in this city do, they disdain emotion; whenever they give a lecture they never speak emotionally about their subject because it is distasteful to them. Emotion, they believe, clouds the intellect instead of enhancing it. They ignore, they fail to develop an entire part of themselves. This is nothing to do with religion *per se*: even if they are not religious they face the same conflict.

What we are looking for is synthesis. The rebbe is not a deity, he is someone who embodies within him heaven and earth. He has developed both of those facets, both of those faculties; he is a great scholar of the word of God and a great human being.

Comparisons with the Pope

DAVID: Do you have that inner harmony, Shmuley? Or the Pope, what about him, surely he's got that same synthesis? After all, for the Catholics he's God's representative on earth.

SB: I must disagree with you, and I'll tell you why. Because the Pope may not marry, I say to myself, 'That mountain that he climbed, the spirituality he has attained, is it because he neglected an entire part of himself, or is it because he really is an exalted human being?' I don't know. What I do know is that he doesn't challenge me, even if I were to be a Catholic, because he has not gone through the same tests and tribulations I have, or the rebbe has. The rebbe lived a normal life and yet he still climbed that mountain, he still remained completely human and completely heavenly showing that the two pose no contradiction. That is his greatness.

To me a great religious leader has been through everything that I have, so that he embodies all aspects of life. Ultimately the Pope is someone I can look up to, and say he is a great man, but he doesn't inspire me to follow. A true leader is someone who on the one hand challenges you and says you should be up here, on the other hand says to you, when you climb, don't leave part of yourself down there. Bring all of you up. In other words, grow!

The idea of leadership is radically different in Catholicism and Judaism. As I said before, leadership in Judaism means challenging others to follow you. When they come to you and say, 'Rabbi, I can't', you can say, 'What do you mean you can't? I've been through that.' In Catholicism those worthy of leadership are said to be those who have retained their purity because they have never done the things that other human beings have done. In other words, we have leaders who grow up from the midst of our nation, whereas I believe the Catholic clergy tries to create, understandably, a separation between God and Man. There is a qualitative gap which also separates the clergy from the lay people so that they are seen to be on two different tiers. It is a completely different structure of leadership.

I'm going to turn my attention to your concern about the deification and the commercialization of the rebbe. Any Chasid who deifies the rebbe has missed the point. Again, any Chasid who looks at the rebbe as a being having great spiritual power, that has been given to him as a gift almost like Jesus' deity, so that he has not had to work to develop it because he was born of a special birth and everything else, misses the point.

A Commercial Symbol

I want to take it step by step, but I want to deal first with the commercialization of the rebbe, which is an easier subject. I think it is absolutely hideous. But as far as having a picture of the rebbe, I think that is absolutely necessary. I would have it that we should be able to surround ourselves with objects of innocence. I don't know another human being I can look at and feel that kind of inspiration. Surrounding yourself with objects of deification is not the same as looking at objects of inspiration: we don't look at the rebbe and sit there in awe and reverence; we look at the rebbe and are reminded of our task. It is pointless to have a leader who doesn't affect my life, so I bring the rebbe in my life to whatever extent I can, and if that means a two-dimensional photograph, then so be it.

Every human being looks in the mirror at their face. Is there something wrong with wanting to see yourself? Even to ourselves we are objects of adoration! The rebbe is my leader, and he has inspired me from my earliest days in Lubavitch. He has helped me get through some very difficult times. I think it would have been very cruel if God did not give us a leader, if He didn't give someone to comfort us, and to say 'Look, I've been through all that, and I have emerged whole, you can do the same.' I want to bring that

leader into my life, not as an object of glorification or deification, but as an object of inspiration. I want to know that someone has done it before.
LISA: So is that why you became Lubavitch?
SB: I became Lubavitch for one reason. I saw Lubavitchers were living for something, whereas I thought my life at the time meant nothing. That is the honest truth. In a Jewish day school I felt I was literally getting up and just going through the motions of living. It was all more than a bit silly. Some people just have a sense of mission. I felt, not everyone feels the same thing, that Lubavitchers were completely devoted to something which was very wonderful. That is what I saw in it, and other people can maybe see something else. I personally cannot imagine, if I believe in a God who created me, that life is about leisure and about being casual. Sometimes the intensity of the Lubavitch lifestyle can consume you as well, but at the same time I live for a reason. People have told me in the past that is a flaw in my own character. I couldn't care less. I don't care what the reason is, I do not, as Robin Williams's character says in the film *Dead Poets Society*, want to come to before I die and discover that I haven't lived. Judaism and Lubavitch afford an individual the opportunity of leading a glorious life and not just existing.

The Sea of Moses

Let me just cover some of the things mentioned before: asking the rebbe about an operation or about where to live and everything else. The question is, how could you forfeit your own identity to a human being? As I said before, if you can imagine God created you, you can also imagine he makes absolute demands of our lives. Our Sages proclaim in the Talmud, 'Know God in all your ways.' We come to the rebbe, by dint of the fact that the rebbe is a spiritual master; when you ask him a question, you are asking a master of the Torah, in study and lifestyle, to tell you what God requires of you. He is in the seat of Moses, as it were.

For instance, the Jewish community has different needs in every generation. If I were living in the USA in 1940, I can venture to say what God would have wanted me to do, because I know what the Halakha would say. If I had the choice either of going to yeshivah or doing Jewish relief efforts in Europe to save lives, I would be obligated to save life; even if it meant forgoing the study of Torah, so be it. Does anyone not accept that, if you were able to, you should have devoted yourself to saving Jewish lives in 1940? So at twenty-one years old, recently married, I came to the rebbe and I said to him, 'What should I do with my life?' I wanted to know, it was consulting an expert in the Torah. 'What is the need of this generation? Should I be a doctor, are there too many people who are sick? Should I be a lawyer, are there Jews that are being persecuted in the courts? Or should I be a *shliach*, because there are Jews who just don't know they're Jewish?' And the rebbe said to me that I should be a *shliach*. You are not consulting the rebbe, you are consulting the needs of that generation as he reveals them.

This is not a yeshivah audience, and so I am not looking to prove that it must be so because the Torah says so. I want to rationalize, to give meaning to all of this. In Judaism there is this concept of a *tzadik*, and it comes from the word for a righteous person, someone who has devoted his or her life beyond the call of duty to God's work. What that means is that the *tzadik* has special credit upstairs. God listens to their prayers because just as the *tzadikim* made the effort to bring God into their life, God makes the effort to bring them into His will.

Blessings on Behalf of Other Humans

In Berachos there is a story about the time that Rabbi Yochanan ben Zakai fell ill; in fact, he was so sick he was going to die. Rabbi Chanina ben Dosa prayed for him and Rabbi Yochanan lived. Rabbi Yochanan, who was the teacher of Israel then, said to his wife, 'If I had stuck my head between my legs and prayed all day long, no notice would have been taken of me.' So his wife then asked, 'Is that because Rabbi Chanina ben Dosa, the person who prayed for you, is a greater Sage than you?' And he answered, 'No, the difference is that he is like a servant before the king, while I am like a nobleman; he is a *tzadik* and I am a scholar.' A servant can always ask for things because he always has the king's attention, but the nobleman can only enter at certain times.

When we come to the rebbe and request his prayers, or when we ask, 'Should I have the operation now?' we are inviting him to intercede for us. This concept is not at all alien to Judaism. It makes sense that someone who is far more devoted to the Jewish cause than myself should be able to supplicate God for something on my behalf. This is what we ask of the rebbe. It in no way replaces our direct relationship with God nor does it imply any sense of divinity on the part of the Rebbe himself.

Let me tell you how the Chasam Sofer dealt with this problem. People used to come to him to ask for blessings for health. Other people said to him, 'Wait a second, do you think you are God? How could you give blessings for health? Let them pray to God themselves.' In reply he told them that the Jews do not need any intermediary between them and God, they are like God's children. The Midrash says that they are higher than the ministering angels, and because of that they can pray to God directly. 'So how is it they come to me?' He likened the Jews to one big body. 'When I pray to God, it is as the leader of the community; it is like the head praying that the torso be healthy.' Likewise, it is not as if the rebbe serves to mediate between us and God: when a Jewish person is going to die, we as a collective whole will suffer, and therefore the rebbe as the leader of that collective people has the right to intercede and pray – for himself, as it were. It doesn't disturb the God–Man relationship.

I'm afraid this is getting really heavy. Are there any other comments before I go on? In fact I'm not going to go on much; I could bring you precedents, but I don't want to deal with precedents, I want to deal with the uncomfortable parts, why people feel uneasy. Basically, I would like this to be more of a personal thing than just imparting knowledge that I gleaned from other places. I have tried to be like a Chasidic rebbe for many years; he really is my inspiration, my guiding light, my mentor, and I see him as such, so I'd like to focus on that.

Pictures of the Rebbe

CHARLES: Why all the pictures of the rebbe? Surely just having them verges on idolatry?
SB: Do you carry a picture of your family around with you? Do you do that because you feel lonely without them? Does it makes you feel less lonely when you carry a picture of them? That is the way I feel about the rebbe. He sent me here, and he gave me what is not an easy job, and I want to know that I am connected with him.

The rebbe said something very interesting a few years back. In Judaism ritual purity is achieved by going to a *mikvah*, a pool of water, or a *ma'ayon*, a spring. If a married woman has undergone her menses and she wants to live with her husband again, she has to go to a *mikvah* or a *ma'ayon* to achieve ritual purity. In Judaism, death is impurity, life is purity, and you step into living water to be cleansed. There are very different laws governing these two. A *mikvah* has to have a certain amount of water: 40 selah, which is equivalent to about 200 gallons. It also has to have walls which enclose it as a pool, and it cannot have any perceivable loss of water. Of course, it is OK to dip in and get out, bringing water out of it, but you can't have a leak or anything like that. None of those restrictions apply to a spring. If you go into a spring of water, a stream, river or the ocean, it doesn't have to have any minimum amount of water, doesn't have to be enclosed, and it can lose water.

Connection to a Source

What is the difference between the two? A *mikvah* is water that you have taken from one place and put into another, it is not attached to any source, and as such, whatever it has must be protected. But a *ma'ayon* – every stream, river and sea – is always attached to a source of running water. Deep within the earth there are springs that shoot forth water, and the rain falls from the sky and waters the earth and seas. And the rebbe said this is the difference between a rabbi who goes to work for Judaism on his own and the *shluchim*. A rabbi who has no leader, who has no rebbe, has no source and is like a *mikvah*. He studies in yeshivah for ten-twelve-fifteen years, gains a certain amount of water, a certain amount of knowledge, and he goes to live somewhere. He'd better be damn careful that the water he has, whatever knowledge he has, whatever purity he has, is not lost, because then he will have nothing to impart. On the contrary, instead of making an impact on the people they will make an impact on him, he might even lose his own spiritual stature. But when you are a *ma'ayon*, when you are a river attached to a source, none of those things apply. We as *shluchim* go out, and so long as we know we are attached to the rebbe as our source, as our inspiration, we know we cannot be infiltrated and lose our spiritual character. We cannot be harmed, because we are not just as a pool of water that is imparting something to the people, but rather we are attached to a source, and our strength and our knowledge and our spirituality emanate from that source.

When God gives us a leader he gives us something concrete with which we can identify. Every human being knows that faith is not enough. Faith tells you that you have to accept two different realities, and that is what the average Christian accepts. From the way I understand it, a Christian accepts from the very onset that heaven on earth are irreconcilable. That the most you can do is achieve merit on earth and win a place in heaven. The Christian looks to find enough virtue to go to heaven, entry into the Garden of Eden, until such time as Jesus will come down and make a kingdom of heaven on earth, and that will be judgement day.

Tell me something, does Christianity have a greater emphasis on sin or on *mitzvah*, on positive deeds or on abstention from negative deeds? I think Christianity, and this is something which makes me personally uneasy, has a tremendous preoccupation with sin. Whereas Judaism says, 'Forget sin! Sin is darkness, so if you want to get rid of darkness, turn on the lights; do something good and it will disappear.' Whereas Christians go and confess their sin. Judaism sees that as anathema. We don't want to talk about sin, we want it to be completely overwhelmed by goodness.

Differences From a Deity

The point is this, we are looking for something concrete. Faith on its own says, 'God is up there, and faith is down here, and accept that and one day either the Messiah will come or we will all die, but that is the best you can hope for.' That is faith. A complete form of identifying something on earth tells you that is not what it is about. It is about bringing Godliness into our world. Judaism was not created so that people can serve God with faith. Judaism was created so that people can cause God to materialize here on earth. To bring God into our world. That is what a *mitzvah* is about. We have a wooden box in every synagogue which we call a holy ark. How does a box become holy? Because we move God to dwell in a physical object and that transforms it into something special. That is why we need something concrete, something to identify with. What is the difference between that and faith in Jesus? Jesus is an end in himself for a Christian. He is a deity. If you love Jesus, you love God. Whereas the rebbe is a mere arrow, all of his authority is only by virtue of the fact that he has dedicated himself so fully to Godliness, and by respecting the rebbe we are automatically channelling our efforts to a higher source.

The Servant of a King is a King

As an example, there is a famous story told about Franklin Roosevelt. He had a black maid, who was from the Deep South and couldn't read, and she used to push him around in his wheelchair every day. Once, when he was going to a state dinner to welcome a former head of government, he was wheeled in to the room and then the bigwigs told the black maid to get out. He got furious and said, 'She has to stay.' They couldn't believe it: 'Why, she's only a maid.' He said, 'When you don't respect her, you don't respect me. She is the person who pushes around the President of the USA. The reason she stays, and the reason you have to respect her, is because she is attached to me. The day she is fired you won't have to keep her any more, but if you throw her out, you are disrespecting me.' All of her authority derived from the fact that she was attached to the President, otherwise she was a nobody. That is what the rebbe is. I know the story because she later recorded this and many other fascinating stories in the famous book, *Backstairs at the White House*.

People say to me, what happens if the rebbe one day says that you should kill yourselves, do you do it? I say to them, 'That's a ridiculous question. If the rebbe said such a thing then he would not be the rebbe any more.' The day he says 'Don't listen to the Torah' is the day all of his authority will be lost. He is only something because he is an arrow that points us towards heaven. He is not a Jesus, he is not a deity himself, he reminds us of our mission on earth to serve God, because he does it himself. The day he stops serving God, I won't listen any more. He won't be the rebbe, he will just be a person who failed. Maimonides says it another way. He says, 'A servant to a king is treated like a king.' If he left the king's service he would lose all that respect, just like Roosevelt's maid. Of course we believe firmly that such a scenario with the Rebbe is preposterous and that all of the Rebbe's actions indicate that he is totally committed to the call of heaven.

Influence of Lubavitch

Lubavitch numbers in total maybe up to 40,000 people, and that includes children, and yet in the space of forty years it has had the most extraordinary impact on Jewish life. In the history of the Jewish people there has never been a group that has done so much. We do not say that we are nothing without the rebbe, but I know that this feat could never have been done without him. To achieve such great things, you need to be attached to some source of outstanding inspiration, of remarkable power, and also someone who prays for your success. You have to believe in something to achieve things in life. Something outside just yourself. We are simply incapable of transforming our world on our own. People have tried and what they have brought to the world is probably more harm than goodness, and we want to avoid that as well. I don't want to be another Karl Marx.

LISA: Isn't there a danger, though, of forgetting God and only remembering the rebbe?

SB: It's funny that you ask that because every single day in prayer we quote a verse from the book of Exodus that says . . . in Hebrew: 'And they [the Jews] believed in God and in Moses His servant.' When the Jews saw the splitting of the Red Sea and the destruction of the Egyptian armies, they believed then, as a result of all these things they had witnessed, in God and Moses. The Talmud says moreover that 'believing in Moses was the equivalent of believing in God'.

I'll give you another example, which is even more fascinating. If you are Jewish, have you said the Shemah? Even if you are not a religious Jew, once in your life you have probably said the Shemah, the most fundamental Jewish prayer which should be said three times a day. If you have said it then I expect you are very perplexed at its words, because they're incredible, almost frightening. Listen to the second paragraph: 'And it will be, if you will diligently obey my commandments, which I enjoin you this day to love the Lord your God . . .' This is from the book of Deuteronomy, which anyone knows is Moses' monologue: it is Moses speaking the entire time. Now, it seems as if Moses is speaking about rewards that can only be given by God: 'I will give rain for your land at the proper time . . . I will give grass in your fields', but apparently Moses himself is promising them these things. He says that if you love God and you do what God wants, 'I will give.' Is he claiming to be a deity? The Talmud answers: 'The heavenly spirits spoke from Moses' mouth.'

God and Moses

In other words, Moses so completely nullified himself to what God wanted that it was as if he and God were indistinguishable. You couldn't identify Moses and say he wasn't a part of God. He had so completely lost his will to God's will, he was such a loyal servant, that everything he said was taken as if it were God saying it. If Moses had said, 'I will give it to you', and he thought he himself had the power to do so, then he would be attributing deity to himself, and would have transgressed the strictest law in Judaism, the commandment that you are not to think that you are a god. However, because he had no will, and he had so completely sublimated himself to God's desires, he was just an extension of God.

Let me give you another Halakhic example of this. Although the idea of slavery is abhorrent to us, the laws concerned with it are still useful for interpreting the world. In the times when Jews were allowed to keep slaves, anything a slave picked up belonged to the slave's owner. If my slave were to walk down the street and find a watch, the watch would belong to me. Now why is that? The Talmud explains this by saying that when the slave puts out his arm, it is as if I put out my arm, because he belongs to me. Likewise it is ridiculous to ask why the wool belongs to me when my sheep grows its fleece. Obviously, it is because the sheep is mine. A true servant is completely devoted to his or her master, he or she has no will, and that was the case with Moses. He had no will and spoke for his Master.

Let me ask you a question. Did you ever notice this paradox? If you want to be a good student, you have to have an empty mind. If you walk into a lecture and your mind is preoccupied with something else, you can forget learning anything. You can't listen and you can't concentrate. Even more than this, you have to remain empty the whole time the lecture is going on. If you walk in with an empty mind, you still have to keep a clear head to absorb the lecture. If you immediately get hooked on one idea and the first thing you say is, 'I disagree', then throughout the lecture you will try to solve that initial riddle: you won't hear the lesson much. That's an amazing fact, but it's only surprising when you think about it. It is saying that for you to use your rational faculty you have to be completely passive.

Active and Passive at Once

Everything in life is paradoxical. We are receivers and givers almost simultaneously. The Talmud says that before God created the universe, God was everywhere; but how could God create a world if there was no empty space for the world to exist in? Even a void, a vacuum of space would have allowed the universe to exist, but the case was that *nothing* was empty because God filled it all. Ever since God created the universe, we, who were created in the image of God, reflect His being. Whenever we want to create something, we have to be able to absorb someone else's existence and to make space in ourselves for them too. If you want to be able to hear a lecture from a professor, you can't go into the room thinking you know everything. You have to make space.

What I am trying to say in answer to your question, Lisa, is that in the beginning of every relationship, surrender is the first step. You ask me, 'Is that what this is all about, just surrendering myself?' Initially, obviously. How can you get into a relationship and just say, 'I am going to impress this person'? If you are only doing and doing, and not receiving, then there is no relationship. The beginning of any interaction is surrender: two people open themselves up to each other. Once that surrender is established, then you can undertake responsibility, then you can project yourself and participate actively. Before you can be a teacher you have to first be a student and learn your ABC. Because you receive something, you have greater ability for a more enhanced projection. By listening to a teacher, you can teach yourself and others. If you have listened to nothing, if you have never surrendered yourself, then you can never give.

Love and Fear

The same thing applies to God. If you are not open to God's spirituality, how can you have any spirituality of your own? Once you have that, then you can come to God and say, 'Now I want to use what You have taught me, I want to use what You have given me, to understand You further.' It is like this. God asks a hell of a lot from us in serving Him. He asks for two contradictory emotions. He wants both love and fear. In order to love someone, you have to have some participation yourself. God asks me to love Him. Simultaneously, God says, 'Fear me.' Fear means, 'You are not here, nullify yourself': you just sit there panicking, you don't think, all you want to do is get out alive. How can love and fear coexist? They coexist–exist in stages. First there is fear, and that is why God scared the hell out of the Jews at Mount Sinai. He really did frighten us. First you have to create a receptacle. If you want to fill a glass up, first you have to empty whatever is inside. Once it is emptied, then you have something to work with.

Beginning as Children

Ultimately, the respect which arises from fear engenders a greater capacity to love. This is why the way in which God created humankind is so beautiful. First we are children, babies who are always receivers from our parents. As a child grows up and is gradually severed from dependency on the parents, she has to learn that there is such a thing as obedience in the world. Mummy and Daddy start to say, 'No, I'm too busy to do that right now, I'll help you later', or, 'You can't do that because you might get hurt.' At first there are tantrums and tears, the toddler lies kicking and screaming on the supermarket floor, and the parents look on utterly embarrassed. It seems so easy to give in, but that would not be fair on the child.

Children don't have to be taught love, they just absorb it from their parents and their loving environment: we don't say, 'Listen here, I love you', because we show them our love in everything we do. The first thing they really have to be *taught* is discipline. As children we are told 'You can't do this' and 'You can't do that' before we even understand. The first thing we have drummed into us is obedience and responsibility, but this hard lesson opens us up to build on all the love that our parents ever bestow upon us. Then we can grow up to reciprocate that love to them and to other human beings. We learn that we do not have the right to have the whole world revolve around us.

The amazing thing is that children who are never disciplined, whose parents give them too much love, are spoilt. They think that all love and all fear should be directed towards them alone. Later in life they will never have the ability to love anyone else because they are completely selfish and self-centred. When you don't know respect, when you haven't been emptied as a receptacle, you have nothing to give. That is the sequence. First there is fear, or the lesson of acquiring responsibility, but then it is followed by real love. First you create a vacuum, then this void becomes filled. You retain something and go on to distribute it to others. Now with children you see it the most. The kids who were never disciplined, never learned the lesson of sharing love, become lousy parents and lousy spouses.

Why is it so quiet? Everyone can wake up now!

Chapter Seventy-four

ANSWERS ABOUT MOSHIACH

The Lubavitch Messianic campaign has engendered many questions and a deep sense of fascination among our students at Oxford. They all ask me whether I truly believe that the Messiah will come, as well as if I believe that the Lubavitcher Rebbe, Rabbi Menachem Schneerson is indeed the Messiah. The following is an interview which I gave to the *Jewish Book News* on the publication of my second book, *The Wolf Shall Lie with the Lamb: The Messiah in Hasidic Thought*. The book was chosen as the Book of the Month by the Jewish Book Club for February 1993, and received a wide range of publicity as the topic is so immediate in the collective Jewish mind.

1: *Is there a simple way to explain the difference between the Jewish and the Christian understanding of the Messiah?* The Jewish understanding of the Messiah has always been that he will be a physical human being who, by virtue of his wisdom and diligence, will influence the world towards a better time. Rabbi Nacham of Bratslav explained that the Messiah would convince the world of the stupidity of war, the same way that they have come to understand the stupidity of idolatry. The Messiah will be a descendant of King David and will restore the Davidic monarchy and re-establish the Jewish commonwealth. Thus we can envision a great leader whose wisdom is respected throughout the world, bringing about a cure to the world's ills through miraculous and non-miraculous means. Furthermore, the Jewish understanding has always been that the Messiah is someone who at present lives in our midst and indeed there is a Messiah in every generation. Whether or not he reveals himself as such, or indeed lives up to his calling, depends on whether or not the generation is worthy, and whether the Messiah himself is worthy. For instance, Rabbi Akiva, one of the foremost Jewish authorities of all time, declared Bar Kochba to be the messianic king. Yet when he later blasphemed and forsook the aid of God in vanquishing the Romans, as related in the Jerusalem Talmud, he was stripped of the title.

The Christian Messiah, in sharp contrast, has assumed the role of deity and is indistinguishable from a god. The concept is, of course, anathema to

Judaism and serves as one of the reasons why Jews harbour such a profound sense of unease for messianism in general. They fail to distinguish between the Christian and Jewish Messiah. A Christian is someone who believes that Jesus was God incarnate. This would tend, by definition, to ascribe to the messianic endeavour a much sharper spiritual focus. Thus we find that the role of the Christian Messiah is to bring about a spiritual redemption whereas the purpose of the Jewish Messiah is a physical redemption, that is, gathering in the dispersed remnants of the Jewish people, removing the yoke of bondage and oppression from them, and re-establishing the Jewish commonwealth along with the Temple.

2: *Is it common knowledge that there have been many instances throughout Jewish history when people identified someone as the Messiah? Shouldn't all these mistakes have taught us not to be preoccupied with the Messiah and just let him come when he comes?* Because a concept has been abused does not mean that it should suffer, especially when it constitutes one of the cardinal articles of Jewish faith. For instance, few would argue that because the land of Israel has been such a hotbed of controversy and rage in the Middle East that it should therefore be dismissed from the Jewish agenda, or that we should not be prepared to fight for it. The most eminent of Jewish Sages throughout history have all written pointedly that the Jewish people must supplicate their Creator for the advent of the messianic era.

Furthermore, countless Jewish Sages have pointed out that the Messiah differs from other Jewish precepts because there is an imperative that a Jew must not only believe, but *await* his coming. Maimonides makes it clear in his codification of the thirteen principles of Jewish faith where he writes, 'and although he may tarry I will await his coming'. Moshiach must be made the focus of the Jewish agenda.

The concept of Moshiach is what gives us perspective on the big picture. It shows that Judaism long ago embarked on a slow but steady journey, the destination being the perfection of the world via a messianic awakening. And it is towards that goal that every effort must be directed.

3: *We understand from your book that you identify yourself as a Chasid of the Lubavitcher Rebbe. What's the official word: do people consider the Lubavitcher Rebbe to be the Messiah? Please explain.* In a clear pronouncement on how a messianic figure can be identified, Maimonides writes that there are two stages: first there are the qualifications for the candidacy. 'If a king shall arise from the House of David who delves deeply in the study of the Torah and observes its *mitzvot* like David, his ancestor; if he, by his personal excellence within the realm of Torah, will compel all of Israel to walk in the way of the Torah, and reinforce the breaches [in its observance among the entire Jewish people]; and if he will fight the wars of God [thus removing all obstacles to Torah observance in the world at large], we may, with assurance, consider him the Messiah.' If a prospective candidate meets these criteria, he is said to be a possible Messiah, *bechezkas Moshiach*.

Secondly, once the candidate rebuilds the Temple and gathers in the dispersed remnants of the Jewish people, that is, actually executes the functions that the messianic redeemer was always meant to fulfil, he is declared definitively to be the true Messiah. Thus Maimonides continues with this: 'If he succeeds in the above . . . builds the Temple on its site, and gathers in the dispersed remnant of Israel, he is definitely the Messiah, *Moshiach vadai*. At this stage, when it becomes possible to observe the Torah and its *mitzvot* in their totality, the era of the Messiah will have actually begun' (*Kings and Wars*, 11:4).

As stated above, the Jewish belief is that there is a potential Messiah in each generation. While no one, not even the rebbe's greatest admirers, could identify him as the *Moshiach vadai*, the definitive Messiah, until such time as he fulfils the messianic prophecies, we can speculate about his fitting the qualifications. Surely there is no Jewish leader alive today who has done more to promote global Jewish observance and awareness as the rebbe. And few would doubt his supreme scholarship, piety and excellence in the realm of the Torah. So it seems that the rebbe could easily be identified as being *bechezkas Moshiach*, possessing the qualifications for the Messiah, as have other great Jewish leaders in generations gone by. But, and I say this emphatically, none can identify him as *Moshiach vadai* until he indeed fulfils the messianic prophecies. At the same time, the rebbe is truly unique in Jewish history as being the first to have launched a campaign to reach all Jews, in every part of the world, to inspire them to greater Jewish commitment. It was and still is quite a bold undertaking.

4: *We understand that your entire book is about the Messiah but can you provide us with a short explanation of this concept in Jewish thought?* Since everything is created by God it must necessarily be perfected. As God is perfect, so must His handiwork be perfect. So why is the world so deeply flawed? Because God desired that humankind be his partner in the perfection of Creation. Man has the choice to improve the world and the lot of his fellow man, or tear the world asunder. In his kindness, God provided us with the Torah, a blueprint, as it were, indicating which contributions towards society enhance the world and which lead to its detriment. Many Jewish thinkers understand the sin of the tree of knowledge to have been the main cause for the world's deterioration. But really Adam's sin was part of a Divine plan. God wanted us to better the world. Through the steady perfection of society and civilization, through the performance of more and more acts of kindness and *mitzvot*, the world achieves perfection.

The actualization of that process in its entirety is the messianic era. When the world reaches a critical mass of goodness, God promised that he would provide the finishing touches. He would root out those things that people are incapable of fully accomplishing on their own, such as the eradication of illness and all forms of hatred. The result is a better world – people who treat each other better, and a manifestation of the underlying Godliness of creation. A world in which all people can maximize their potential without intimidation and without contention. A world in which no tears of sorrow or tragedy will ever again be shed. A world in which the dreaded diseases of the past are nothing more than a memory. A world in which no parent will ever be bereaved of a child, or a wife of her husband.

5: *Maimonides included belief in the Messiah as a fundamental precept for Jews. Do any significant Jewish personalities disagree?* In short, to disagree with this would be to disagree with the entire Torah, both written and oral. Countless statements and references to the messianic era abound in the Pentateuch and the prophets. There can be no dissenter. To be sure, Jewish messianism has elicited a negative response in many quarters because of its enigmatic nature and the fear people naturally have of the unknown. But no serious student of Judaism can ever accept a dissenter as speaking in the name of authentic tradition. That is not to say that many Jewish people do not harbour a profound sense of unease towards messianism, and especially speculation as to the identity of the Messiah. Perhaps it was easier for Jews living in pogrom-infested Russia and eastern Europe to hope for a messianic redeemer than it is for today's suburban Americans whose lifestyle is comfortable enough without necessitating relocation to Israel. But any negative emotional sentiment from any Jewish quarter towards the concept of the Messiah cannot in any way degrade the centrality of messianism to Judaism.

6: *During the Gulf War there was much talk in some circles about predictions of the Messiah's arrival. We even heard some people predict specific dates. How do you view such speculation?* I cannot imagine that it is ever healthy actually to set forth a date. Specifying a date can only serve severely to undermine the credibility of the entire enterprise if the date passes and the Messiah has still not come. I cannot speak in the name of Lubavitch, but the rebbe, who is the only credible spokesman for the movement on issues of this magnitude, has never specified any date, other than it should happen today rather than tomorrow. The Talmud severely rebukes those individuals who are intent on calculating a date. What is desirable is that every individual exerts his and her utmost effort in ushering in a messianic era, be it through study, acts of kindness, or anything else that serves to better the world as part of a Divine plan. The central message in the preparation for the Messiah is this: whereas before, Jews have not necessarily emphasized how all of their actions are part of an overall strategy, today this must be emphasized. Every *mitzvah* one performs and every prayer one offers should resonate with an overwhelming desire to bring the world that much closer to achieving the original goal of creation – a perfect world. No act of charity and no religious duty is done in isolation. Each serves as a brick in what will eventually culminate in a flawless and magnificent structure.

7: *According to Jewish thought, what's going to happen when the Messiah comes?* As my book, *The Wolf Shall Lie with the Lamb*, discusses at length, there is a significant dispute between the Sages, primarily Maimonides and Nachmonides. Maimonides had a very rational approach to the messianic era, and allegorized many of the messianic prophecies. For example, 'The wolf shall lie with the lamb' was interpreted not as indicating a transformation in animal nature, but as an allegorical reference to the peaceful coexistence that would ensue between the Jewish people and its tormenters throughout the ages.

But Nachmonides takes Maimonides to task for his naturalistic view of the messianic era and understands all of the messianic prophecies as being literal.

Be this as it may, what is clear is that once the Messiah is positively identified and rebuilds the Temple, and gathers in the dispersed remnants of the Jewish people, the resurrection of the dead will take place forty years later, and even those who are alive will need to experience momentary death. Thereafter, all of humanity will live an everlasting existence, one which will be dedicated to the pursuit of the knowledge of God. In realization of that goal, the world will be a perfect place, one in which disease and suffering will never again affect us so that we can devote all of our energy to ascending the subliminal heights of Divine awareness. Maimonides understands the messianic era as one in which material plenty will abound, only in order to free us of mundane pursuits and dedicate our existence to transcendental concerns.

There will still be both Jewish and non-Jewish nations and all righteous Gentiles, defined as those who adhere to the universal code of ethics and morality, known as the Seven Noachide Laws, will merit a place in the messianic world that it is to come, just like the Jews.

APPENDIX

Programme of main events organised by the Oxford University L'Chaim Society.

1989

Rabbi Manis Friedman: author of *Doesn't Anyone Blush Anymore* lectured on 'The Jew and the Non-Jew'; 'The Feminist Mystique'; 'The Quest For Innocence'.

Rabbi Shmuel Boteach: 'Man's Freedom of Choice vs God's omnipotence'; 'Dream Psychology and Interpretation'; 'Aborting a Life'; 'Philosophy of the Immaterial'.

1990

Shlomo Carlebach: the famous Chasidic musician and singer performed at a lively concert to a capacity academic audience.

Senator Rudy Boschwitz: 'The US, Israel and the World'; Oxford Union.

Benjamin Netanyahu: 'Defending Israel and its Policies'; Oxford Union.

Rabbi Manis Friedman: 'Intimacy, Sexuality and Modesty'; Oxford Union.

Lord Young: Secretary of State for Trade and Industry, 'Combining Jewish Identity with a Political Career'.

Elie Wiesel: 1986 Nobel Peace Prize laureate spoke on 'The Story of Esther, or God in Hiding'; Oxford Union Debating Chamber with Lord Jenkins, Chancellor of the University, in attendance.

Adin Steinsaltz: well-known translator of the Steinsaltz edition of the Talmud, spoke on 'What the Soviets Must Do to Prevent Anarchy Amidst Radical Reform'.

Rabbi Shmuel Boteach: weekly Friday night lectures on 'Franco, Spain, the Jews and the Holocaust'; 'Limits of Forgiveness: Simon Wiesenthal's *The Sunflower*'; 'Rabbinical Responsa during the Holocaust'; 'Gradations of Evil: Did Eichmann reach a point of no return?'; 'When is Violence acceptable in Jewish law'; 'The Deafening Silence in London and New York'; 'Jewish Activism During the Holocaust'; Weekly Sunday night lectures on 'Child Custody in Jewish Law'; 'The Case for the Mechitza'; 'The Place of Secular Learning in Judaism'; 'Animal Experimentation in Jewish Law'; 'God and Evil'; 'The Mitzvah to Live in the Land of Israel: An Halachic Survey'; 'Mathematics and Mystics: Nature's Underlying Layer'.

1991

Jon Voight: Oscar-winning actor, star of films such as *Midnight Cowboy, Coming Home* and *The Champ*, was on a five-day visit to help the Oxford University L'Chaim Society. He spoke on 'Searching the Heart of Humanity for the Common Bond'. He is a professing Christian and has been closely associated with Lubavitch and Chabad in a Californian drug rehabilitation programme.

Dennis Prager: leading American radio personality and ethical monotheist. 'Why Liberalism has become a Dirty Word'; Randolph Hotel, Oxford.

Benny Begin: Member of Knesset and son of the late Israeli Prime Minister, Menachem Begin, Mr Begin describes himself as a 'geologist moonlighting in politics'. He spoke on prospects for Middle East peace at the University Examination Schools.

Professor Geza Vermes: a world expert on the Dead Sea Scrolls, discussed the significance of the scrolls in the understanding of Judaism and Christianity.

Simon Wiesenthal: the well-known Nazi hunter spoke on 'Justice Not Vengeance'; Oxford Town Hall to a crowd of 2,000 Oxford students.

Danah Zohar: 'Quantum Mind from Quantum Matter . . .'; the acclaimed author of *The Quantum Self* and *The Quantum Society* discussed the implication of quantum physics for life and religion.

Boaz Modai: Israeli Embassy official spoke on 'Israel: Another Year, Another Crisis'.

Professor George Schlesinger of the University of North Carolina: this world-renowned philosopher talked on 'Vicious Circles in Secular and in Jewish Logic'.

Dr Jonathan Webber, senior research fellow at the University of Cracow and fellow of the Oxford Centre for Jewish and Hebrew Studies: he discussed 'The Auschwitz Site: Its Future and to Whom It Belongs'.

Rabbi Shmuel Boteach: classes included Torah teachings; 'Maimonides's *Thirteen Principles of Faith*'; principles of the Talmud (three times weekly); 'Halakha and Medical Advance'; 'Sin as Neurosis, and Neurosis as Sin'; 'Nietzsche's Critique of Religion'; 'Electricity and the Shabbat'; 'Modern Caricatures of Leading Biblical Women'; 'Determinism and Free-will';

'Maimonides's Epistle on Martyrdom'; 'An Examination of Proofs for God'.

Ariel Sharon: former Israeli General and war hero, former Minister of Defence and Minister of Housing, spoke on Israel's security to a large gathering with extensive media coverage at the Oxford Union.

Clare Short MP and Avigdor Kahalani (former Brigadier General and hero of the Yom Kippur War): debate on 'Should Israel Exchange Land for Peace?'

Leonard Nimoy: premiere and talk on the film *Never Forget* about the Holocaust. The actor and director, famous for the *Star Trek* films and television series, portrayed a concentration camp survivor based on a true account.

Sir Brian Cartledge: British Ambassador to the USSR in 1985–8 and President of Linacre College, discussed 'Does the Soviet Union have a Future?'

Professor Herman Branover, Professor Velvl Green and Danah Zohar: debate and weekend seminar on 'Science and Judaism'. Professor Branover, research leader of strategic defence initiative in the US; Professor Green, former director of NASA life science research centre; Danah Zohar, well-known physics author.

Dr Richard Dawkins, Professor Colin Blakemore and Dr Peter Atkins: five-hour, memorable debate on 'Science vs Religion'. Dr Richard Dawkins, author of *The Selfish Gene*; Professor Colin Blakemore, Oxford Professor of Physiology and world-expert on the human brain; Dr Peter Atkins, lecturer in Physical Chemistry at Oxford University. A large audience of students and academics attended in the Gulbenkian Theatre.

Ned Temko, Editor of the *Jewish Chronicle*: spoke on 'My Five Interviews with Yasser Arafat'.

Rabbi Shmuel Boteach: Thursday night classes on the weekly Torah reading.

1992

Michael Winner: 'A Night at the Movies with Michael Winner', director of the film *Death Wish*.

John Schlesinger: the famous film director of *Midnight Cowboy* and other classics gave a general talk on his work.

Dr Richard Dawkins, Professor John Maynard-Smith, Professor of Evolutionary Biology at Sussex University, Professor Herman Bondi, President of the British Humanist Society, versus Professor Robert Winston, Professor of Fertility Studies at University College, London, and Professor David Berlinsky: part two of 'Science versus Religion' debate

- on 'Darwinism, its Scientific Validity and Social Consequences'; Gulbenkian Theatre. Heated debate ends after four hours.

Benjamin Netanyahu, leader of the Israeli opposition Likud party: 'Can Democracies Negotiate with Dictatorships?'; Oxford Union. 1,500 students attended.

Professor Robert Winston: 'Modern Cures for Infertility'; a discussion by the pioneer of in vitro fertilisation.

Dr Christiaan Barnard: 'How I Prepared and Performed the World's First Heart Transplant'.

Dr Christiaan Barnard vs Lord Immanuel Jakobovits (Emeritus Chief Rabbi of the UK and Commonwealth): debate on 'The Ethics of Euthanasia'; Oxford Union.

General Robert Oaks: NATO Commander of the Allied Air Forces in Europe, discussed 'Common Values of Religion and the Professional World'.

Issar Harel: founder of Shin Bet and Mossad, the Israeli Secret Service, director of Mossad for twenty years and leader of the kidnapping of Adolf Eichmann, talked to a large audience on 'The Capture of Adolf Eichmann, and Other Mossad Exploits'; Oxford Union.

Elyakim Rubenstein: head of Israeli peace delegation in Washington, talked on 'Will the Middle East Peace Conference Succeed'; Oxford Union.

Natan Scharansky: famous 'refusenik' from the former USSR, discussed 'Who Will the Soviet Jewish Immigrants Install into Power in the Israeli Elections?'; Oxford Union.

Rabbi Shmuel Boteach and invited speakers and/or students, in Point-Counter-Point special debates: 'Should There Be One Standard of Jewish Conversion?'; 'Should Women be Rabbis?'; 'Is There Life After Death? – Addressing Humanism'; 'Should Life Be Dedicated to the Pursuit of Pleasure?'; 'Is the "Land For Peace" Movement "Kosher"?'; 'Should All Jews Live in Israel?'; 'Jewish Identity: Religion or Culture?'; 'The "2001 Principle": Is There a Design in Creation?'; 'Should Judaism Allow Abortion?'; 'Should Judaism Accept Homosexuality As An Alternative Lifestyle?'; 'Are Progressive and Reform Authentic Expressions of Judaism?'; 'Does the Existence of Suffering Contradict God's Existence?'; 'Is Judaism Fair to Women; Does It Treat Women as Men's Equals?'; 'Multiculturalism: Is it Healthy For Jews to Lead Different Lives to the Rest of Society?'.

Rabbi Shmuel Boteach: daily lunchtime lesson on the Talmud – 'Tractate Bava Metzia'; Thursday night lectures on the weekly Torah reading for the community.

Classes by Chabad scholars: Dr Naftali Loewenthal, 'Chasidic and Jewish Mystical Thought'; Rabbi Aryeh Forta, 'Philosophical and Psychological Examination of the *Mitzvot* (Commandments)'; Rabbi Zvi Telsner,

Sunday regular Shiurim on the Talmud.

1993

Mark Almond: well-known lecturer in Modern History, Oxford University, spoke on 'Nazism in Germany – overcoming the past twice'; L'Chaim Centre.

Amir Maimon: the co-ordinator of the remarkable air lift of Ethiopian Jews, codenamed 'Operation Solomon', discussed 'How Israel Brought about the Miracle of the Ethiopian Exodus'; L'Chaim Centre.

Seymour Hersch and Ephraim Karsh: adjudicated by Ned Temko, Editor of the *Jewish Chronicle*. Mr Hersch, author of *The Sampson Option* and double winner of the Pulitzer Prize, and Professor Karsh, Professor of War Studies at King's College, London, debated 'The Morality of Israel's Nuclear Arsenal'.

Dennis Prager and Dr Jonathan Glover: Mr Prager, well-known US radio broadcaster and writer on religion, and Dr Glover, lecturer in Moral Philosophy at Oxford University, debated 'Can we be Good without God?'

Dr Naftali Loewenthal: classes on 'What Will the World Be Like in the Age of the Messiah?'

Gary Senyor: the successful Anglo-Jewish film director lectured on the recent release of his film *Leon the Pig Farmer* and the phenomenon of films of Jewish content.

Rabbi Shmuel Boteach: classes on Jewish medical ethics and on the Talmud tractate Ketuvot.

John Gommes: in his fifties, Mr Gommes discovered he was Jewish and that his family feigned Catholicism during the Portuguese Inquisition. He gave a fascinating talk, 'The Remarkable True Story of a Modern-day Marrano'.

General Robert Oaks: NATO Supreme Commander of Air Forces in Europe, discussed 'Should America Be the World's Global Policeman?'

Sev Fluss: Deputy Director of the World Health Organisation talked on 'Is AIDS Worth All the Fuss?'

Michael Medved: controversial author of *Hollywood versus America* and well-known US film critic, TV host of a film preview show, pursued the theme of his book in a talk, 'Is Hollywood Guilty?'.

Mickey Duff: leading national and international boxing promoter, addressed the question 'Is Boxing Moral?'; Oxford Union.

Chaim Topol: the famous star of *Fiddler on the Roof* answered questions about the Jewish characters in the musical.

Morris Abram: United States Ambassador to the United Nations lectured

on the controversial subject of 'Bias Against Israel at the United Nations'.
Rabbi Zvi Telsner: weekly classes analysing the Talmud.
Dr Naftali Loewenthal: weekly classes on 'Chasidic Prayer – Its Internal Meaning and Its Effect on the Human Soul'.
Rabbi Shmuel Boteach: daily classes on Maimonides's *Guide of the Perplexed*, Judaism's foremost work on Philosophy.
Mikhail Gorbachev: Ex-Soviet President addressed the L'Chaim Society on the huge political changes of the twentieth century, and the role he played in them; Oxford Town Hall.
Professor Norman Stone: famous Professor of Modern History, Oxford University, and a specialist in Russian and East European history, spoke on his exclusive access to previously undisclosed Nazi documents held by the Russian authorities and their content.
Lucy Stone: outstanding divorce lawyer, often representing celebrities, talked about famous divorces and the causes and major issues in divorce.
Mel Mermelstein: author of *By Bread Alone*, his true account as a survivor of Buchenwald and Auschwitz, discussed Leonard Nimoy's film *Never Forget*, based on his story. The film is also about his successful legal action in California against Nazi revisionists there.

1994

Sev Fluss: Chief of Health Legislation Unit, World Health Organisation, talked on 'The Saga of Medical Experiments on Humans – Historical and Contemporary Perspectives'.
Paul Zetter: Chairman of Zetters Group plc, Britain's largest football pools, discussed 'An Account of Blessings'.
Moshe Raviv: Israeli Ambassador to Britain lectured on 'The Middle East Peace Process' to 300 students at the Oxford Union.
Dr Margaret Brearley: well-known speaker of the Institute of Jewish Affairs, discussed 'New Age Thinking'.
Yoram Sheftel: the controversial defence lawyer of John Demjanjuk (allegedly 'Ivan the Terrible') spoke about the case and the issues involved in a highly controversial and emotionally charged exchange with students.
Murray Pantirer: a Holocaust survivor's first-hand account of working in Oskar Schindler's enamel works factory which is featured in Steven Spielberg's film, *Schindler's List*.
Mr and Mrs Augusto Odone: their talk on how they saved the life of their child against all the odds, which was featured in the recent film *Lorenzo's Oil*.
Frank Wells: President of the Disney Corporation on 'The Viability of EuroDisney'.

Mr Yu Jian-Heng: Vice-Chairman of the Institute of China Management Science, on reforms within China's commercial infrastructure.

Point-Counter-Point debates, Rabbi Shmuel Boteach versus student volunteers: 'Should Judaism Be a Liberal Religion?'; 'Is the Concept of the Family Outdated?', 'Does God Care About His World?'; 'Can Religion and Politics Mix?'.

BIBLIOGRAPHY

Abohav, Rabbeinu Yitzchak, trans. Rabbi Y.Y. Reinman, *Menora's Hamaor: The Light of Contentment*, (1982) New Jersey, The Torascript Library.

Abrahams, I., *Jewish Life in the Middle Ages*, ed. C. Roth, (1932) London.

Ausubel, Nathan, *A Treasury of Jewish Folklore*, (1975) New York, Crown Publishers Inc.

Besdin, Rabbi Abraham R., *Man of Faith in the Modern World: Reflections of the Rav*, volume 2, (1989) Hoboken, Ktav Publishing House Inc.

Birnbaum, David, *God and Evil: A Jewish Perspective*, (1989) Hoboken, Ktav Publishing House Inc.

Bloom, Allan, *The Closing of the American Mind*, (1987) London, Penguin Books Ltd.

Boteach, Rabbi Shmuel, *Dreams*, (1991) New York, Bash Publications Inc.

—— *The Wolf Shall Lie With The Lamb: The Messiah in Chasidic Thought*, (1993) London, Jason Aronson Inc.

Carnegie, Dale, *How to Win Friends and Influence People*, (1936) New York, Pocket Books.

Chavel, Rabbi Dr Charles B., *Ramban, Commentary on the Torah*, (1971) New York, Shilo Publishing House.

Darwin, Francis (ed.), *The Life and Letters of Charles Darwin*, (1887).

Dawkins, Richard, *The Blind Watchmaker*, (1986) Harlow, Longman.

—— *The Selfish Gene*, (1976) Oxford, OUP.

Dershowitz, Alan M., *Chutzpah*, (1991) London, Little, Brown & Co.

Diament, Carol (ed.), *Jewish Marital Status*, (1989) New Jersey, Jason Aronson Inc.

Gay, Peter, *A Godless Jew*, (1987) London, Yale University Press.

Gilbert, Martin, *The Holocaust: The Jewish Tragedy*, (1986) London, Collins.

Greenberg, David F., *The Construction of Homosexuality*, (1988) Chicago, Chicago University Press.

Hausner, Gideon, *Justice in Jerusalem*, (1966) New York, Herzl Press.

Herning, Basil F., *Jewish Ethics and Halakhah for our Time*, (1984) New York, Ktav Publishing House Inc.

Heschel, Abraham J., *God in Search of Man: A Philosophy of Judaism*, (1951) New York, Farrar, Straus & Giroux.

—— *Man is Not Alone: A Philosophy of Religion*, (1951) New York, Farrar, Straus & Giroux.

—— *The Prophets*, (1962) New York, Harper & Row.

Hibbert, C. & E. (eds.), *The Encyclopaedia of Oxford*, (1988) London, Macmillan.

Hong, H.V. & E. (ed. and trans.), *Soren Kierkegaard's Journals and Papers*, 7 vols., (1967–78) Indiana, Indiana University Press.

Jakobovits, Lord Immanuel, *Human Fertilisation and Embryology Values and Safeguards*, (1989) in Leylah no. 29 London, Office of Chief Rabbi and Jews College.

—— 'Jewish Views on Abortion' and 'Medical Experimentation on Humans in Jewish Law' in *Jewish Bioethics*, (1979) New York, Hebrew Publishing Co.

Janus, Samuel S., *The Janus Report on Sexual Behaviour*, (1993) New York, John Wiley & Sons Inc.

Johnson, Paul, *A History of the Jews*, (1988) London, Weidenfeld & Nicolson.

Kaplan, Aryeh, *The Real Messiah?*, (1985) New York, The National Conference of Synagogue Youth.

LaGard Smith, Frank, *When Choice Becomes God*, (1990) Oregon, Harvest House Publishers.

Lamm, Norman, *Faith and Doubt: Studies in Traditional Jewish Thought*, (1986) New York, Ktav Publishing Inc.

Levin, Rabbi Faitel, *Halacha, Medical Science and Technology: Perspectives on Contemporary Halacha Issues*, (1987) New York, Maznaim Publishing Corporation.

Lewis, David M., *The Jews of Oxford*, (1992) Oxford, Oxford Jewish Congregation.

Lubavitch House, *Likutei Amarin-Tanya*, (1981) London, Kehot Publication Society.

Mallet, C.E., *A History of the University of Oxford*, 3 vols., (1924) London, out of print.

Malthus, Thomas Robert, 'An Essay on the Principle of Population as it affects the Future Improvement of Society, with remarks on the speculations of Mr Godwin, M. Condorat and many other writers.' (1798).

Maynard Smith, John, *The Evolution of Sex*, (1978) Cambridge, CUP.

—— *The Theory of Evolution*, (1958) Cambridge, CUP.

Milton, Richard, *The Facts of Life*, (1992) London, Fourth Estate Ltd.

Morris, Henry, *Henry Morris: The Collection*, (1984) Cambridge, CUP.

Morris, Jan, *Oxford*, (1965) Oxford, OUP.

Nachshoni, Y., *Studies in the Weekly Parashah*, Vol. 1–5, (1988) New York, Mesorah Publications Ltd.

Netzach, Abraham, *Subbota: My Twenty Years In Soviet Prisons*, (1984) New York, Empire Press.

The New Encyclopaedia Britannica, 15th Edition, (1989) Chicago, Chicago University Press.

Prager, Dennis, *Ultimate Issues*, vol. 6, no. 3, July–Sept 1990.

—— *Culver City*, vol. 8, no. 1.

Prager, Dennis & Telushkin, Joseph, *The Nine Questions People Ask About Judaism*, (1981) New York, Simon & Schuster Inc.

Richardson, H.R., *The English Jewry under Angevin Kings*, (1960) London, Greenwood Press.

Robert, Marthe, *From Oedipus to Moses: Freud's Jewish Identity*, (1977) London, Littman Library of Jewish Civilisation, Routledge & Kegan Paul.

Rosner, F. & Bleich, David J., *Jewish Bioethic*, (1987) New York, Hebrew Publishing Co.

Roth, C. *History of the Jews in England*, (1941) Oxford, Oxford Historical Society.

—— *Intellectual Activities of Medieval Anglo-Jewry*, British Academy supplemental papers no. viii, (1949) London, British Academy.

—— *The Jews of Medieval Oxford*, (1951) Oxford, Oxford Historical Society.

Sacks, Rabbi Jonathan, *Traditional Alternatives*, (1988) London, Jews College Publications.

Schneerson, Rabbi Joseph Issac, *Sefer Hamaamorim Kuntreisim*, vols. 1–3, New York, Kehot Publication Society.

Schneerson, Rabbi Menachem Mendel, *Likuttei Sichos*, vols. 1–25, New York, Kehot Publication Society.

Sharon, Ariel, *Warrior*, (1989) London, Optima.

Smart, N., *Nineteenth Century Religious Thought in the West*, vol. I, (1988) Cambridge, CUP.

Soloveitchik, Rabbi Joseph B., *The Lonely Man of Faith*, (1992) New York, Doubleday.

Spero, Moshe Halevi, *Judaism and Psychology: Halakhic Perspectives*, (1980) New York, Ktav Publishing House.

Steinberg, Avraham, *Jewish Medical Law*, (1989) New York, Beit-Shamai Publications Inc.

Steinsaltz, Adin, *The Strife of the Spirit*, (1988) London, Adin Steinsaltz.

—— *The Long Shorter Way*, (1988) London, Jason Aronson Inc.

—— *The Thirteen Petalled Rose*, (1980) New York, Basic Books Inc.

Tendler, Moses, *Population Control: The Jewish View in Jewish Bioethics*, (1979) New York, Hebrew Publishing Co.

Teplitz, Rabbi Saul J., *Best Jewish Sermons of 5731–5732*, (1972) New York, Jonathan David Publishers.

Wiesel, Elie, *Dawn*, (1973) London, Collins.

—— *Night*, (1972) London, Collins.

—— *The Town Beyond the Wall*, (1975) London, Robson.
Wiesenthal, Simon, *The Sunflower*, (1976) New York, Schocken Books Inc.

INDEX

INDEX

INDEX

INDEX